CONTENTS

EDITOR'S WELCOME

Welcome to HomeDesigns for Indoor-Outdoor Living, an entire book of home designs that capture the outdoors. Homes with patios, decks, porches, verandas, skylights, sunrooms and window show-pieces were gathered in this special issue, dedicated to the outdoor lover.

To create this book, we studied more than 4,000 home plans from 40 of America's leading residential designers. We also carefully reviewed plan sales statistics from the past five years to select only those plans that combine indoor and outdoor living features. If you enjoy outdoor barbecues, relaxing on a sun deck or star-gazing evenings on the porch, you'll love this collection of HomeDesigns for Indoor-Outdoor Living.

At HomeStyles "SOURCE 1" Designers' Network, we not only design home plans, we build dreams. For 45 years (since 1946), we've supplied more than 175,000 home plans to professional builders, home owners, and do-it-yourselfers. All have shared the common goal of building their dream home. The tremendous variety of designs represented in this book allows you to choose the home that best suits your lifestyle, budget, and building site.

Keep in mind that the most important part of a home design is the floor plan — the layout and flow of the rooms. If the floor plan excites you, minor changes are easily made by qualified professionals. Also, exterior styling and appearance can be easily modified. Wood siding can be changed to shakes or even to stucco, for example. Window and trim styles can also be changed. The only limits to creative customizing are your own taste and ingenuity.

As you let your dreams run wild, you'll discover one of the most exciting aspects about this book is the tremendous savings that our home plans give to you. Custom designs cost thousands of dollars, usually 5% to 15% of the cost of construction. The design costs for a $100,000 home, for example, can range from $5,000 to $15,000.

A "SOURCE 1" plan costs only $220 to $520 depending on the size of the home and the number of sets of blueprints that you order. When you order a "SOURCE 1" plan, you save the money you need to truly build your dream — to add a deck, swimming pool, beautiful kitchen, elegant master bedroom, luxurious bathroom, or other extras.

You can be assured of the quality of "SOURCE 1" plans. All of the blueprints are designed by licensed architects or members of the AIBD (American Institute of Building Designers). Each plan is designed to meet the nationally recognized building codes in effect, at the time and place that they were drawn.

Please note that all "SOURCE 1" plans are designed to meet the specifications of seismic zones I or II. Because the United States has such a wide variety of geography and climate, each county and municipality will have its own codes, ordinances, zoning requirements, and building regulations.

Therefore, depending on where you live, your plan may need to be modified to comply with your local building requirements — snow loads, energy codes, seismic zones, etc. If you need information or have questions regarding your specific requirements, call your local contractor, municipal building department, lumber yard, or the American Institute of Building Designers (AIBD 1-800-366-2423). You may also call the National Association of Home Builders (NAHB) (1-800-368-5242) to get the number of your local Home Builders Association, who can recommend a quality member builder in your area.

Building a home is truly the American dream. This book includes articles on how to select the right home design, offers money-saving tips on cutting construction costs, and most importantly, contains over 200 new, up-to-date and best-selling home designs.

"SOURCE 1" doesn't just design homes, we build dreams! We hope that this book brings you one step closer to building yours.

CHOOSING THE DESIGN THAT'S RIGHT FOR YOU

For most of us, our home is the largest investment we will ever make. As a result, the style and type of home that we build is largely an economic decision. But of equal importance are issues of lifestyle, personal taste, and self-expression. Inevitably, our home is both our castle and our captor. We invest in it with the incomes that we earn from our weekday labor, and on the weekends, we invest in it with our saws, hammers, paintbrushes, and lawn tools. Our homes are truly an all-consuming labor of love.

Recognizing that love is in the eyes of the beholder, the following is a helpful guide to follow as you search for your dream home.

BUDGET

As a general rule, building a home costs between $60 and $100 per square foot of living space. However, as with most rules, the exceptions are greater than the rule. The greatest variables are land costs, labor and material costs, and individual tastes and style. The best bet is to contact your local builders association, lumberyard, or contractor.

Once you have an idea of what you can afford, determine any changes that you foresee in your income over the next five to ten years. For many, the future holds a greater income and therefore the possibility of a larger house. For others — young parents considering part-time work or empty-nesters soon to retire, the future may hold a reduction in income. Keep these considerations in mind as you evaluate your home plan needs.

LIFESTYLE

Just as your income may change, so too may your lifestyle. Select a plan that is flexible, versatile and adaptable. Young families may need a design that allows for expansion or flexibility in the floor plan. A 10′ x 10′ nursery may be adequate for a young child but will be terribly cramped for a teenager. On the other hand, a nursery today may become a den tomorrow.

For empty-nesters, there are other considerations. Children leave but they also return with friends, spouses, and grandchildren. The flexibility of the home design is a major consideration in dealing with these changes.

Your final lifestyle consideration is "aging." As we get older stairs become more difficult, doors are harder to open, and kitchens and bathrooms become more difficult to manage (especially in a wheelchair). If you plan on aging with your home, be sure to design your home so that it ages with you. Wider hallways, reinforced bathrooms for handgrips and railings, and gradual slopes in stairways are easy and less expensive to install at the time of construction. Renovating your home for wheelchair accessibility or handicapped living can be extremely costly down the line.

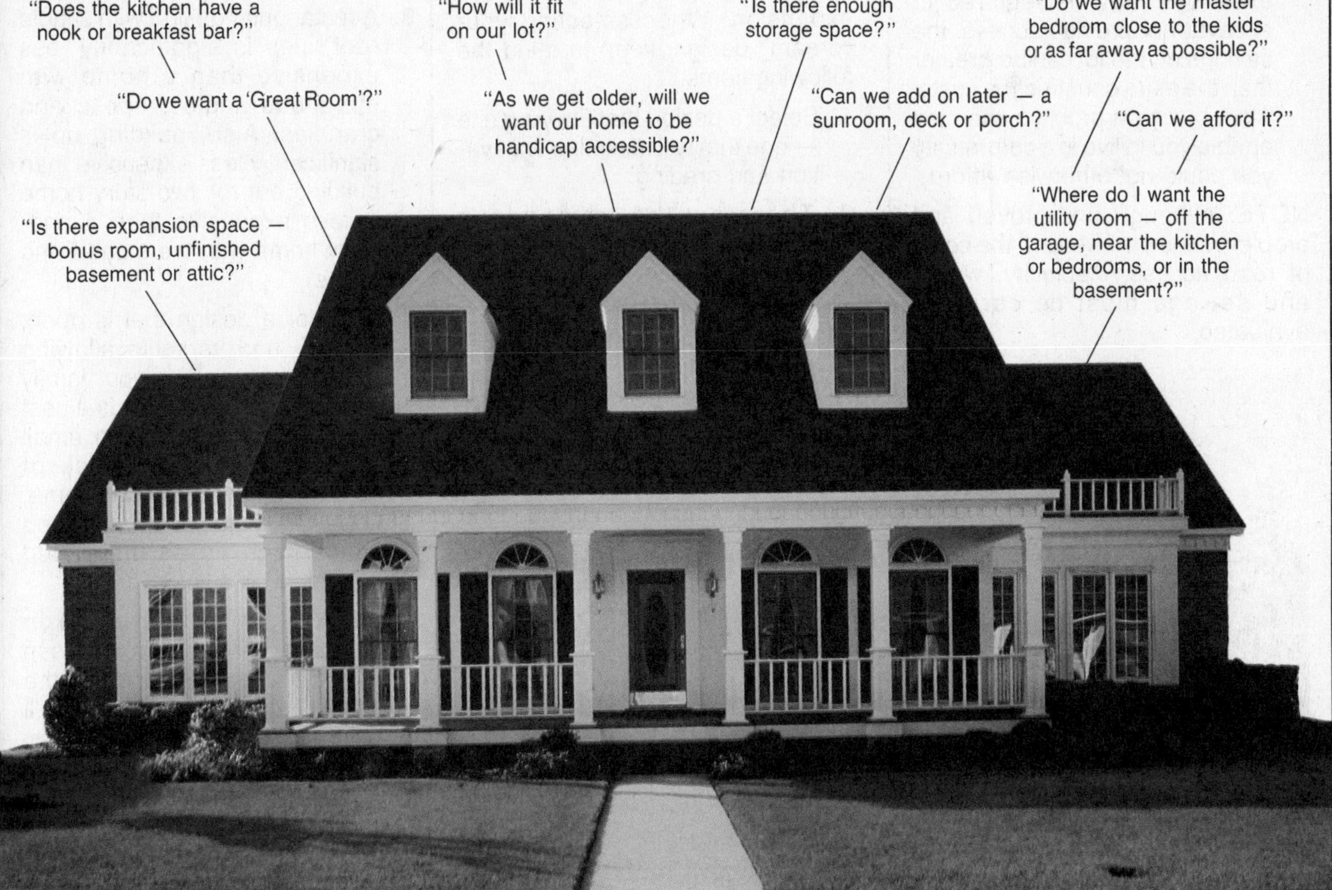

Photo by Gil Ford

Plan E-3000

COST-SAVING TIPS FOR BUILDING A HOME IN THE 90's

With construction costs and land values on the rise, record numbers of home builders are looking for money-saving ideas to build an affordable "dream home." Real estate, design costs, building materials, and contracting are the four areas that offer the greatest savings potential for new home buyers.

REAL ESTATE TIPS

The cost of land will vary depending on its location, whether or not it is developed or undeveloped, and whether the site poses any problems such as a difficult terrain, complicated configuration, or local zoning requirements.

1. When evaluating the land you wish to buy, keep in mind that undeveloped land is generally cheaper than developed land. It also has greater potential for appreciation as the surrounding area develops.
2. Despite potential problems, a difficult site can be a blessing in disguise. Although additional expenses may be required to excavate or provide access, the savings on the lot can be greater than the extra construction costs. Also, buying a problem site may enable you to live in a community you could not otherwise afford.

NOTE: Although unimproved and problem sites are cheaper, the costs of road access, electricity, water, and sewage must be carefully evaluated.

Photo courtesy of Piercy & Barclay Designers

Plan P-7659

DESIGN TIPS

Once you have your lot, you must select a design that fits both your site and your lifestyle.

Identify your family's current and future needs and income. As a gèneral rule, it is much safer to select a design that is within your budget and is flexible for future expansion. When selecting your "dream" design, keep in mind the following items:

1. Select a design that fits your site — one that will minimize excavation and grading.
2. There can be tremendous savings using predesigned blueprints from "SOURCE 1" or other reputable stock blueprint companies. Architects' fees for custom drawn blueprints will range from 5% to 15% of the cost of building your home. Design costs for a $100,000 home, for example, can range from $5,000 to $15,000. However, complete construction blueprints are available from most stock design companies for $190-$490.
3. A rectangular design with simple roof lines is significantly less expensive than a home with numerous angles, nooks and crannies. Also, building up is significantly less expensive than building out. (A two-story home is less expensive than a one-story home with the same living space).
4. Look for a design that is open, flexible, and versatile allowing rooms to change as your family grows. Built-in furniture is a cost effective way of utilizing small spaces. It gives a sense of greater volume in a small home. Look for a home with unfinished space such as an unfinished basement or attic.
5. Decks, patios, screened in porches, greenhouses, and sun rooms add tremendously to the comfort and pleasure that you'll have in living in your home. They also translate to increased value for resale!
6. Design your home for energy efficiency. 2x6 construction of the walls may be more expensive

Plan R-1028

Photo courtesy of Barclay Home Designs

Plan H-930

Photos by Bob Hallinen

in the short run, but these minimal costs will be paid back in energy savings.

Site your house correctly. A southern exposure in colder climates and a northern exposure in warmer climates will have a surprising effect on your fuel bills.

MATERIAL TIPS

The materials used to build your home are the most expensive costs of construction. Don't compromise on materials to save money! Savings can be made in using pre-manufactured materials and standard sizes.

1. Limit custom work! As attractive as elaborate detailing can be, the cost is often exorbitant. Look for mass produced detailing wherever possible.
2. Areas such as the kitchen and the bathroom are often very expensive to build due to the number of appliances, cabinets and features. Your builder and local supplier can design the kitchen and bathroom to take advantage of pre-designed cabinetry and counters.

CONTRACTING TIPS

Cutting construction costs (i.e. labor and materials) requires experience, time, and organizational skills.

As a home builder you have four options:

1. A construction company;
2. A general contractor (carpenter/builder);
3. Act as your own general contractor;
4. Build your own home.

In all of these cases, the contractor is responsible for coordinating the work of all "trades" — electricians, plumbers, painters, builders, etc., securing permits, handling finances and ensuring quality. There are advantages and disadvantages to each option:

1. A general construction company may offer some cost savings because your project will be consolidated with a number of other concurrent projects and there may be labor savings with sub-contractors. However, your house is one of many and you will not have much personal contact with your builder.
2. The general contractor can provide more personalized attention than a construction company. However, you will have to spend more time reviewing and comparing competitive bids and possibly specifying materials. A general contractor usually works on a "cost-plus" basis — the costs of materials and sub-contractors' charges plus the contract fee. This can either be a fixed cost or a percentage of the cost.
3. Acting as your own general contractor significantly reduces costs but also significantly increases the time and responsibility you must commit to the project. In this role, you have the responsibility of hiring, supervising, securing permits, and getting materials. This requires knowledge of local building codes and means working with construction specialists. Although the savings are significant, you must weigh the extensive commitment and time involved against having the work done by a professional.
4. The most cost efficient approach is to act as your own contractor and builder. In this case you eliminate all the costs except for materials. This option can be rewarding but requires a tremendous commitment of time — first in educating yourself, and then in doing it.

Photo by Gil Ford

Plan E-2208

10 Most Popular Elements of a Good Home Desig

1. Eye-Catching Exterior

Your house is a form of self-expression. Whether simple or subdued, stately or elegant, the exterior creates the first impression of your home. Does the exterior appearance of the home suit your tastes? If not, will changing the exterior materials or the color help?

2. Entryway Warmth

An inviting entryway sets the tone and atmosphere of your home. Does the entry have ample closet storage? Are the entrances covered or sheltered from rain or snow?

3. Zoning

There are three major zones in each home: working zones — kitchen, utility room, garage, bathrooms, and entryways; living zones — the living room, dining room, nook, family room, and/or Great Room; quiet zones — master bedroom, secondary bedrooms, library, den, and study.

As you look at your home plan, keep in mind that a good plan buffers the quiet zones from working zones by physically separating them on different levels or by placing living areas between them.

4. Traffic Flow

Another issue to consider is how people will travel between rooms and between zones. This is called traffic flow. You may wish to analyze the floor plan by asking: Is there a convenient path between the garage and the kitchen for carrying groceries and other supplies? How does traffic pass between the kitchen and other eating areas? Are bathrooms easily accessible to bedrooms and the family and recreation areas? Do I want the master bedroom close to or separate from the other bedrooms? Do I want the utility area in the basement, near the kitchen or near the bedrooms?

5. Openness, Flexibility, and Versatility

Look for a design that is open and airy and has rooms with multiple uses to change with your family's needs. For example, the "Great Room" concept has become increasingly popular. In this idea, the kitchen, breakfast room, and family room work together as one large area yet function as separate spaces with their own identities. Also, ask yourself, can a nursery or spare bedroom be converted into a study, library, or parlour? Could the kitchen or Great Room be expanded by adding a sun room or sliding door for a future deck or screened porch?

Photo courtesy of Piercy & Barclay Designers   Plan P-6563

6. Atmosphere

Atmosphere is created by the use of natural light, heightened ceilings, skylights, clerestory windows, and creative use of built-in artificial lights. Heightened ceilings create a greater sense of space and volume without increasing the actual dimensions of the room. A ceiling can also change the entire atmosphere of a room — vaulted and cathedral ceilings provide a contemporary "feel," trayed ceilings are more formal and elegant, and beamed ceilings create a casual and homey atmosphere.

7. Master Suites and Luxurious Master Bathrooms

A spacious, refreshing, and relaxing private bedroom retreat is highly popular. Walk-in closets, dual vanities, skylights, a separate shower and tub are added luxuries in high demand.

8. Kitchens

The kitchen has become a social center often incorporated with a breakfast nook and Great Room. A large, open kitchen with plenty of counter space, an island or peninsula counter, and a breakfast bar are highly desirable features.

9. Storage, Built-ins, and Utility Rooms

Creative use of alcoves, built-in bookshelves, nooks, and wet bars are both popular and cost effective. These small elements can create a larger sense of space in an otherwise small or medium-sized design.

Storage spaces are in high demand. Does the home you are looking for have an unfinished attic, basement, bonus room, or expandable garage? Do the bedrooms have adequate closet space? Does the kitchen have a pantry and sufficient cupboards? Does the utility room have extra storage and sufficient space?

10. Inside/Outside

To bring the outdoors in, new home designs are incorporating sun rooms, solariums, and greenhouses, as well as decks, patios, and porches. Creative window shapes and energy-efficient glass doors allow your home design to capture the beauty and freshness of the outdoors. If your home does not have a backyard deck or patio, could these be added without major expense?

Photo by Mark Englund

Fantastic Floor Plan!

- This is the famous house shown on the PBS "Hometime" television series.
- Impressive floor plan includes a deluxe master suite with a private courtyard, magnificent bath and large closet.
- The large island kitchen/nook combination includes a corner pantry and easy access to a rear deck.
- The spacious family room includes a fireplace and vaulted ceiling.
- The two upstairs bedrooms share a bath with double sinks.
- Note the convenient laundry room in the garage entry area.

Plan B-88015

Bedrooms: 3	**Baths:** 2½
Space:	
Upper floor:	534 sq. ft.
Main floor:	1,689 sq. ft.
Total living area:	2,223 sq. ft.
Basement:	approx. 1,689 sq. ft.
Garage:	455 sq. ft.
Exterior Wall Framing:	2x4

Foundation options:
Standard basement only.
(Foundation & framing conversion diagram available — see order form.)

Blueprint Price Code: C

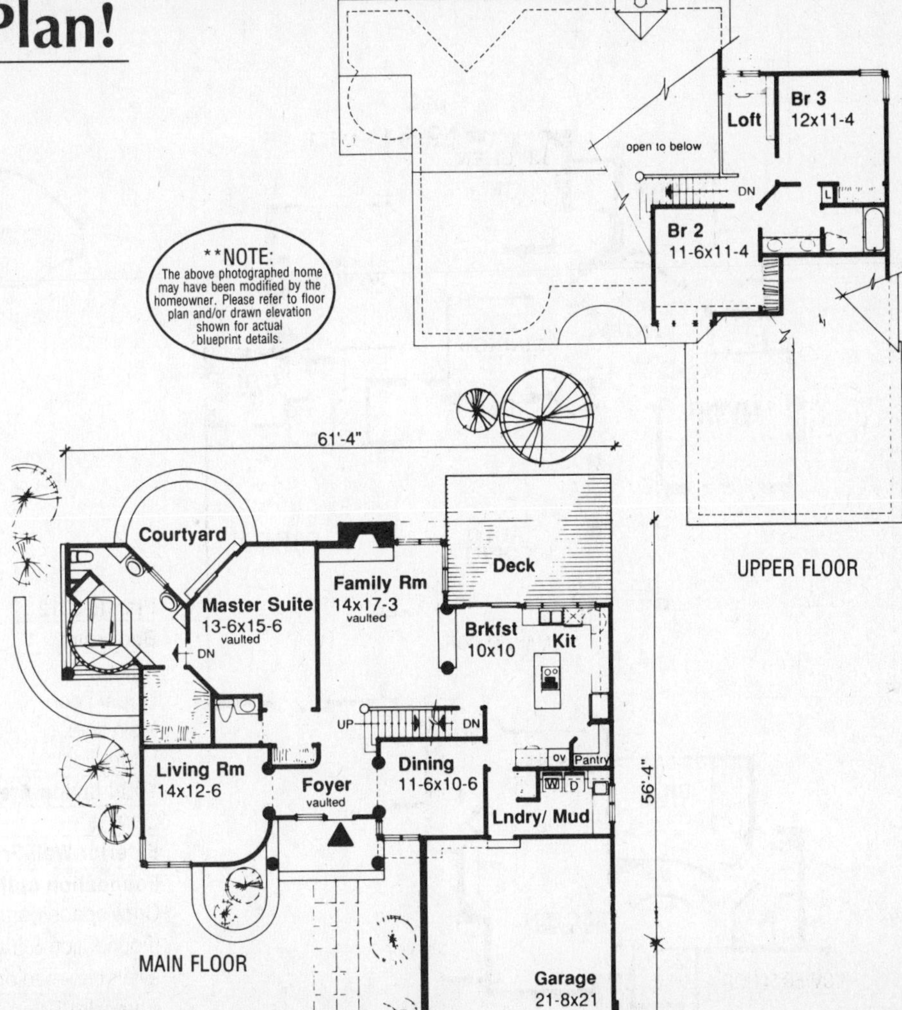

Plan B-88015

TO ORDER THIS BLUEPRINT, CALL TOLL-FREE 1-800-547-5570
(Prices and details on pp. 12-15.)

Exercise Room With Sauna/Spa

- Three levels of luxury are found in this three-level traditional home with beautiful half-round front window and covered entry.
- Archways adorn the entrance to the sunken living room, also with fireplace flanked by windows.
- Coved ceilings are found in the dining room; double doors open to the kitchen, nook and family room areas.
- The sunken family room offers a fireplace and a view to the attached deck. The large island kitchen has a pantry and nook with bay window and sliders to access the deck.
- A spacious master suite is found on the upper level, with bayed sitting area and luxury bath.
- The lower level provides room for a fourth bedroom, a rec room, and an exercise room with bar, sauna, and octagonal spa with bay window view.

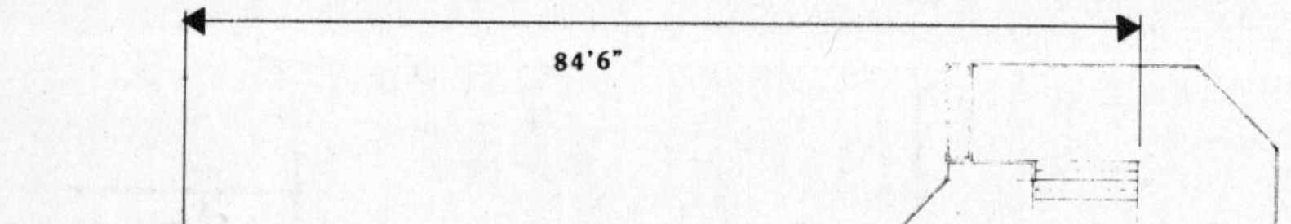

84'6"

83'

NOOK 11/0 X 12/0

KITCHEN 14/8 X 16/6

DECK

STUDY 14/0 X 15/9

SEAT

UP

DN

ENTRY

SUNKEN FAMILY 21/0 X 19/6

DINING 15/6 X 13/0

LIVING 18/0 X 18/0

UTIL. 11/0 X 10/0

AUTO COURT

GARAGE 24/4 X 35/4

MAIN FLOOR

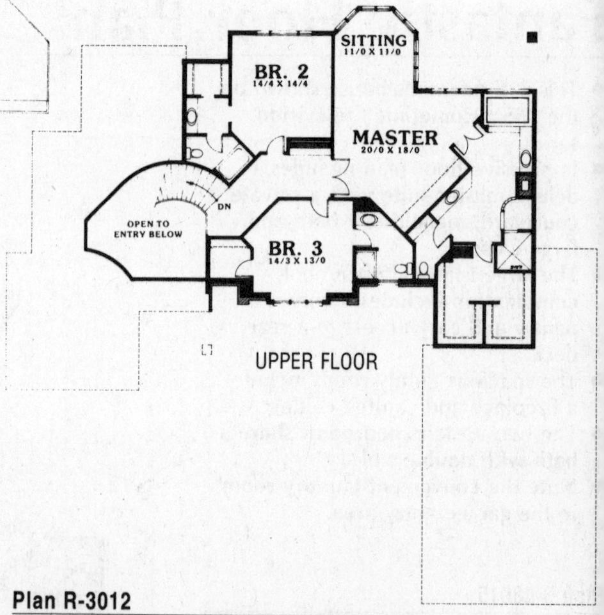

SITTING 11/0 X 11/0

BR. 2 14/4 X 14/4

MASTER 20/0 X 18/0

OPEN TO ENTRY BELOW

BR. 3 14/3 X 13/0

UPPER FLOOR

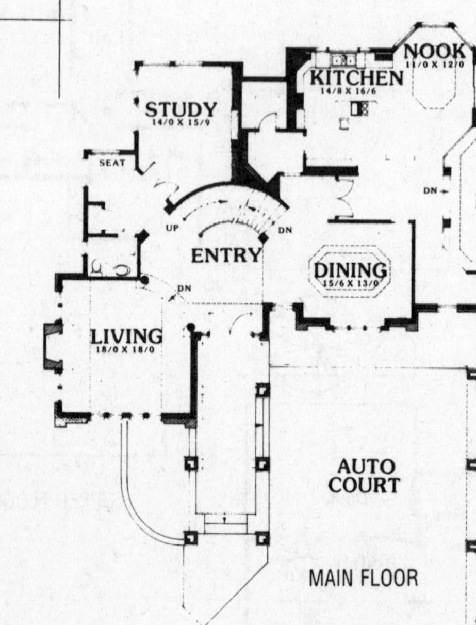

SPA 11/0 X 11/0

EXERCISE 14/0 X 12/6

BR. 4 15/0 X 13/6

BAR

REC. RM. 17/6 X 22/6

STOR.

LOWER FLOOR

Plan R-3012

Bedrooms: 4	**Baths:** 4 full + 2 half
Space:	
Upper floor	1,742 sq. ft.
Main floor	2,864 sq. ft.
Lower floor	1,582 sq. ft.
Total Living Area	**6,188 sq. ft.**
Garage	860 sq. ft.
Exterior Wall Framing	2x6

Foundation options:

Crawlspace/partial daylight basement

(Foundation & framing conversion diagram available—see order form.)

Blueprint Price Code G

TO ORDER THIS BLUEPRINT, CALL TOLL-FREE 1-800-547-5570

(prices and details on pp. 12-15.)

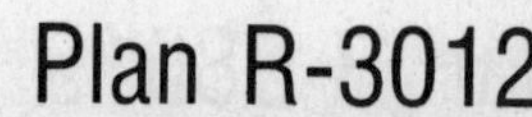

Plan R-3012

Dramatic Interior Makes a Best-Seller

- **An incredible master suite takes up the entire 705 sq. ft. second floor, and includes deluxe bath, huge closet and skylighted balcony.**
- **Main floor design utilizes angles and shapes to create dramatic interior.**
- **Extra-spacious kitchen features large island, sunny windows and plenty of counter space.**
- **Sunken living room focuses on massive fireplace and stone hearth.**
- **Impressive two-level foyer is lit by skylights high above.**

Photo by Karlis Grants

**NOTE: The above photographed home may have been modified by the homeowner. Please refer to floor plan and/or drawn elevation shown for actual blueprint details.

MASTER SUITE 20/0X15/0
SKYLIGHT
WALK-IN W'ROBE
OPEN TO GREAT RM. BELOW
SKYLIGHT
DN
SKYLIGHTS
SUNKEN TUB
SH
ENTRY BELOW

UPPER FLOOR

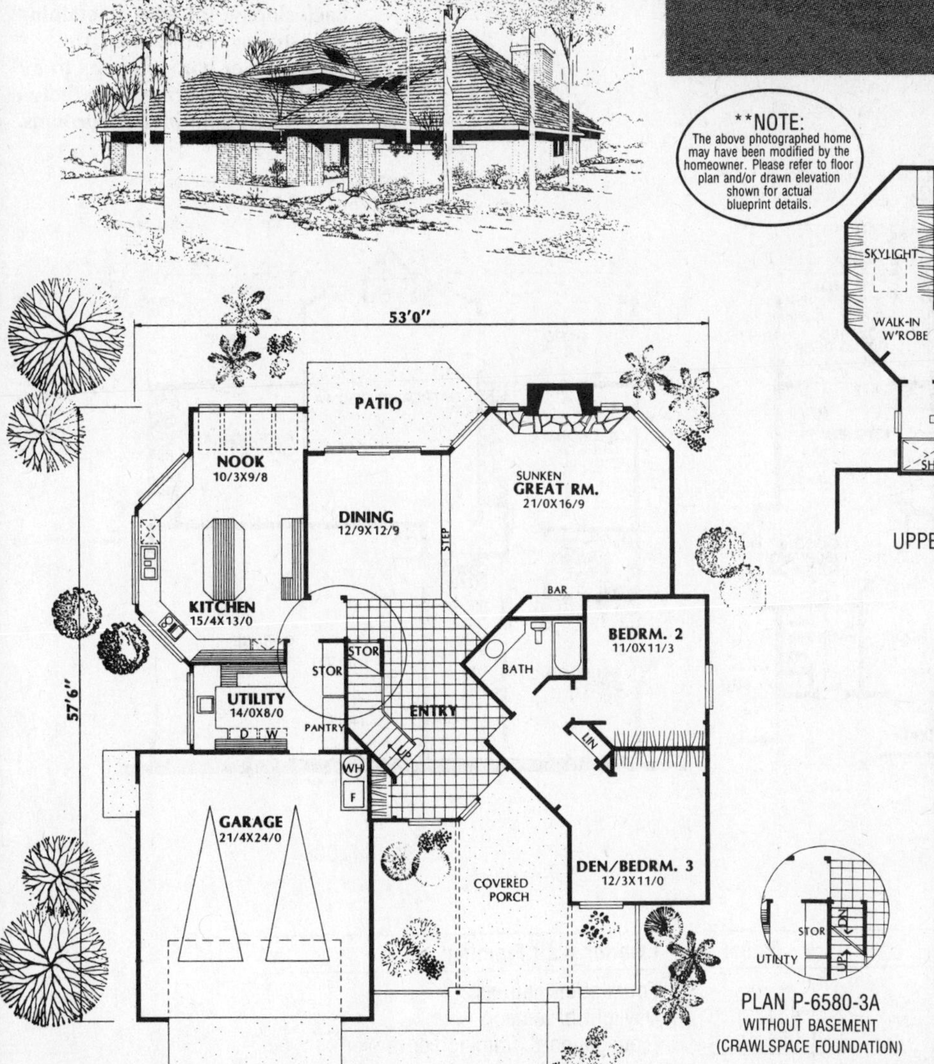

MAIN FLOOR

STOR
UTILITY
DN
UP

PLAN P-6580-3A
WITHOUT BASEMENT
(CRAWLSPACE FOUNDATION)

Plans P-6580-3A & -3D

Bedrooms: 2-3	**Baths:** 2
Space:	
Upper floor:	705 sq. ft.
Main floor:	1,738 sq. ft.
Total living area:	2,443 sq. ft.
Basement:	1,738 sq. ft.
Garage:	512 sq. ft.
Exterior Wall Framing:	2x4

Foundation options:
Daylight basement (Plan P-6580-3D).
Crawlspace (Plan P-6580-3A).
(Foundation & framing conversion diagram available — see order form.)

Blueprint Price Code:	C

Plans P-6580-3A & -3D

TO ORDER THIS BLUEPRINT, CALL TOLL-FREE 1-800-547-5570
(Prices and details on pp. 12-15.)

Dazzling Entry Impact

- A quaint cottage-like entry with lattice-trimmed covered front porch opens into a dazzling grand room and dining room with high cathedral vaulted ceiling, fireplace and view decks seen through flanking French doors. High transom windows add further to the dramatics.
- The island kitchen overlooks a good morning room and an outdoor covered dining deck.
- The master suite features a cathedral ceiling leading the eye to a covered privacy deck and views beyond. The spacious master bath is highlighted by a spa tub under corner windows.
- The lower level walks out to a patio, accommodating a front-to-back sloping lot with a retaining wall shown on the plan. The tuck-under garage opens to a central gathering room between three additional bedrooms.

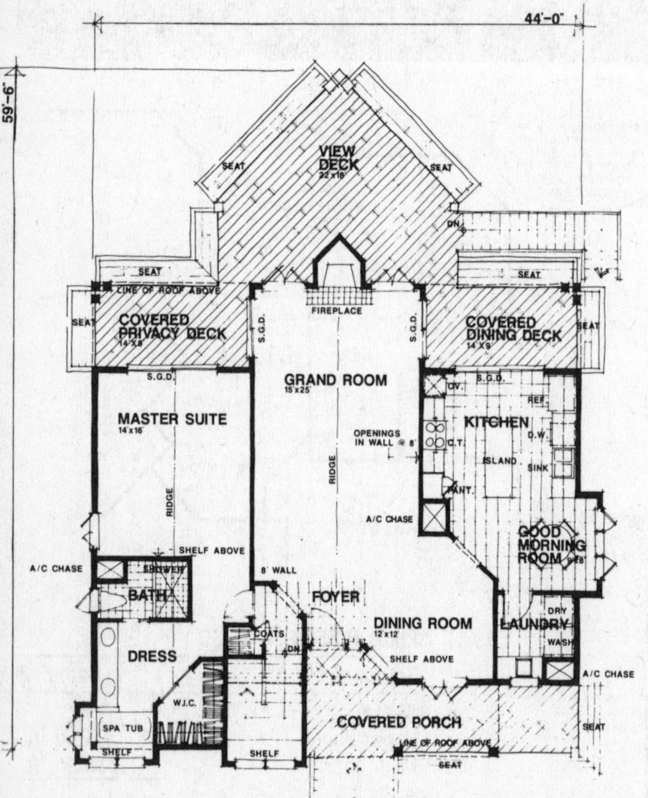

UPPER FLOOR

PATIO
22'x18'
LINE OF SEAT ABOVE
STOVE
PATIO
14'x9'
PATIO
14'x9'
GATHERING ROOM
15'x19'
BEDROOM 3/ GUEST
11'x12'
BEDROOM 4/ OFFICE
11'x11'
METER
LINE OF FLOOR ABOVE
LINEN
BATH
LOWER FOYER
GARAGE
24'x20'
BEDROOM 2/ GUEST
11'x11'
STOR.
CURB
A/C
FURNACE
RETAINING WALL

MAIN FLOOR

Plan EOF-14

Bedrooms: 4	**Baths:** 2
Space:	
Upper floor:	1,431 sq. ft.
Main floor:	1,054 sq. ft.
Total living area:	2,485 sq. ft.
Garage:	480 sq. ft.

Exterior Wall Framing: 2x4

Foundation options:
Daylight basement.
(Foundation & framing conversion diagram available — see order form.)

Blueprint Price Code: C

TO ORDER THIS BLUEPRINT, CALL TOLL-FREE 1-800-547-5570
(prices and details on pp. 12-15.)

Plan EOF-14

Spacious Elegance

Lower level:	1,944 sq. ft.
Upper level:	1,427 sq. ft.
Total living area:	3,371 sq. ft.
Garage, storage & exterior bar:	732 sq. ft.
Porches & balcony:	769 sq. ft.
Total under roof:	4,872 sq. ft.

Exterior walls are 2x6 construction.
Specify basement, crawlspace or slab foundation.

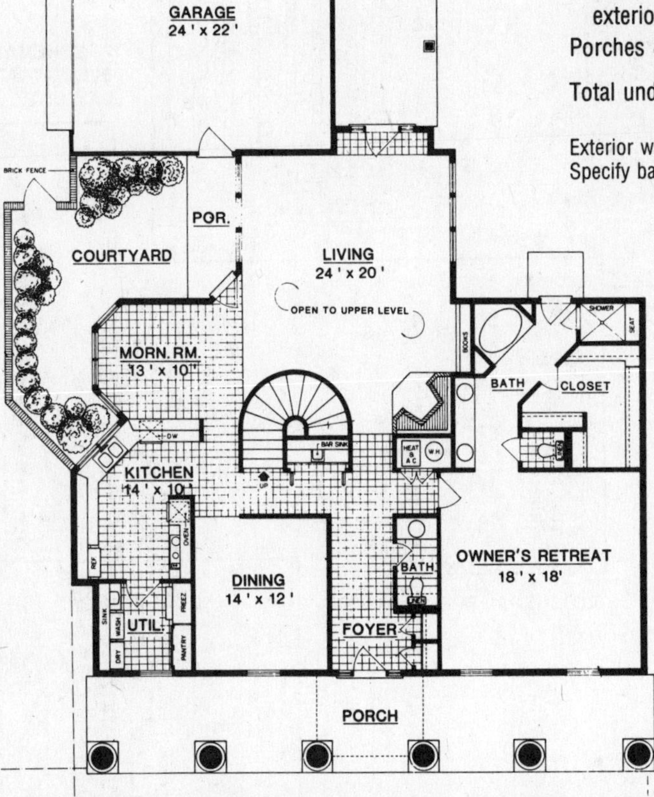

FIRST FLOOR

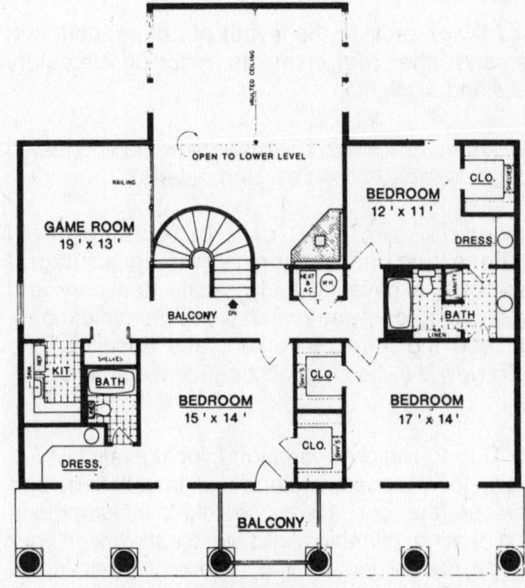

SECOND FLOOR

An Energy Efficient Home

Blueprint Price Code E

Plan E-3301

TO ORDER THIS BLUEPRINT, CALL TOLL-FREE 1-800-547-5570
(Prices and details on pp. 12-15.)

THE "SOURCE 1" PLANS PACKAGE — COMPLET

WHAT OUR PLANS INCLUDE

"SOURCE 1" construction blueprints are detailed, clear and concise. All blueprints are designed by licensed architects or members of the A.I.B.D. (American Institute of Building Designers), and each plan is designed to meet the nationally recognized building codes (either the Uniform Building Code, Standard Building Code or Basic Building Code) at the time and place they were drawn.

Although blueprints will vary depending on the size and complexity of the home and on the individual designer's style, each set will include the following elements:

1. **Exterior Elevations** show the front, rear, and the sides of the house including exterior materials, details, and measurements.

2. **Foundation Plans** include drawings for a full or daylight basement, crawlspace, or slab foundation. All necessary notations and dimensions are included. (Foundation options will vary for each plan. If the home you want does not have the type of foundation you desire, a foundation conversion diagram is available from "SOURCE 1".)

3. **Detailed Floor Plans** show the placement of interior walls and the dimensions for rooms, doors, windows, stairways, etc. of each level of the house.

4. **Cross Sections** show details of the house as though it were cut in slices from the roof to the foundation. The cross sections detail the home's construction, insulation, flooring and roofing details.

5. **Interior Elevations** show the specific details of cabinets (kitchen, bathroom, and utility room) fireplaces, built-in units, and other special interior features.

6. **Roof Plans** provide the layout of rafters, dormers, gables, and other roof elements including clerestory windows and skylights.

7. **Schematic Electrical Layouts** show the suggested location for switches, fixtures, and outlets.

8. **General Specifications** provide general instructions and information regarding structural specifications, excavating and grading, masonry and concrete work, carpentry and wood specifications, thermal and moisture protection, and specifications about drywall, tile, flooring, glazing, caulking and sealants.

NOTE: Due to regional variations, local availability of materials, local codes, methods of installation, and individual preferences, it is impossible to include much detail on heating, plumbing, and electrical work on your plans. The duct work, venting, and other details will vary depending on the type of heating and cooling system (forced air, hot water, electric, solar) and the type of energy (gas, oil, electricity, solar) that you use. These details and specifications are easily obtained from your builder, contractor, and/or local suppliers.

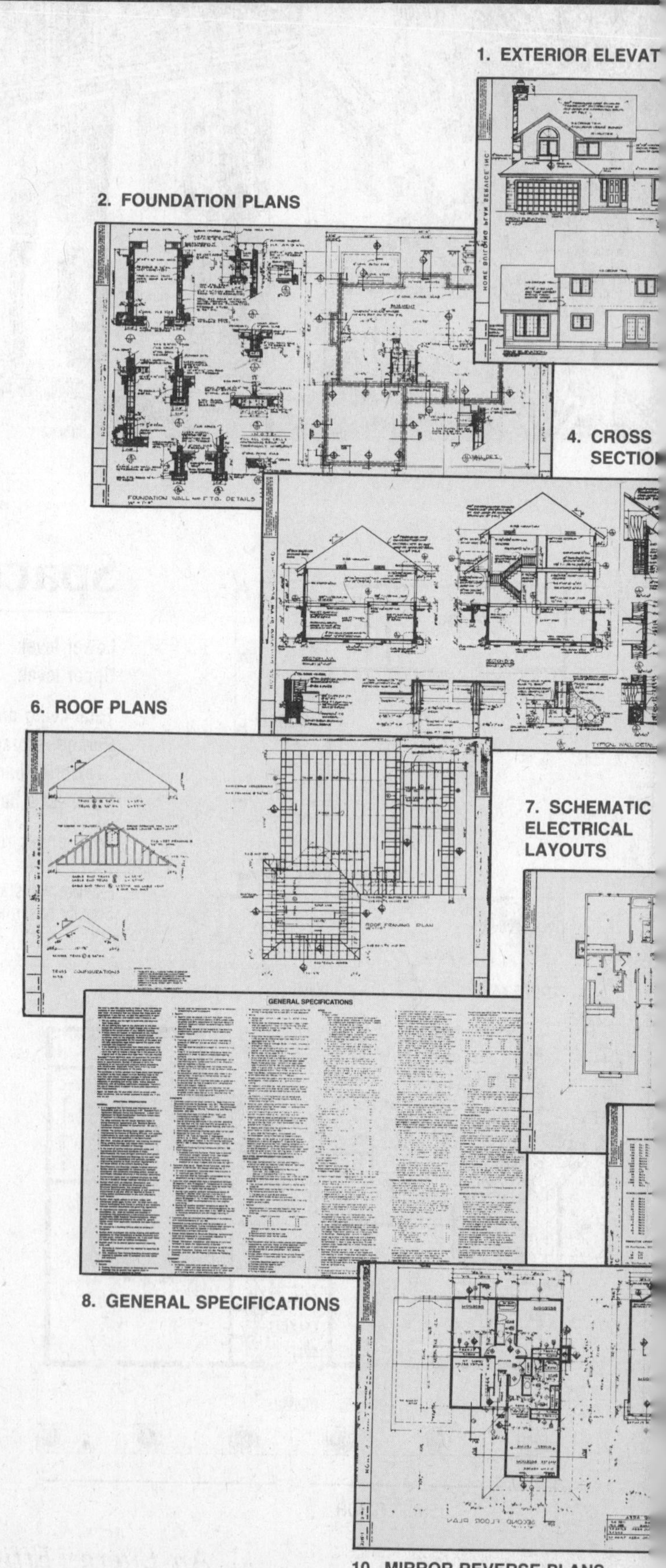

CONSTRUCTION BLUEPRINTS TO BUILD YOUR HOME

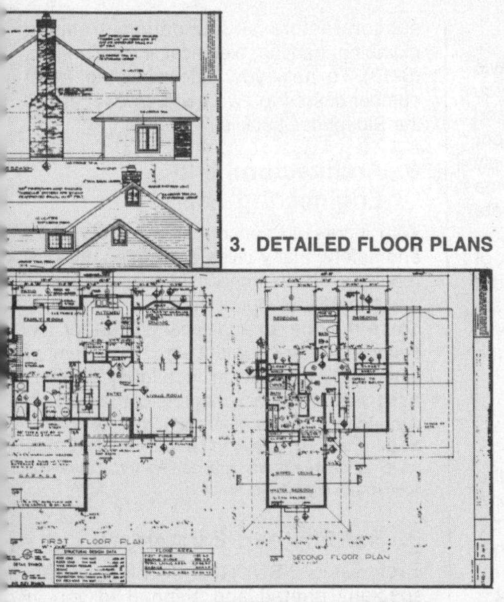

3. DETAILED FLOOR PLANS

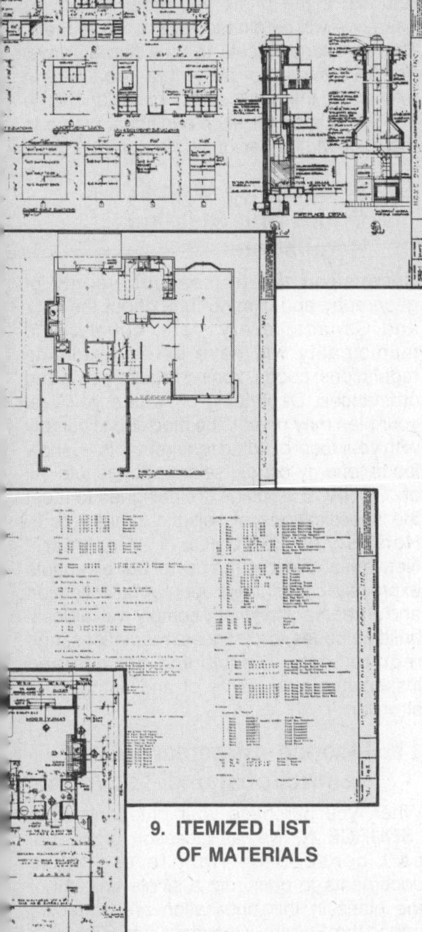

5. INTERIOR ELEVATIONS

9. ITEMIZED LIST OF MATERIALS

11. HELPFUL "HOW-TO" DIAGRAMS

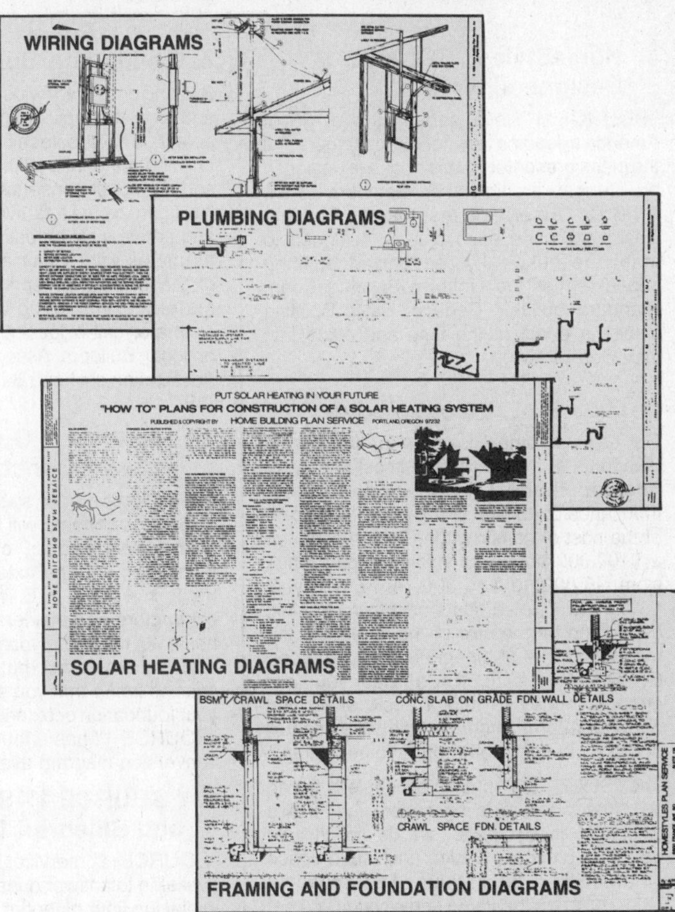

Important Extras and Helpful Building Aids

(Sold Separately)

Every set of plans that you order will contain all the details that your builder will need. However, "Source 1" provides additional guides and information as follows:

9. **Itemized List of Materials** details the quantity, type, and size of materials needed to build your home. (This list is extremely helpful in acquiring an accurate construction estimate. It is not intended for use to order materials.)

10. **Mirror Reverse Plans** are useful if you want to build your home in the reverse of the plan that is shown. Reverse plans are available for an additional charge. However, since the lettering and dimensions will read backwards, we recommend that you order at least one regular-reading set of blueprints.

11. **Helpful "How-To" Diagrams — Plumbing, Wiring, Solar Heating, and Framing and Foundation Conversion Diagrams**

Each of these diagrams details the basic tools and techniques needed to plumb, wire, and install a solar heating system, convert plans with 2 x 4 exterior walls to 2 x 6 (or vice versa), or adapt a plan for a basement, crawlspace, or slab foundation.

WHAT YOU NEED TO KNOW BEFORE YOU ORDER

1. HomeStyles "SOURCE 1" Designers' Network

"SOURCE 1" is a consortium of 35 of America's leading residential designers. All the plans presented in this book are designed by licensed architects or members of the A.I.B.D. (American Institute of Building Designers), and each plan is designed to meet the nationally recognized building codes (either the Uniform Building Code, Standard Building Code or Basic Building Code) in effect at the time and place that they were drawn.

2. Blueprint Price Schedule

Our sales volume allows us to offer quality blueprints at a fraction of the cost it takes to develop them. Custom designs cost thousands of dollars, usually 5 to 15 percent of the cost of construction. Design costs for a $100,000 home, for example, can range from $5,000 to $15,000. A HomeStyles "SOURCE 1" plan costs only $190 to $490 depending on the size of the home and the number of sets of blueprints that you order. By ordering a "SOURCE 1" plan, you save enough money to add a deck, swimming pool, beautiful kitchen, luxurious master bedroom, elegant bathroom, or other extras.

The "SOURCE 1" pricing schedule is based on "total finished living space." When we calculate "living space" we do not include garages, porches, decks, unfinished space or unfinished basements. The schedule below outlines the value and savings you get from ordering "SOURCE 1" plans and multiple sets:

NUMBER OF SETS	PRICE CODE GROUP BY SQUARE FEET						
	A Under 1,500	B 1,500-1,999	C 2,000-2,499	D 2,500-2,999	E 3,000-3,499	F 3,500-3,999	G 4,000 & Up
*7	$265	$315	$350	$385	$420	$455	$490
4	$235	$275	$305	$340	$375	$410	$445
1	$190	$225	$255	$285	$320	$355	$390

*Prices guaranteed to December 31, 1991.

3. Revisions, Modifications, and Customizing

The tremendous variety of designs available through "SOURCE 1" allows you to choose the home that best suits your lifestyle, budget and building site. Your home can be easily customized through your choice of siding, roof, trim, decorating, color, and other non-structural alterations and materials.

Most "SOURCE 1" plans are easily modified by qualified professionals. Minor changes and material substitutions can be made by any professional builder without the need for expensive blueprint revisions. However, if you are considering making major changes to your design, we strongly recommend that you seek the services of an architect or professional designer to assist you.

Also, every state, county, and municipality has its own codes, zoning requirements, ordinances, and building regulations. Modifications may be necessary to comply with your specific requirements — snow loads, energy codes, seismic zones, etc.

4. Estimating Building Costs

Building costs vary widely depending on style and size, the type of finishing materials you select, and the local rates for labor and building materials. With an average cost per square foot of construction, you can multiply this figure by the total living area of your home and derive a rough estimate. More accurate estimates will require a professional review of the working blueprints and the types of materials you choose. To get a rough estimate, call a local contractor, your state or local Builders Association, the National Association of Home Builders (NAHB), or the AIBD.

5. Foundation Options and Exterior Construction

Depending on your specific geography and climate, your home will be built with either a slab, crawlspace, or basement type foundation and the exterior walls will either be 2 x 4 or 2 x 6. Most professional contractors and builders can easily adapt a home to meet the foundation and exterior wall requirements that you desire. If the specific home that you select does not meet your foundation or exterior wall requirements, "SOURCE 1" has a foundation and framing conversion diagram available.

6. "SOURCE 1" Service Policy and Blueprint Delivery

"SOURCE 1" service representatives are available to answer questions and assist you in placing your blueprint order. All telephone orders are entered directly into our computer. Mail orders are entered upon receipt. We try to process and ship every order within 48 hours. For regular mailing (US First Class Mail or UPS Second Day Air) you should receive your blueprints within 4 to 5 working days. For express mail (UPS Next Day Air or Federal Express) please expect 1 to 2 days for delivery.

7. How Many Blueprints Should I Order?

BLUEPRINT CHECKLIST

_____ **OWNER'S SET(S)**
_____ **BUILDER** (usually requires at least three sets: one for legal document, one for inspections, and a minimum of one set for subcontractors.)
_____ **BUILDING PERMIT DEPARTMENT** (at least one set; check with your local governing body for number of sets required.)
_____ **LENDING INSTITUTION** (usually one set for conventional mortgage; three sets for FHA or VA loans.)
_____ **TOTAL NUMBER OF SETS NEEDED**

A single set of blueprints is sufficient to study and review a home in greater detail. However, if you are planning to get cost estimates or are planning to build, you will need a minimum of 4 sets and more likely 7 sets — sometimes more. Once you begin the process of building your home, everyone seems to need a set. As the owner, you will want to retain a set (1), your lending institution (2), the local building authorities (3), your builder/contractor (4), and of course, subcontractors — foundation, framing, plumbing, heating, electrical, insulation, etc. (5-10) To help you determine the exact number of sets you will need, please refer to the Blueprint Checklist.

8. Architectural and Engineering Seals

With increased concern over energy costs and safety, many cities and states are now requiring that an architect or engineer review and "seal" a blueprint prior to construction. There may be an additional charge for this service. Please contact your local lumber yard, municipal building department, Builders Association, or local chapters of the AIBD or American Institute of Architecture (AIA).

Note: (Plans for homes to be built in Nevada may have to be re-drawn and sealed by a Nevada-licensed design professional.)

9. Returns and Exchanges

Each set of "SOURCE 1" blueprints is specially printed and shipped to you in response to your specific order; consequently, we cannot honor requests for refunds. If the prints you order cannot be used, we will be pleased to exchange them. Please return all sets to us within 30 days. For the new set of plans that you select in exchange, there will simply be a flat charge of $50 (plus $5 for each additional set up to the original number of sets ordered).

10. Compliance With Local Codes and Building Regulations

Because of the tremendous variety of geography and climate throughout the U.S. and Canada, every state, county, and municipality will have its own building regulations, codes, zoning requirements and ordinances. Depending on where you live, your plan may need to be modified to comply with your local building requirements — snow loads, energy codes, seismic zones, etc. All of "SOURCE 1" plans are designed to meet the specifications of seismic zones I or II. HomeStyles "SOURCE 1" Designers' Network authorizes the use of our blueprints expressly conditioned upon your obligation and agreement to strictly comply with all local building codes, ordinances, regulations, and requirements — including permits and inspections at the time of and during construction.

11. License Agreement, Copy Restrictions, and Copyright

When you purchase your blueprints from "SOURCE 1," we, as Licensor, grant you, as Licensee, the right to use these documents to construct a single unit. All of the plans in this publication are protected under the Federal Copyright Act, Title XVII of the United States Code and Chapter 37 of the Code of Federal Regulations. Each "Source 1" designer retains title and ownership of the original documents. The blueprints licensed to you cannot be used, resold to any other person, copied or reproduced by any means.

Order Form and Price Schedule

hone: Call in your order and credit card payment information to our toll-free number, 1-800-547-5570.
ax: Fax your order form with credit card payment information to our International Fax number, 612-338-1626.
ail: Fill out the order form below and mail it to HomeStyles at the address shown at the top of the form.
OLIDAY SAVINGS! SAVE $30 OFF ANY PLAN: To receive discount, mention it with your phone order, or check Box on the Order Form below.

Holiday Savings! $30 Off Plan Orders

BLUEPRINT ORDER FORM

Mail to:
HomeStyles "Source 1"
275 Market St., Suite 521
Minneapolis, MN 55405

For Faster Service
Call Toll-Free
1-800-547-5570

Please send me the following:

Plan Number ______________ **Price Code** ________

Foundation ______________________

(Please review your plan carefully for foundation options — basement, crawlspace, or slab. Many plans offer all three options, others offer only one.)

Number of Sets	A	B	C	D	E	F	G	Amount
☐ 7	$295	$345	$380	$415	$450	$485	$520	$ ______
☐ 4	$265	$305	$335	$370	$405	$440	$475	$ ______
☐ 1	$220	$255	$285	$315	$350	$385	$420	$ ______

*Prices guaranteed to December 31, 1992.

☐ **HOLIDAY SAVINGS**—Deduct $30 if you order before Dec. 31, 1991. $ ______

☐ **Additional Sets** of this plan, $25 now; $35 later, each. (Number of sets ______) $ ______

☐ **Itemized List of Materials,** $30, each additional set $10. $ ______
Lists are available only for plans with prefix letters AH, AM*, AX, B, C, CDG*, CPS, DD*, DG, E, H, I, J, K, N, NW*, P, R, S, SD, U, W
*Please ask when ordering, not available on all plans

☐ **Description of Materials:** Two sets $25 $ ______
(For use in obtaining FHA or VA financing)
(Only available for Plans with prefix letters C, H, J, K, N, P, U)

☐ **Mirror Reverse Surcharge,** $25 $ ______
(Number of sets to be reversed ______.)
*The writing on Mirror Reverse plans will be backwards. Order at least one regular set.

☐ **Typical How-To Diagrams** $ ______
☐ Plumbing ☐ Wiring ☐ Solar Heating
☐ Framing & Foundation Conversion
One set @ $12.50, any two @ $23.00, any three @ $30.00, all four only $35.

☐ **Sales Tax** (MN Residents, please add 6.5%) $ ______

Please Add Postage Charges (Check One)

☐ First-Class Priority or UPS Blue Label (U.S. only), $12.00 $ ______
Allow 4-5 working days for delivery. *Must have street address for UPS delivery.

☐ First-Class Priority (Canada only) $12.00 $ ______
Allow 2-3 weeks for delivery.

☐ Overnight Express Delivery (U.S. only) $25.00 $ ______
Allow 1-2 working days for delivery. *Must have street address.

☐ Express Delivery (Canada only) $40.00 $ ______
Allow 4-5 working days for delivery. *Must have street address.

☐ Overseas Airmail Delivery $50.00 $ ______
Allow approx. 7 working days.

Payment **TOTAL ORDER** $ ______

☐ Check/money order enclosed (in U.S. funds)
☐ VISA ☐ MasterCard ☐ AmEx ☐ Discover Exp. Date ______

Card Number ______________________

Signature ______________________

Name ______________________

Street ______________________

City ______________ State ____ Zip ______

Daytime Telephone (____) ______________

☐ Builder-Contractor ☐ Home Owner ☐ Renter PG-21

BLUEPRINT ORDER FORM

Mail to:
HomeStyles "Source 1"
275 Market St., Suite 521
Minneapolis, MN 55405

For Faster Service
Call Toll-Free
1-800-547-5570

Please send me the following:

Plan Number ______________ **Price Code** ________

Foundation ______________________

(Please review your plan carefully for foundation options — basement, crawlspace, or slab. Many plans offer all three options, others offer only one.)

Number of Sets	A	B	C	D	E	F	G	Amount
☐ 7	$295	$345	$380	$415	$450	$485	$520	$ ______
☐ 4	$265	$305	$335	$370	$405	$440	$475	$ ______
☐ 1	$220	$255	$285	$315	$350	$385	$420	$ ______

*Prices guaranteed to December 31, 1992.

☐ **HOLIDAY SAVINGS**—Deduct $30 if you order before Dec. 31, 1991. $ ______

☐ **Additional Sets** of this plan, $25 now; $35 later, each. (Number of sets ______) $ ______

☐ **Itemized List of Materials,** $30, each additional set $10. $ ______
Lists are available only for plans with prefix letters AH, AM*, AX, B, C, CDG*, CPS, DD*, DG, E, H, I, J, K, N, NW*, P, R, S, SD, U, W
*Please ask when ordering, not available on all plans

☐ **Description of Materials:** Two sets $25 $ ______
(For use in obtaining FHA or VA financing)
(Only available for Plans with prefix letters C, H, J, K, N, P, U)

☐ **Mirror Reverse Surcharge,** $25 $ ______
(Number of sets to be reversed ______.)
*The writing on Mirror Reverse plans will be backwards. Order at least one regular set.

☐ **Typical How-To Diagrams** $ ______
☐ Plumbing ☐ Wiring ☐ Solar Heating
☐ Framing & Foundation Conversion
One set @ $12.50, any two @ $23.00, any three @ $30.00, all four only $35.

☐ **Sales Tax** (MN Residents, please add 6.5%) $ ______

Please Add Postage Charges (Check One)

☐ First-Class Priority or UPS Blue Label (U.S. only), $12.00 $ ______
Allow 4-5 working days for delivery. *Must have street address for UPS delivery.

☐ First-Class Priority (Canada only) $12.00 $ ______
Allow 2-3 weeks for delivery.

☐ Overnight Express Delivery (U.S. only) $25.00 $ ______
Allow 1-2 working days for delivery. *Must have street address.

☐ Express Delivery (Canada only) $40.00 $ ______
Allow 4-5 working days for delivery. *Must have street address.

☐ Overseas Airmail Delivery $50.00 $ ______
Allow approx. 7 working days.

Payment **TOTAL ORDER** $ ______

☐ Check/money order enclosed (in U.S. funds)
☐ VISA ☐ MasterCard ☐ AmEx ☐ Discover Exp. Date ______

Card Number ______________________

Signature ______________________

Name ______________________

Street ______________________

City ______________ State ____ Zip ______

Daytime Telephone (____) ______________

☐ Builder-Contractor ☐ Home Owner ☐ Renter PG-21

Gracious Open-Concept Floor Plan

- A striking and luxurious contemporary, this home offers great space and modern styling.
- A covered entry leads to a spacious foyer which flows into the sunken dining and stunning Great Room area.
- A spectacular two-story high fireplace dominates the vaulted Great Room.
- A bright nook adjoins the open kitchen, which includes a corner window above the sink.
- The den, which may be an optional guest bedroom, also opens onto the expansive deck.
- The majestic master bedroom on the second floor offers a 10′ high coved ceiling, splendid bath, large closet and a private deck.
- Two other upstairs bedrooms share a second bath and a balcony hallway overlooking the Great Room and entry below.

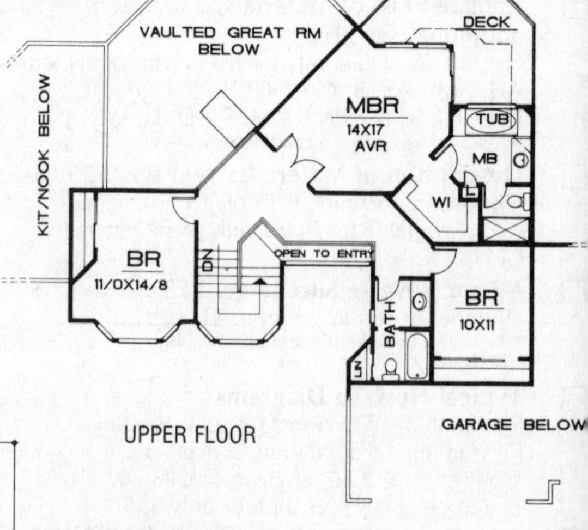

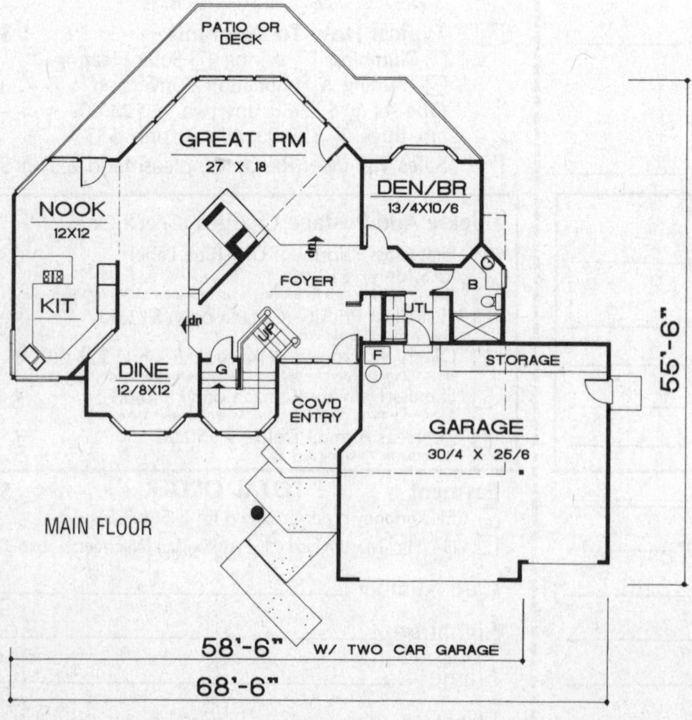

Plan S-41587

Bedrooms: 3-4	**Baths:** 3
Space:	
Upper floor:	1,001 sq. ft.
Main floor:	1,550 sq. ft.
Total living area:	2,551 sq. ft.
Basement:	1,550 sq. ft.
Garage (triple):	773 sq. ft.
Exterior Wall Framing:	2x6

Foundation options:
Daylight basement.
Standard basement.
Crawlspace.
(Foundation & framing conversion diagram available — see order form.)

Blueprint Price Code: D

TO ORDER THIS BLUEPRINT, CALL TOLL-FREE 1-800-547-5570
(prices and details on pp. 12-15.)

Plan S-41587

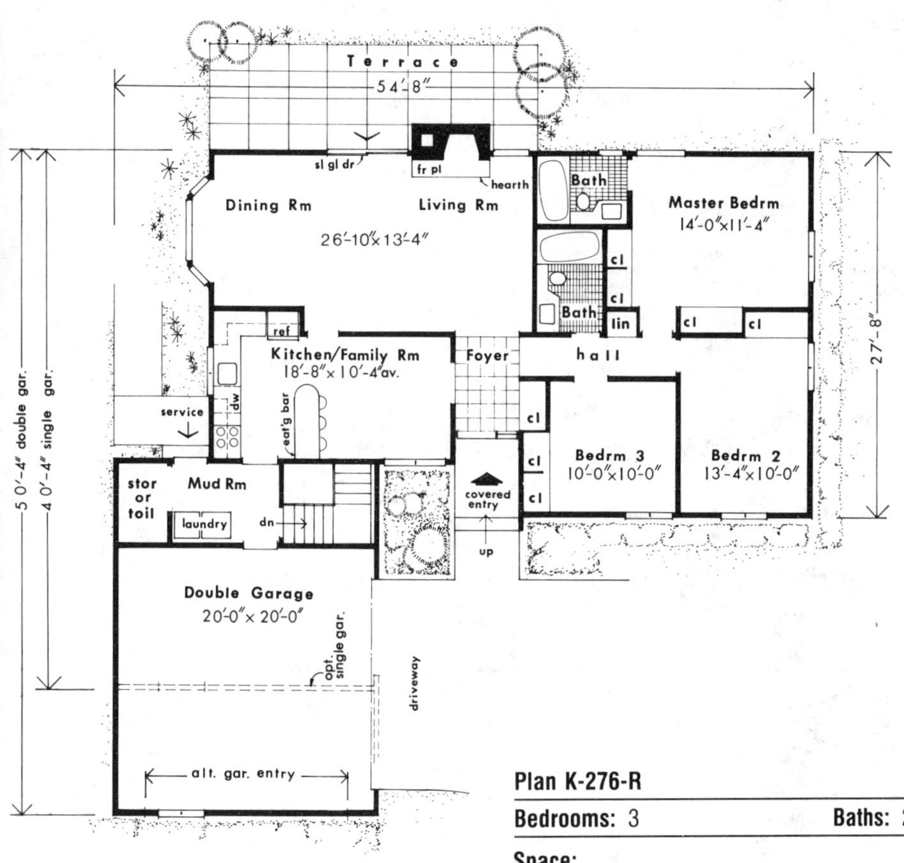

Compact, Economical to Build

- This economically-structured L-shaped ranch puts a great many desirable features into a mere 1,193 sq. ft. of living space. A wood-burning fireplace highlights the living area. Sliding glass doors open to the backyard terrace.
- The kitchen/family room features an eating bar.
- Covered entry welcomes you to the central foyer for easy channeling to any part of the house.
- Located in a wing of their own are three bedrooms and two baths.
- For a narrow lot, the garage door could face the front.

Plan K-276-R

Bedrooms: 3 **Baths:** 2

Space:

Total living area:	1,193 sq. ft.
Basement:	1,193 sq. ft.
Garage, mud room, etc.:	551 sq. ft.
Exterior Wall Framing:	2x4 or 2x6

Foundation options:
Standard basement.
Crawlspace.
Slab.
(Foundation & framing conversion diagram available — see order form)

Blueprint Price Code: A

Plan K-276-R

TO ORDER THIS BLUEPRINT, CALL TOLL-FREE 1-800-547-5570
(prices and details on pp. 12-15.)

Practical and Cozy

This three-bedroom, two-bath eye-catcher blends plenty of practicality with a hideaway coziness. Its multi-level design places two bedrooms and one bath upstairs, ideal as the separate children's area that many parents prize. They will also enjoy the lavish master suite that awaits on the main floor, complete with its pass-through walk-in wardrobe and over-sized vanity counter.

Within outside dimensions of 34' width by 48' depth, this home appears to far exceed its 1,346 sq. ft. Vaulted ceilings sweep up to meet an exposed beam that spans the entire diagonal length of the immense great room and dining areas. Another exposed beam merges with the first to extend its vaulted ceilings over a sunny morning room that opens to an intimate private patio. Note the stylish kitchen design, with its convenient access to the two adjacent eating areas.

Main floor:	963 sq. ft.
Upper floor:	383 sq. ft.
Total living area: (Not counting garage)	1,346 sq. ft.

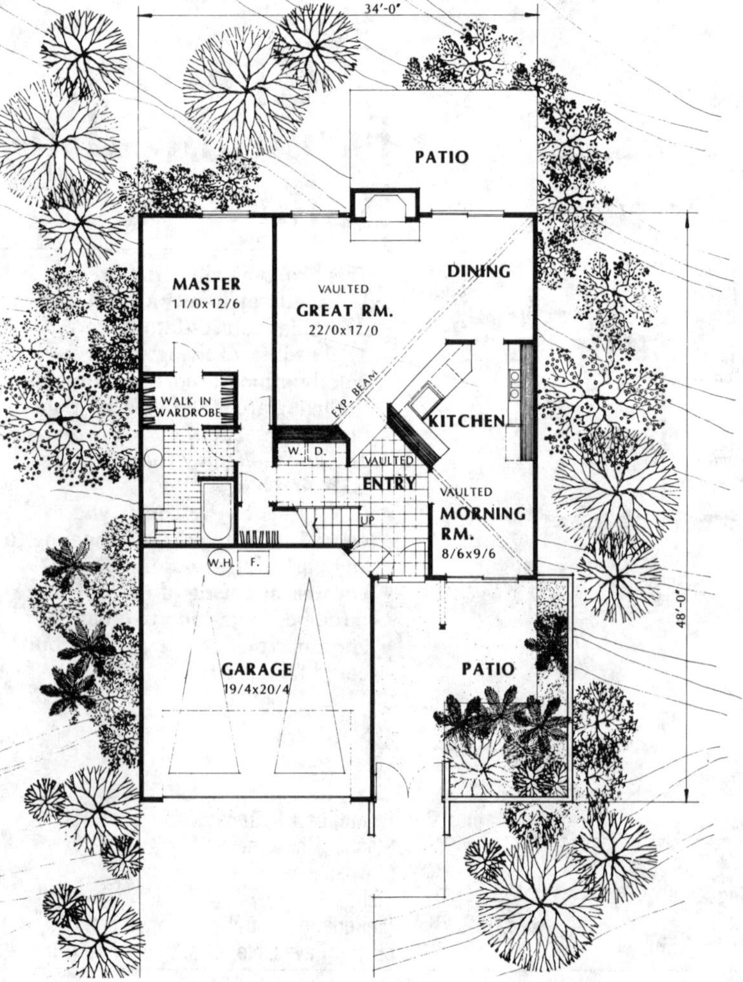

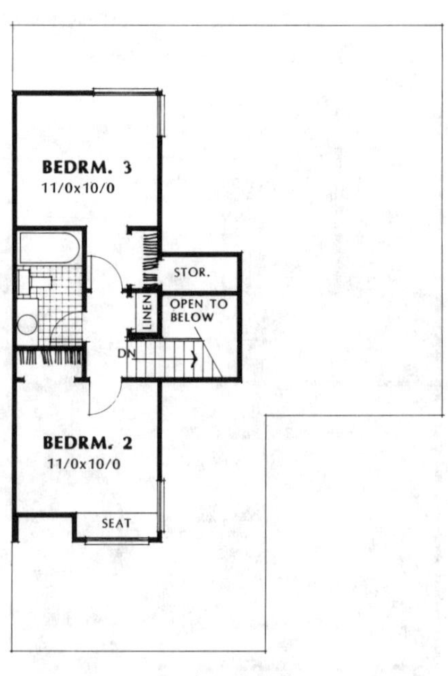

PLAN P-6564-3A
WITHOUT BASEMENT

TO ORDER THIS BLUEPRINT, CALL TOLL-FREE 1-800-547-5570
(prices and details on pp. 12-15.)

Blueprint Price Code A

Plan P-6564-3A

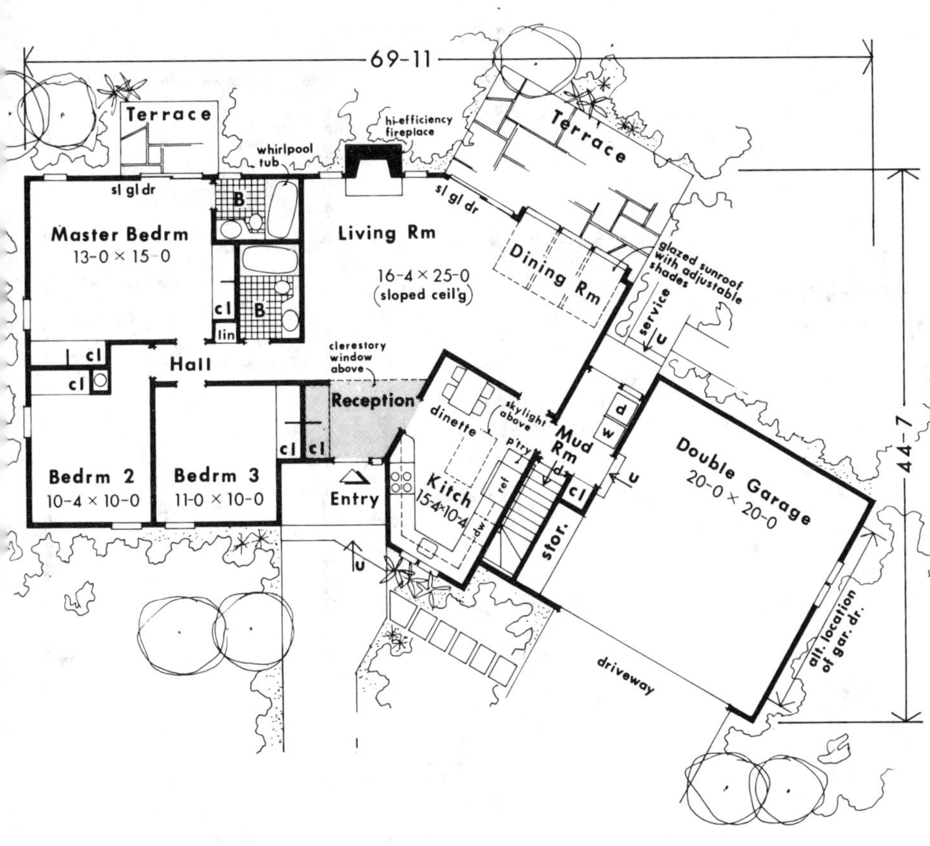

Angled Design Captures the Sun

Finished in traditional clapboard siding and rustic roof shingles, this single-story passive solar design is deliberately angled at its core to capture optimum sunlight and to accommodate regular as well as irregular sites.

The living room is highlighted by a dramatic sloped ceiling and a wood-burning fireplace. The adjacent dining room is accentuated by the glazed ceiling and wall that flood the area with sunshine and solar warmth. The glazed ceiling panels have adjustable screens for summer shading. The U-shaped kitchen features a dinette area, crowned with a large skylight above.

Three bedrooms are isolated in a wing of their own. The master bedroom has a terrace and a private bath, equipped with a whirlpool tub. For best benefits, it is recommended that the rear of house faces south, or nearly south. Total living area is 1,237 sq. ft.; garage, mud room, etc., 525 sq. ft.; optional basement is 1,264 sq. ft.

Total living area: (Not counting basement or garage)	1,237 sq. ft.
Garage, mud room:	525 sq. ft.
Basement (optional):	1,264 sq. ft.

Blueprint Price Code A

Plan K-523-C

TO ORDER THIS BLUEPRINT, CALL TOLL-FREE 1-800-547-5570

(prices and details on pp. 12-15.)

Two-Story Masonry Design

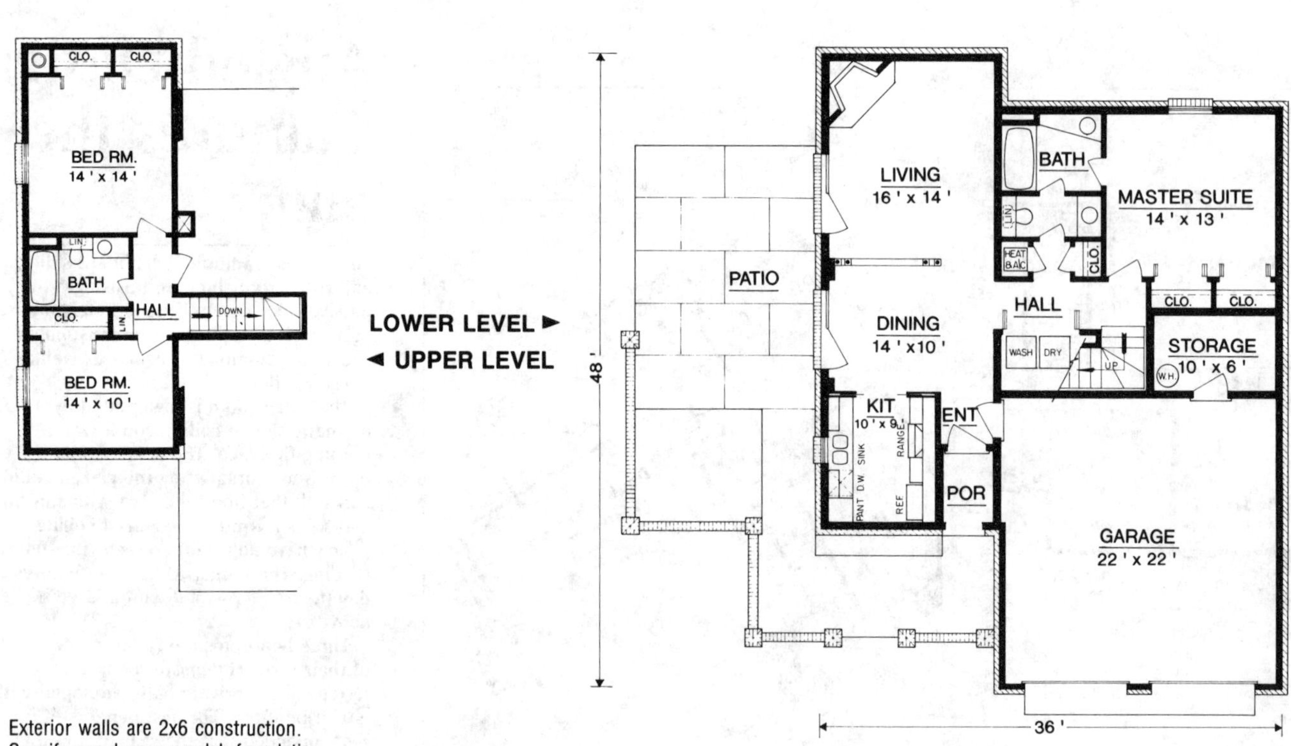

Exterior walls are 2x6 construction.
Specify crawlspace or slab foundation.

AREAS

Living	1452 sq. ft.
Garage & Storage	547 sq. ft.
Porch	27 sq. ft.
Total	2026 sq. ft.

An Energy Efficient Home

Blueprint Price Code A

TO ORDER THIS BLUEPRINT, CALL TOLL-FREE 1-800-547-5570

(prices and details on pp. 12-15.)

Plan E-1422

Cozy, Rustic Comfort

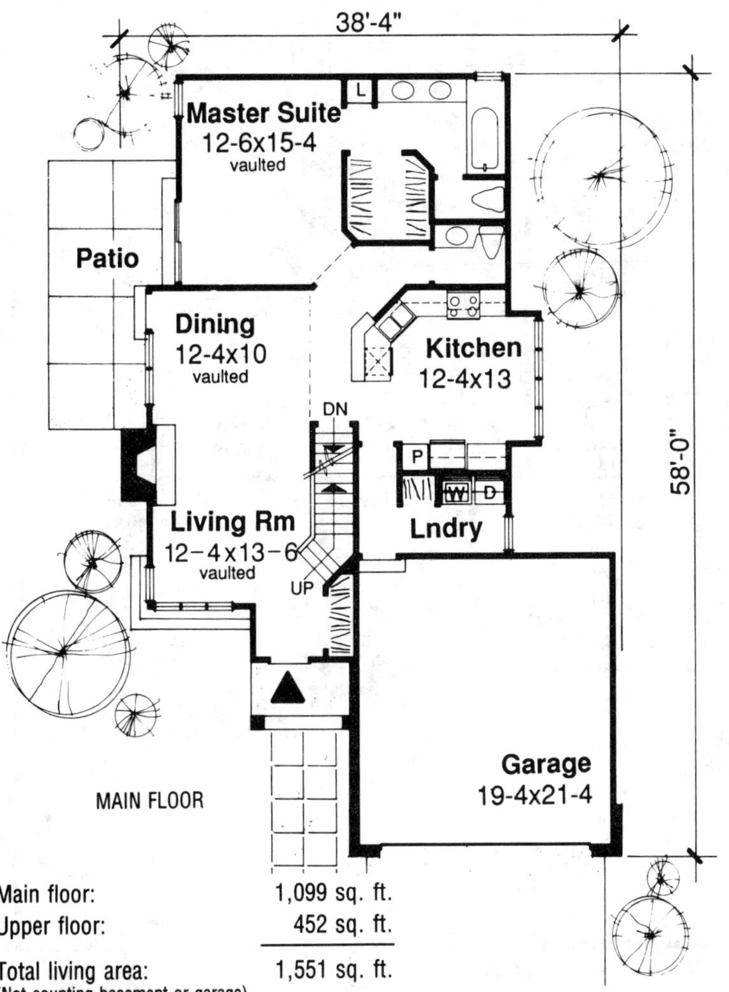

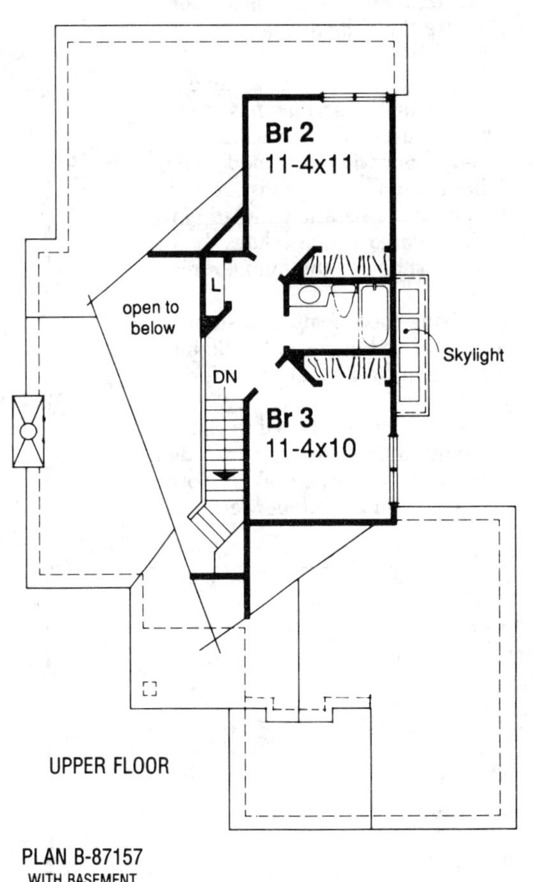

PLAN B-87157
WITH BASEMENT

Main floor:	1,099 sq. ft.
Upper floor:	452 sq. ft.
Total living area: (Not counting basement or garage)	1,551 sq. ft.

Blueprint Price Code B

Plan B-87157

TO ORDER THIS BLUEPRINT, CALL TOLL-FREE 1-800-547-5570
(prices and details on pp. 12-15.)

Open Plan Includes Circular Dining Room

- **Innovative architectural features and a functional, light-filled floor plan are the hallmarks of this attractive design.**
- **The facade is graced by a stone chimney and a circular glass bay which houses the spectacular dining room with its domed ceiling.**
- **A bright, sunny kitchen is set up for efficient operation and adjoins a dinette area which echoes the circular shape of the formal dining room.**
- **The living room features a stone fireplace, and opens to the dining room to make a great space for entertaining.**
- **The bedrooms are zoned to the left, with the master suite including a private bath, large walk-in closet and access to an outdoor terrace.**

Plan K-663-N

Bedrooms: 3	**Baths:** 2
Space:	
Total living area:	1,560 sq. ft.
Basement:	1,645 sq. ft.
Garage:	453 sq. ft.
Mudroom & stairs:	122 sq. ft.
Exterior Wall Framing:	2x4/2x6

Foundation options:
Standard basement.
Slab.
(Foundation & framing conversion diagram available — see order form.)

Blueprint Price Code:	B

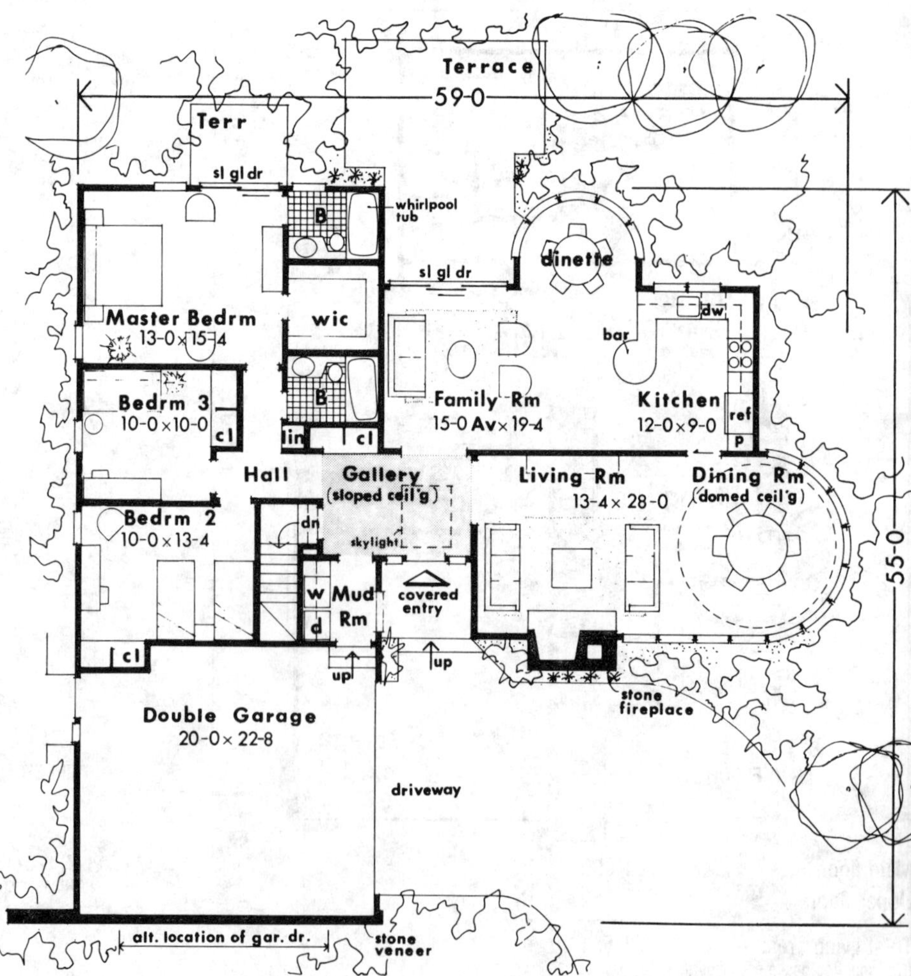

TO ORDER THIS BLUEPRINT, CALL TOLL-FREE 1-800-547-5570
(prices and details on pp. 12-15.)

Plan K-663-N

Let the Sun Shine In!

- This exciting energy-efficient design uses a southern exposure window-wall to take advantage of the warmth of the sun, and gives a dramatic exterior look in the process.
- A trellis beam and built-in insulated shutters or drapes for summer shade, a concrete slab and trombe wall to store the sun's heat, full insulation and some earth berming all add to the energy efficiency and cost savings.
- The main floor includes a vast Great Room for living, dining and entertaining. It has a dramatic cathedral ceiling leading up to an optional study loft with balcony overlook.
- The kitchen is large enough for an informal eating arrangement.
- The main floor master bedroom has dual closets and handy access to the bathroom and laundry facilities.
- The upper level can be finished now or later and includes two bedrooms and a second full bathroom.

28'0"

CL
UP
MASTER BEDRM 12'4" x 13'6"
MASONRY "TROMBE" WALL
CL
CL
BATH
LIVING/ DINING RM 25'0" x 14'4"
D W
PANTRY
REF
LINE OF BALCONY ABOVE
KITCHEN 12'4" x 13'4"
DW
CL
DN
FOYER
36'0"

MAIN FLOOR

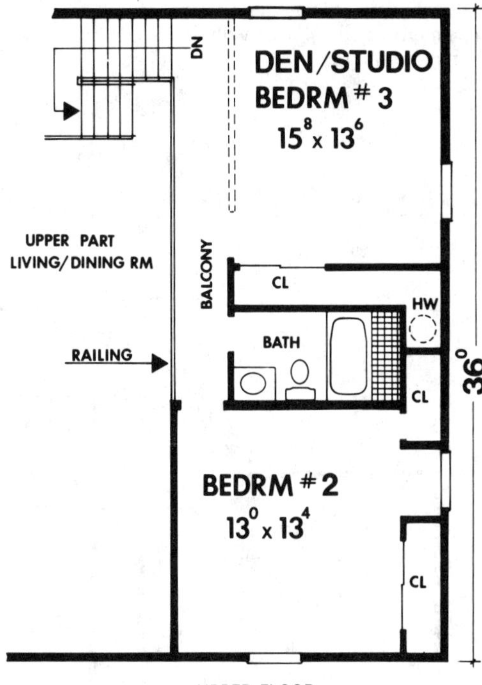

UPPER FLOOR

Plan AX-98055

Bedrooms: 3	**Baths:** 2	**Exterior Wall Framing:**	2x6
Space:		**Foundation options:**	
Upper floor:	582 sq. ft.	Slab.	
Main floor:	1,008 sq. ft.	(Foundation & framing conversion diagram available — see order form.)	
Total living area:	1,590 sq. ft.		
One-car garage:	288 sq. ft.		
Two-car garage:	480 sq. ft.	**Blueprint Price Code:**	B

Plan AX-98055

TO ORDER THIS BLUEPRINT, CALL TOLL-FREE 1-800-547-5570
(prices and details on pp. 12-15.)

Design Reflects Finesse

This especially handsome yet simple ranch house attracts admiration with its exterior facade of stone, shingles, and natural tone (unpainted) wood, all used with finesse. The house layout is practical, but with many imaginative touches. There are two entries to the house, one through the mud room, the other a formal, covered front entranceway.

To the left of the welcoming gallery is the dining room-living room area, with elegant cathedral ceiling. The living room has an optional entrance to the family room, covered by folding doors. The dinette, with a curved wall of stock-size windows overlooking the terrace, also has a screen or partition shielding it from the family room. The family room offers a sliding glass exit to the terrace and a built-in fireplace.

To the right of the gallery lie the three bedrooms. The master suite contains a walk-in closet and a surprise: a skylight above the dressing alcove. The master bedroom has its own bath while the other two bedrooms share a bath. There is plenty of closet and storage space throughout. The basic house is 1,672 sq. ft.; optional basement is 1,672 sq. ft.; garage, etc., is 546 sq. ft.

Living area:	1,672 sq. ft
Basement (opt.):	1,672 sq. ft
Garage, mud rom, etc.:	546 sq. ft

(Alternate slab-on-grade foundation plan included.)

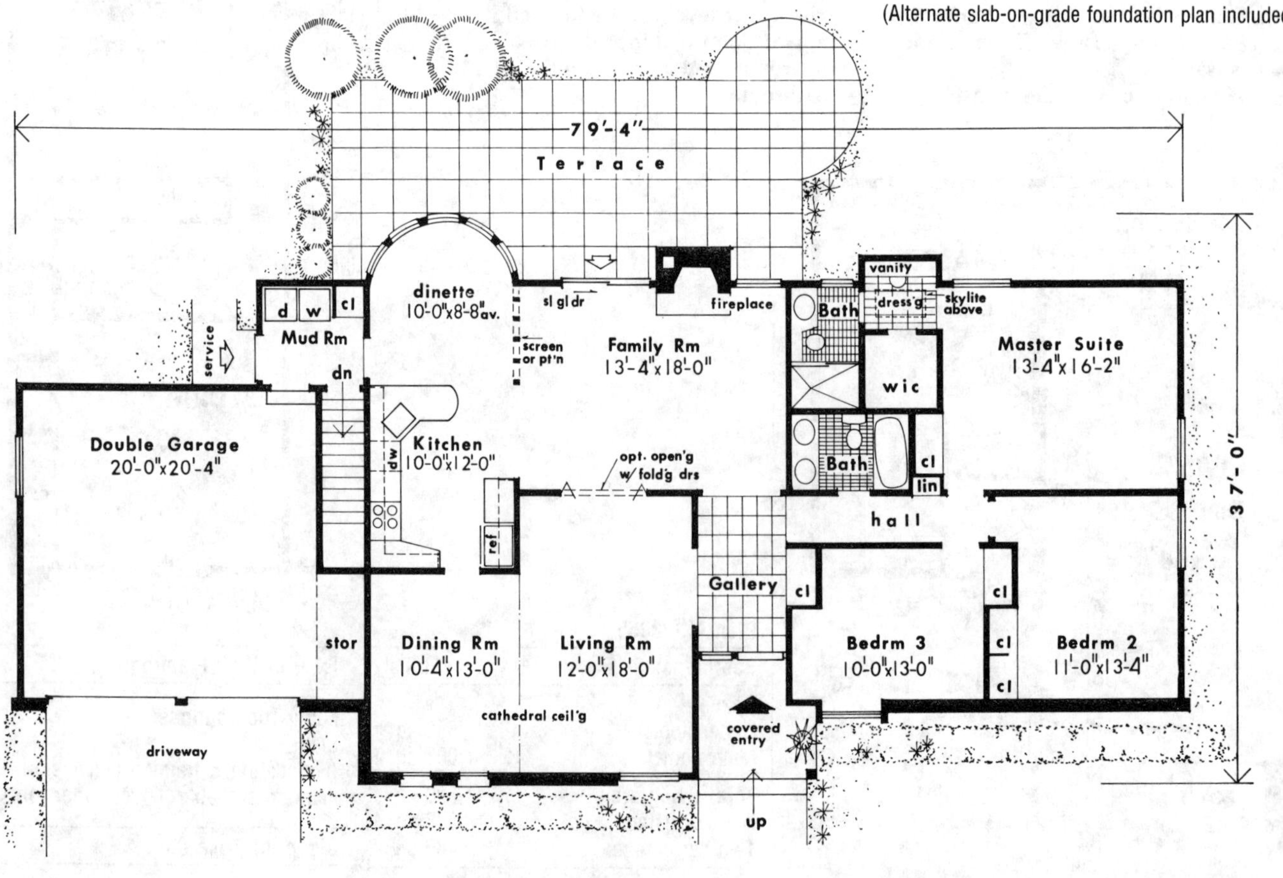

79'-4"
Terrace
dinette 10'-0"x8'-8"av.
sl gl dr
fireplace
screen or pt'n
Family Rm 13'-4"x18'-0"
d w cl
Mud Rm
service
dn
Double Garage 20'-0"x20'-4"
Kitchen 10'-0"x12'-0"
dw
ref
opt. open'g w/ fold'g drs
vanity
Bath
dress'g
skylite above
Master Suite 13'-4"x16'-2"
wic
Bath
cl
lin
hall
37'-0"
Gallery
cl
cl
cl
cl
stor
Dining Rm 10'-4"x13'-0"
Living Rm 12'-0"x18'-0"
Bedrm 3 10'-0"x13'-0"
Bedrm 2 11'-0"x13'-4"
cathedral ceil'g
covered entry
driveway
up

TO ORDER THIS BLUEPRINT, CALL TOLL-FREE 1-800-547-5570
(prices and details on pp. 12-15.)

Blueprint Price Code B

Plan K-162-J

Compact Two-Story Features Front Courtyard

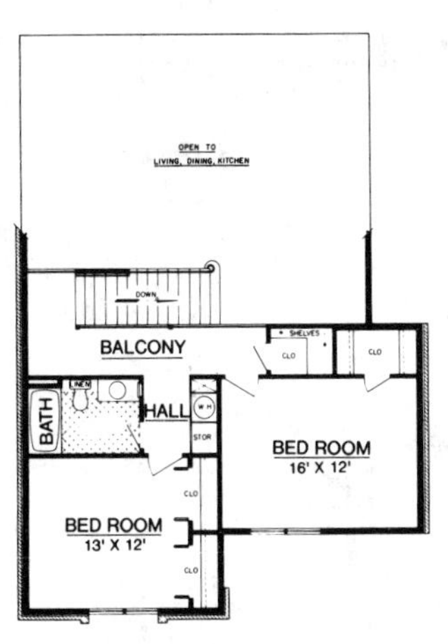

LOWER LEVEL ►

◄ UPPER LEVEL

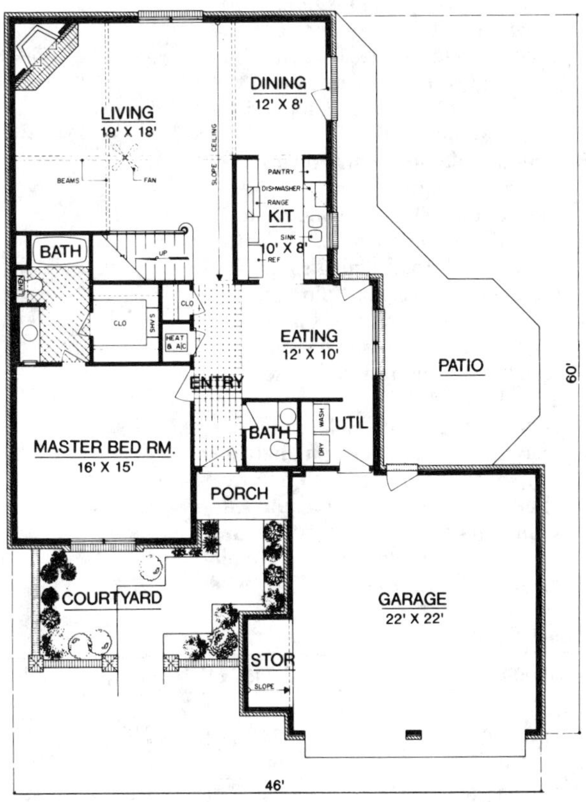

AREAS

Living-Lower Level	1224 sq. ft.
Living-Upper Level	608 sq. ft.
Living-Total	1832 sq. ft.
Garage & Storage	516 sq. ft.
Porch	32 sq. ft.
Total	2380 sq. ft.

Exterior walls are 2x6 construction.
Specify crawlspace or slab foundation.

An Energy Efficient Home

Blueprint Price Code B

Plan E-1817

TO ORDER THIS BLUEPRINT, CALL TOLL-FREE 1-800-547-5570
(prices and details on pp. 12-15.)

Visual Surprises

- The exterior of this two-story, four-bedroom design is boldly accented with a dramatic roof cavity, while the inside features wall angles that enhance the efficiency of the floor plan and offer visual variety.
- The double-door entry opens into a bright reception area, leading to the sloped-ceilinged living room.
- The efficient kitchen conveniently serves the formal dining room and the cheerful breakfast dinette.
- Off the reception area is a powder room and a large laundry space which could be finished to serve as a hobby room.
- Four bedrooms are isolated on the second level; a connecting balcony is open to the living room below.
- The master suite is fully equipped; sliding glass doors yield access to the open wood deck that is literally carved into the roof.

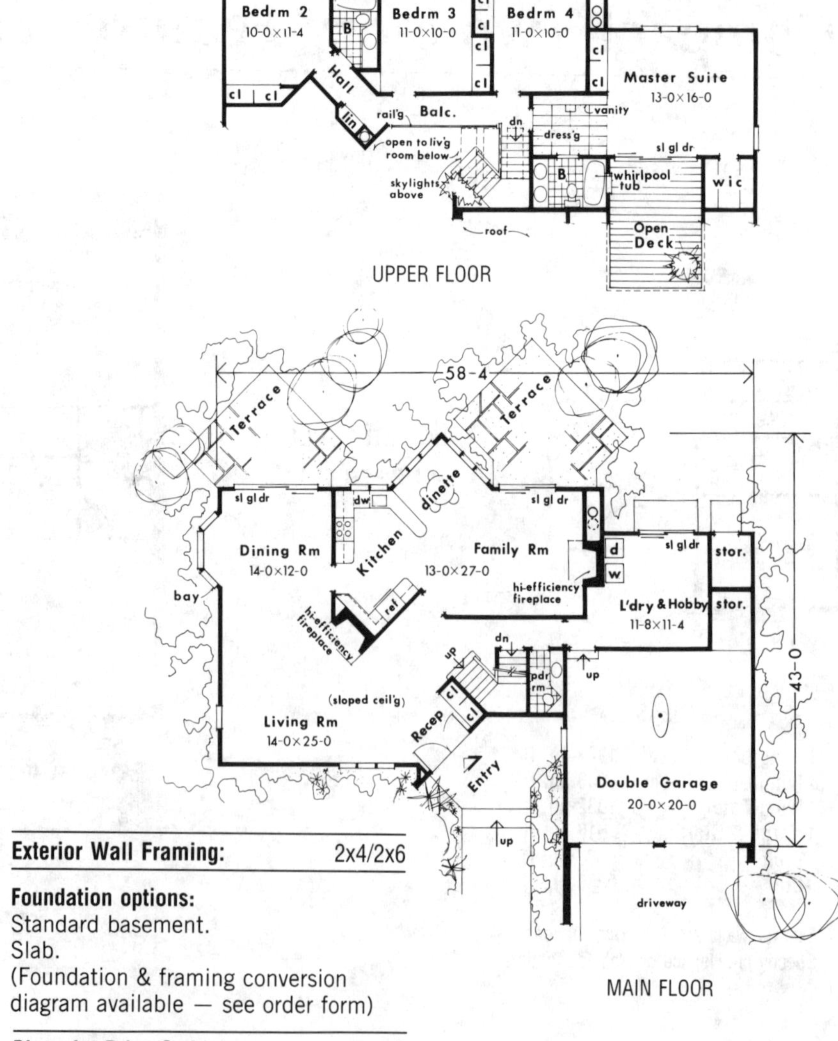

Plan K-540-L

Bedrooms: 4	Baths: 2½
Space:	
Upper floor:	884 sq. ft.
Main floor:	1,106 sq. ft.
Total living area:	1,990 sq. ft.
Basement:	1,106 sq. ft.
Garage:	400 sq. ft.
Storage, laundry:	254 sq. ft.

Exterior Wall Framing:	2x4/2x6

Foundation options:
Standard basement.
Slab.
(Foundation & framing conversion diagram available — see order form)

Blueprint Price Code:	B

TO ORDER THIS BLUEPRINT, CALL TOLL-FREE 1-800-547-5570
(prices and details on pp. 12-15.)

Plan K-540-L

A Garden Home with a View

- This clever design proves that privacy doesn't have to be compromised even in high-density urban neighborhoods. From within, all views are oriented to the sideyard and to a lush entry courtyard.
- The exterior view is sheltered, but still offers a warm, welcoming look.
- The innovate interior design centers on a unique kitchen, which directs traffic away from the working areas while still serving the entire home.
- The large sunken family room features a vaulted ceiling and large fireplace.
- The master suite is highlighted by a sumptuous master bath, with separate shower and whirlpool tub, plus a large walk-in closet.
- The formal living room is designed and placed in such a way that it can become a third bedroom, den, office or study room, depending on family needs and lifestyles.

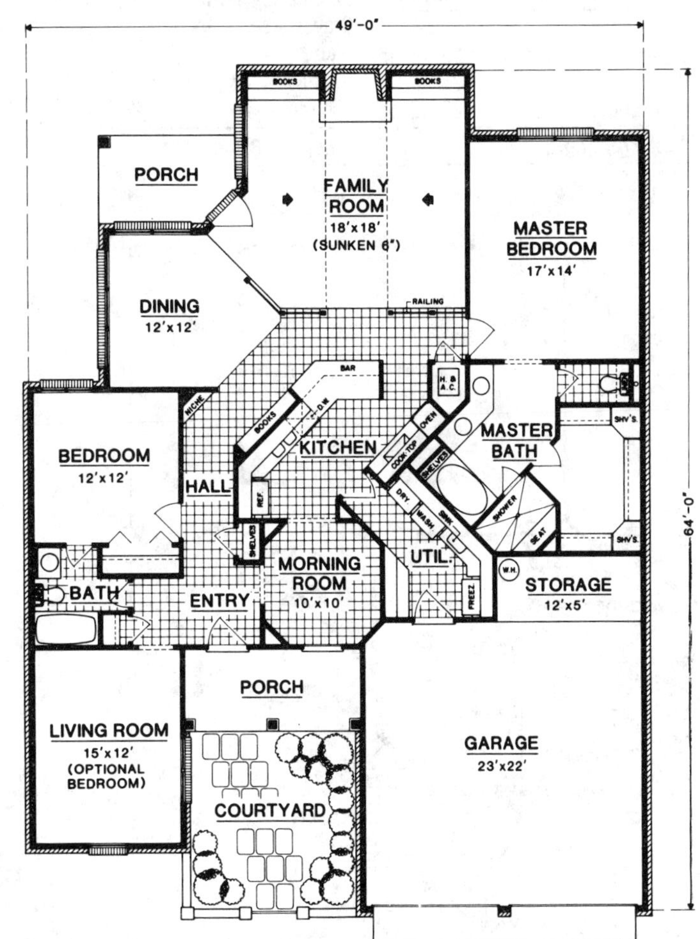

Plan E-1824

Bedrooms: 2-3	**Baths:** 2
Space:	
Total living area:	1,891 sq. ft.
Garage:	506 sq. ft.
Storage:	60 sq. ft.
Porches:	184 sq. ft.
Exterior Wall Framing:	2x6

Ceiling Heights::	9'
Foundation options:	
Crawlspace.	
Slab.	
(Foundation & framing conversion diagram available — see order form.)	
Blueprint Price Code:	B

Plan E-1824

TO ORDER THIS BLUEPRINT, CALL TOLL-FREE 1-800-547-5570

(prices and details on pp. 12-15.)

Plan E-2004

Bedrooms: 3	Baths: 2
Space:	
Total living area:	2,023 sq. ft.
Garage:	484 sq. ft.
Storage & Porches:	423 sq. ft.
Exterior Wall Framing:	2x6

Foundation options:
Crawlspace.
Slab.
(Foundation & framing conversion diagram available — see order form.)

Blueprint Price Code: C

Exciting Floor Plan In Traditional French Garden Home

- Creative, angular design permits an open floor plan.
- Living and dining rooms open to a huge covered porch.
- Kitchen, living and dining rooms feature impressive 12′ ceilings accented by extensive use of glass.
- Informal eating nook faces a delightful courtyard.
- Luxurious master bath offers a whirlpool tub, shower, and walk-in closet.
- Secondary bedrooms also offer walk-in closets.

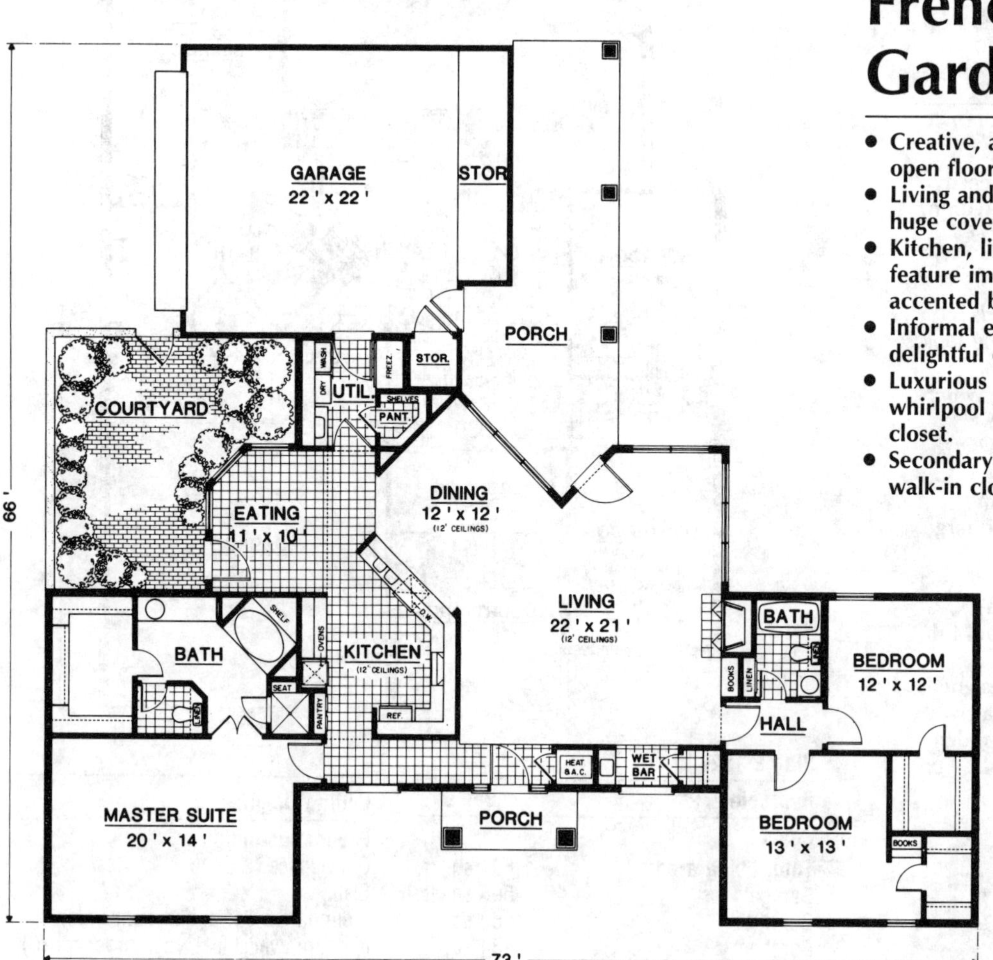

TO ORDER THIS BLUEPRINT, CALL TOLL-FREE 1-800-547-5570 (prices and details on pp. 12-15.)

Plan E-2004

Sunny Octagon Dining Room

- A cathedral ceiling, French doors to a side patio, and a fireplace accentuate the living room, which joins a quaint octagon dining room.
- The U-shaped kitchen opens to the dining room, and has access to the rear covered porch.
- Secluded to the rear is the master suite with walk-in closet and private bath with his 'n her vanities and luxury tub.
- The main floor also includes a guest room or extra bedroom with private bath access.
- A sitting area and dual closets are featured in one of the two upper floor bedrooms.

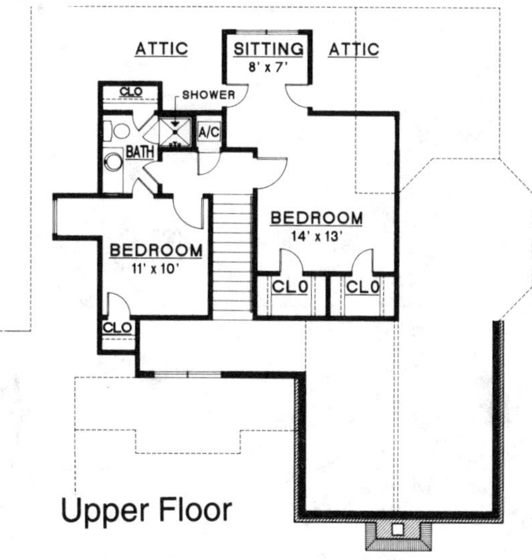

Upper Floor

Main Floor

Plan E-2005	
Bedrooms 4	**Baths** 3
Space:	
Upper floor	582 sq. ft.
Main floor	1,465 sq. ft.
Total Living Area	**2,047 sq. ft.**
Garage	484 sq. ft.
Exterior Wall Framing	2x6
Foundation options:	
Crawlspace	
Slab	
(Foundation & framing conversion diagram available—see order form.)	
Blueprint Price Code	C

HomeStyles SOURCE 1 Designers' Network

Plan E-2005

TO ORDER THIS BLUEPRINT, CALL TOLL-FREE 1-800-547-5570

(prices and details on pp. 12-15.)

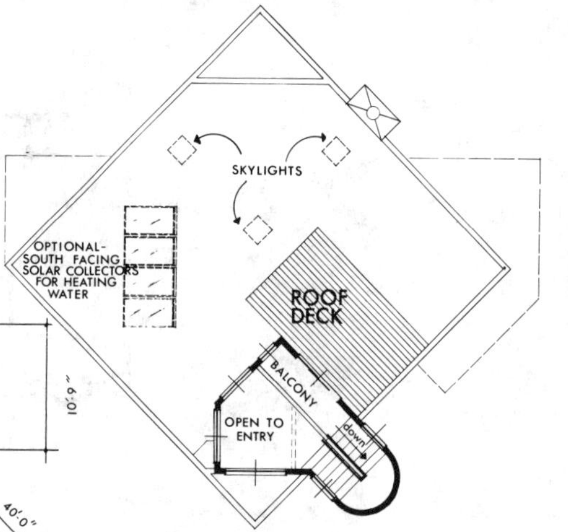

OPTIONAL- SOUTH FACING SOLAR COLLECTORS FOR HEATING WATER

SKYLIGHTS

ROOF DECK

BALCONY

OPEN TO ENTRY

down

ROOF TOP
UPPER LEVEL

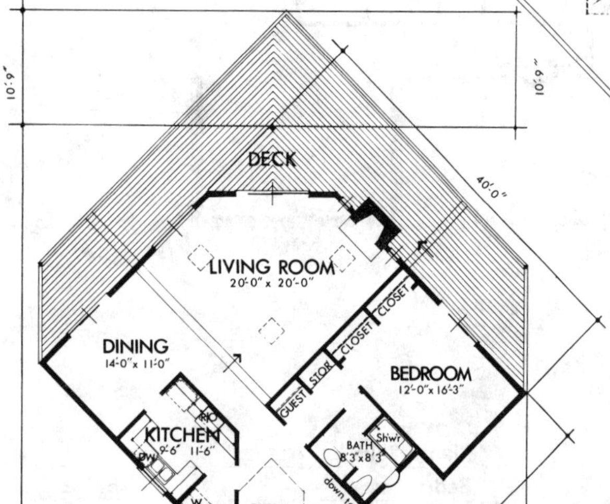

10'-9"

DECK

40'-0"

LIVING ROOM
20'-0" x 20'-0"

DINING
14'-0" x 11'-0"

CLOSET

CLOSET

GUEST

STOR

BEDROOM
12'-0" x 16'-3"

KITCHEN
9'-6" 11'-6"

BATH
8'3"x8'3"

Shwr

ENTRY

W

D

down to bsmt

up

36'-0"

75'-6"

CARPORT
21'-6" x 24'-0"

MAIN FLOOR

54'-0"

36'-0"

36'-0"

SKYLIGHTS

BEDROOM
14'-6" x 11'-0"

OPEN TO LIVING RM.

CLOSET

CLOSET

BEDROOM
12'-0" x 12'-0"

CLOSET

CLOSET

STORAGE

BALCONY RAILING

LIN

BATH

WH

WS

HEAT

OPEN TO ENTRY

up

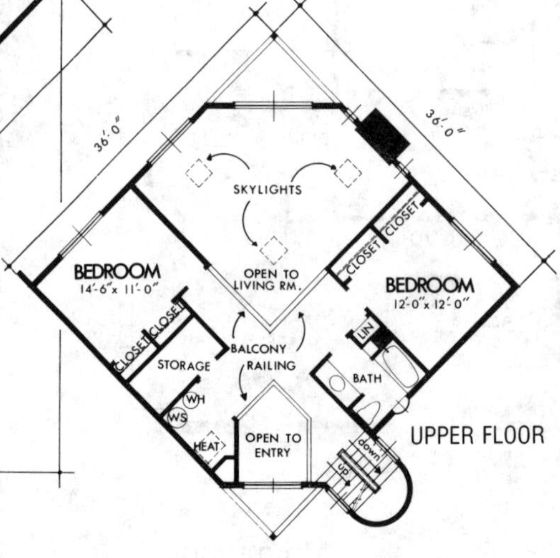

UPPER FLOOR

Striking Vertical Design

- Unique roof deck and massive wrap-around main level deck harbor an equally exciting interior.
- Large sunken living room is brightened by a three-window skylight and also features a log-sized fireplace.
- U-shaped kitchen is just off the entry, adjacent to handy laundry area.
- Second-story balcony overlooks the large living room and entryway below.

Plans H-935-1 & -1A

Bedrooms: 3	**Baths:** 2
Space:	
Upper floor:	844 sq. ft.
Main floor:	1,323 sq. ft.
Total living area:	2,167 sq. ft.
Basement:	approx. 1,323 sq. ft.
Carport:	516 sq. ft.
Exterior Wall Framing:	2x6

Foundation options:
Standard basement (Plan H-935-1).
Crawlspace (Plan H-935-1A).
(Foundation & framing conversion diagram available — see order form.)

Blueprint Price Code: C

TO ORDER THIS BLUEPRINT, CALL TOLL-FREE 1-800-547-5570
(prices and details on pp. 12-15.)

Plans H-935-1 & -1A

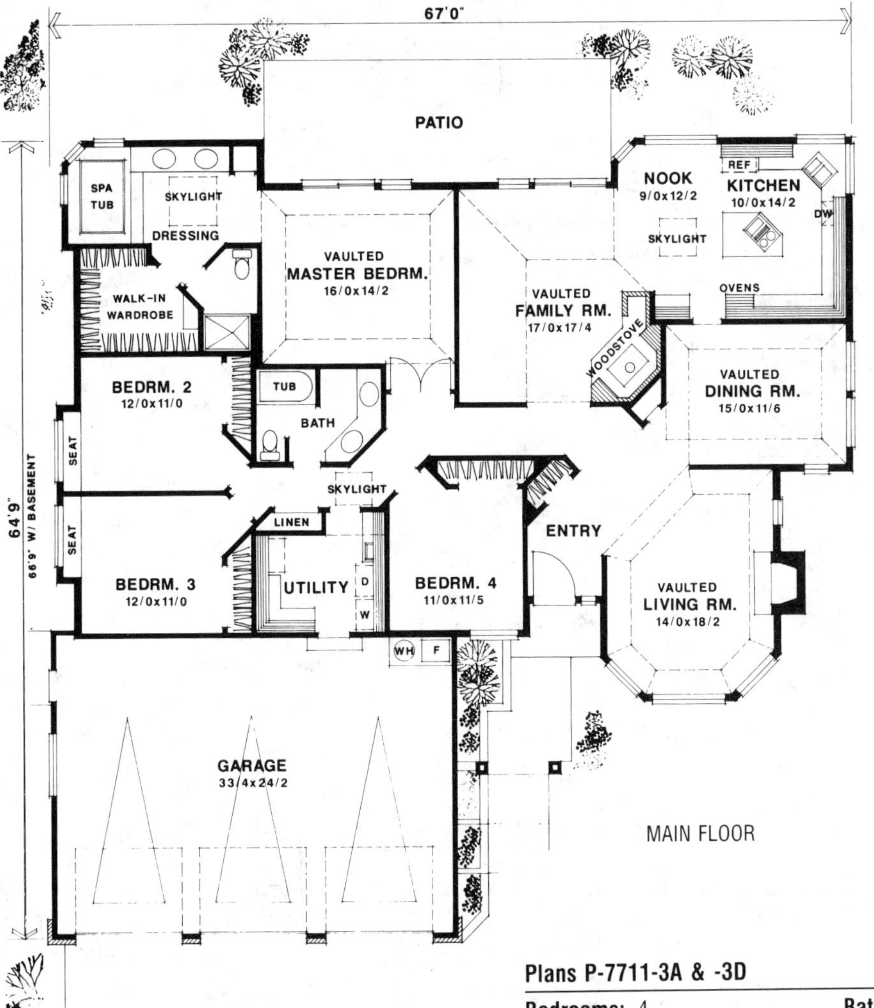

UTILITY
W
DN
GARAGE

PLAN P-7711-3D
WITH DAYLIGHT BASEMENT

Full of Surprises

- While dignified and reserved on the outside, this plan presents delightful surprises throughout the interior.
- Interesting angles, vaulted ceilings, surprising spaces and bright windows abound everywhere you look in this home.
- The elegant, vaulted living room is off the expansive foyer, and includes an imposing fireplace and large windows areas.
- The delightful kitchen includes a handy island and large corner windows in front of the sink.
- The nook is brightened not only by large windows, but also by a skylight.
- The vaulted family room includes a corner wood stove area plus easy access to the outdoors.
- A superb master suite includes an exquisite bath with a skylighted dressing area and large walk-in closet.
- Three secondary bedrooms share another full bath, and the large laundry room is conveniently positioned near the bedrooms.

Plans P-7711-3A & -3D

Bedrooms: 4 **Baths:** 2

Space:

Main floor (non-basement version):	2,510 sq. ft.
Main floor (basement version):	2,580 sq. ft.
Basement:	2,635 sq. ft.
Garage:	806 sq. ft.

Exterior Wall Framing: 2x6

Foundation options:
Daylight basement (Plan P-7711-3D).
Crawlspace (Plan P-7711-3A).
(Foundation & framing conversion diagram available — see order form.)

Blueprint Price Code: D

Plans P-7711-3A & -3D

TO ORDER THIS BLUEPRINT, CALL TOLL-FREE 1-800-547-5570
(prices and details on pp. 12-15.)

Stunning Exterior, Breathtaking Interior

- Here's a modern plan with Mediterranean design touches on the exterior and an interior that provides abundant space for entertaining as well as private family life.
- A covered porch leads into an expansive foyer which directs traffic to a sunken vaulted parlor on the one side or forward into the more casual portions of the home.
- A sunny reading room protrudes off to the side of the parlor and dining room.
- The huge sunken family room includes a wet bar, fireplace and vaulted ceiling.
- An imaginatively designed kitchen includes a skylight above the center island and a large pantry, in addition to abundant counter and cabinet space.
- A bright breakfast nook adjoins the kitchen and overlooks the family room two steps below.
- The expansive second floor includes a fantastic master suite with a vaulted ceiling, private balcony, huge closet and sumptuous bath.

Plan Q-3769-1A

Bedrooms: 3 | **Baths:** 4

Space:

Upper floor:	1,364 sq. ft.
Main floor:	2,405 sq. ft.
Total living area:	3,769 sq. ft.
Garage:	668 sq. ft.

Exterior Wall Framing: 2x4

Foundation options:
Slab only.
(Foundation & framing conversion diagram available — see order form.)

Blueprint Price Code: E

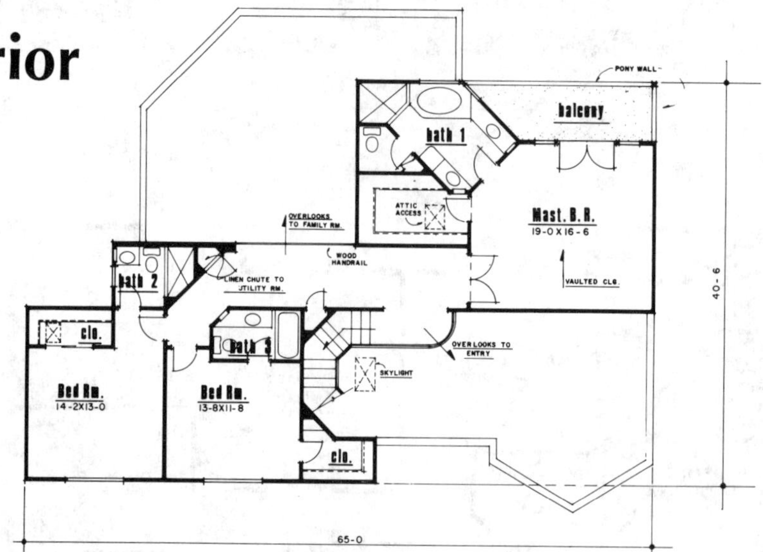

UPPER FLOOR

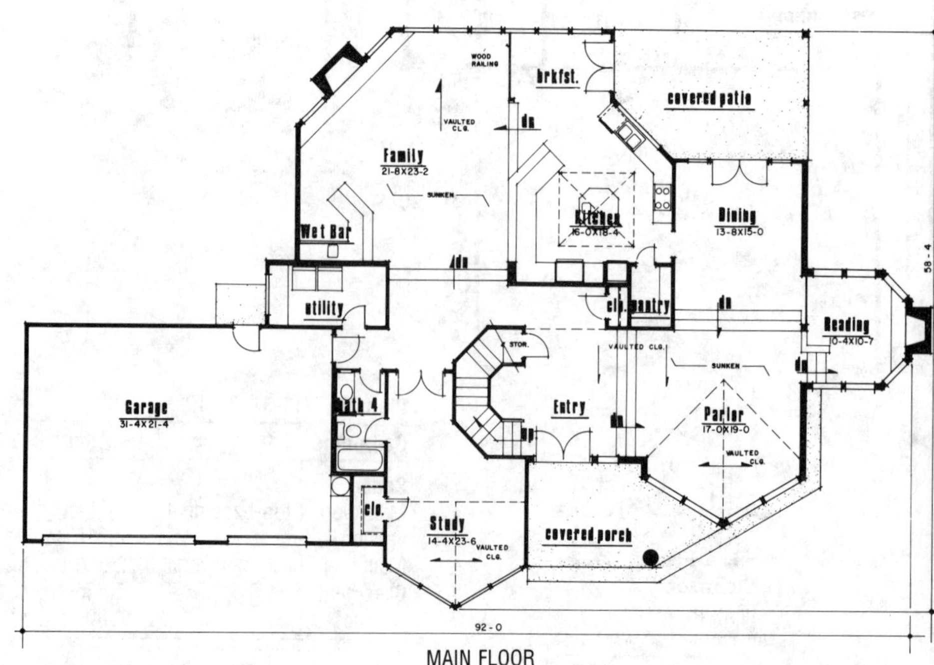

MAIN FLOOR

TO ORDER THIS BLUEPRINT, CALL TOLL-FREE 1-800-547-5570
(prices and details on pp. 12-15.)

Plan Q-3769-1A

PLAN H-2114-1B FRONT VIEW

MAIN FLOOR

Designed for Outdoor Living

- Dining room, living room, and spa are oriented toward the full-width deck extending across the rear of the home.
- Floor-to-ceiling windows, vaulted ceilings, and a fireplace are featured in the living room.
- Spa room has tile floor, operable skylights, and private access through connecting master suite.
- Upper level offers two bedrooms, spacious bathroom, and a balcony view of the living room and scenery beyond.

PLAN H-2114-1A
WITHOUT BASEMENT

Plans H-2114-1A & -1B

Bedrooms: 3-4	**Baths:** 2½-3½
Space:	
Upper floor:	732 sq. ft.
Main floor:	1,682 sq. ft.
Sun room:	147 sq. ft.
Total living area:	2,561 sq. ft.
Basement:	approx. 1,386 sq. ft.
Garage:	547 sq. ft.
Exterior Wall Framing:	2x6

Foundation options:
Daylight basement (Plan H-2114-1B).
Crawlspace (Plan H-2114-1A).
(Foundation & framing conversion diagram available — see order form.)

Blueprint Price Code:

Without basement:	D
With basement:	F

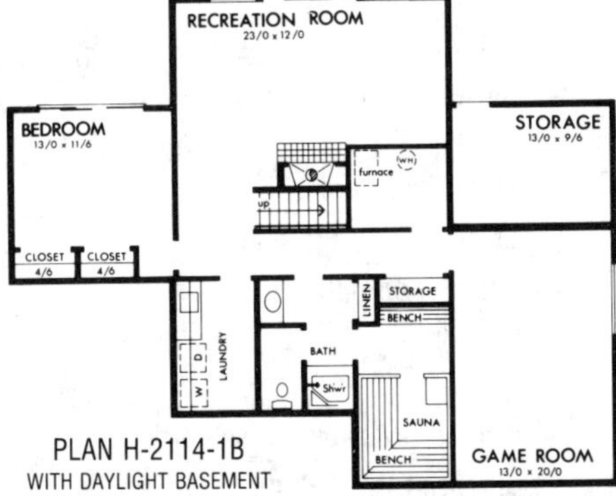

PLAN H-2114-1B
WITH DAYLIGHT BASEMENT

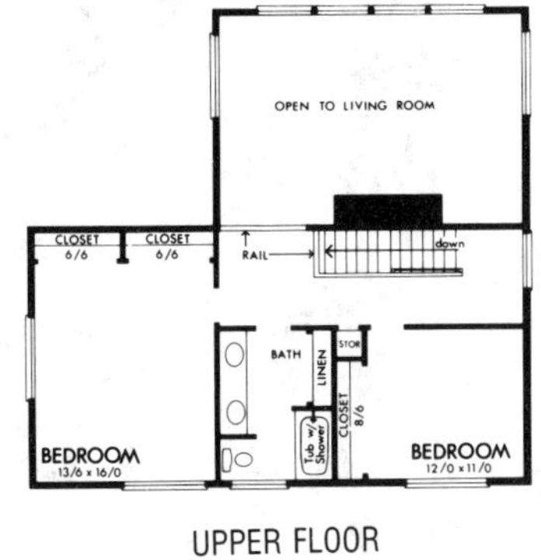

UPPER FLOOR

Plans H-2114-1A & -1B

TO ORDER THIS BLUEPRINT, CALL TOLL-FREE 1-800-547-5570
(prices and details on pp. 12-15.)

Lighthouse Recall

- For the lake or ocean-view lot, this unique home offers just the right look with its lighthouse recall.
- The plan's octagonal shape allows the family to take full advantage of breathtaking views, with plenty of windows, and even a crow's nest.
- The raised entry opens to a panoramic view of the main living area encircling the central fireplace and spiral stairs.
- The kitchen overlooks the breakfast nook and beyond to the dining room.
- The living room is steps down from the rest of the main level for a more spacious feel.
- The second floor houses three bedrooms and two full baths, while the entire third floor is a kids' activity room.

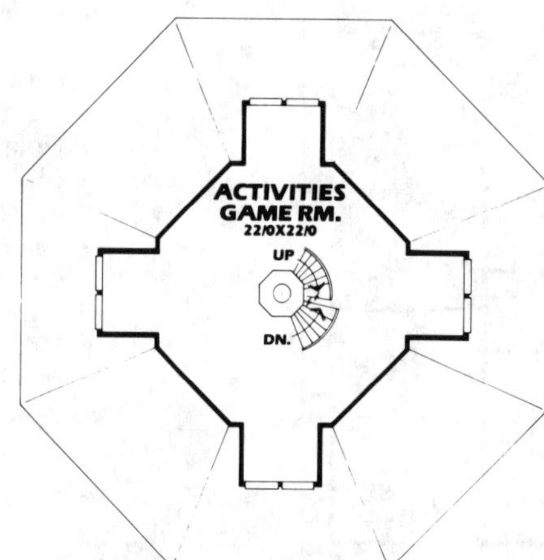

THIRD LEVEL

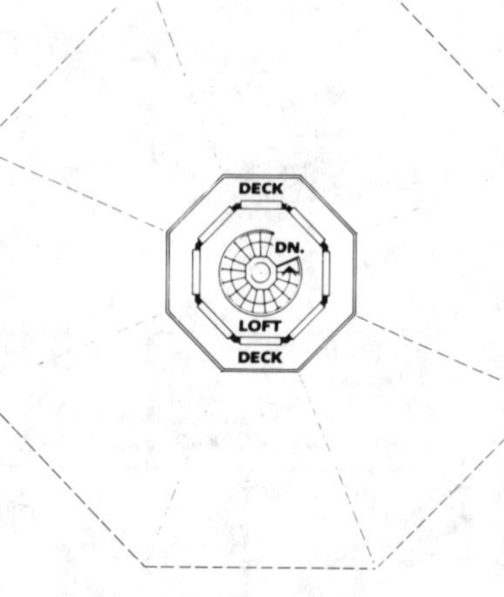

UPPER LEVEL

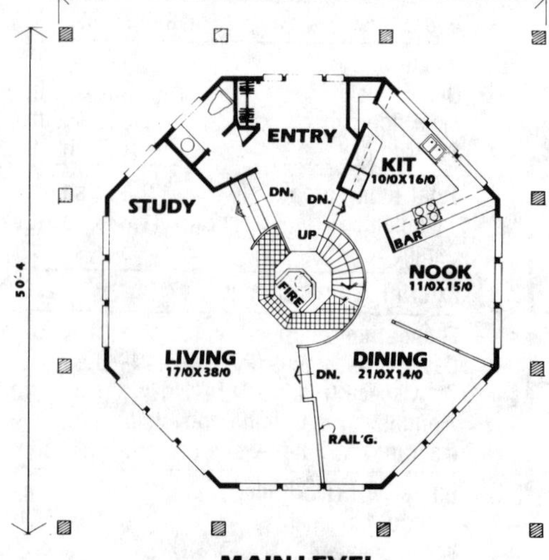

MAIN LEVEL

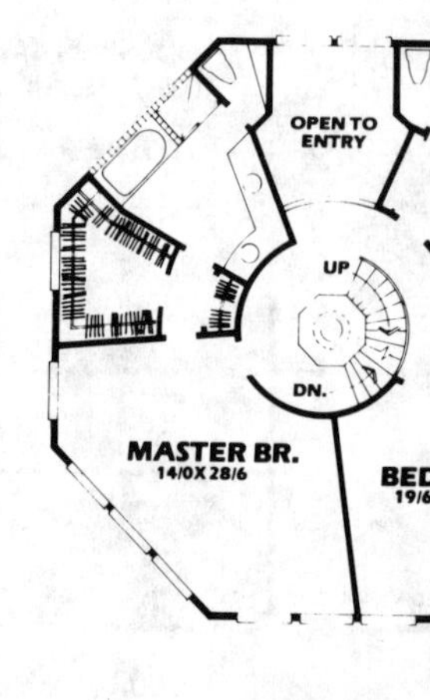

SECOND LEVEL

Plan SD-9009	
Bedrooms: 3	**Baths:** 2½
Space:	
Crow's nest:	100 sq. ft
Third floor:	597 sq. ft
Second floor:	1,294 sq. ft
Main floor:	1,393 sq. ft
Total living area:	3,384 sq. ft
Exterior Wall Framing:	2x4
Foundation options:	
Standard basement.	
Crawlspace.	
(Foundation & framing conversion diagram available — see order form.)	
Blueprint Price Code:	E

TO ORDER THIS BLUEPRINT, CALL TOLL-FREE 1-800-547-5570
(prices and details on pp. 12-15.)

Plan SD-9009

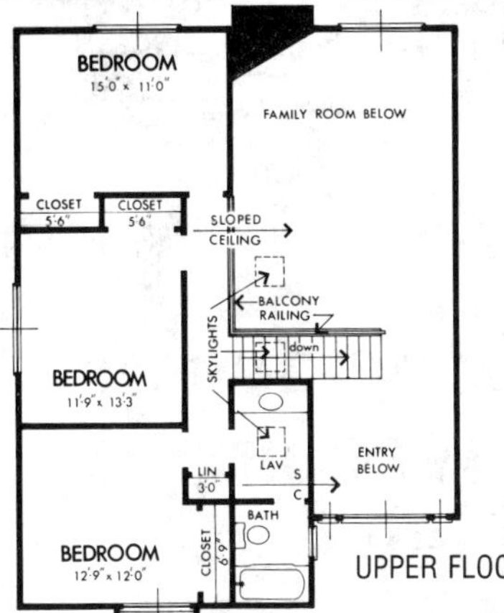

Pure Luxury in a Choice of Styles

- Southwestern colonial or Western contemporary exteriors are available when deciding if this spacious design is for you.
- Elaborate master suite features attached screened spa room, regular and walk-in closets, and luxurious bath with skylight.
- Study, large family and living room with sloped ceilings and rear patio are other points of interest.
- Three additional bedrooms make up the second level.
- The Spanish version (M2A) offers a stucco exterior and slab foundation.

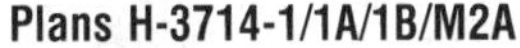

Plans H-3714-1/1A/1B/M2A

Bedrooms: 4	**Baths:** 3
Space:	
Upper floor:	740 sq. ft.
Main floor:	2,190 sq. ft.
Total living area:	2,930 sq. ft.
Basement:	1,153 sq. ft.
Garage:	576 sq. ft.
Exterior Wall Framing:	2x6

Foundation options:
Daylight basement (Plan H-3714-1B).
Standard basement (Plan H-3714-1).
Crawlspace (Plan H-3714-1A).
Slab (Plan H-3714-M2A).
(Foundation & framing conversion diagram available — see order form.)

Blueprint Price Code: D

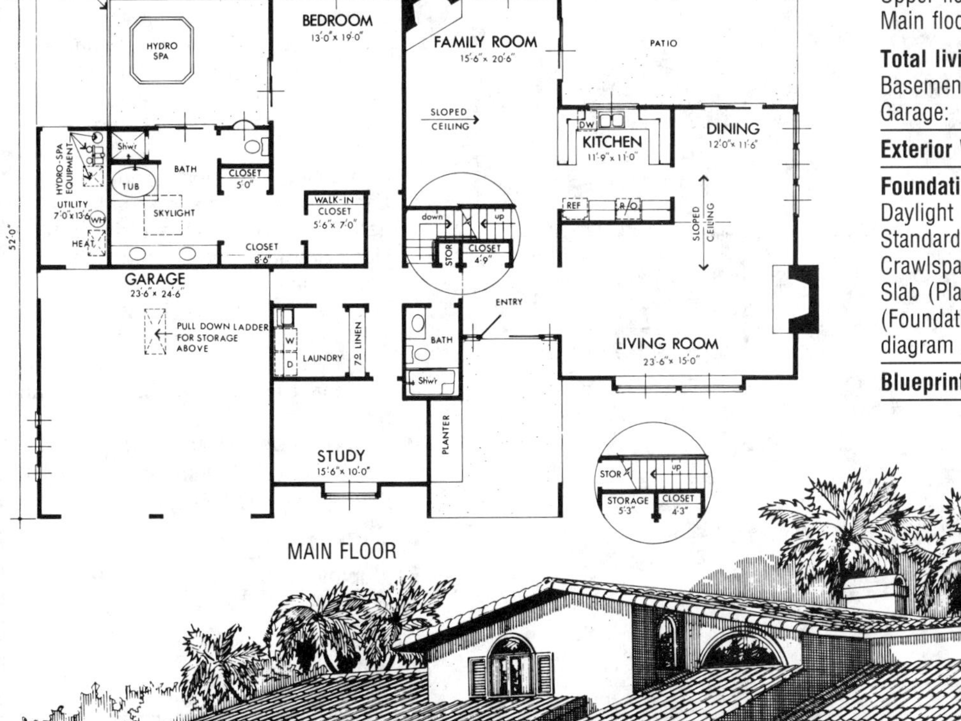

PLAN H-3714-M2A FRONT VIEW

Spectacular Sweeping Views

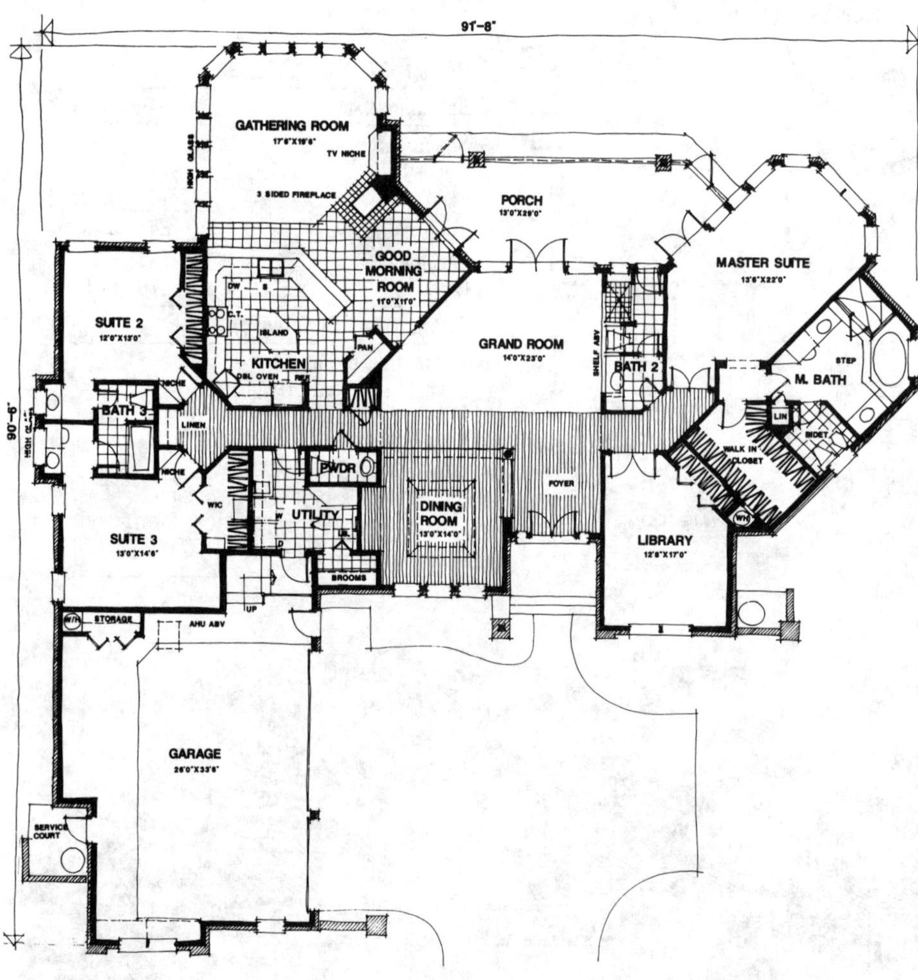

- The elegant brick facade of this exciting home conceals a highly contemporary interior.
- The foyer opens to a huge Grand Room that further opens to a delightful rear porch, also accessed through the morning room, pool bath and master suite.
- Completely surrounded in windows and high fixed glass is a spacious gathering room, also featuring a three-sided fireplace and built-in entertainment center.
- The spectacular master suite is secluded to the rear of the home, but wrapped in windows and offering its own fantastic bath with luxury tub and bidet.
- Two additional sleeping suites found at the other end of the home share a bath with private vanities.

Plan EOF-8

Bedrooms: 3-4	**Baths:** 3 ½
Space:	
Main floor	3,392 sq. ft.
Total Living Area	**3,392 sq. ft.**
Garage	871 sq. ft.
Exterior Wall Framing	2x6
Foundation options:	
Slab	
(Foundation & framing conversion diagram available—see order form.)	
Blueprint Price Code	**E**

TO ORDER THIS BLUEPRINT, CALL TOLL-FREE 1-800-547-5570
(prices and details on pp. 12-15.)

Plan EOF-8

Splashy Master Bath

- Beautiful bay windows protruding from the living and dining rooms that flank the foyer add a classic touch to the facade of this stately home.
- Equally attractive is its interior, with an exciting sunken family room featuring a huge fireplace and wet bar.
- A large wood deck with octagonal conversation area is nestled between the family room and adjoining breakfast area set in a large bay window.
- The modern, roomy kitchen has an island worktop and extended counter bar.
- Three secondary bedrooms and a master suite with a spectacular private bath featuring a tray ceiling, separate vanities and an oversized luxury tub set in a bay window are found on the upper level.

Plan A-2255-DS

Bedrooms: 4	**Baths:** 3 ½
Space:	
Upper floor	1,880 sq. ft.
Main floor	1,643 sq. ft.
Total Living Area	**3,523 sq. ft.**
Basement	1,643 sq. ft.
Garage	962 sq. ft.
Exterior Wall Framing	2x6
Foundation options:	
Standard Basement	
(Foundation & framing conversion diagram available—see order form.)	
Blueprint Price Code	F

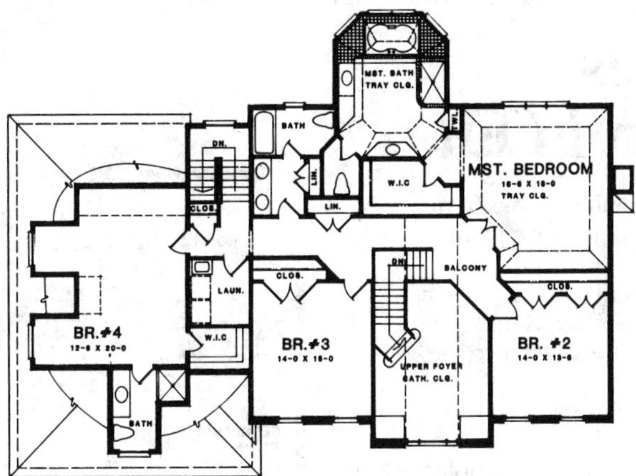

UPPER FLOOR

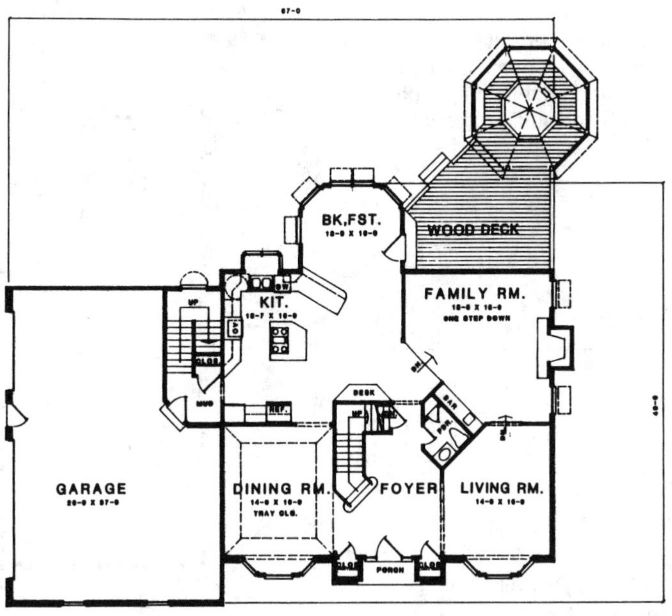

MAIN FLOOR

Plan A-2255-DS

Luxurious Inside and Out

- A beautiful barrel vault stretches from the foyer through to the sunken Grand Room of this stately ranch; pillars accentuate the entrance of the home as well as the entrance to the Grand Room, which also offers access to the rear porch.
- Rounded walls and designer niches soften some room and wall divisions; high arched wall openings add another touch to the sunken Gathering room, also featuring a corner fireplace and corner window seat.
- The spectacular master suite has a private, sunken entertainment retreat with fireplace and an adjoining bath with luxury tub and sunken shower; a personal library lies opposite the bedroom.
- A guest suite also features a private bath and courtyard.

Plan EOF-1	
Bedrooms: 4-5	**Baths:** 4
Space:	
Main floor	3,903 sq. ft.
Total Living Area	**3,903 sq. ft.**
Garage	748 sq. ft.
Exterior Wall Framing	2x4
Foundation options:	
Slab	
(Foundation & framing conversion diagram available—see order form.)	
Blueprint Price Code	F

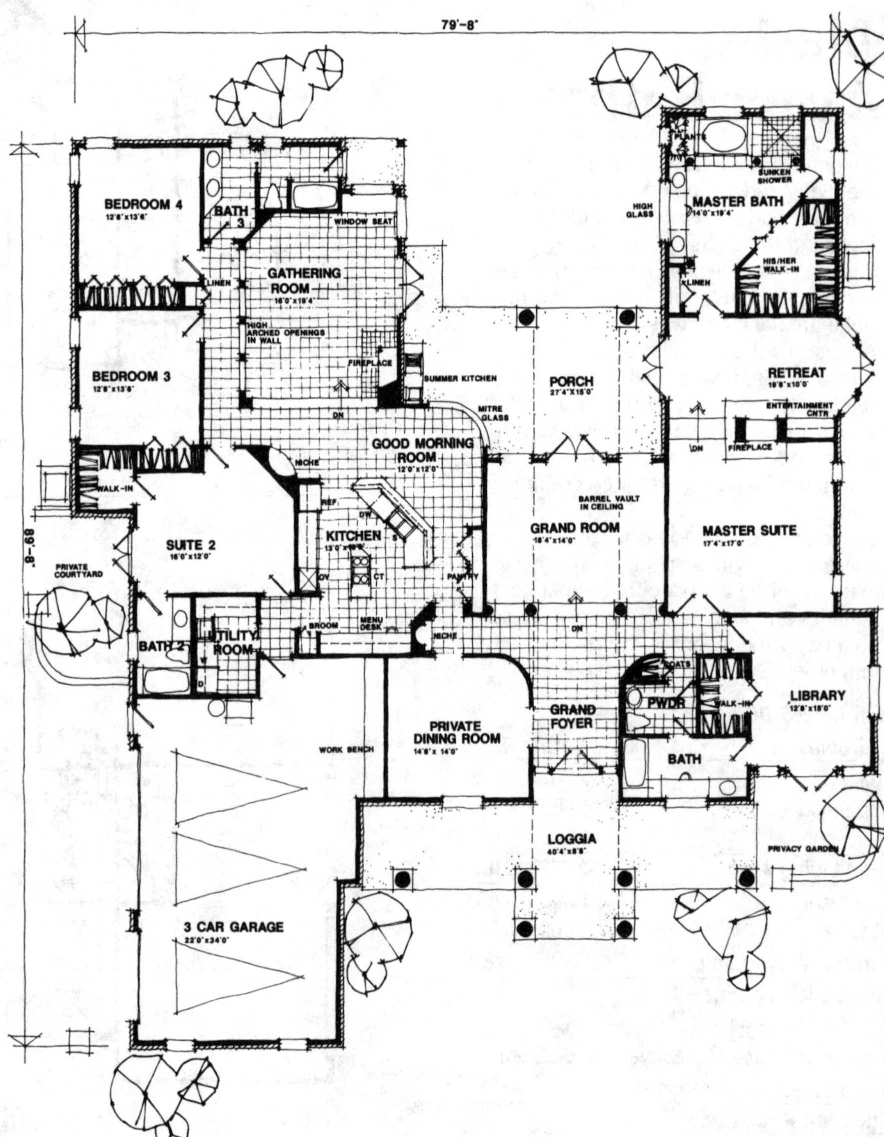

TO ORDER THIS BLUEPRINT, CALL TOLL-FREE 1-800-547-5570
(prices and details on pp. 12-15.)

Plan EOF-1

Ultimate Elegance

- The gracious foyer of this distinguished Southern home reveals a sweeping staircase and a direct view to the pool environment beyond.
- The grand parlour at center has a two-story ceiling, high-fixed glass, ale bar and fireplace.
- Open to the equally large gathering room is the gourmet island kitchen with menu desk, walk-in pantry and octagonal morning room which offers a second route to the upper level.
- Bright and luxurious, the master suite features a convenient morning kitchen, sunny octagonal sitting area that overlooks the covered veranda and optional pool, and a lavish bath.
- Three bedroom suites are located off the circular staircase and hall-bridge that overlooks the parlour; a sunset deck adjoins two of them.

Plan EOF-3	
Bedrooms: 4-5	**Baths:** 5 ½
Space:	
Upper floor	1,150 sq. ft.
Main floor	3,045 sq. ft.
Total Living Area	**4,195 sq. ft.**
Garage	814 sq. ft.
Exterior Wall Framing	2x6
Foundation options:	
Slab	
(Foundation & framing conversion diagram available—see order form.)	
Blueprint Price Code	G

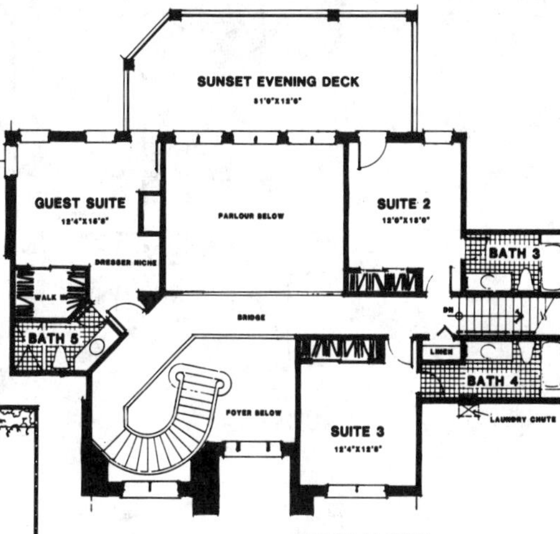

UPPER FLOOR

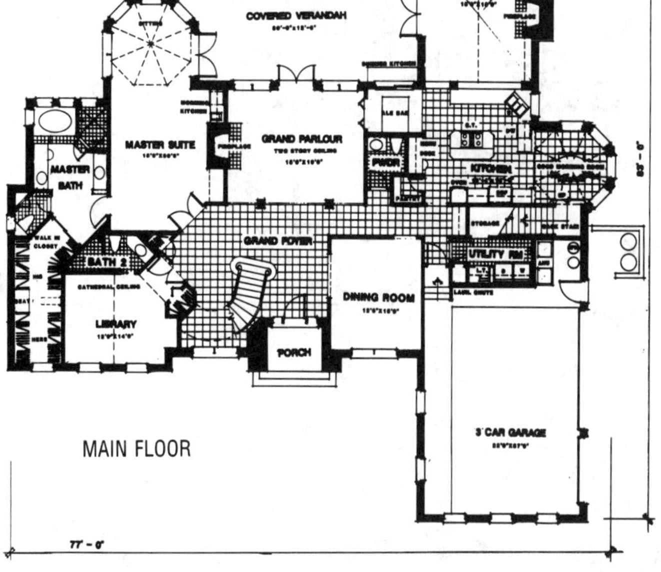

MAIN FLOOR

Plan EOF-3

Grand Parlour

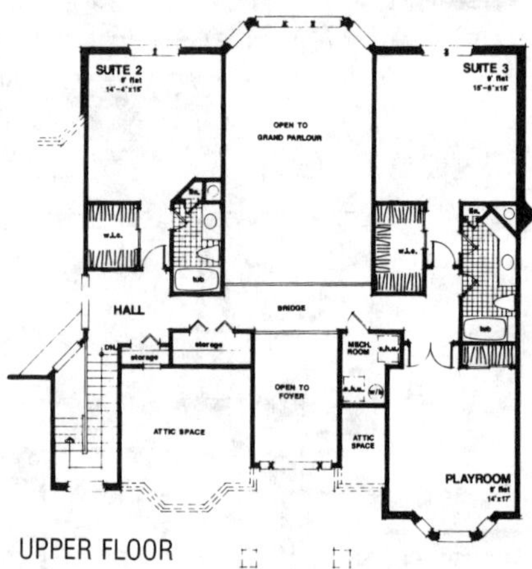

UPPER FLOOR

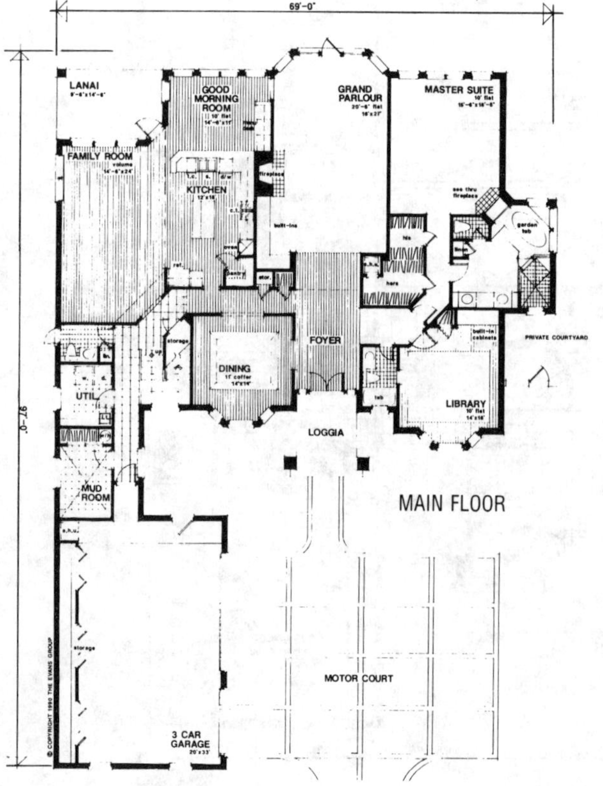

MAIN FLOOR

- A great deal of windows and outdoor light is captured in this luxurious two-story, beginning with the foyer and grand parlour, both open to the upper level.
- The luxury island kitchen offers an eating counter and adjoining morning room enclosed in glass; the merging family room has volume ceiling and access to a rear porch.
- Ten foot flat ceilings hover above the secluded master suite that boasts a stunning see-thru fireplace to the garden tub on the other side; the private bath offers separate his 'n her walk-in closets and a generous shower with seat. A personal library with bay window is steps away.
- Two secondary bedrooms on the upper level are divided by an interior balcony bridge that overlooks the parlour below; both have a private bath.
- Double doors open to a playroom.

Plan EOF-4	
Bedrooms: 3	**Baths:** 4 ½
Space:	
Upper floor	1,397 sq. ft.
Main floor	3,088 sq. ft.
Total Living Area	**4,485 sq. ft.**
Garage	660 sq. ft.
Exterior Wall Framing	2x4
Foundation options:	
Slab	
(Foundation & framing conversion diagram available—see order form.)	
Blueprint Price Code	G

TO ORDER THIS BLUEPRINT, CALL TOLL-FREE 1-800-547-5570
(prices and details on pp. 12-15.)

Plan EOF-4

Country Charm Revisited

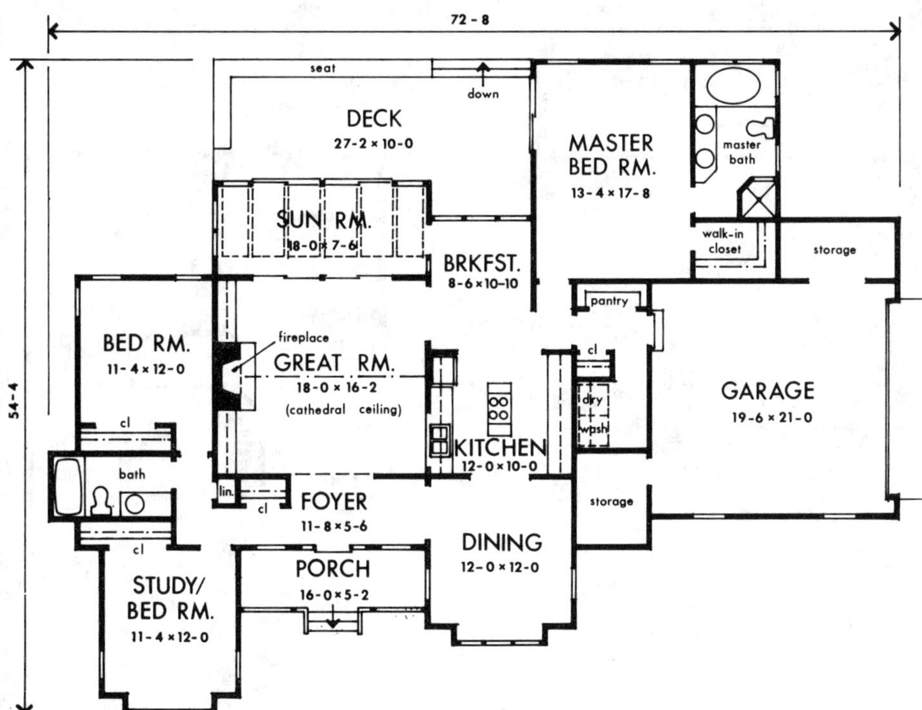

- A covered front porch, dormers, multi-paned windows and two projected windows at the dining room and study offer a welcoming front exterior with country charm revisited.
- The Great Room is the heart of this plan, featuring a cathedral ceiling, fireplace with flanking bookshelves and direct access to the rear sun room through dual sliders.
- The kitchen with cooking island serves both the formal dining room and the breakfast eating area.
- The master suite opens onto the rear deck via sliders.
- The master bath has double vanities and separate shower and tub under corner windows.
- Two other bedrooms are located at the other end of the house for privacy, with the front bedroom doubling as a study.

Plan DG-161

Bedrooms: 2-3 — **Baths:** 2

Space:

Total living area:	1,899 sq. ft.
Garage:	410 sq. ft.
Storage area:	approx. 125 sq. ft.

Exterior Wall Framing: 2x4

Foundation options:
Crawlspace.
(Foundation & framing conversion diagram available — see order form.)

Blueprint Price Code: B

REAR VIEW

Plan DG-161

TO ORDER THIS BLUEPRINT, CALL TOLL-FREE 1-800-547-5570
(prices and details on pp. 12-15.)

HDS-90-820-A

HDS-90-820-B

HDS-90-820-C

Three Attractive Facades

- The impressive entrance to this versatile one-story reveals the openness and pleasantries found throughout.
- A lovely kitchen and breakfast nook offer a pass-thru to the busy, vaulted Great Room beyond.
- The family room section features a cozy fireplace and a generous view of the attached patio outside.
- An attractive solarium lies between the master bedroom and bath, the bedroom with vaulted ceilings and a full-length closet, the bath with dual vanities and a separate shower and tub.
- The two secondary bedrooms share a bath.
- NOTE: All three elevation choices are included in the plans.

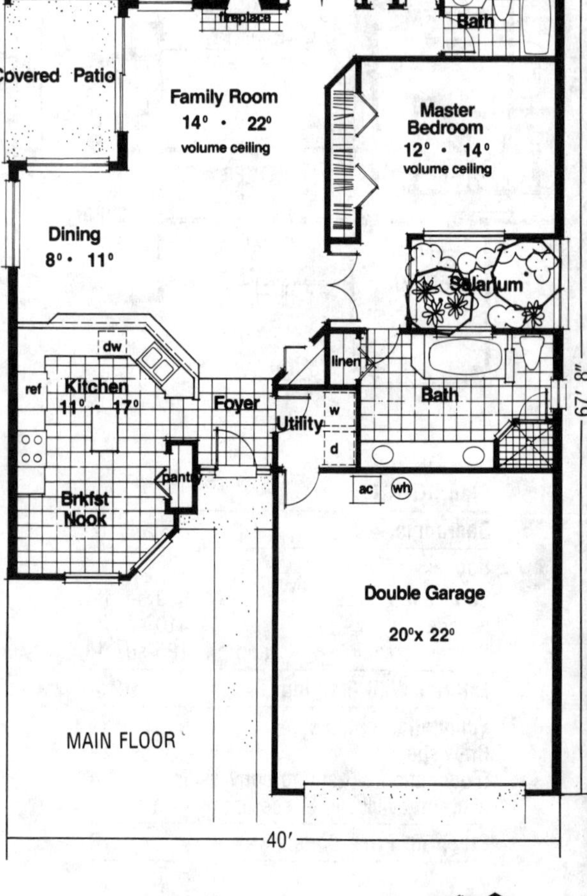

Plan HDS-90-820

Bedrooms: 3	**Baths:** 2
Space:	
Total living area:	1,576 sq. ft.
Garage:	440 sq. ft.
Exterior Wall Framing:	concrete block
Foundation options: Slab. (Foundation & framing conversion diagram available — see order form.)	
Blueprint Price Code:	B

TO ORDER THIS BLUEPRINT, CALL TOLL-FREE 1-800-547-5570
(prices and details on pp. 12-15.)

Plan HDS-90-820

FRONT VIEW

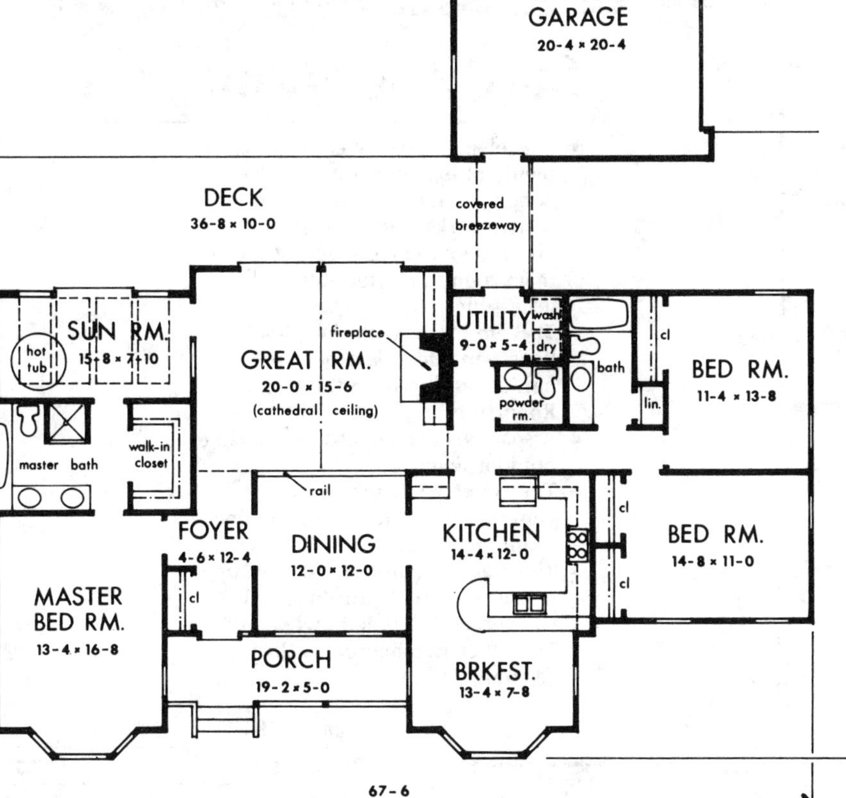

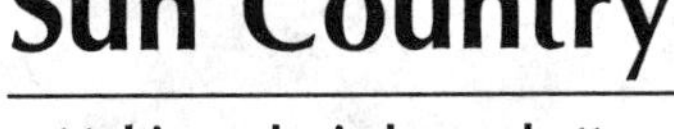

Sun Country

- Multipaned windows, shutters, dormers, bay windows and a covered porch dress up this country cottage.
- A sun room with hot tub adjacent to the deck, with access from the Great Room and the master bath, updates this intriguing home and can incorporate passive solar heating advantages.
- The Great Room has a fireplace, cathedral ceiling and sliding glass doors with an arched window above to allow natural light penetration.
- The kitchen is convenient, situated between the formal dining room and the bay-windowed breakfast room.
- A generous master bedroom has a walk-in closet and spacious master bath with double-bowl vanity, shower, and garden tub. The other two bedrooms are located at the other end of the house for privacy.
- The garage is connected to the house by a breezeway for flexibility of lot sizes and shapes.

REAR VIEW

Plan DG-159

Bedrooms: 3	**Baths:** 2½
Space:	
Total living area:	2,021 sq. ft.
Garage:	413 sq. ft.
Exterior Wall Framing:	2x4
Foundation options: Crawlspace. (Foundation & framing conversion diagram available — see order form.)	
Blueprint Price Code:	C

Plan DG-159

TO ORDER THIS BLUEPRINT, CALL TOLL-FREE 1-800-547-5570

(prices and details on pp. 12-15.)

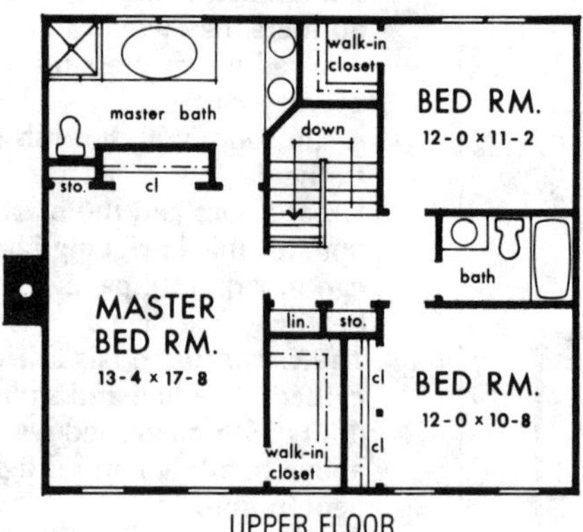

UPPER FLOOR

seat
DECK
down
skylights
BRKFST.
9-8 x 10-0
down
SUN RM.
12-0 x 9-0
wet bar
KITCHEN
12-0 x 14-8
storage
up
wash dry
36-2
fireplace
GREAT RM.
13-4 x 23-2
GARAGE
20-0 x 20-8
pd. rm.
FOYER
6-8 x 13-2
DINING
12-0 x 12-6
cl
62-6

MAIN FLOOR

Sun Room Surprise

- This elegant 2-story colonial has plenty of extras including a well-zoned passive solar sun room which works and looks great.
- From the entrance foyer, all of the main rooms are viewable and accessible.
- The sun room, with skylights, boasts an added luxury of a wet bar, accessible from the Great Room and breakfast eating area.
- A spacious deck opens the house to outdoor living.
- The country kitchen, with island cooktop, serves the formal dining room, breakfast room and deck.
- The master bedroom offers a large master bath with whirlpool tub, shower, and double bowl vanity. The other two bedrooms share a separate bath.

Plan DG-185

Bedrooms: 3	**Baths:** 2½
Space:	
Upper floor:	917 sq. ft
Main floor:	1,168 sq. ft
Total living area:	2,085 sq. ft
Garage:	413 sq. ft
Storage area:	approx. 25 sq. ft
Exterior Wall Framing:	2x

Foundation options:
Crawlspace.
(Foundation & framing conversion diagram available — see order form.)

Blueprint Price Code: C

TO ORDER THIS BLUEPRINT, CALL TOLL-FREE 1-800-547-5570
(prices and details on pp. 12-15.)

Plan DG-185

FRONT VIEW

Wrap It Up, 'll Take It

A wrap-around covered porch at the front and sides of the house and an open deck at the back with storage provide plenty of outside living area.

Arched rear windows and a sun room add exciting visual elements to the exterior while updating this country plan.

The spacious Great Room has a fireplace, cathedral ceiling and clerestory with arched windows.

The second level balcony overlooks the Great Room.

The kitchen is centrally located between the dining area and Great Room for maximum flexibility in layout and has a food preparation island for convenience.

The generous master bedroom with fireplace has direct access to the sun room and covered wrap-around porch. A large walk-in closet and double bowl vanity add to the master suite's appeal.

The sun room has a hot tub with access to back deck, Great Room, and master bedroom to allow dispersal of solar heat during winter months.

The second level has two bedrooms, storage and a full bath.

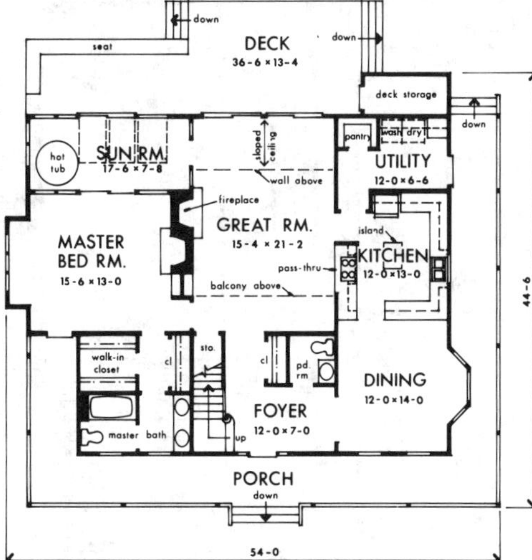

MAIN FLOOR

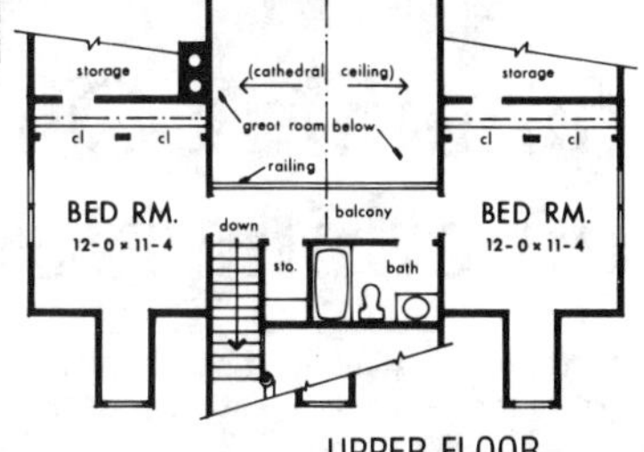

UPPER FLOOR

Plan DG-163

Bedrooms: 3	**Baths:** 2½
Space:	
Upper floor:	537 sq. ft.
Main floor:	1,562 sq. ft.
Total living area:	2,099 sq. ft.
Exterior Wall Framing:	2x4

Foundation options:
Crawlspace.
(Foundation & framing conversion diagram available — see order form.)

Blueprint Price Code:	C

REAR VIEW

Plan DG-163

TO ORDER THIS BLUEPRINT, CALL TOLL-FREE 1-800-547-5570
(prices and details on pp. 12-15.)

FRONT VIEW

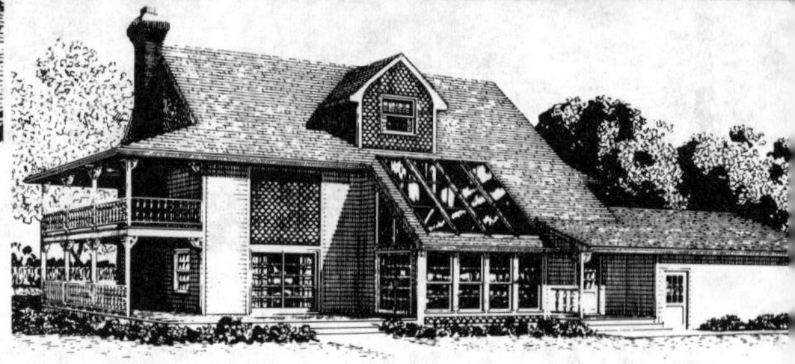

REAR VIEW

Something Old, Something New

"Something old, something new" aptly describes the flavor and sentiment of this replica of earlier times.

Beveled oval plate glass with heavy oak surrounds and appropriate hand-carved wreaths and borders make entering the home the delightful experience it was meant to be. Inside one finds the huge central entry hall with the magnificent open staircase with turned balusters and shapely handrails.

With all bedrooms being on the second floor, the main level is entirely devoted to daily living in a generous atmosphere. The 14′ x 23′ living room and 14′ x 13′ dining room give one an idea of the spaciousness of this home.

Notice the 80 cubic foot pantry closet and the adjacent storage closet with an equal amount of space. A two-thirds bath and well equipped laundry room complete the mechanical area of the home.

Certainly the most provocative room on the main floor is the beautiful glass-enclosed morning or breakfast room. Huge skylight panels augment the bank of windows and sliding doors to create a delightful passive solar room suitable for many uses while contributing greatly to the heating efficiency of the entire building.

Upstairs two good-sized bedrooms with adjoining bathroom serve the junior members of the family while the parents enjoy the spacious master suite with walk-in wardrobes and private bath.

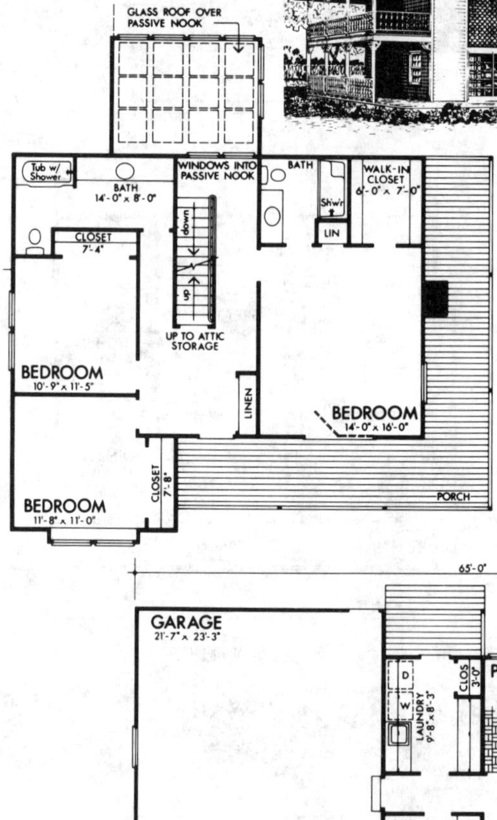

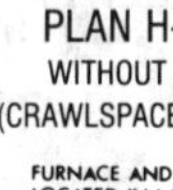

GLASS ROOF OVER PASSIVE NOOK

Tub w/ Shower

BATH 14′-0″ x 8′-0″

WINDOWS INTO PASSIVE NOOK

BATH

WALK-IN CLOSET 6′-0″ x 7′-0″

CLOSET 7′-4″

UP TO ATTIC STORAGE

BEDROOM 10′-9″ x 11′-5″

LINEN

BEDROOM 14′-0″ x 16′-0″

BEDROOM 11′-8″ x 11′-0″

CLOSET 7′-8″

PORCH

PLAN H-3729-1A
WITHOUT BASEMENT
(CRAWLSPACE FOUNDATION)

FURNACE AND WATER HEATER TO BE LOCATED IN LAUNDRY ROOM

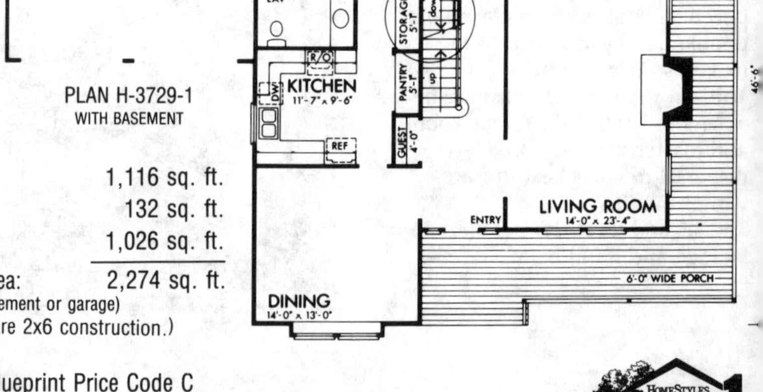

65′-0″

GARAGE 21′-7″ x 23′-3″

LAUNDRY 9′-8″ x 8′-3″

PASSIVE NOOK 12′-10″ x 9′-8″

BRICK FLOOR

SUN DECK

FRENCH DOORS

LAV

STORAGE 5′-1″

PANTRY 5′-1″

KITCHEN 11′-7″ x 9′-6″

GUEST 4′-0″

ENTRY

LIVING ROOM 14′-0″ x 23′-4″

6′-0″ WIDE PORCH

DINING 14′-0″ x 13′-0″

46′-6″

PLAN H-3729-1
WITH BASEMENT

First floor:	1,116 sq. ft.
Sun nook:	132 sq. ft.
Second floor:	1,026 sq. ft.
Total living area:	2,274 sq. ft.

(Not counting basement or garage)
(Exterior walls are 2x6 construction.)

TO ORDER THIS BLUEPRINT, CALL TOLL-FREE 1-800-547-5570
(prices and details on pp. 12-15.)

Blueprint Price Code C

Plans H-3729-1 & H-3729-1A

Back Home Again

- Decorative columns enhance the beauty of this country-style home with wraparound porch for total outdoor living.
- Three or four bedroom versions (192 & 191) offer affordability and family size flexibility.
- All rooms on the main level have direct access to the front and rear covered porches.
- The Great Room and the master suite both have access to a side sunroom.
- The kitchen has a large cooktop and serving island and a breakfast eating area.
- The master bedroom includes a walk-in closet and private bath with double vanity and separate tub and shower.

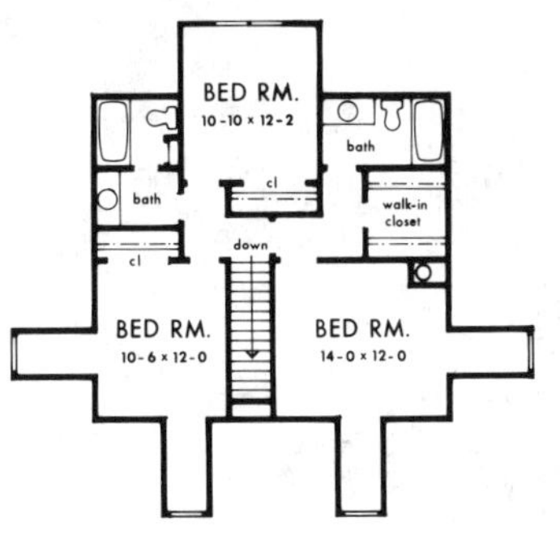

UPPER FLOOR

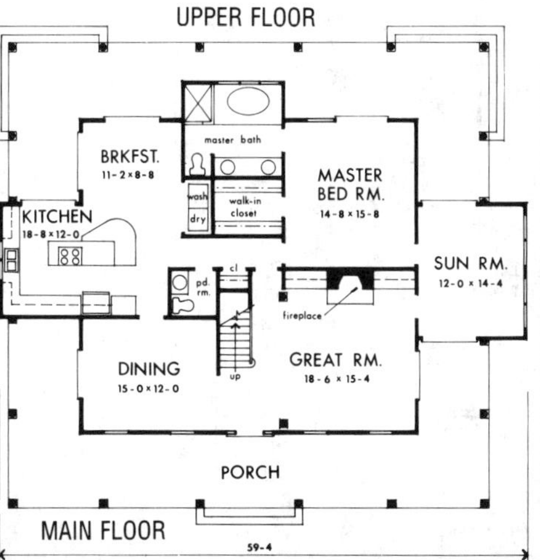

DG-191

Plans DG-191, -192	
Bedrooms: 4/3	**Baths:** 3½/2½
Space:	
Upper floor:	870/674 sq. ft.
Main floor:	1,637/1,564 sq. ft.
Total living area:	2,507/2,238 sq. ft.
Exterior Wall Framing:	2x4
Foundation options: Crawlspace. (Foundation & framing conversion diagram available — see order form.)	
Blueprint Price Code:	191-D, 192-C

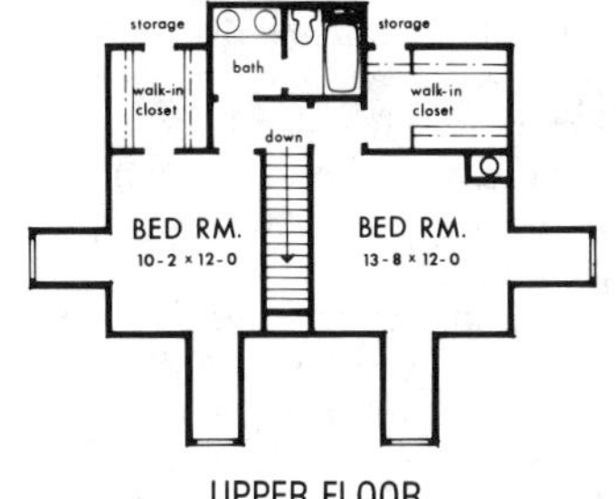

UPPER FLOOR

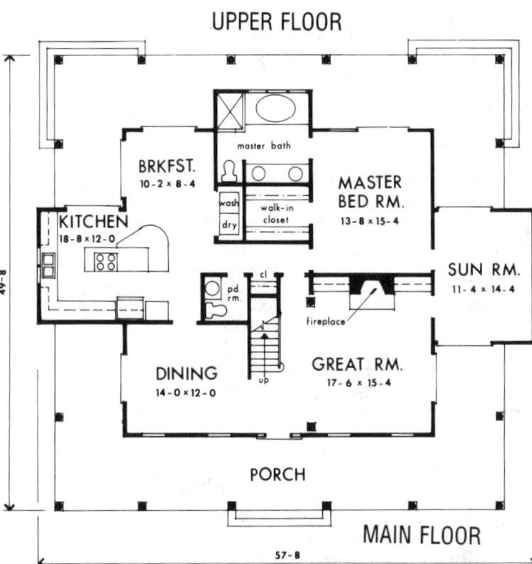

DG-192

REAR VIEW

Charm of Yesteryear

- Wrap-around porches, dormers, narrow-lap siding, and divided windows capture the charm of yesteryear.
- The Great Room is the centerpiece of the floor plan, complete with vaulted ceiling, clerestory with arched window, balcony overlook and cozy fireplace.
- The kitchen is conveniently placed between the formal dining room, the breakfast bay and the utility room.
- The main-floor master suite features a splendid, bay-windowed bath with a walk-in closet.
- The sun room, with hot tub under greenhouse windows, is accessed from the Great Room and master suite.

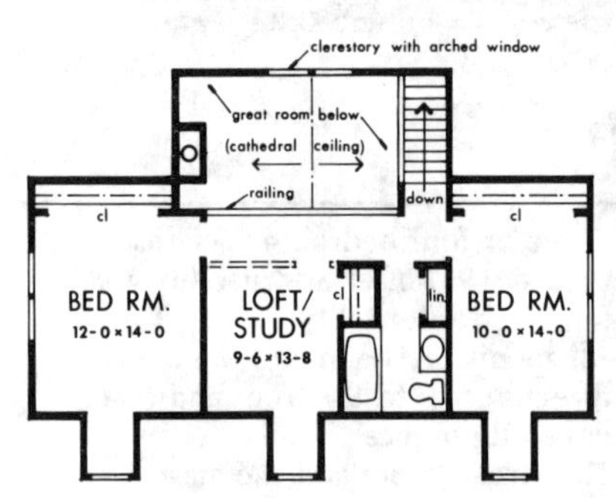

UPPER FLOOR

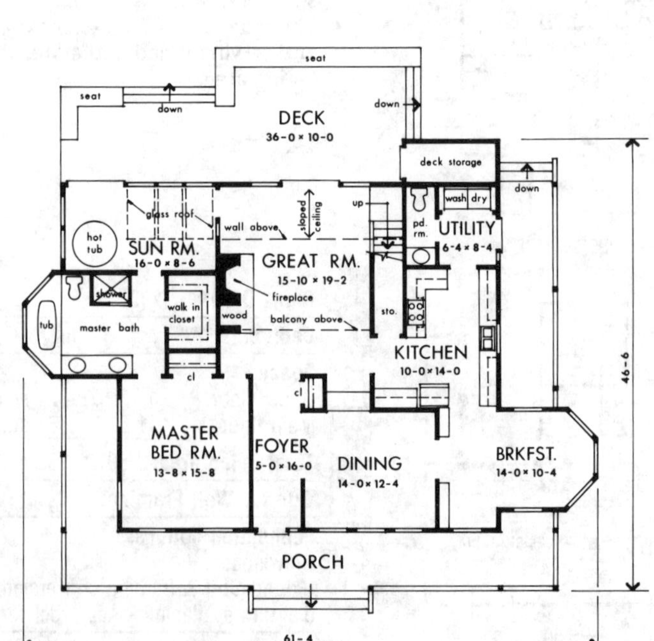

MAIN FLOOR

Plan DG-158

Bedrooms: 3-4	**Baths:** 2½
Space:	
Upper floor:	674 sq. ft.
Main floor:	1,659 sq. ft.
Total living area:	2,333 sq. ft.
Exterior Wall Framing:	2x4

Foundation options:
Crawlspace.
(Foundation & framing conversion diagram available — see order form.)

Blueprint Price Code:	C

TO ORDER THIS BLUEPRINT, CALL TOLL-FREE 1-800-547-5570
(prices and details on pp. 12-15.)

Plan DG-158

Dormered Delight

- A large covered front porch with decorative columns and triple dormers above add a delightful country look to this family home.
- Formal and informal living spaces flank the open stairway at the entry. To the left is the dining/Great Room with fireplace and sun room beyond. To the right of the entry is the island kitchen with breakfast bar and family room opening to a screened porch leading to the garage.
- The stunning master suite offers a second fireplace, walk-in closet with natural light and open master bath with whirlpool tub and private deck access. There are three additional bedrooms sharing two full bathrooms upstairs.

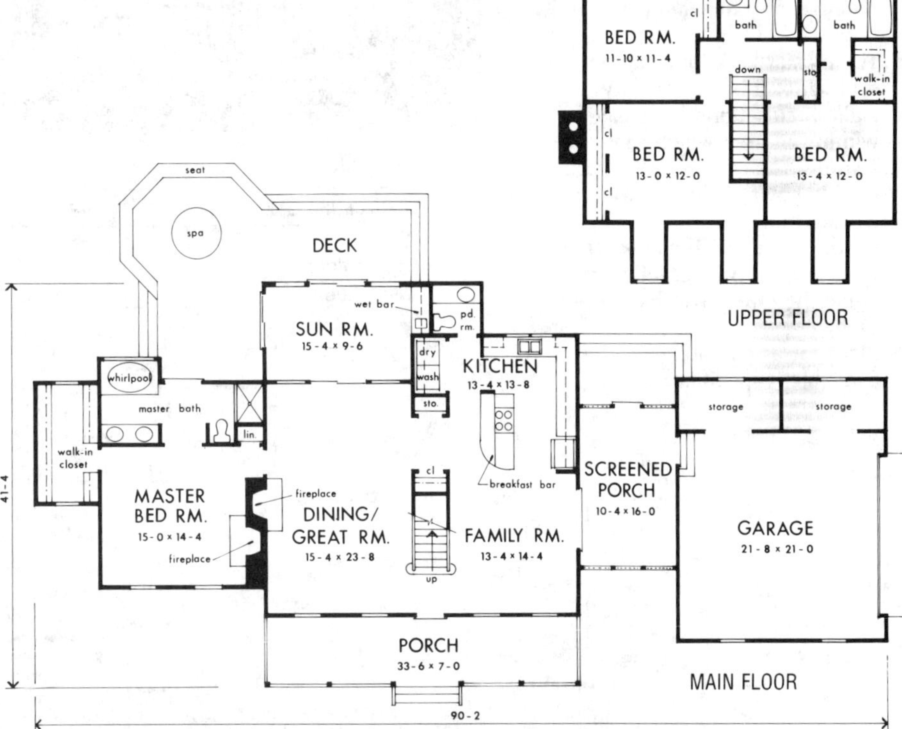

Plan DG-197

Bedrooms: 4	**Baths:** 3½
Space:	
Upper floor:	867 sq. ft.
Main floor:	1,584 sq. ft.
Total living area:	2,451 sq. ft.
Garage:	455 sq. ft.
Storage area: approx.	100 sq. ft.
Exterior Wall Framing:	2x4

Foundation options:
Crawlspace.
(Foundation & framing conversion diagram available — see order form.)

Blueprint Price Code:	C

Plan DG-197

(prices and details on pp. 12-15.)

Elegant Victorian

- This elegant Victorian of the Queen Anne era displays an exterior of distinctive decorative detailing consistent with its time, while offering an interior plan layout that satisfies today's standards.
- A spacious living room incorporates a large bay-windowed area and a fireplace overlooking the wrap-around veranda.
- The generous kitchen with island counter is centrally located to the dining, family and sun rooms, providing efficient servicing. Breakfast can be served in any of the three areas.
- The partially covered rear deck with hot tub is accessible from the dining room, sun room and family room.
- The master bedroom suite on the second level has a fireplace, walk-in closet and large bay-windowed area which can serve as a study. The master bath boasts a double bowl vanity, shower and garden tub.
- Of the three additional bedrooms, one enjoys a private full bath, while the other two share a full bath.
- Plans for a separate garage are available if specified.

FRONT VIEW

Plan DG-171

Bedrooms: 3½ **Baths:** 4

Space:

Upper floor:	1,195 sq. ft.
Main floor:	1,393 sq. ft.
Total living area:	2,588 sq. ft.

Exterior Wall Framing: 2x

Foundation options:
Crawlspace.
(Foundation & framing conversion diagram available — see order form.)

Blueprint Price Code:

BED RM. 11-0 x 13-0
cl
BED RM. 11-4 x 11-6
cl
BED RM. 11-0 x 13-0
bath
lin.
bath
fireplace
MASTER BED RM. 13-4 x 18-0
down
cl
cl
study
master bath

UPPER FLOOR

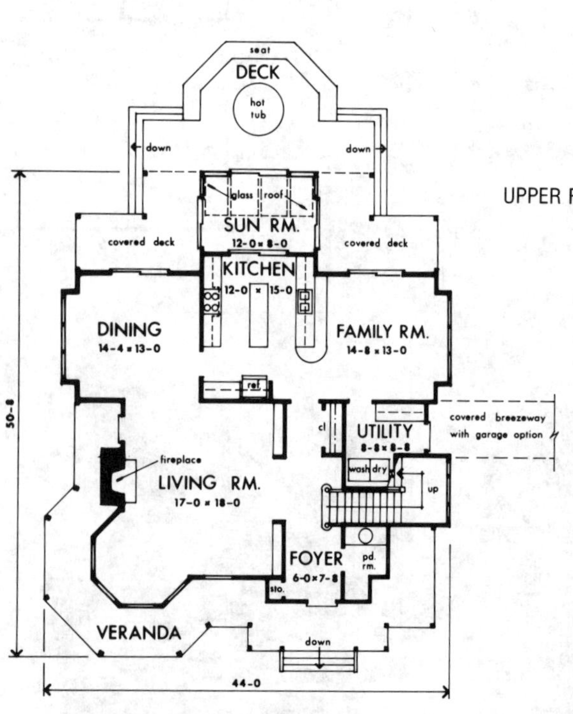

MAIN FLOOR

REAR VIEW

TO ORDER THIS BLUEPRINT, CALL TOLL-FREE 1-800-547-5570
(prices and details on pp. 12-15.)

Plan DG-171

Deluxe Kitchen Is Major Highlight

- Foyer and living room are open to the upper level, 17′ high.
- Kitchen and breakfast area are positioned to enjoy outside view normally obstructed by carport or garage.
- Glass walls wrap around a cozy atrium.
- Upper level offers three additional bedrooms and a balcony to view lower living area.

Plan E-2503

Bedrooms: 4	**Baths:** 2½
Space:	
Upper floor:	811 sq. ft.
Main floor:	1,708 sq. ft.
Total living area:	2,519 sq. ft.
Carport and storage:	715 sq. ft.
Porch:	36 sq. ft.
Exterior Wall Framing:	2x6

Foundation options:
Standard basement.
Crawlspace.
Slab.
(Foundation & framing conversion diagram available — see order form.)

Blueprint Price Code: D

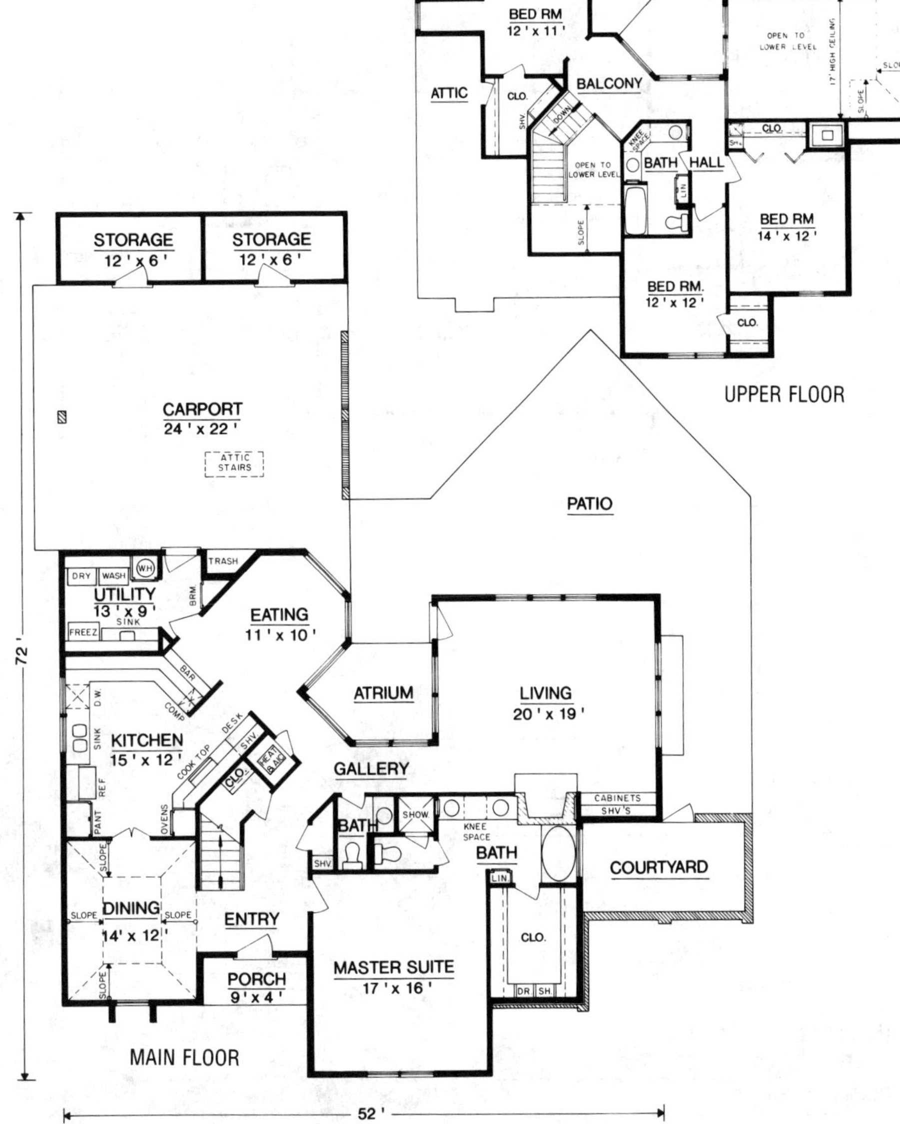

Plan E-2503

(prices and details on pp. 12-15.)

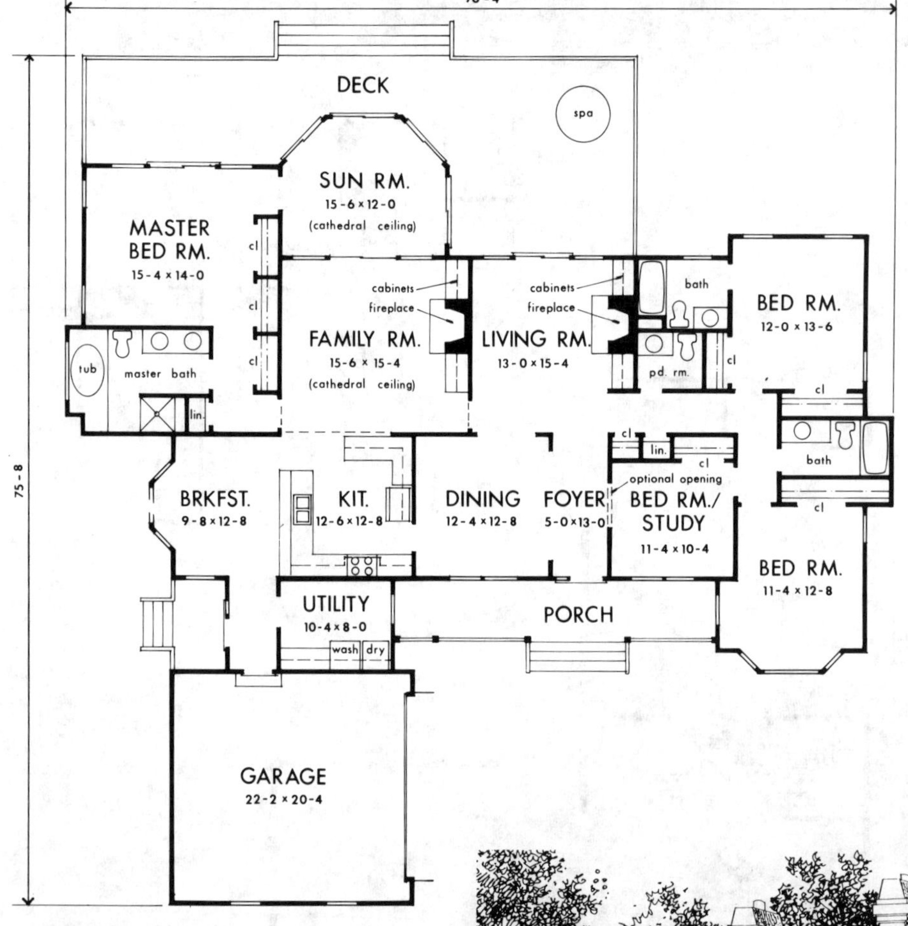

Porches and Dormers and Bays, Oh My!

- A country charm is effectively created by a covered porch, dual dormers and multiple bay windows.
- Both the formal living room and the family room offer cozy fireplaces with built-in flanking cabinets.
- The family room has a dramatic cathedral ceiling with arched window opening to a bright sun room with mirrored arched window.
- The central kitchen conveniently serves the formal dining room and the breakfast bay.
- The master suite has an abundance of closets, access to the sun room and rear deck, and a bold master bath.
- The other three bedrooms are located at the other side of the plan.

Plan DG-204

Bedrooms: 4	**Baths:** 3½
Space:	
Total living area:	2,621 sq. ft.
Garage:	451 sq. ft.
Exterior Wall Framing:	2x4
Foundation options: Crawlspace. (Foundation & framing conversion diagram available — see order form.)	
Blueprint Price Code:	D

(prices and details on pp. 12-15.)

A Stately Statement

- This distinctive two-story colonial has an updated plan which includes a sun room with passive solar capability.
- The central entrance foyer allows a convenient circulation pattern throughout the entire house.
- Formal entertaining is accomplished in the front-facing living and dining rooms, while casual living takes place in the family room, sun room, covered porch and deck.
- The spacious country kitchen offers a large island and breakfast area, with direct access to the sun room and deck as well as handy garage access through the mud room.
- The second level includes the master bedroom with a pair of walk-in closets and a master bath which offers a double-bowl vanity, shower, and whirlpool tub.
- There are three additional bedrooms, a second full bath and an open stairwell with natural light.

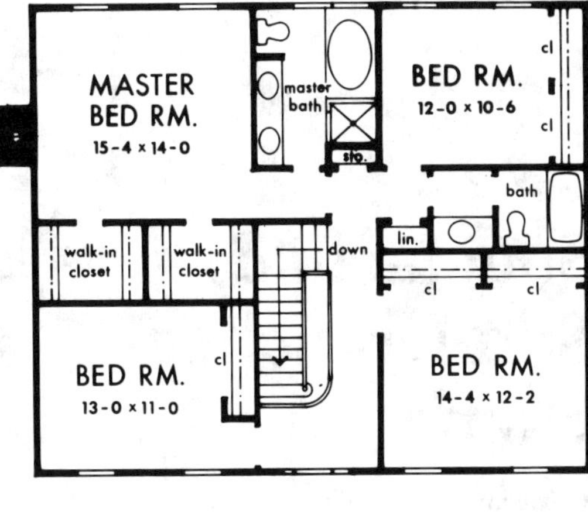

UPPER FLOOR

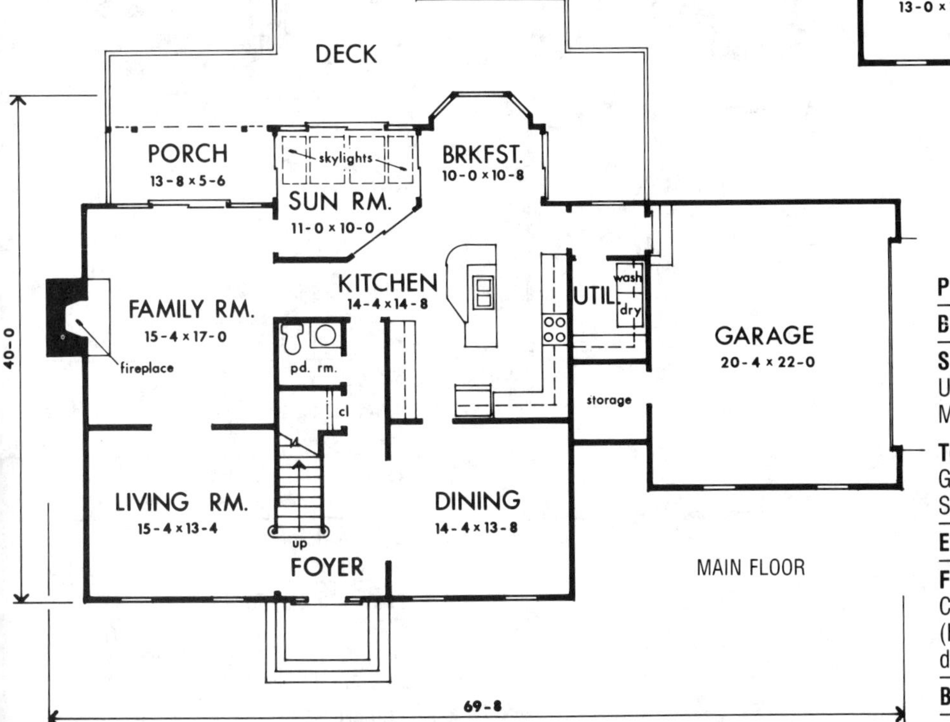

MAIN FLOOR

Plan DG-189

Bedrooms: 4	**Baths:** 2½
Space:	
Upper floor:	1,180 sq. ft.
Main floor:	1,475 sq. ft.
Total living area:	2,655 sq. ft.
Garage:	447 sq. ft.
Storage area:	Approx. 25 sq. ft.
Exterior Wall Framing:	2x4

Foundation options:
Crawlspace.
(Foundation & framing conversion diagram available — see order form.)

Blueprint Price Code: D

Plan DG-189

TO ORDER THIS BLUEPRINT, CALL TOLL-FREE 1-800-547-5570
(prices and details on pp. 12-15.)

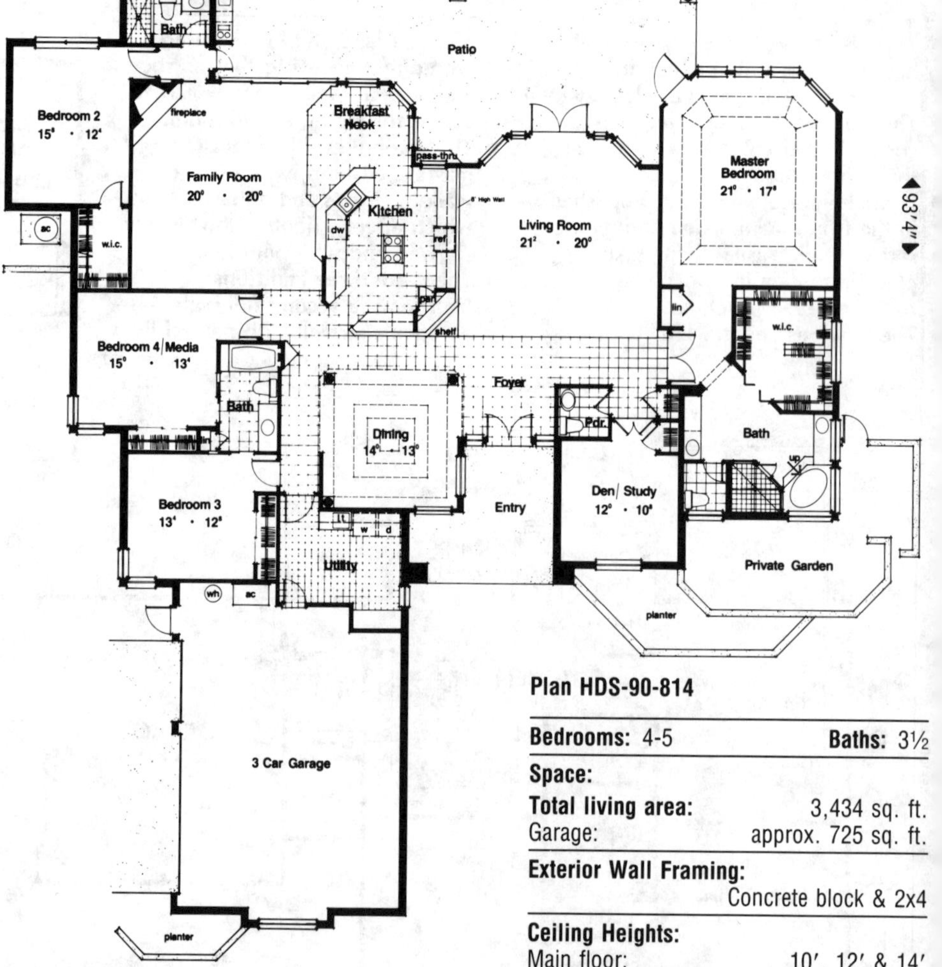

Spectacular Sun-Drenched Home

- Sweeping hip rooflines, stucco siding with interesting quoins and banding, and interesting arched transom windows give this exciting sunbelt design a special flair.
- From an important 1½ story covered entry leading into the foyer, guests are greeted with a stunning view. A bay-window-wall opens the living room, straight ahead, to the covered patio, rear yard, and possible pool. To the left is an open-feeling formal dining room with columns and spectacular receding tray ceiling.
- The island kitchen overlooks the large family room with corner fireplace and breakfast bay.
- The master wing, well separated from the secondary bedrooms, features a coffered ceiling, sitting area with patio access, massive walk-in closet, and sun-drenched garden bath.

Plan HDS-90-814

Bedrooms: 4-5 **Baths:** 3½

Space:
Total living area: 3,434 sq. ft.
Garage: approx. 725 sq. ft.

Exterior Wall Framing:
Concrete block & 2x4

Ceiling Heights:
Main floor: 10', 12' & 14'

Foundation options:
Slab.
(Foundation & framing conversion diagram available — see order form.)

Blueprint Price Code: E

Plan HDS-90-814

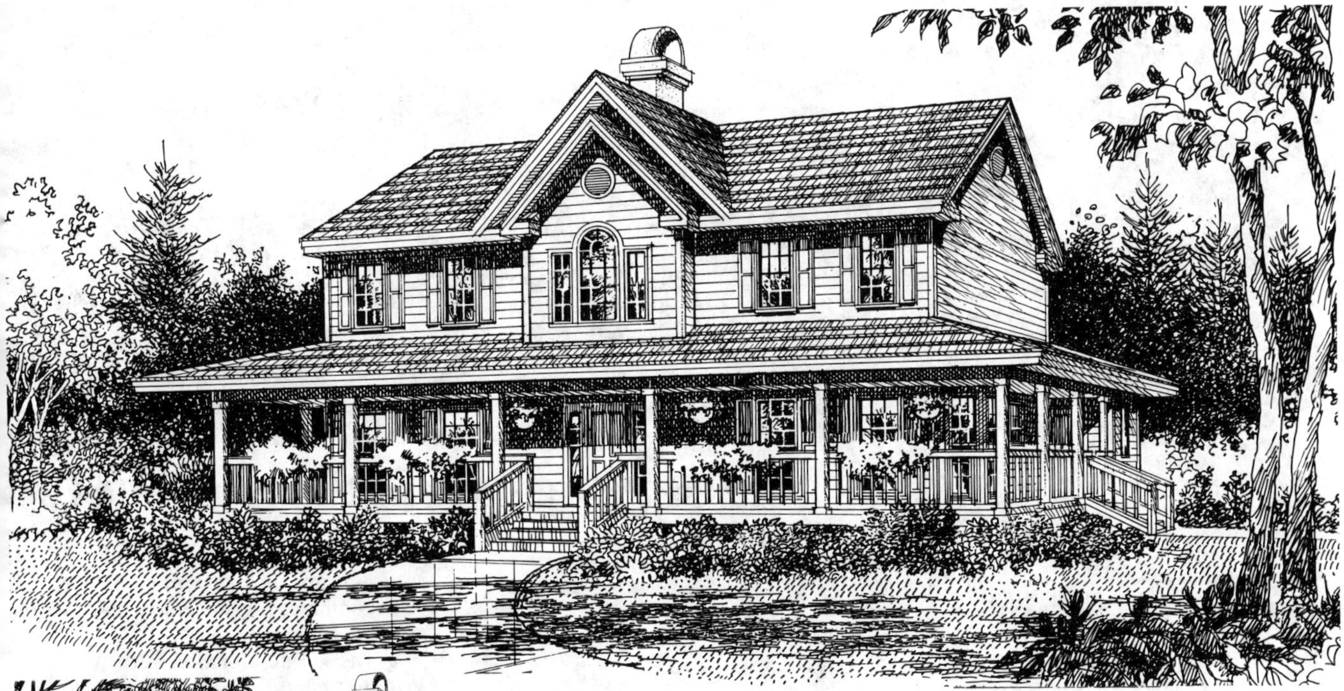

FRONT VIEW

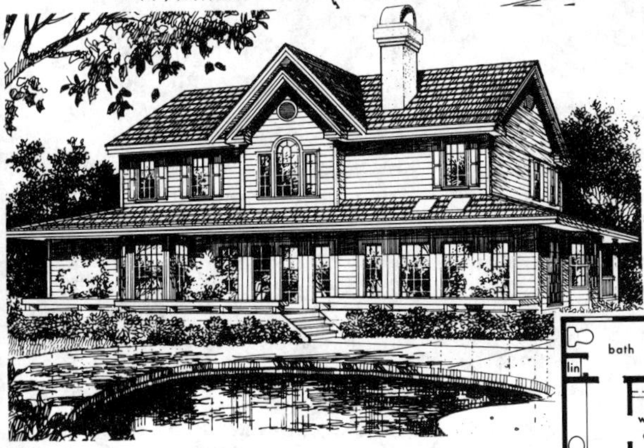

REAR VIEW

Indoor/ Outdoor Emphasis

- A wrap-around covered porch at the front and sides of house and an open deck at back with spa and seating provide plenty of outside living area.
- Front and rear Palladian windows add exciting visual elements to the exterior as well as provide natural light to interior.
- The entrance foyer and spacious Great Room are dramatic two-story vaulted spaces with Palladian windows at the second level.
- The kitchen is centrally located for maximum flexibility in layout and has food preparation island for convenience. The formal dining and breakfast rooms each have bay window highlights.
- The generous master bedroom has access to the sun room thru the master bath. The master bath has a garden tub, shower, double bowl vanity, and large walk-in closet.
- The sun room has operable skylights for natural light as well as air flow.
- A loft/study on second level overlooks the foyer and the Great Room below.
- The second level has three bedrooms. One large bedroom has a private bath and walk-in closet and the two other bedrooms share a full bath.

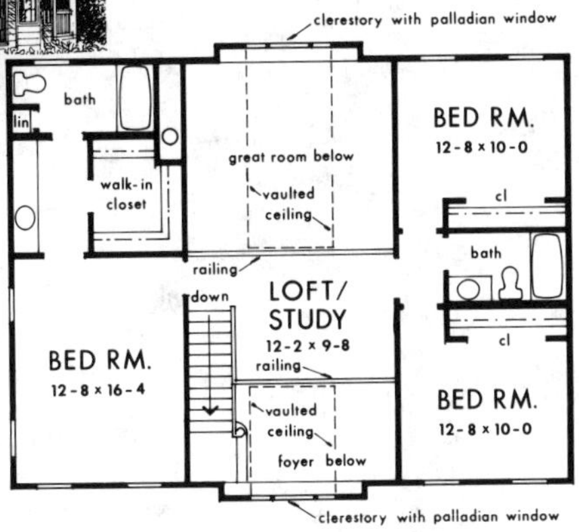

UPPER FLOOR

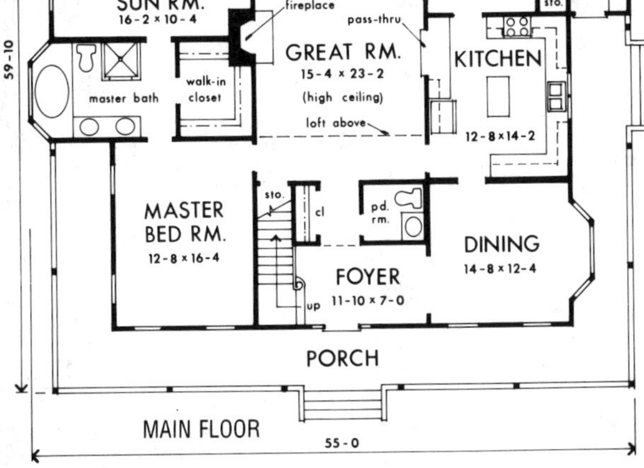

MAIN FLOOR

Plan DG-225

Bedrooms: 4	**Baths:** 3½
Space:	
Upper floor	958 sq. ft.
Main floor:	1,734 sq. ft.
Total living area:	2,692 sq. ft.
Exterior Wall Framing:	2x4

Foundation options:
Crawlspace.
(Foundation & framing conversion diagram available—see order form.)

Blueprint Price Code:	D

Plan DG-225

TO ORDER THIS BLUEPRINT, CALL TOLL-FREE 1-800-547-5570

(prices and details on pp. 12-15.)

Elegance & Grace Perfected

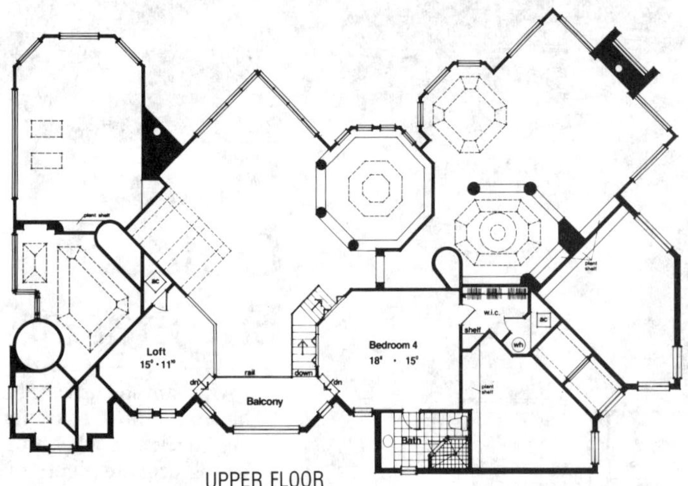

UPPER FLOOR

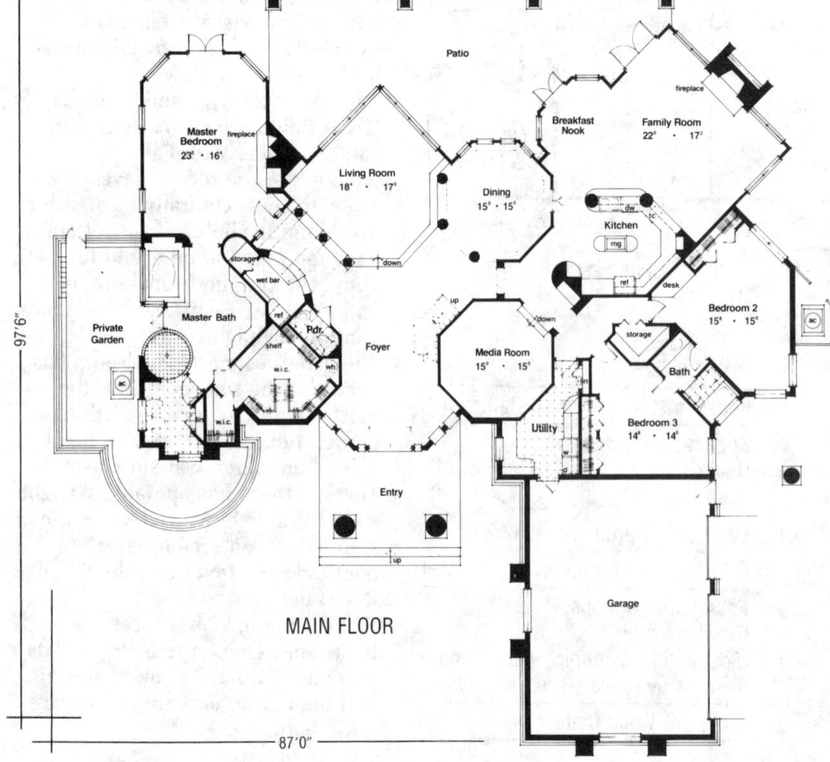

MAIN FLOOR

- The grand style, both inside and out, of this luxurious residence combines elegance and grace to perfection.
- The gothic contemporary architecture exudes an aura of grandeur, drawing the eye to a stately 2½ story entry portico.
- The interior is equally stunning with open high flowing spaces featuring coffered ceilings with columns defining room changes.
- The formal zone impresses with the vast foyer overlooking the sunken living room under corner window walls. The octagonal dining room, loft overlook, and curved wet bar complete the formal area.
- The informal zone of island kitchen, breakfast nook, family room, and octagonal media room make the most of precious family time together.
- The master suite continues the elegance, with a fireplace, endless walk-in closet, and garden bath which brings the outdoors in.

Plan HDS-90-819

Bedrooms: 4+	**Baths:** 3½
Space:	
Upper floor:	765 sq. ft.
Main floor:	3,770 sq. ft.
Total living area:	4,535 sq. ft.
Garage:	approx. 750 sq. ft.
Exterior Wall Framing:	2x4
Ceiling Heights:	
Upper floor:	9'
Main floor:	9'
Foundation options:	
Slab.	
(Foundation & framing conversion diagram available — see order form.)	
Blueprint Price Code:	G

TO ORDER THIS BLUEPRINT, CALL TOLL-FREE 1-800-547-5570
(prices and details on pp. 12-15.)

Plan HDS-90-819

Farmhouse with Victorian Touch

- Scalloped shingles and horizontal siding accented by detailed brackets define the Victorian exterior. The sides and rear of the home are brick.
- Both the master bedroom and guest bedroom are located on the lower level. A third bedroom and game room is located on the upper level. The game room doubles as a fourth bedroom when needed.
- Both the living room and dining room feature ceilings open to the upper level game room.
- The master suite is spacious and has an adjoining bath with twin vanities, angled tub and large walk-in closet.
- Typical ceilings heights are 8′.
- This home is energy efficient.

PLAN E-1910
WITHOUT BASEMENT

Exterior walls are 2x6 construction.
Specify crawlspace or slab foundation.

Heated area:	1,974 sq. ft.
Unheated area:	821 sq. ft.
Total area:	2,795 sq. ft.

LOWER LEVEL
FLOOR PLAN

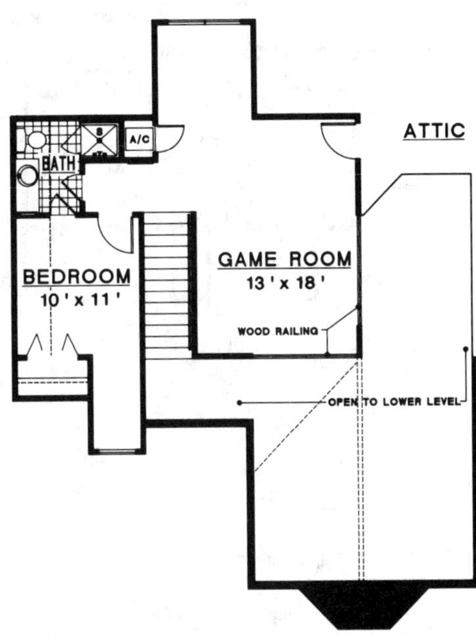

UPPER LEVEL
FLOOR PLAN

Blueprint Price Code B

Plan E-1910

TO ORDER THIS BLUEPRINT, CALL TOLL-FREE 1-800-547-5570
(prices and details on pp. 12-15.)

Open, Fresh and Modern Interior

- Stucco is used for the subtle finish of the porch walls and columns. Brick is used for the balance of the exterior.
- The interior is open, fresh and modern, featuring minimal division between the main living areas. The foyer contains an elegant circular stairwell.
- The master suite has an adjoining sitting area complete with TV space. The master bath is spacious.
- The country kitchen offers a large butler's pantry, adjoining eating area and utility room.
- Two upstairs bedrooms have a bath and a balcony which overlooks the lower level.
- This home is energy efficient.
- The living room and foyer have 17′ ceilings. The sitting area and eating area feature sloped ceilings of varied heights. Typical ceiling heights are 8′.

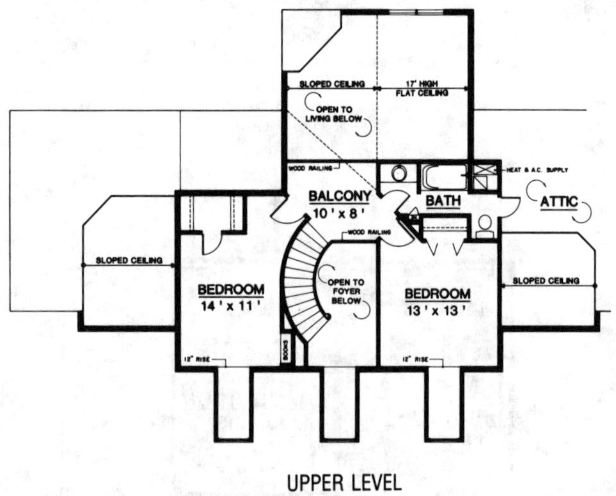

UPPER LEVEL

Exterior walls are 2x6 construction.
Specify basement, crawlspace or slab foundation.

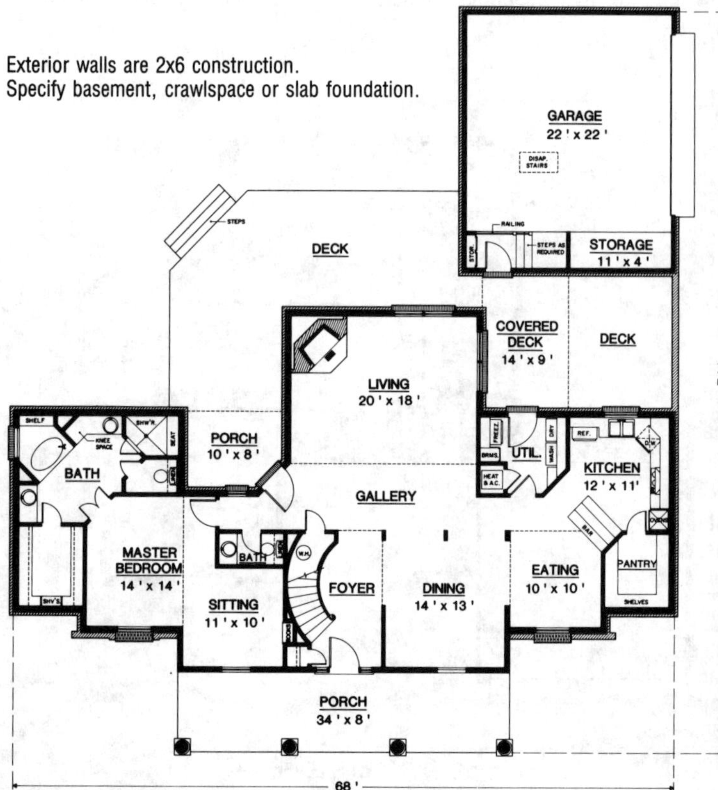

Heated area:	2,330 sq. ft.
Unheated area:	1,035 sq. ft.
Total area: (Not counting basement)	3,365 sq. ft.

TO ORDER THIS BLUEPRINT, CALL TOLL-FREE 1-800-547-5570
(prices and details on pp. 12-15.)

Blueprint Price Code C

Plan E-2305

HomeStyles SOURCE 1 DESIGNERS' NETWORK

Rustic Home Offers Comfort, Economy

- Rustic and compact, this home offers economy of construction and looks at home in any setting.
- The homey front porch, multi-paned windows, shutters and horizontal siding combine to create a rustic exterior.
- An L-shaped kitchen is open to the dining room and also to the living room to create a Great Room feel to the floor plan.
- The living room includes a raised-hearth fireplace.
- Main floor master suite features a large walk-in closet and a double vanity in the master bath.
- An open two-story high foyer leads to the second floor, which includes two bedrooms with walk-in closets and a full bath with two linen closets.

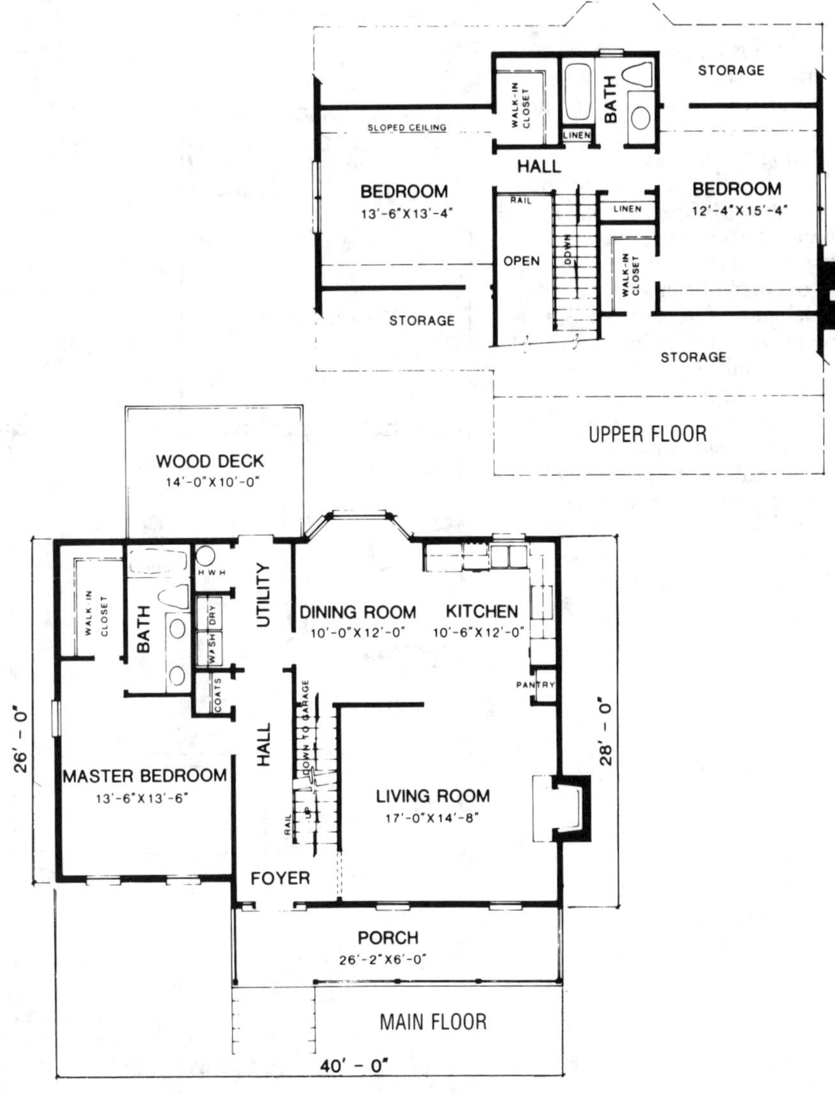

Plan C-8339

Bedrooms: 3	**Baths:** 2
Space:	
Upper floor:	660 sq.ft.
Main floor:	1,100 sq.ft.
Total living area:	1,760 sq.ft.
Basement:	Approx. 1,100 sq.ft.
Garage:	Included in basement.
Exterior Wall Framing:	2x4
Foundation options:	
Standard basement only. (Foundation & framing conversion diagram available — see order form.)	
Blueprint Price Code:	B

Plan C-8339

TO ORDER THIS BLUEPRINT, CALL TOLL-FREE 1-800-547-5570
(prices and details on pp. 12-15.)

Southern Country

- This home is distinctly Southern Country in style, from its wide front porch to its multi-paned and shuttered windows.
- The living room boasts a 12′ cathedral ceiling, a fireplace and French doors to the rear patio.
- The dining room is open, but defined by three massive columns with overhead beams.
- The delightful kitchen/nook area is spacious and well-planned for both efficiency and pleasant kitchen working conditions.
- A handy utility room and half-bath are on either side of a short hallway leading to the carport.
- The master suite offers his and hers walk-in closets and an incredible bath which incorporates a plant shelf above the garden tub.

Plan J-86140

Bedrooms: 3	**Baths:** 2½
Total living area:	2,177 sq. ft.
Basement:	2,177 sq. ft.
Carport:	440 sq. ft.
Storage:	120 sq. ft.
Porch:	233 sq. ft.
Exterior Wall Framing:	2x4
Ceiling Heights:	9′

Foundation options:
Standard basement.
Crawlspace.
Slab.
(Foundation & framing conversion diagram available — see order form.)

Blueprint Price Code: C

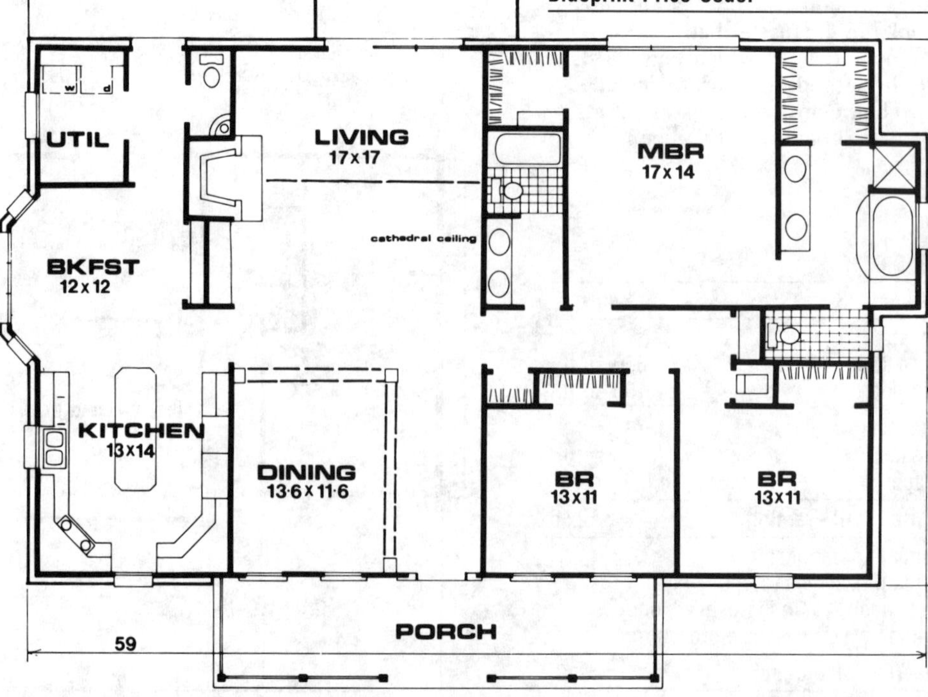

Plan J-86140

Open Plan in Traditional Design

- This modest-sized design is popular for its simple yet stylish exterior, making it suitable for either country or urban settings.
- A covered front porch and gabled roof extension accent the facade while providing sheltered space for outdoor relaxing.
- Inside, the living room with a cathedral ceiling and fireplace is combined with an open dining area and kitchen with island to create one large gathering spot for family and guests.
- The master bedroom features a private bath, large closet and ample sleeping area.
- Two other bedrooms share a second full bath.
- A convenient utility area and walk-in pantry are found in the passageway to the carport; also note the large outdoor storage closet.

Plan J-86155

Bedrooms: 3	**Baths:** 2
Total living area:	1,385 sq. ft.
Basement:	1,385 sq. ft.
Carport:	380 sq. ft.
Exterior Wall Framing:	2x4

Foundation options:
Standard basement.
Crawlspace.
Slab.
(Foundation & framing conversion diagram available — see order form.)

Blueprint Price Code:	A

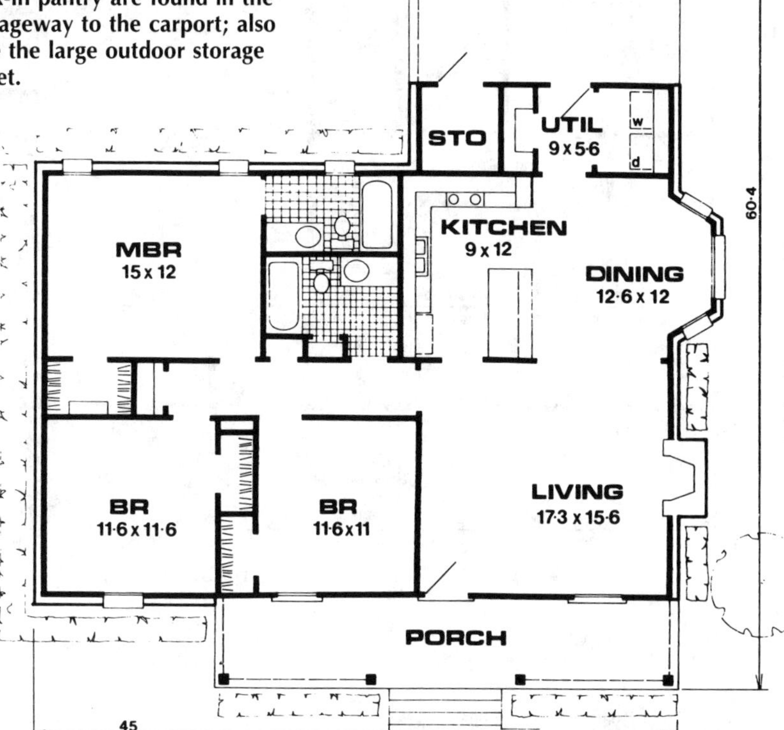

Plan J-86155

TO ORDER THIS BLUEPRINT, CALL TOLL-FREE 1-800-547-5570
(prices and details on pp. 12-15.)

Full-Width Veranda Welcomes Visitors

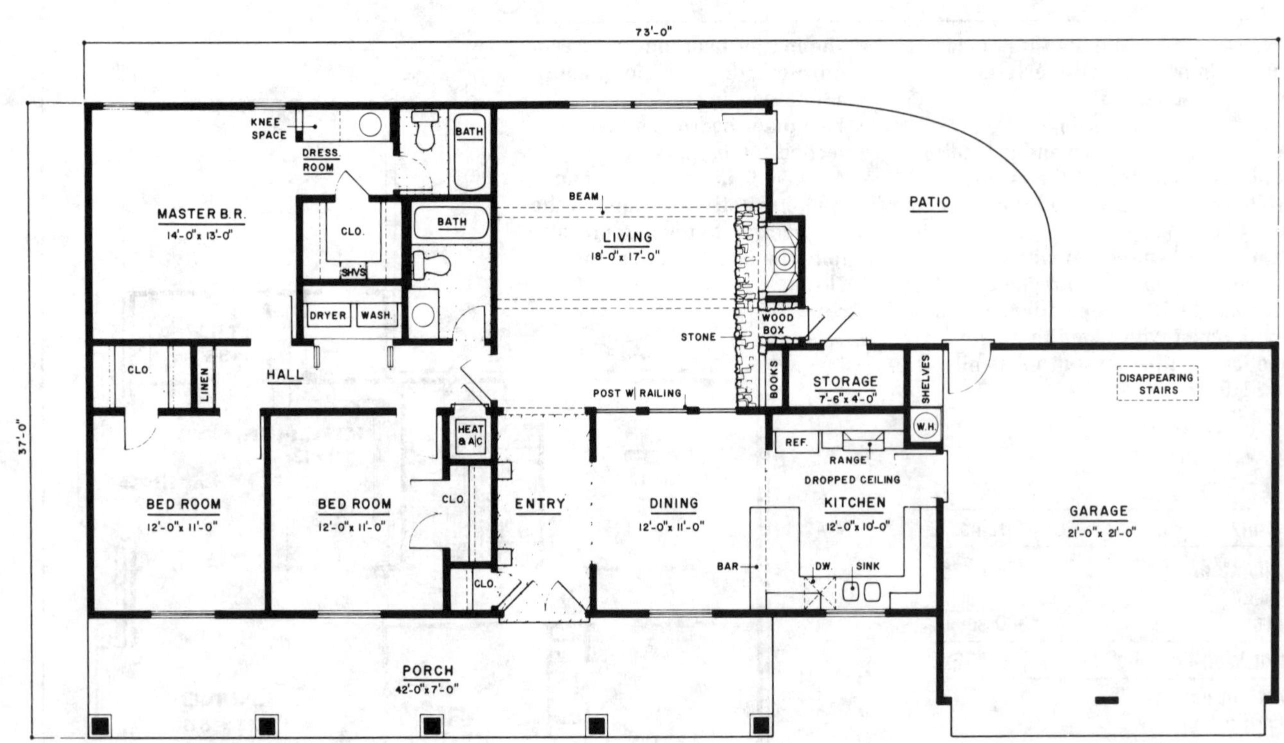

PLAN E-1304
WITHOUT BASEMENT

Specify crawlspace or slab foundation.

Total living area:	1,395 sq. ft.
Garage & storage:	481 sq. ft.
Porch:	294 sq. ft.
Total area:	2,170 sq. ft.

TO ORDER THIS BLUEPRINT, CALL TOLL-FREE 1-800-547-5570
(prices and details on pp. 12-15.)

Blueprint Price Code A

Plan E-1304

Compact, Cozy, Inviting

- Liberal-sized living room is centrally located and features corner fireplace and sloped ceilings.
- Separate two-car garage is included with plan.
- Two-bedroom loft overlooks living room and entryway below.
- Full-width porches, both front and rear, invite guests and family alike for leisure time rest and relaxation.

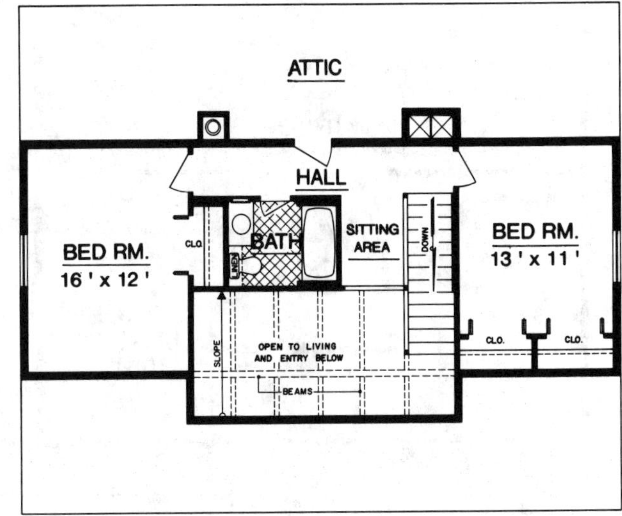

UPPER FLOOR

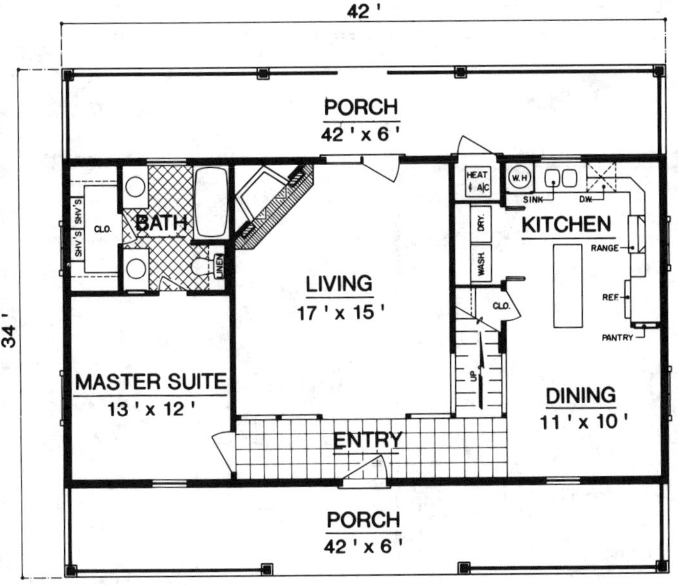

MAIN FLOOR

Plan E-1421

Bedrooms: 3	**Baths:** 2
Space:	
Upper floor:	561 sq. ft.
Main floor:	924 sq. ft.
Total living area:	1,485 sq. ft.
Basement:	approx. 924 sq. ft.
Porches:	504 sq. ft.
Exterior Wall Framing:	2x6

Foundation options:
Standard basement.
Crawlspace.
Slab.
(Foundation & framing conversion diagram available — see order form.)

Blueprint Price Code: A

Plan E-1421

TO ORDER THIS BLUEPRINT, CALL TOLL-FREE 1-800-547-5570
(prices and details on pp. 12-15.)

Log Cabin Appeal

- A simple, relaxing log cabin appeal is created with wood siding over conventional wall construction.
- The dramatic living/dining room has dual sliding glass doors overlooking a full-length deck, a sloped ceiling with loft above, and a stone fireplace focal point.
- The spacious kitchen can easily accommodate a breakfast table with a view of the side screened porch.
- The main floor bedroom has a walk-in closet and private access to the full bath.
- The upstairs bedroom suite throws in such goodies as a private deck and a wood stove.

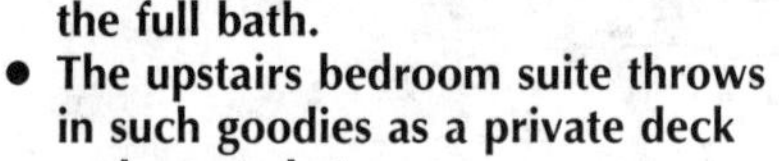

REAR VIEW

Plan AX-8162-A

Bedrooms: 2-3	**Baths:** 2
Space:	
Upper floor:	544 sq. ft.
Main floor:	952 sq. ft.
Total living area:	1,496 sq. ft.
Basement:	952 sq. ft.
Optional screened porch area:	271 sq. ft.
Garage:	366 sq. ft.
Storage area:	84 sq. ft.
Exterior Wall Framing:	2x4
Foundation options:	
Standard basement.	
Slab.	
(Foundation & framing conversion diagram available — see order form.)	
Blueprint Price Code:	A

UPPER FLOOR

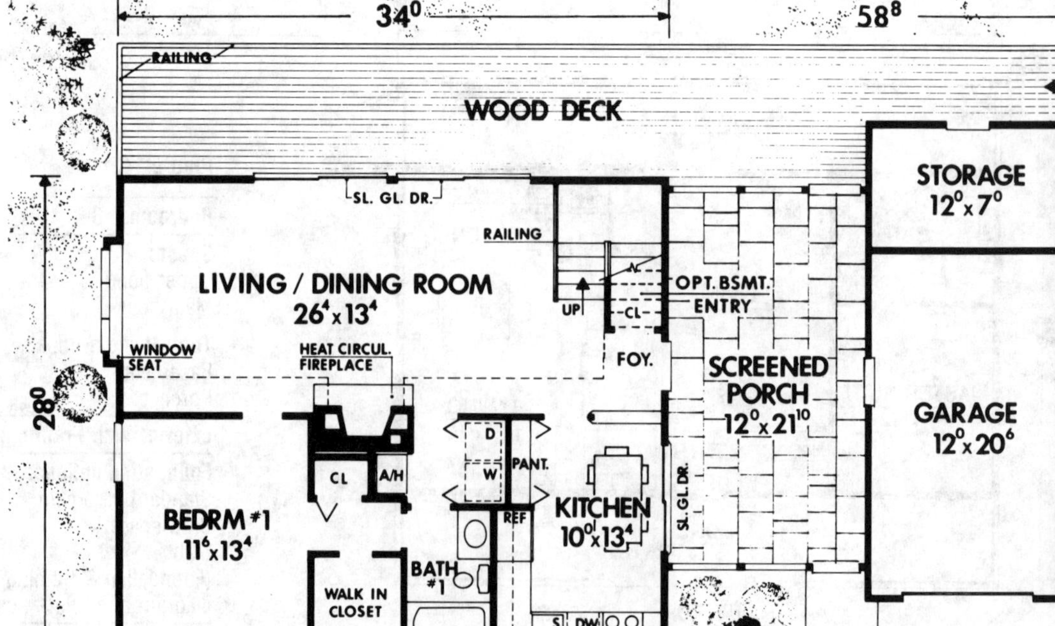

MAIN FLOOR

TO ORDER THIS BLUEPRINT, CALL TOLL-FREE 1-800-547-5570
(prices and details on pp. 12-15.)

Plan AX-8162-A

Panoramic Porch

- A gracious, ornate rounded front porch and a two-story turreted bay lend a Victorian charm to this home.
- A two-story foyer with round-top transom windows and plant ledge above greets guests at the entry.
- The living room enjoys a panoramic view overlooking the front porch and yard.
- The formal dining room and den each feature a bay window for added style.
- The kitchen breakfast room incorporates an angled island cooktop, from which the sunken family room with corner fireplace can be enjoyed.
- The three bedrooms and two full baths upstairs are highlighted by a stunning master suite. The master bath offers a quaint octagonal sitting area within the turret bay.

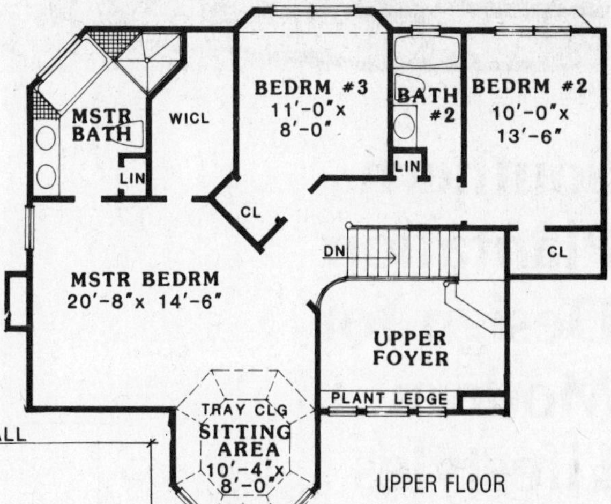

MSTR BATH
WICL
LIN
BEDRM #3 11'-0"x 8'-0"
BATH #2
LIN
BEDRM #2 10'-0"x 13'-6"
CL
DN
CL
MSTR BEDRM 20'-8"x 14'-6"
UPPER FOYER
TRAY CLG
SITTING AREA 10'-4"x 8'-0"
PLANT LEDGE

UPPER FLOOR

69'-2" OVERALL
PATIO
SUNKEN FAMILY RM 21'-4"x 14'-8"
BRKFST RM 9'-0"x 14'-0"
KITCHEN 11'-0"x 14'-0"
S
DW
OV
DN
DINING RM 13'-0"x 11'-0"
FIREPLACE
DN TO BSMT
UP
REF
BATH #3
CL
WET BAR
UTIL
W D
MUD RM
STORAGE
HIGH CEIL FOYER
UP
HIGH CEIL LIVING RM 15'-8"x 16'-4"
TWO CAR GARAGE 20'-0"x 20'-6"
DEN/GUEST RM 13'-4"x 11'-8"
PORCH
UP
PORCH

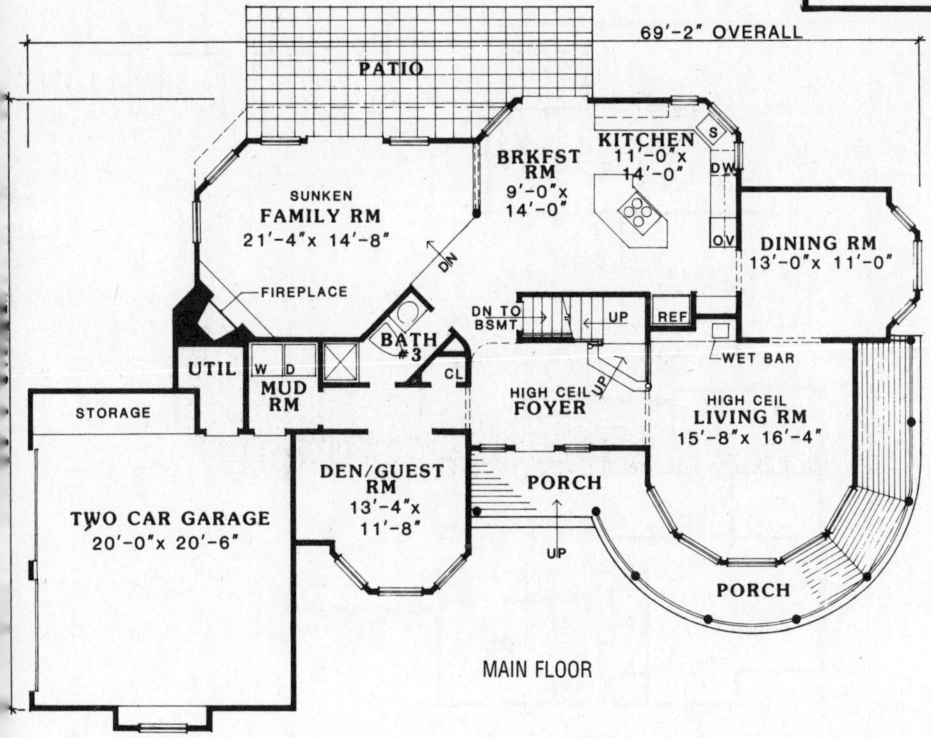

MAIN FLOOR

Plan AX-90307

Bedrooms: 3-4	**Baths:** 3
Space:	
Upper floor:	956 sq. ft.
Main floor:	1,499 sq. ft.
Total living area:	2,455 sq. ft.
Basement:	1,499 sq. ft.
Garage:	410 sq. ft.
Exterior Wall Framing:	2x4

Foundation options:
Standard basement.
Slab.
(Foundation & framing conversion diagram available — see order form.)

Blueprint Price Code: C

Plan AX-90307

TO ORDER THIS BLUEPRINT, CALL TOLL-FREE 1-800-547-5570
(prices and details on pp. 12-15.)

Southern Plantation Design for Modern Lifestyles

Typical of its earlier ancestors, this raised plantation home features a wrap-around porch complete with detailed columns and railings. An impressive entry boasts a circular stairwell and high, dramatic ceilings. A balcony overlooks the lower level. The unusual angled kitchen shares a view to the outside with the cozy eating area.

The oversized master suite has a sitting area perfect for relaxation. An enormous master bath offers his/her bath and closet facilities.

This luxury story-and-a-half home is an energy-efficient design. It is drawn on a raised crawlspace foundation. An alternate concrete slab foundation is available.

Areas:	
Lower level:	2,575 sq. ft.
Upper level:	911 sq. ft.
Total heated area:	3,486 sq. ft.
Unheated area:	1,623 sq. ft.
Total area:	5,109 sq. ft.

Exterior walls are 2x6 construction.
Specify crawlspace or slab foundation.

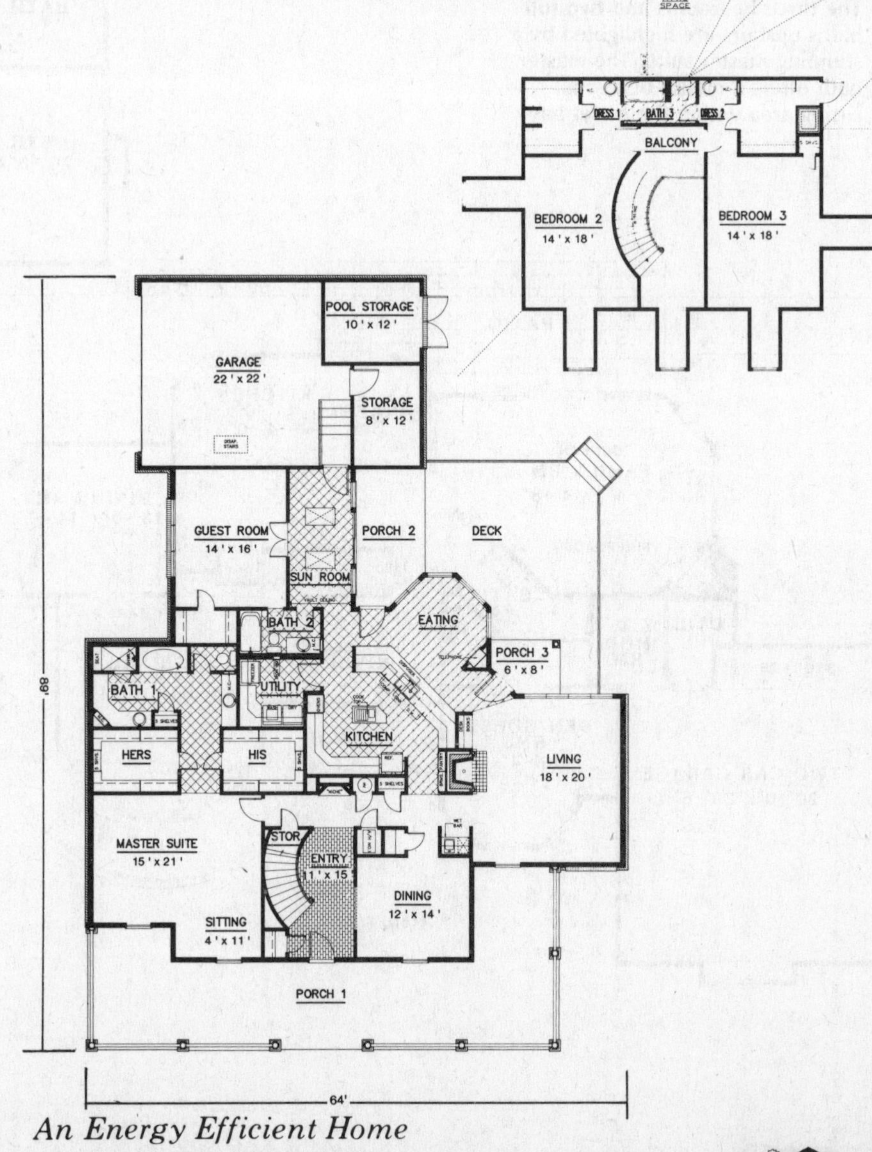

An Energy Efficient Home

Blueprint Price Code E

Plan E-3400

TO ORDER THIS BLUEPRINT, CALL TOLL-FREE 1-800-547-5570 (prices and details on pp. 12-15.)

Wrap-around Porch Accents Victorian Farmhouse

- Fish-scale shingles and horizontal siding team with the detailed front porch to create this look of yesterday. The sides and rear are brick.
- The main level features a center section of informal family room and formal living and dining rooms. They can all be connected via French doors.
- A separate workshop is located on the main level and connected to the main house by a covered breezeway.
- The master bath ceiling is sloped and has built-in skylights. The kitchen and eating area have high sloped ceilings also. Typical ceiling heights are 8′ on the basement and upper level and 10′ on the main level.
- This home is energy efficient.
- This home is designed on a full daylight basement. The two-car garage is located under the workshop.

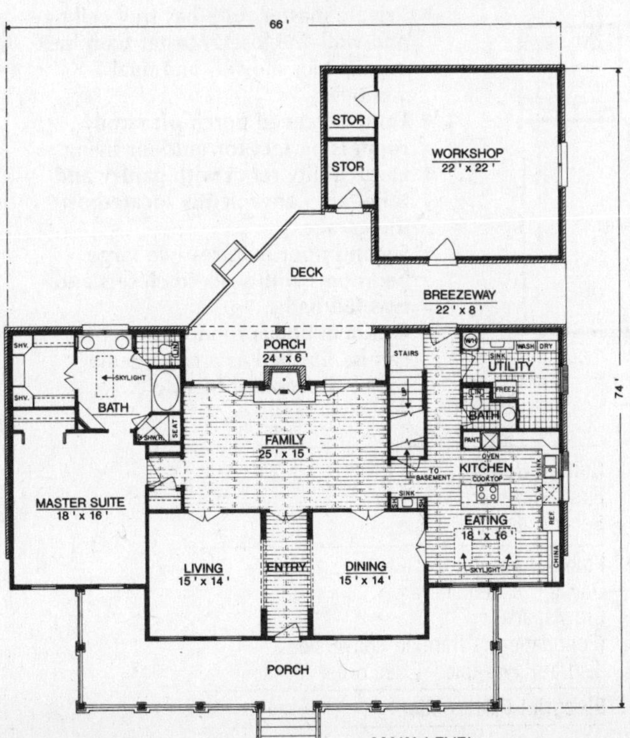

MAIN LEVEL

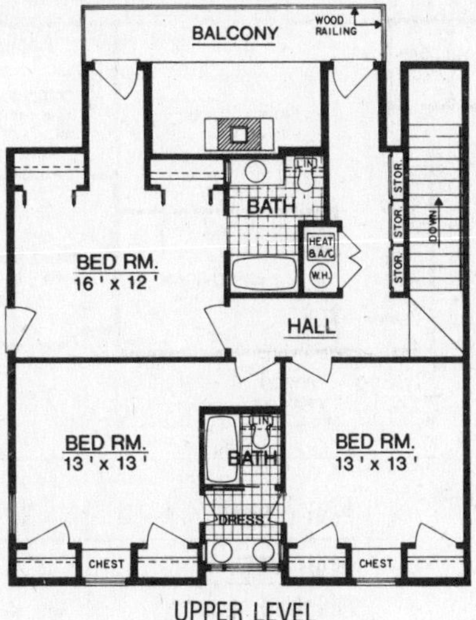

UPPER LEVEL
PLAN E-3103
WITH DAYLIGHT BASEMENT

Exterior walls are 2x6 construction.

Heated area:	3,153 sq. ft.
Unheated area	2,066 sq. ft.
Total area: (Not counting basement)	5,219 sq. ft.

Blueprint Price Code E

Plan E-3103

TO ORDER THIS BLUEPRINT, CALL TOLL-FREE 1-800-547-5570
(prices and details on pp. 12-15.)

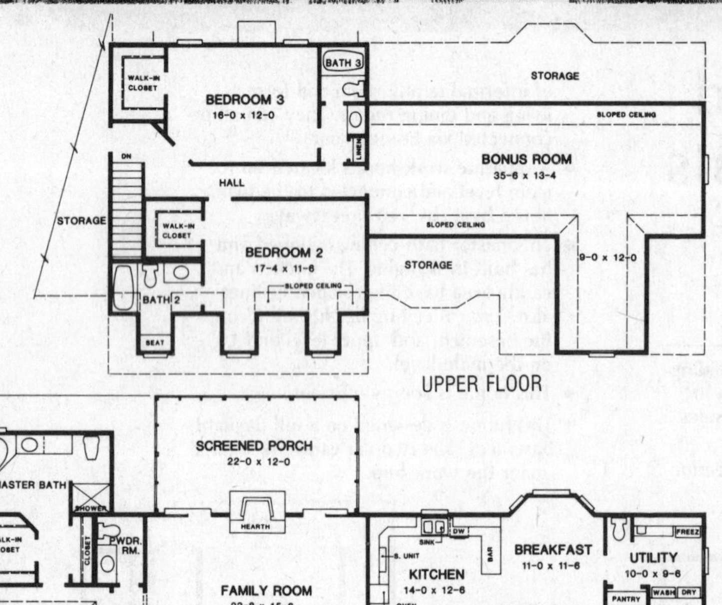

UPPER FLOOR

MAIN FLOOR

Deluxe Main Floor Master Suite

- Traditional style exterior with modern floor plan. Dormers and stone add curb appeal to this home.
- Formal entry with staircase leads to formal living or large family room.
- Large kitchen is conveniently located between formal dining room and secluded breakfast nook with bay window.
- Private master suite has trey ceiling and walk-in closet. Master bath has corner tub, shower, and dual vanities.
- Large screened porch off family room is perfect for outdoor living.
- Large utility room with pantry and toilet are conveniently located off the garage.
- Second floor features two large bedrooms with walk-in closets and two full baths.
- Optional bonus room (624 sq. ft.) can be finished as a large game room, bedroom, office, etc.

Plan C-8915

Bedrooms: 3	**Baths:** 3½
Finished space:	
Upper floor:	832 sq. ft.
Main floor:	1,927 sq. ft.
Total living area:	2,759 sq. ft.
Bonus area:	624 sq. ft.
Basement:	1,674 sq. ft.
Garage:	484 sq. ft.
Exterior Wall Framing:	2x4

Ceiling Height:	
First floor:	9′
Second floor:	8′
Foundation options:	
Daylight basement.	
Crawlspace.	
(Foundation & framing conversion diagram available — see order form.)	
Blueprint Price Code:	D

TO ORDER THIS BLUEPRINT, CALL TOLL-FREE 1-800-547-5570
(prices and details on pp. 12-15.)

Plan C-8915

Three-Bedroom Home Features Screened-In Porch

- This classic story-and-a-half design encompasses a thoroughly modern interior on a compact foundation area.
- Living and dining rooms flow together, yet are divided by a screened porch which provides more space in nice weather.
- Deluxe master bedroom is larger than you might expect in a home this size, and includes a big walk-in closet and a dressing area.
- The large kitchen includes abundant counter space, and adjoins a roomy utility area.
- The upstairs includes two nice-sized bedrooms and a convenient bath.

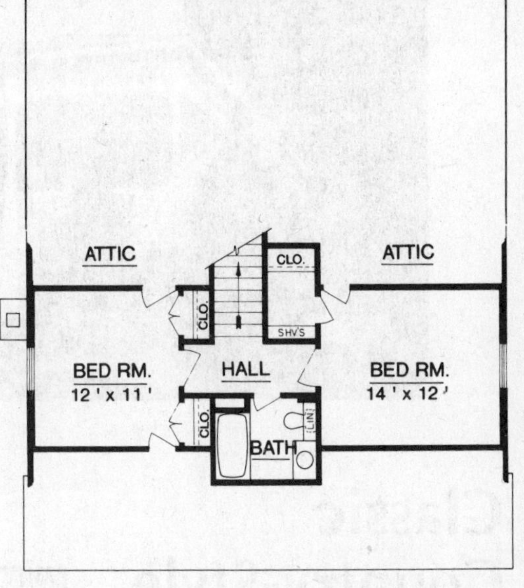

UPPER FLOOR

Plan E-1626

Bedrooms: 3 **Baths:** 2

Space:

Upper floor:	464 sq. ft.
Main floor:	1,136 sq. ft.
Total living area:	1,600 sq. ft.
Porches:	393 sq. ft.
Garage:	462 sq. ft.
Storage:	11 sq. ft.

Exterior Wall Framing: 2x6

Foundation options:
Crawlspace.
Slab.
(Foundation & framing conversion diagram available — see order form.)

Blueprint Price Code: B

58 '
42 '
PORCH
14 ' x 12 '
DINING
13 ' x 12 '
UTIL
9 ' x 6 '
W.H.
WASH
DRY
STORAGE
22 ' x 5 '
BRM
REF
SINK
BATH
GARAGE
22 ' x 21 '
UP
RANGE
D.W.
KIT
11 ' x 9 '
LIN
PANTRY
VANITY
LIVING
24 ' x 14 '
SHV
MASTER SUITE
15 ' x 14 '
HEAT & A/C
CLO.
ENTRY
PORCH
36 'x 6 '

MAIN FLOOR

**NOTE:
The above photographed home may have been modified by the homeowner. Please refer to floor plan and/or drawn elevation shown for actual blueprint details.

Plan E-1626

TO ORDER THIS BLUEPRINT, CALL TOLL-FREE 1-800-547-5570
(prices and details on pp. 12-15.)

Photo by Felice Photographers

Classic Country-Style Home

- Almost completely surrounded by an expansive wrap-around porch that measures almost 1,200 sq. ft., this classic plan exudes warmth and grace.
- The foyer is liberal in size and leads guests to a formal dining room at left or the large living room at right.
- A large country kitchen includes a sunny, bay-windowed breakfast nook.
- The main floor also includes a utility area and full bath.
- Upstairs, the master suite is impressive, with its large sleeping area, big closet and magnificent bath.
- Three secondary bedrooms with ample closets share a full bath with double sinks.
- Also note stairs leading up to an attic, useful for storage space.

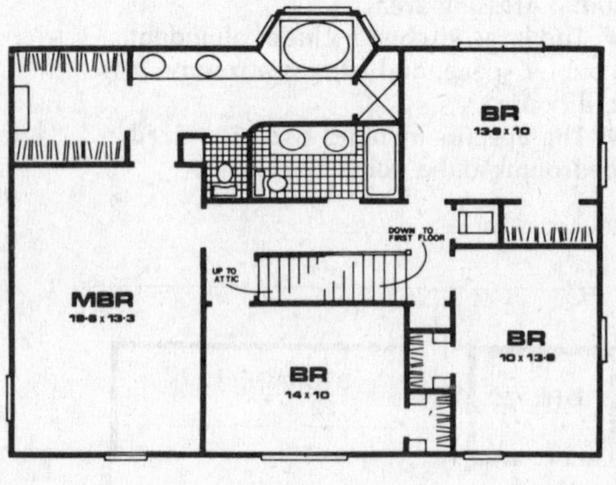

UPPER FLOOR

Plan J-86134	
Bedrooms: 4	**Baths:** 3
Space:	
Upper floor:	1,195 sq. ft.
Main floor:	1,370 sq. ft.
Total living area:	2,565 sq. ft.
Basement:	1,370 sq. ft.
Garage:	576 sq. ft.
Storage:	144 sq. ft.
Porch:	1,181 sq. ft.
Exterior Wall Framing:	2x4
Foundation options:	
Standard basement.	
Crawlspace.	
Slab.	
(Foundation & framing conversion diagram available — see order form.)	
Blueprint Price Code:	D

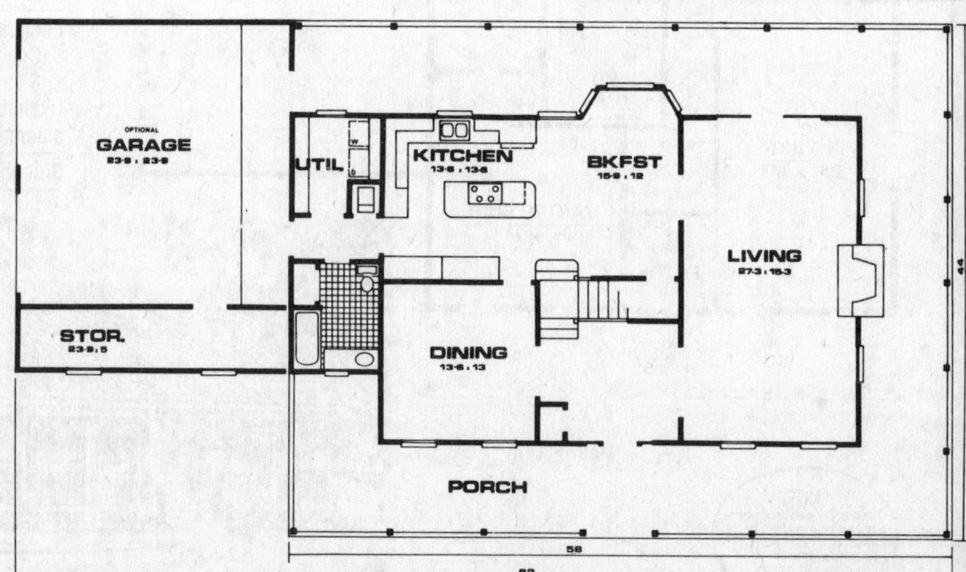

MAIN FLOOR

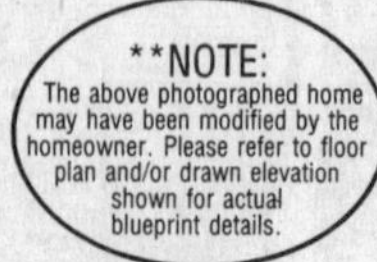

**NOTE: The above photographed home may have been modified by the homeowner. Please refer to floor plan and/or drawn elevation shown for actual blueprint details.

TO ORDER THIS BLUEPRINT, CALL TOLL-FREE 1-800-547-5570
(prices and details on pp. 12-15.)

Plan J-86134

**NOTE: The above photographed home may have been modified by the homeowner. Please refer to floor plan and/or drawn elevation shown for actual blueprint details.

All-American Country Home

- Romantic, old-fashioned and spacious living areas combine to create this modern home.
- Off the entryway is the generous living room with fireplace and French doors which open onto the traditional rear porch.
- Country kitchen features an island table for informal occasions, while the adjoining family room is ideal for family gatherings.
- Practically placed, a laundry/mud room lies off the garage for immediate disposal of soiled garments.
- This plan is available with garage (H-3711-1) or without garage (H-3711-2) and with or without basement.

PLANS H-3711-2 & H-3711-2A
(WITHOUT GARAGE)

PLANS H-3711-1 & H-3711-1A
(WITH GARAGE)

WALK-IN CLOSET 7'6" x 7'6"
BATH
Shwr
LINEN 6'0"
BATH
STOR
BEDROOM 13'3" x 11'0"
CLOSET 4'9"
CLOSET 4'9"
UP TO ATTIC
up
down
CLOSET 4'9"
CLOSET 4'9"
BEDROOM 13'0" x 19'0"
BEDROOM 15'0" x 10'0"
BEDROOM 10'0" x 13'3"

UPPER FLOOR

Plans H-3711-1/1A & -2/2A	
Bedrooms: 4	**Baths:** 2½
Space:	
Upper floor:	1,176 sq. ft.
Main floor:	1,288 sq. ft.
Total living area:	2,464 sq. ft.
Basement:	approx. 1,288 sq. ft.
Garage:	505 sq. ft.
Exterior Wall Framing:	2x6
Foundation options: Standard basement (Plans H-3711-1 & -2). Crawlspace (Plans H-3711-1A & -2A). (Foundation & framing conversion diagram available — see order form.)	
Blueprint Price Code:	C

74'0"
FRENCH DRS.
DINING 11'9" x 13'3"
DW
REF.
D
W
LAUNDRY 13'0" x 7'6"
STORAGE 15'8" x 13'6"
ISLAND
PANTRY
COUNTRY KITCHEN 15'0" x 27'0"
WH
down
up
down
GARAGE 23'6" x 21'6"
44'0"
LIVING ROOM 13'0" x 27'0"
ENTRY
LAV
FAMILY ROOM
CLOS 3'0"
8' WIDE COVERED PORCH

MAIN FLOOR

Plans H-3711-1/1A & -2/2A

TO ORDER THIS BLUEPRINT, CALL TOLL-FREE 1-800-547-5570
(prices and details on pp. 12-15.)

Old Homestead

Almost everyone has a soft place in his heart for a certain home in his childhood. A home like this one, with understated farmhouse styling and wrap-around porch, may be the image of "Home" that your children remember.

Two versions of the first floor plan provide a choice between a country kitchen and a more formal dining room.

All versions feature 2x6 exterior wall framing.

First floor:	1,359 sq. ft.
Second floor:	626 sq. ft.
Total living area:	1,985 sq. ft.
(Not counting basement or garage)	
(Non-basement versions designed with crawlspace)	
Garage:	528 sq. ft.

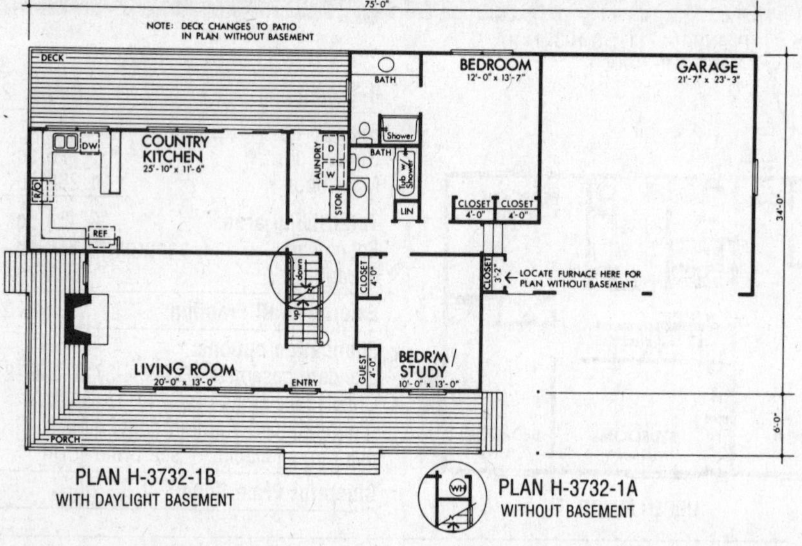

PLAN H-3732-1B
WITH DAYLIGHT BASEMENT

PLAN H-3732-1A
WITHOUT BASEMENT

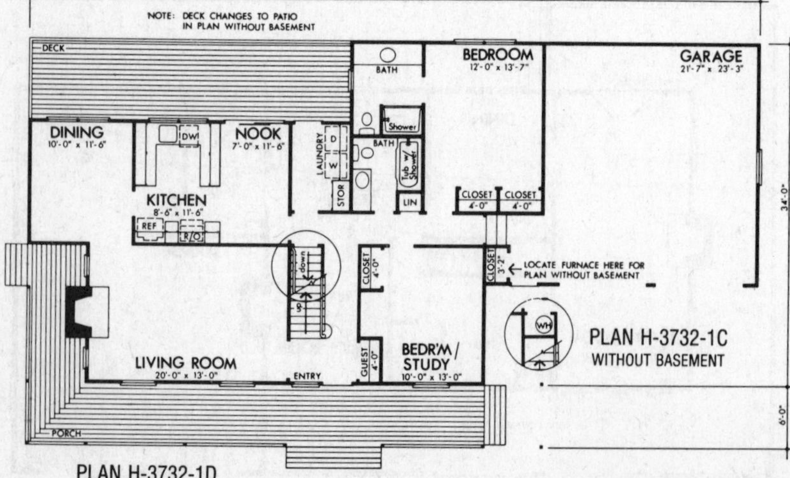

PLAN H-3732-1C
WITHOUT BASEMENT

PLAN H-3732-1D
WITH DAYLIGHT BASEMENT

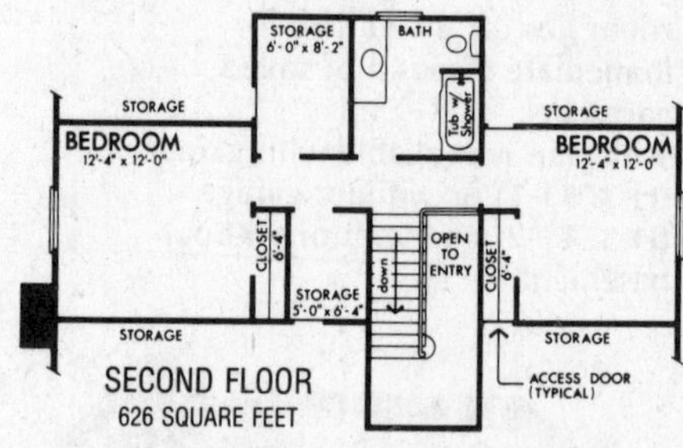

SECOND FLOOR
626 SQUARE FEET

Blueprint Price Code B

Plans H-3732-1A, H-3732-1B, H-3732-1C & H-3732-1D

TO ORDER THIS BLUEPRINT, CALL TOLL-FREE 1-800-547-5570
(prices and details on pp. 12-15.)

High Luxury in One-Story Plan

- 12′ ceilings are featured in the entryway and living room.
- 400 sq. ft. living room boasts a massive fireplace and access to the rear porch.
- Corridor-style kitchen has angled eating bar and convenient nearby laundry facilities.
- Master suite incorporates unusual bath arrangement consisting of an angled whirlpool tub and separate shower.
- Secondary bedrooms are zoned for privacy and climate control.

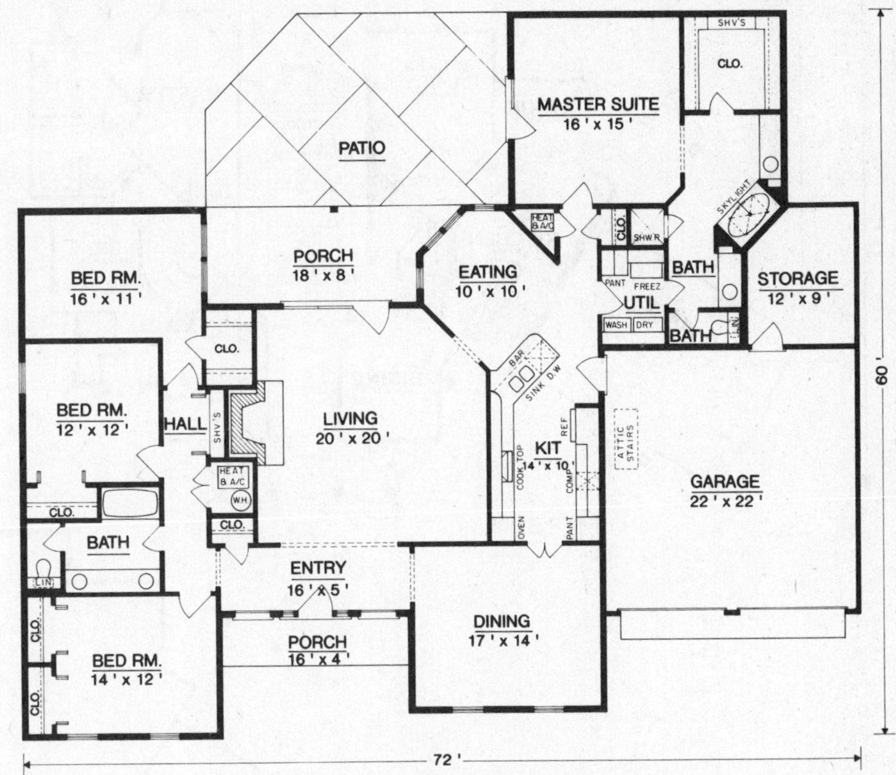

Plan E-2302

Bedrooms: 4	**Baths:** 2
Space:	
Total living area:	2,396 sq. ft.
Garage and storage:	590 sq. ft.
Porches:	216 sq. ft.
Exterior Wall Framing:	2x6

Foundation options:
Standard basement.
Crawlspace.
Slab.
(Foundation & framing conversion diagram available — see order form.)

Blueprint Price Code:	C

Plan E-2302

TO ORDER THIS BLUEPRINT, CALL TOLL-FREE 1-800-547-5570
(prices and details on pp. 12-15.)

Distinguished Indoor/Outdoor Living

- A very formal exterior and foyer highlight this distinguished home.
- Coved ceilings are found in the entry and sunken living room beyond, along with planters on either side; a fireplace and adjoining deck are also featured.
- A second deck joins an island kitchen and nook.
- Double doors access the elegant master bedroom with bay window, deck and luxury bath.
- A generous rec room with fireplace, patio, mini-kitchen and bar, plus two additional bedrooms make up the lower

Plan R-3010	
Bedrooms: 4	**Baths:** 3 ½
Space:	
Main floor	3,823 sq. ft.
Lower floor	1,285 sq. ft.
Total Living Area	**5,108 sq. ft.**
Garage	811 sq. ft.
Exterior Wall Framing	2x6
Foundation options:	
Crawlspace/partial daylight basement	
(Foundation & framing conversion diagram available—see order form.)	
Blueprint Price Code	G

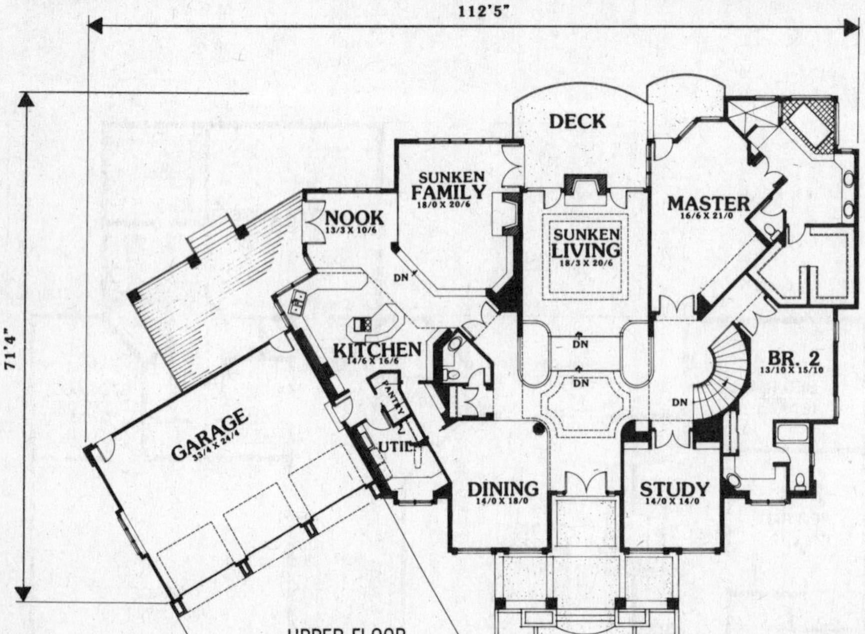

112'5"

71'4"

DECK

SUNKEN FAMILY 18/0 X 20/6

NOOK 13/3 X 10/6

SUNKEN LIVING 18/3 X 20/6

MASTER 16/6 X 21/0

KITCHEN 14/6 X 16/6

BR. 2 13/10 X 15/10

GARAGE 33/4 X 24/4

PANTRY

UTIL.

DINING 14/0 X 18/0

STUDY 14/0 X 14/0

UPPER FLOOR

PATIO

BR. 3 12/4 X 15/0

REC RM 32/0 X 27/0

BAR

BR. 4 11/10 X 12/0

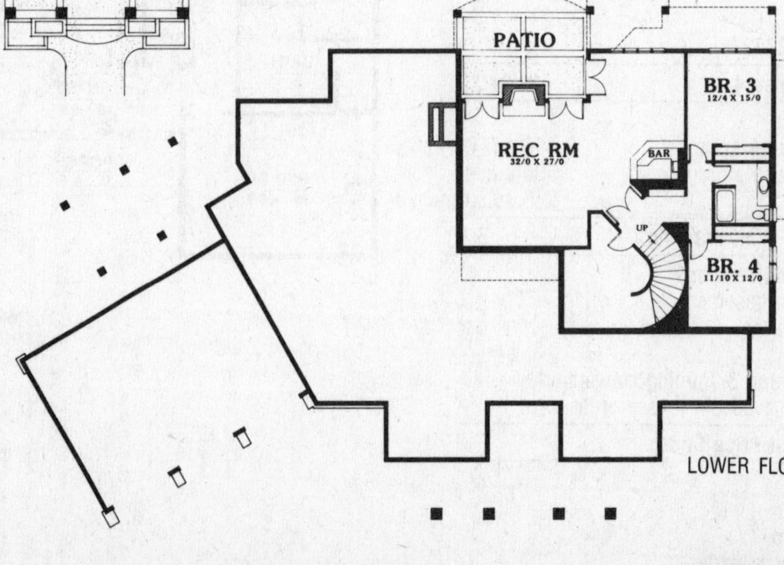

LOWER FLOOR

TO ORDER THIS BLUEPRINT, CALL TOLL-FREE 1-800-547-5570
(prices and details on pp. 12-15.)

Plan R-3010

Stately Traditional

- A stately traditional exterior is greeted inside by an equally dramatic two-story foyer with circular stairway.
- A formal living room and fireplace join a sunken dining room; a butler's pantry separates the dining room from the large island kitchen with pantry, breakfast nook with rounded window wall, and the rear deck.
- The large sunken family room features a fireplace flanked by books or entertainment equipment and a rounded rear window wall.
- Access to the upper level is possible through the foyer or through a second staircase near the kitchen.
- An elegant master bedroom with window seat, see-through fireplace, and luxury bath, is joined on the second floor by three additional bedrooms with private baths and a large bonus area for an extra bedroom, work area, or playroom.

Plan R-2146	
Bedrooms: 4-5	**Baths:** 4 ½
Space:	
Upper floor	2,149 sq. ft.
Main floor	2,605 sq. ft.
Bonus room	856 sq. ft.
Total Living Area	**5,610 sq. ft.**
Garage	1,206 sq. ft.
Exterior Wall Framing	2x6
Foundation options:	
Crawlspace	
(Foundation & framing conversion diagram available—see order form.)	
Blueprint Price Code	G

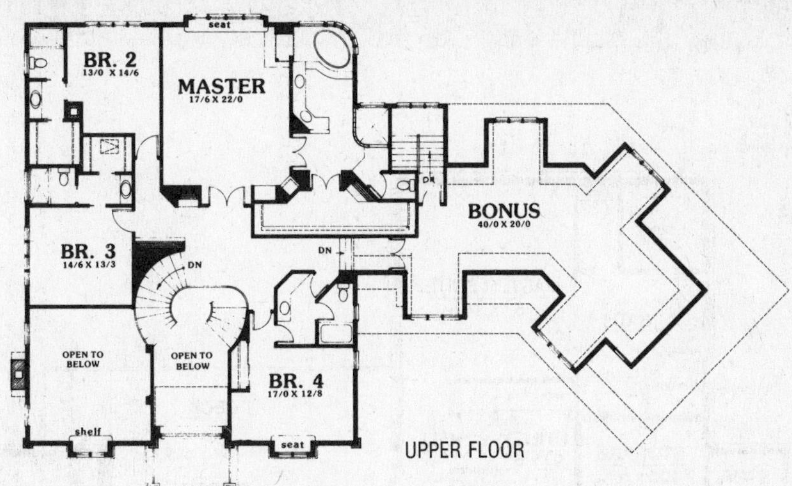

UPPER FLOOR

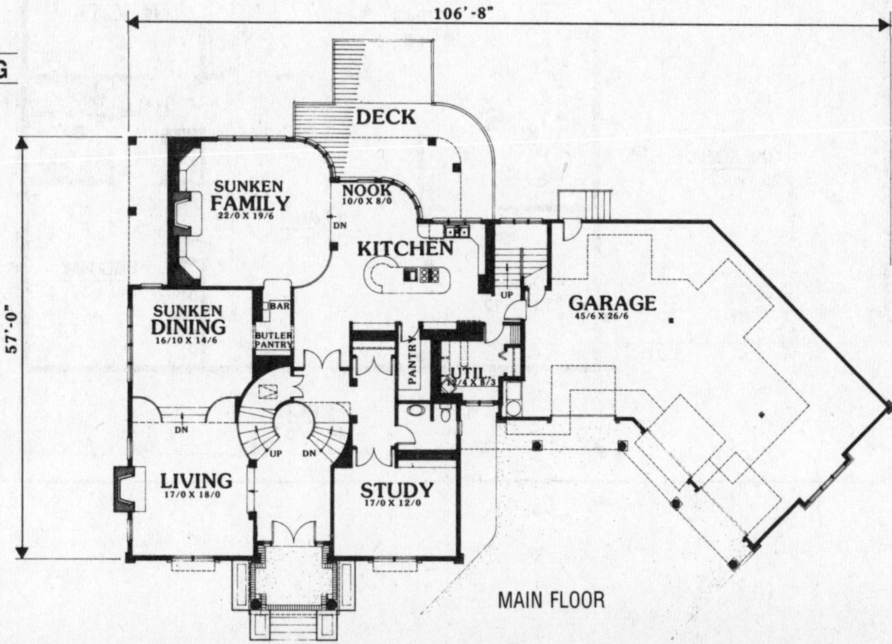

MAIN FLOOR

Plan R-2146

TO ORDER THIS BLUEPRINT, CALL TOLL-FREE 1-800-547-5570
(prices and details on pp. 12-15.)

Raised Cottage Design Offers Large Covered Porches

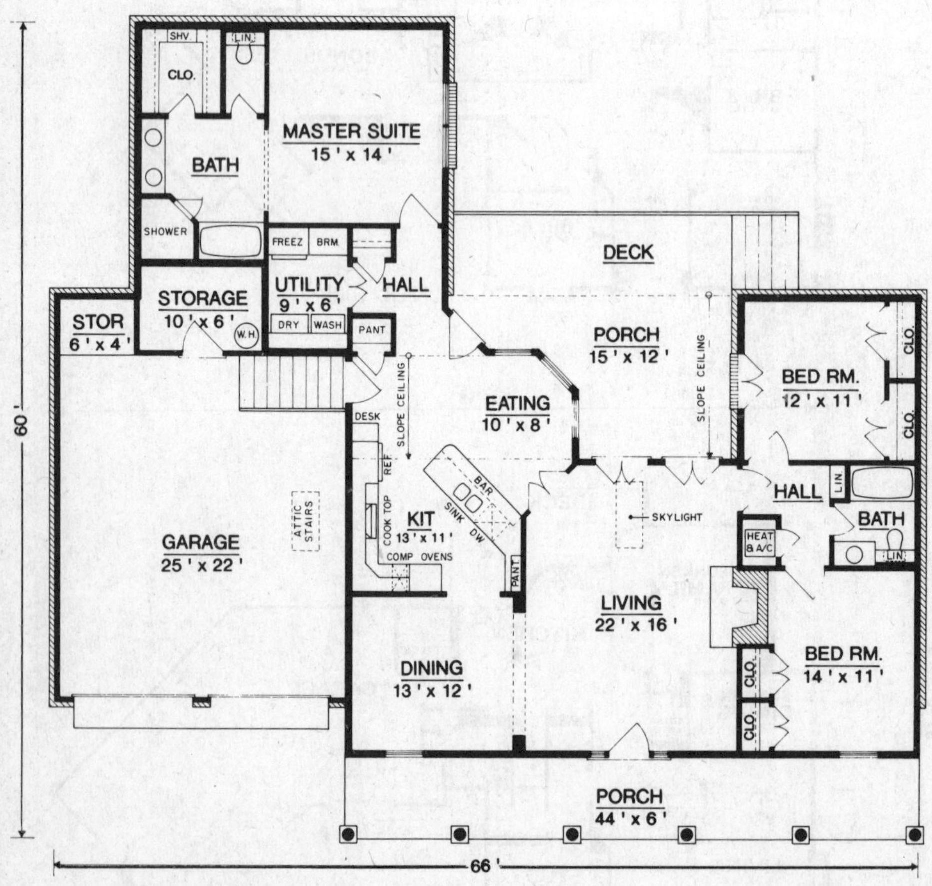

- Twin dormers and covered porch add drama to this raised one-story.
- Large centered living room features 12′ ceilings and built-in skylights.
- Kitchen has unusual but functional angular design, sloped ceilings, bar, and eating area that overlooks the adjoining deck.
- Elegant master suite is conveniently located near kitchen.

Plan E-1826

Bedrooms: 3	**Baths:** 2
Space:	
Total living area:	1,800 sq. ft.
Garage:	550 sq. ft.
Storage:	84 sq. ft.
Porches:	466 sq. ft.
Exterior Wall Framing:	2x6

Foundation options:
Crawlspace.
Slab.
(Foundation & framing conversion diagram available — see order form.)

Blueprint Price Code: B

TO ORDER THIS BLUEPRINT, CALL TOLL-FREE 1-800-547-5570 (prices and details on pp. 12-15.)

Plan E-1826

Splendor of the Old South

- Designed after "Monteigne", an italinate home from the Nachez area, this reproduction utilizes modern stucco finishes for the exterior.
- The formal foyer is accented by the large circular stairwell. The foyer is open to the upper level balcony.
- The full width sun room stretches across the rear of the main house and overlooks the center courtyard.
- A uniquely located entertainment center serves the main activity rooms.
- The master suite and bath are super plush and contain every imaginable feature — including his and her vanities, separate mirrored make-up vanity, super closets and a glassed-in garden tub. The king-sized bedroom suite even utilizes the adjoining study.
- Two additional bedrooms with private baths are located on the upper level. They share a study and veranda. A fourth, ground-level, bedroom serves as a guest room or nursery.
- The living room and study have 14′ ceilings. Typical ceiling heights are 9′ at the lower level and 8′ on the upper level.
- This home is completely energy efficient.

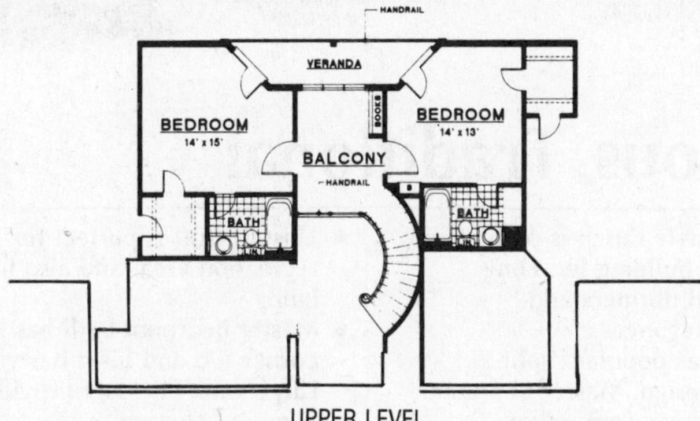

UPPER LEVEL

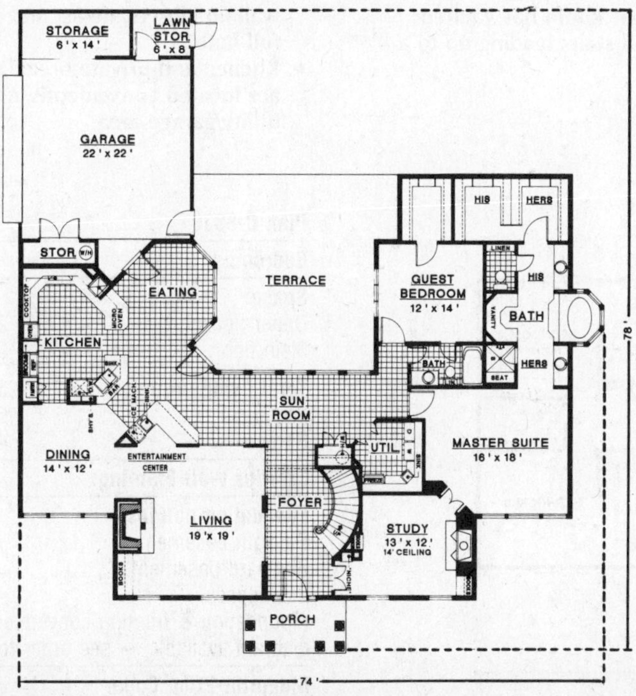

LOWER LEVEL

Heated area:	3,284 sq. ft.
Unheated area:	817 sq. ft.
Total area:	4,101 sq. ft.

(Not counting basement)

Exterior walls are 2x6 construction.
Specify basement, crawlspace or slab foundation.

Blueprint Price Code E

Plan E-3200

TO ORDER THIS BLUEPRINT, CALL TOLL-FREE 1-800-547-5570
(prices and details on pp. 12-15.)

Gracious Traditional

- Traditional style ranch is perfect for a corner building lot. Long windows and dormers add distinctive elegance.
- Floor plan has popular "split-bedroom" design. Master bedroom is secluded away from other bedrooms.
- Large Great Room has vaulted ceiling and stairs leading up to a loft.
- Upstairs loft is perfect for recreation area, and also has a full bath.
- Master bedroom bath has large corner tub and his-n-her vanities. Large walk-in closet provides plenty of storage.
- Two other bedrooms have large walk-in closets, desks, and share a full bath.
- Kitchen and private breakfast nook are located conveniently near the utility/garage area.

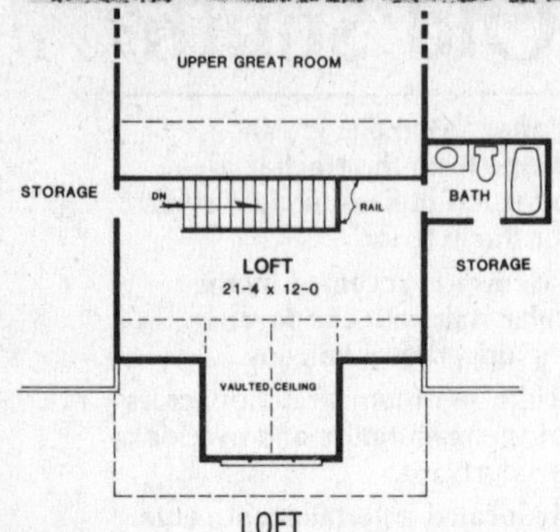

LOFT

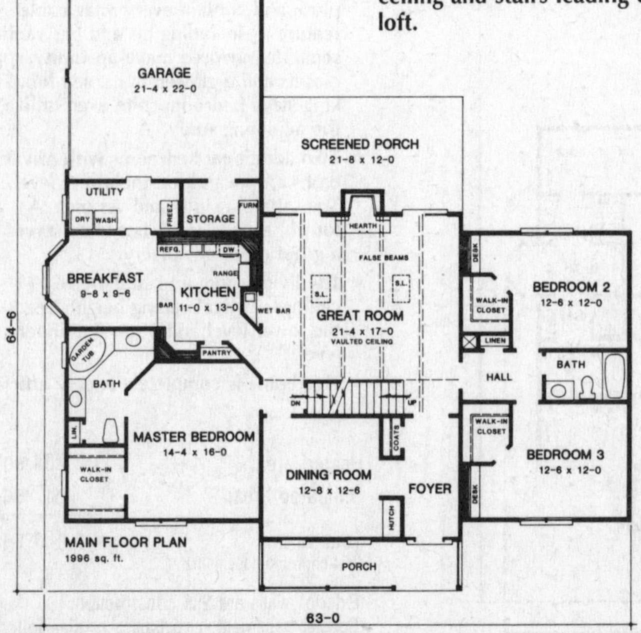

MAIN FLOOR

Plan C-8920

Bedrooms: 3	**Baths:** 3
Space:	
Upper floor:	305 sq. ft.
Main floor:	1,996 sq. ft.
Total living area:	2,301 sq. ft.
Basement:	1,996 sq. ft.
Garage:	469 sq. ft.
Exterior Wall Framing:	2x4

Foundation options:
Daylight basement.
Standard basement.
Crawlspace.
(Foundation & framing conversion diagram available — see order form.)

Blueprint Price Code: C

TO ORDER THIS BLUEPRINT, CALL TOLL-FREE 1-800-547-5570
(prices and details on pp. 12-15.)

Plan C-8920

HomeStyles SOURCE 1 Designers' Network

Country Kitchen and Deluxe Master Bath

- Front porch, dormers and shutters give this home a decidedly country look on the outside, which is complemented by an informal modern interior.
- The roomy country kitchen connects with a sunny breakfast nook and utility area on one hand and a formal dining room on the other.
- The central portion of the home consists of a large family room with a fireplace and easy access to a rear deck.
- The downstairs master suite is particularly impressive for a home of this size, and features a majestic master bath with two walk-in closets and double vanities.
- Upstairs, you will find two more ample-sized bedrooms, a double bath and a large storage area.

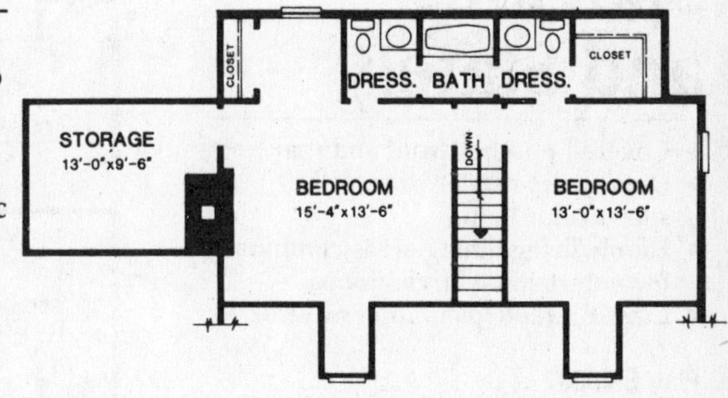

UPPER FLOOR

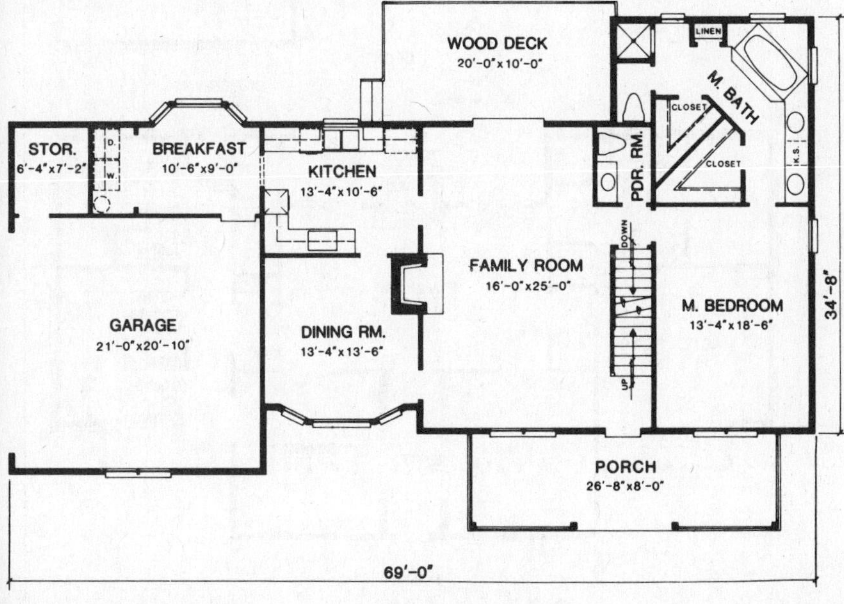

MAIN FLOOR

Plan C-8645

Bedrooms: 3	**Baths:** 2½
Space:	
Upper floor:	704 sq.ft.
Main floor:	1,477 sq.ft.
Total living area:	2,181 sq.ft.
Basement:	Approx. 1,400 sq.ft.
Garage:	438 sq.ft.
Storage:	123 sq.ft.
Exterior Wall Framing:	2x4

Foundation options:
Standard basement.
Crawlspace.
Slab.
(Foundation & framing conversion diagram available — see order form.)

Blueprint Price Code: C

Plan C-8645

TO ORDER THIS BLUEPRINT, CALL TOLL-FREE 1-800-547-5570
(prices and details on pp. 12-15.)

Spacious and Stately

- Covered porches front and rear.
- Downstairs master suite with spectacular bath.
- Family/living/dining areas combine for entertaining large groups.
- Classic Creole/plantation exterior.

Plan E-3000

Bedrooms: 4	**Baths:** 3½
Space:	
Upper floor:	1,027 sq. ft.
Main floor:	2,008 sq. ft.
Total living area:	3,035 sq. ft.
Porches:	429 sq. ft.
Basement:	2,008 sq. ft.
Garage:	484 sq. ft.
Storage:	96 sq. ft.
Exterior Wall Framing:	2x6
Typical Ceiling Heights:	
Upper floor:	8′
Main floor:	9′

Foundation options:
Standard basement.
Crawlspace.
Slab.
(Foundation & framing conversion diagram available — see order form.)

Blueprint Price Code: E

**NOTE:
The above photographed home may have been modified by the homeowner. Please refer to floor plan and/or drawn elevation shown for actual blueprint details.

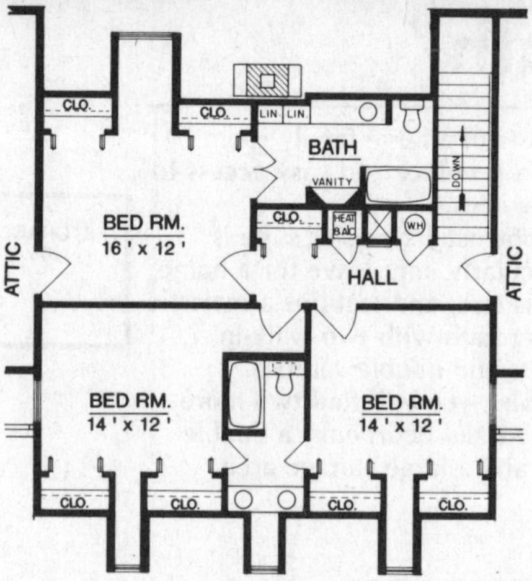

CLO. CLO. LIN LIN BATH VANITY DOWN BED RM. 16' x 12' ATTIC CLO. HEAT BAC WH HALL ATTIC BED RM. 14' x 12' BED RM. 14' x 12' CLO. CLO. CLO. CLO.

UPPER FLOOR

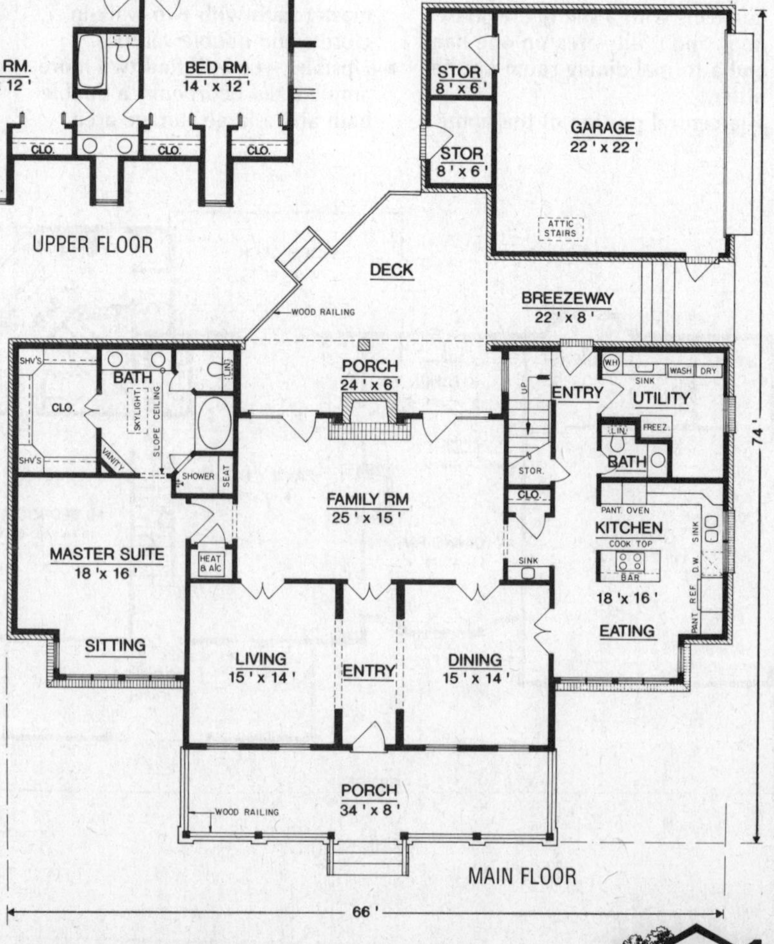

STOR 8' x 6' GARAGE 22' x 22' STOR 8' x 6' ATTIC STAIRS DECK BREEZEWAY 22' x 8' WOOD RAILING

SHV'S BATH LIN CLO. SKYLIGHT SLOPE CEILING VANITY SHV'S SHOWER SEAT PORCH 24' x 6' UP ENTRY UTILITY WH SINK WASH DRY LIN FREEZ. BATH STOR. CLO. FAMILY RM 25' x 15' PANT. OVEN KITCHEN COOK TOP BAR SINK D.W. REF. 18' x 16' MASTER SUITE 18' x 16' HEAT & A/C SINK PANT. EATING SITTING LIVING 15' x 14' ENTRY DINING 15' x 14' 74'

PORCH 34' x 8' WOOD RAILING

MAIN FLOOR

66'

TO ORDER THIS BLUEPRINT, CALL TOLL-FREE 1-800-547-5570
(prices and details on pp. 12-15.)

Plan E-3000

HomeStyles SOURCE 1 DESIGNERS' NETWORK

Great Room Featured

- In this rustic design, the centrally located Great Room features a cathedral ceiling with exposed wood beams. Living and dining areas are separated by a massive fireplace.
- The isolated master suite features a walk-in closet and compartmentalized bath.
- The gallery type kitchen is between the breakfast room and formal dining area. A large utility room and storage room complete the garage area.
- On the opposite side of the Great Room are two additional bedrooms and a second full bath.

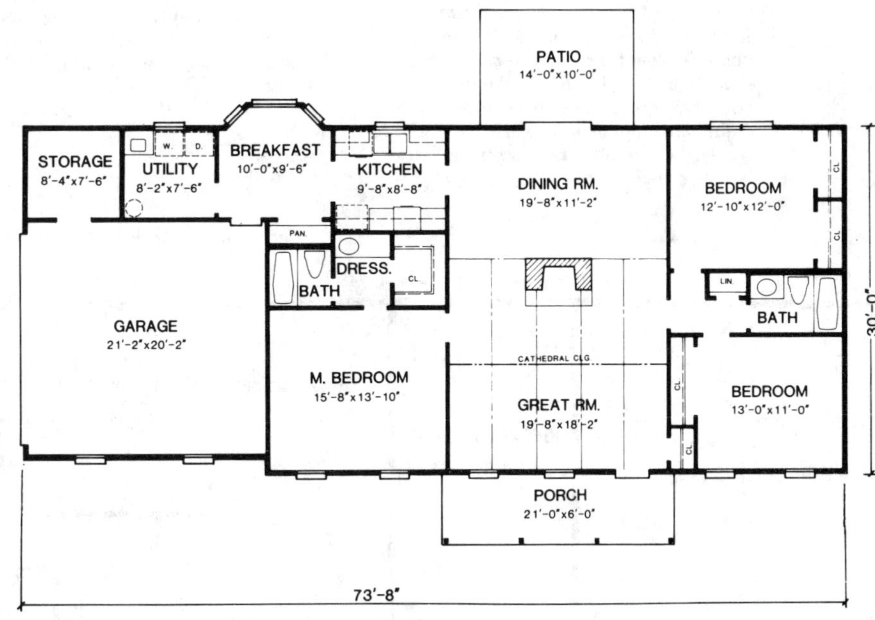

Plan C-8460

Bedrooms: 3	**Baths:** 2
Space:	
Total living area:	1,670 sq. ft.
Basement:	approx. 1,600 sq. ft.
Garage:	427 sq. ft.
Storage:	63 sq. ft.
Exterior Wall Framing:	2x4

Foundation options:
Standard basement.
Crawlspace.
Slab.
(Foundation & framing conversion diagram available — see order form)

Blueprint Price Code: B

Plan C-8460

TO ORDER THIS BLUEPRINT, CALL TOLL-FREE 1-800-547-5570
(prices and details on pp. 12-15.)

Rustic Home With Porches Means Relaxation

A spacious screened porch serves as a great place to eat out during warm summer days and nights, while the front porch is ideal for relaxed rocking or a swing. The Great Room to the left of the entry has a fireplace and connects to the dining area and country kitchen. The large master bedroom features a private bath and ample closets.

For entertaining large groups, the combined dining area, living room and screened porch provide lots of space. Also note the large kitchen/utility and pantry area.

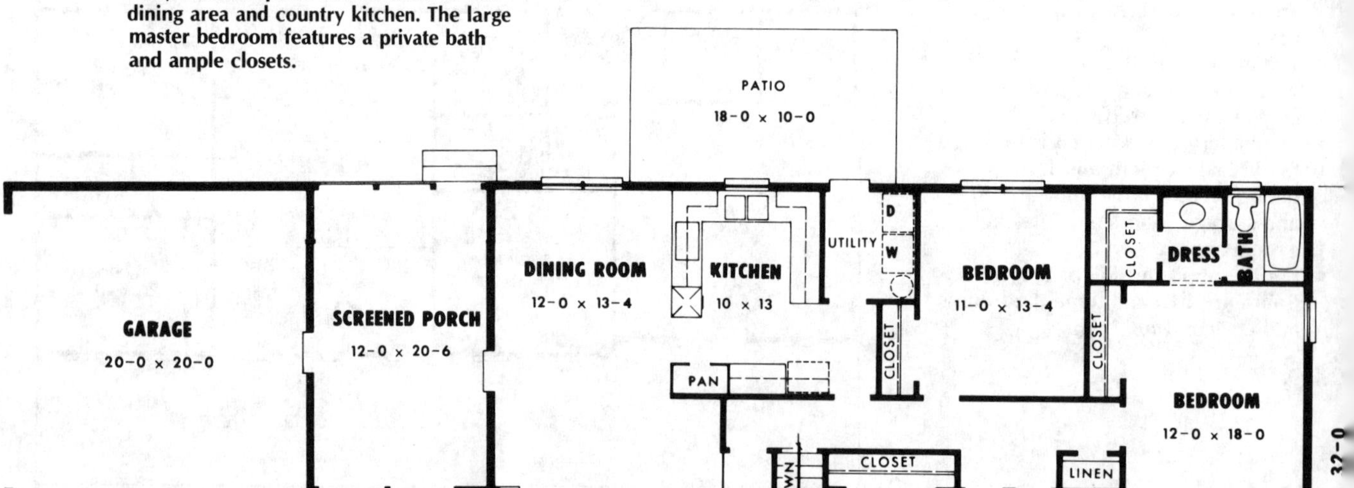

PATIO
18-0 x 10-0

GARAGE
20-0 x 20-0

SCREENED PORCH
12-0 x 20-6

DINING ROOM
12-0 x 13-4

KITCHEN
10 x 13

UTILITY

D

W

PAN

BEDROOM
11-0 x 13-4

CLOSET

CLOSET

DRESS

BATH

CLOSET

BEDROOM
12-0 x 18-0

LIVING ROOM
15-6 x 17-8

DOWN

COAT

CLOSET

BEDROOM
12-0 x 11-4

LINEN

DRESSING

BATH

FOYER

PORCH
26 x 6

32-0

88-8

Total living area: 1,688 sq. ft.
(Not counting basement or garage)

Specify slab, crawlspace or basement foundation.

TO ORDER THIS BLUEPRINT, CALL TOLL-FREE 1-800-547-5570
(prices and details on pp. 12-15.)

Blueprint Price Code B

Plan C-7557

Rustic Home for Relaxed Living

A screened-in breezeway provides a cool place to dine out on warm summer days and nights, and the rustic front porch is ideal for relaxed rocking or a swing. A Great Room to the left of the entry has a fireplace and connects the dining area to the country kitchen.

The large master suite contains separate shower, garden tub, vanities and walk-in closets.

Total living area: 1,773 sq. ft.
(Not counting basement or garage)
(Specify basement, crawlspace or slab foundation)

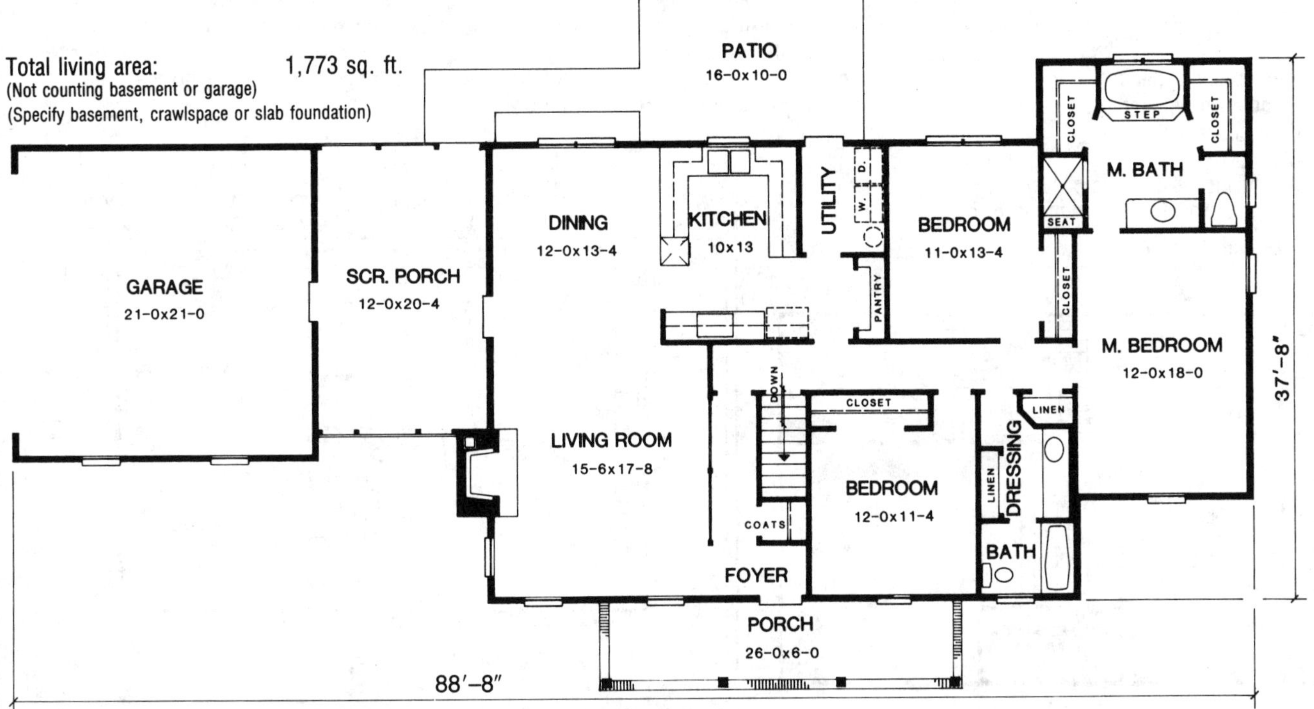

Blueprint Price Code B

Plan C-8650

TO ORDER THIS BLUEPRINT, CALL TOLL-FREE 1-800-547-5570
(prices and details on pp. 12-15.)

Plan J-8895	
Bedrooms: 3	**Baths:** 2½
Space:	
Upper floor:	860 sq. ft.
Main floor:	919 sq. ft.
Total living area:	1,779 sq. ft.
Basement:	919 sq. ft.
Optional carport:	462 sq. ft.
Porch:	466 sq. ft.
Exterior Wall Framing:	2x4
Foundation options:	
Standard basement.	
Crawlspace.	
Slab.	
(Foundation & framing conversion diagram available — see order form.)	
Blueprint Price Code:	B

Expansive Porch Offers Warm Welcome

- This gracious design conjures up images of family and friends sipping iced tea on the veranda during warm summer evenings.
- Inside, a relatively compact floor plan still offers abundant space for family life and entertaining.
- The spacious living room includes a fireplace and built in cabinetry.
- The open kitchen/dining room design provides space for food preparation, eating and cleanup without the confined feeling found in many kitchens.
- The second floor consists of three good-sized bedrooms, two mirror-image baths and a hobby area.

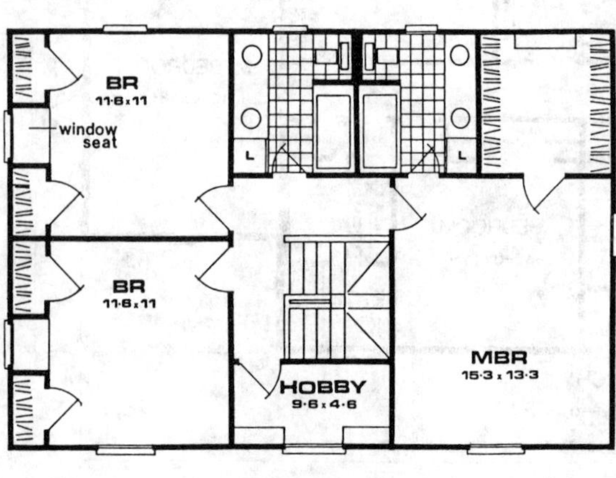

UPPER FLOOR

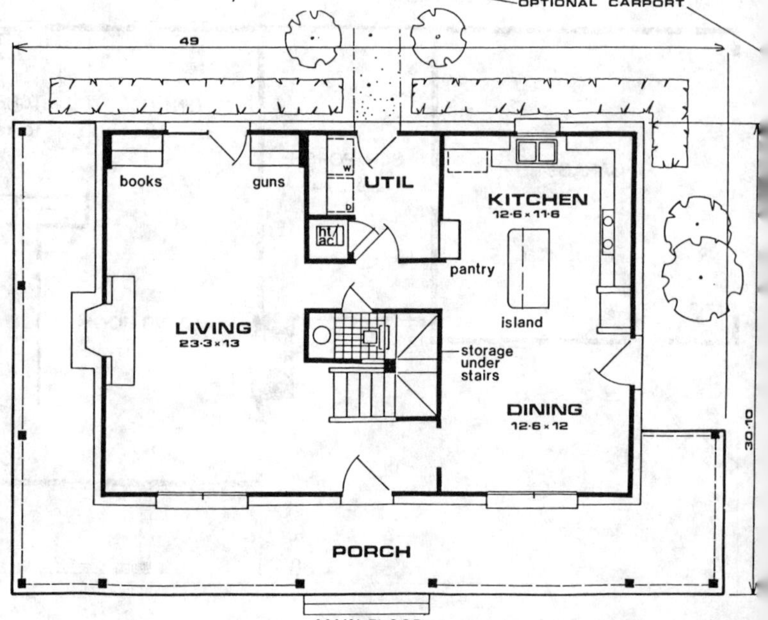

MAIN FLOOR

TO ORDER THIS BLUEPRINT, CALL TOLL-FREE 1-800-547-5570
(prices and details on pp. 12-15.)

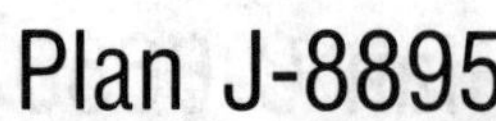
Plan J-8895

HomeStyles SOURCE 1 Designers' Network

Cozy Country Cottage

- This two-story cozy country cottage is perfect for the growing family with the availability of an unfinished basement and bonus room above the garage.
- The two-story entrance foyer has a palladian window in the clerestory dormer above to let the natural light flood in.
- The Great Room has a fireplace and columned division from the formal dining room.
- The master suite is on the first level for privacy and accessibility. The master bath boasts a whirlpool tub with skylight above, shower and double bowl vanity. The second level consists of two bedrooms, a full bath and plenty of storage.
- A spacious bonus room can be finished off above the garage for a host of activities.

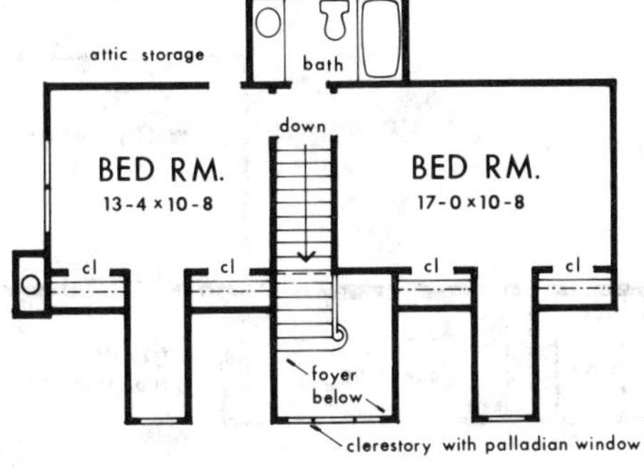

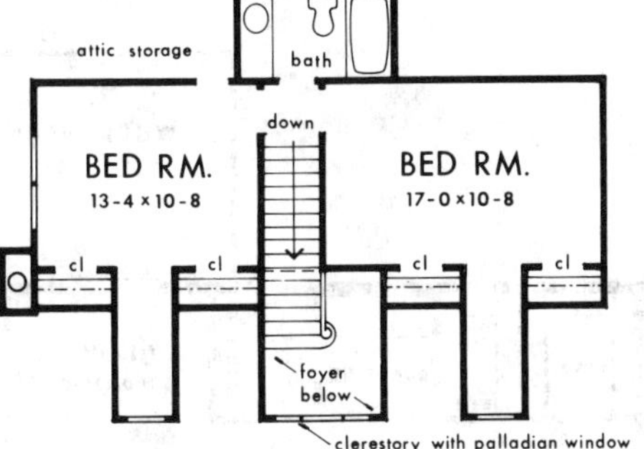

UPPER FLOOR

Plan DG-224

Bedrooms: 3	**Baths:** 2½
Space:	
Upper floor:	542 sq. ft.
Main floor:	1,289 sq. ft.
Total living area:	1,831 sq. ft.
Basement:	1,289 sq. ft.
Garage:	441 sq. ft.
Storage area: approx.	50 sq. ft.
Exterior Wall Framing:	2x4
Ceiling Height:	
Main floor:	9′

Foundation options:
Standard basement.
Crawlspace.
(Foundation & framing conversion diagram available — see order form.)

Blueprint Price Code: B

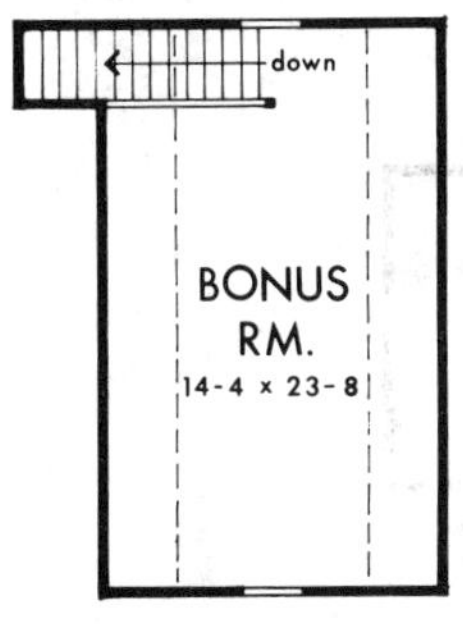

UPPER FLOOR (ABOVE GARAGE)

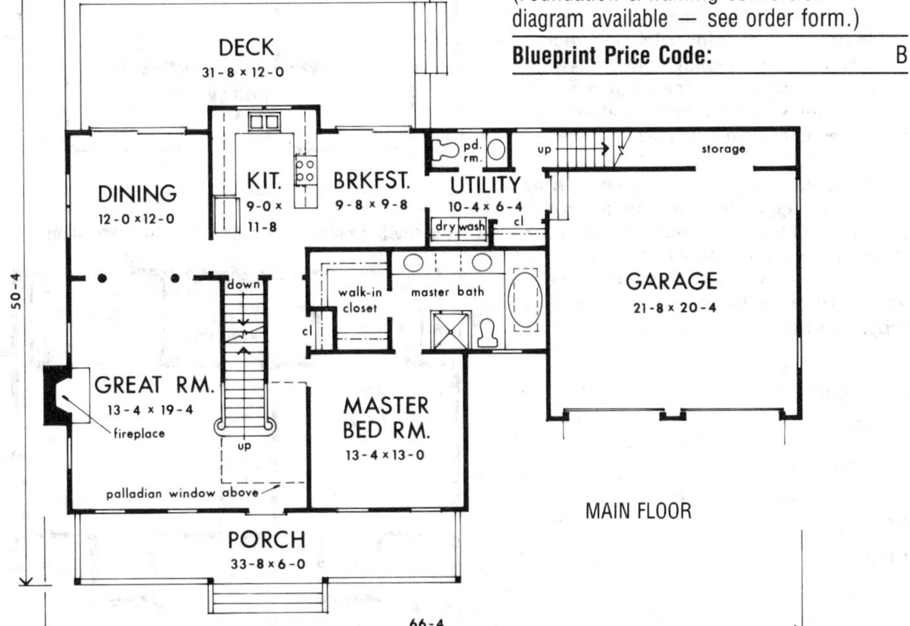

MAIN FLOOR

Plan DG-224

TO ORDER THIS BLUEPRINT, CALL TOLL-FREE 1-800-547-5570
(prices and details on pp. 12-15.)

Country Kitchen and Great Room

Cozy front porch, dormers, shutters and multi-paned windows on the exterior of this Cape Code design are complemented by an informal interior. The 1,318 sq. ft. of heated living area on the main floor is divided into three sections. In the first section is an eat-in country kitchen with island counter and bay window and a large utility room which can be entered from either the kitchen or garage. The second section is the Great Room with inside fireplace, an informal dining nook and double doors opening onto the rear deck. The third section consists of a master suite, which features a walk-in closet and compartmentalized bath with linen closet.

An additional 718 sq. ft. of heated living area on the upper floor includes a second full bath and two bedrooms with ample closet space and window seats. A large storage area is provided over the garage. All or part of the basement can be used to supplement the main living area.

First floor:	1,318 sq. ft.
Second floor:	718 sq. ft.
Total living area: (Not counting basement or garage)	2,036 sq. ft.
Basement:	1,221 sq. ft.
Garage:	436 sq. ft.

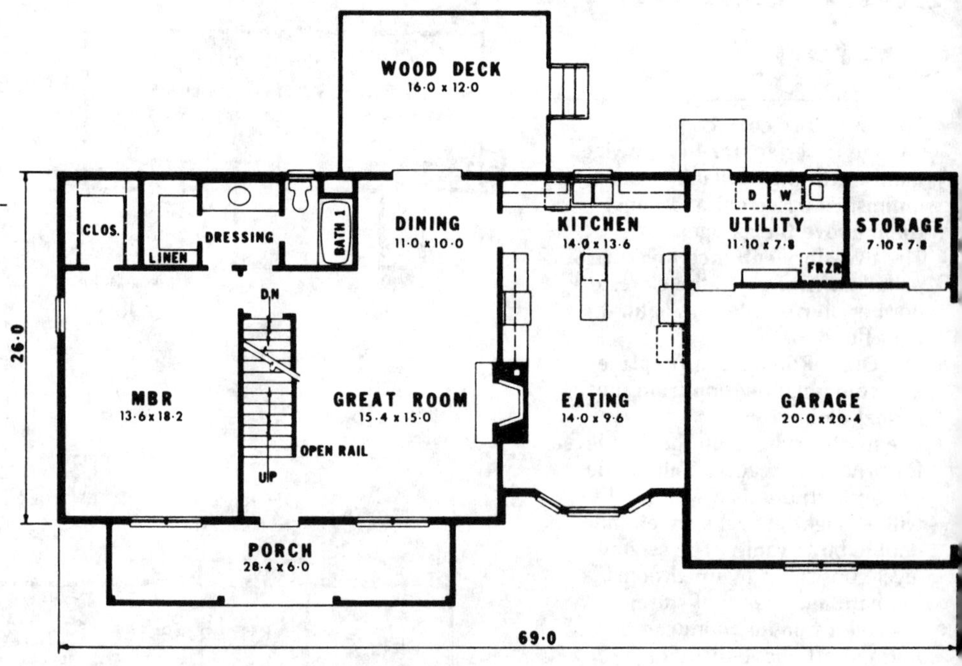

Specify basement, crawlspace or slab foundation when ordering.

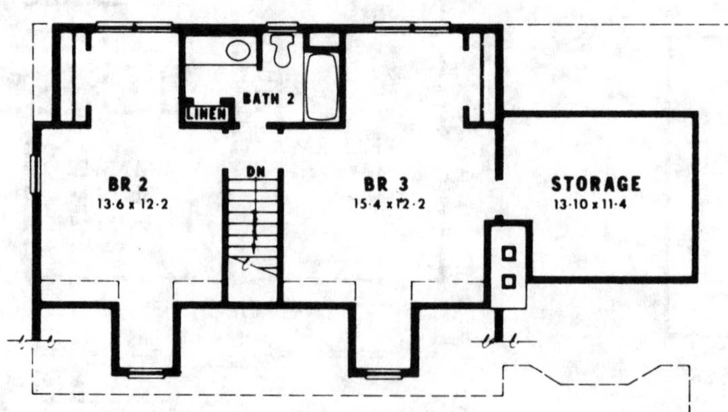

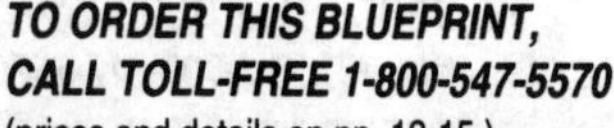

TO ORDER THIS BLUEPRINT, CALL TOLL-FREE 1-800-547-5570
(prices and details on pp. 12-15.)

Blueprint Price Code C

Plan C-8040

Style and Charm on all Four Sides

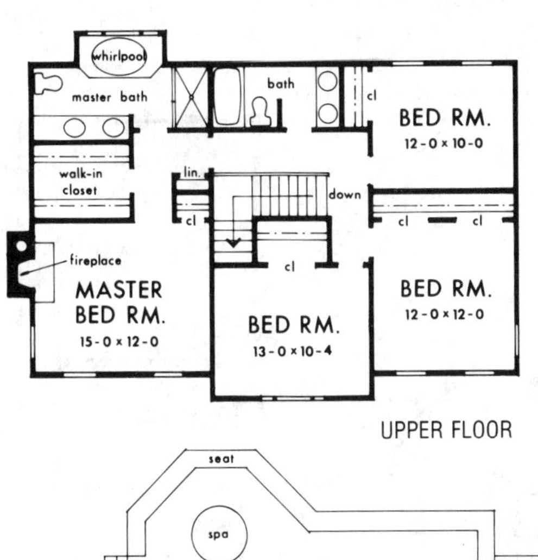

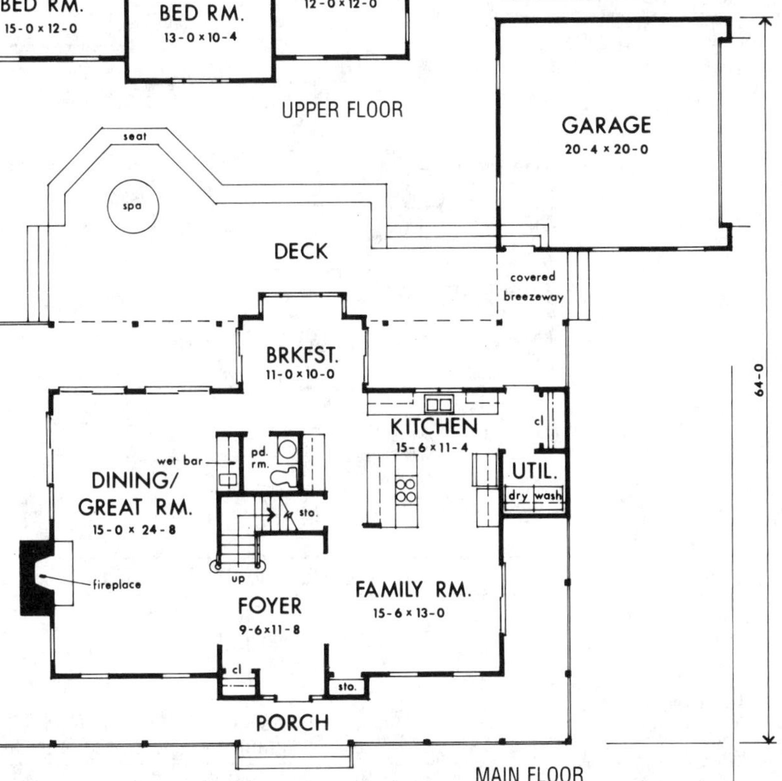

- This stylish country farm house displays its exterior beauty both front and rear.
- A wrap-around porch allows sheltered access to all first-level areas along with a covered breezeway to the garage.
- The first level boasts a spacious open plan layout with all the latest features.
- The Great Room has a fireplace and plenty of glass.
- The kitchen overlooks the family room and rear yard.
- The Master bedroom on second level has fireplace, large walk-in closet, and master bath with shower, whirlpool tub and double bowl vanity. The other three bedrooms share a full bath with double bowl vanity.
- An expansive deck allows space for a spa tub.

Plan DG-199

Bedrooms: 4	**Baths:** 2½
Space:	
Upper floor:	1,060 sq. ft.
Main floor:	1,254 sq. ft.
Total living area:	2,314 sq. ft.
Garage:	407 sq. ft.
Exterior Wall Framing:	2x4
Foundation options:	
Crawlspace.	
(Foundation & framing conversion diagram available — see order form.)	
Blueprint Price Code:	C

Plan DG-199

(prices and details on pp. 12-15.)

You Asked For It!

- Our most popular plan in recent years, E-3000, has now been downsized for affordability, without sacrificing character or excitement.
- Exterior appeal is created with a covered front porch with decorative columns, triple dormers and rail-topped bay windows.
- The floor plan has combined the separate living and family rooms available in E-3000 into one spacious family room with corner fireplace, which flows into the dining room through a columned gallery.
- The kitchen serves the breakfast eating room over an angled snack bar, and features a huge walk-in pantry.
- The stunning main-floor master suite offers a private sitting area, a walk-in closet and a dramatic, angled master bath.
- There are two large bedrooms upstairs accessible via a curved staircase with bridge balcony.

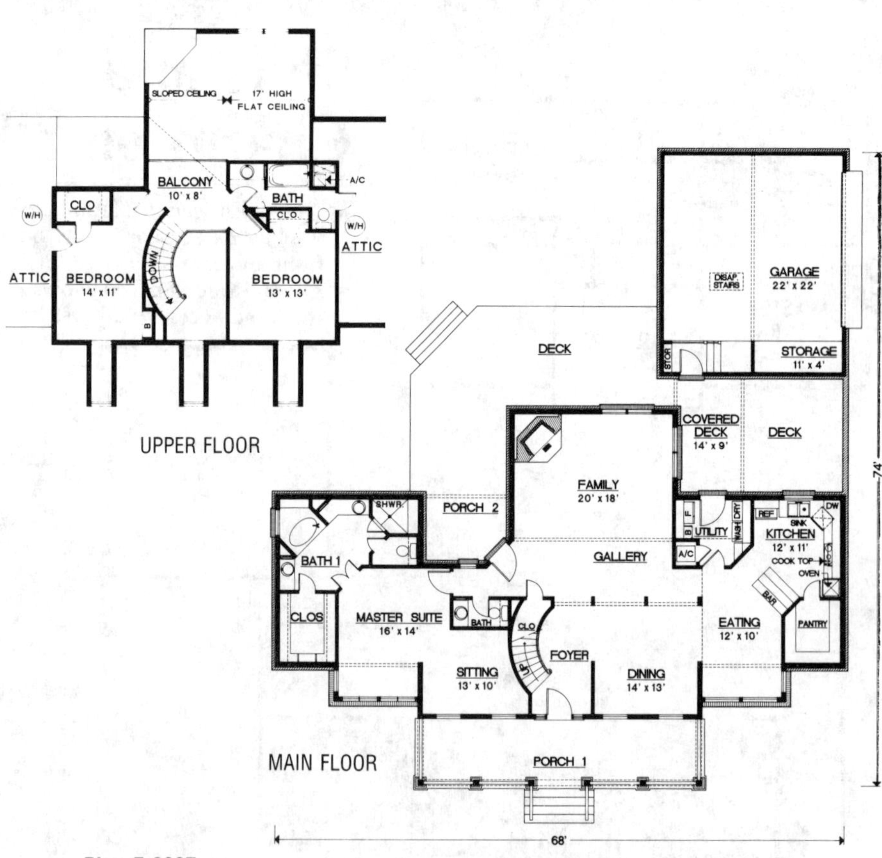

Plan E-2307

Bedrooms: 3	**Baths:** 2½
Space:	
Upper floor:	595 sq. ft.
Main floor:	1,765 sq. ft.
Total living area:	2,360 sq. ft.
Basement:	1,765 sq. ft.
Garage:	484 sq. ft.
Storage area:	44 sq. ft.

Exterior Wall Framing: 2x6

Foundation options:
Standard basement.
Crawlspace.
Slab.
(Foundation & framing conversion diagram available — see order form.)

Blueprint Price Code: C

TO ORDER THIS BLUEPRINT, CALL TOLL-FREE 1-800-547-5570
(prices and details on pp. 12-15.)

Plan E-2307

Traditional Touches Dress Up a Country Cottage

Multipaned windows, shutters and a covered porch embellish the traditional exterior of this country cottage. The floor plan incorporates a central Great Room. A raised-hearth stone fireplace forms part of a wall separating the Great Room from the kitchen.

The large country kitchen features an island and abundant counter space. The breakfast room includes a bay window. A large dining room faces the front.

First-level master bedroom has its own super bath with separate shower, garden tub, twin vanities and walk in closets. Two large bedrooms, separate dressing areas and compartment tub occupy the second level.

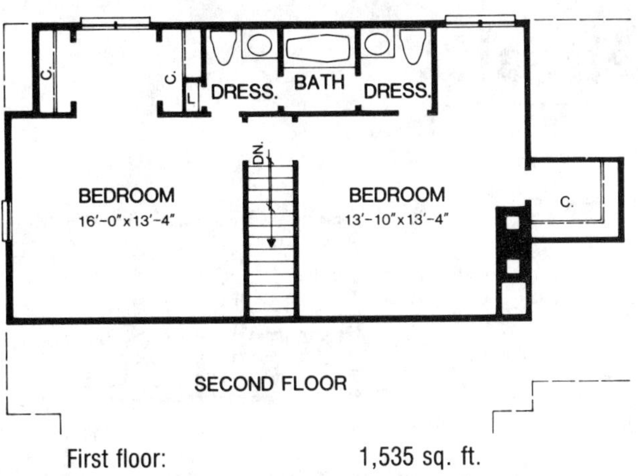

First floor:	1,535 sq. ft.
Second floor:	765 sq. ft.
Total living area: (Not counting basement or garage)	2,300 sq. ft.

PLAN C-8535
WITH BASEMENT

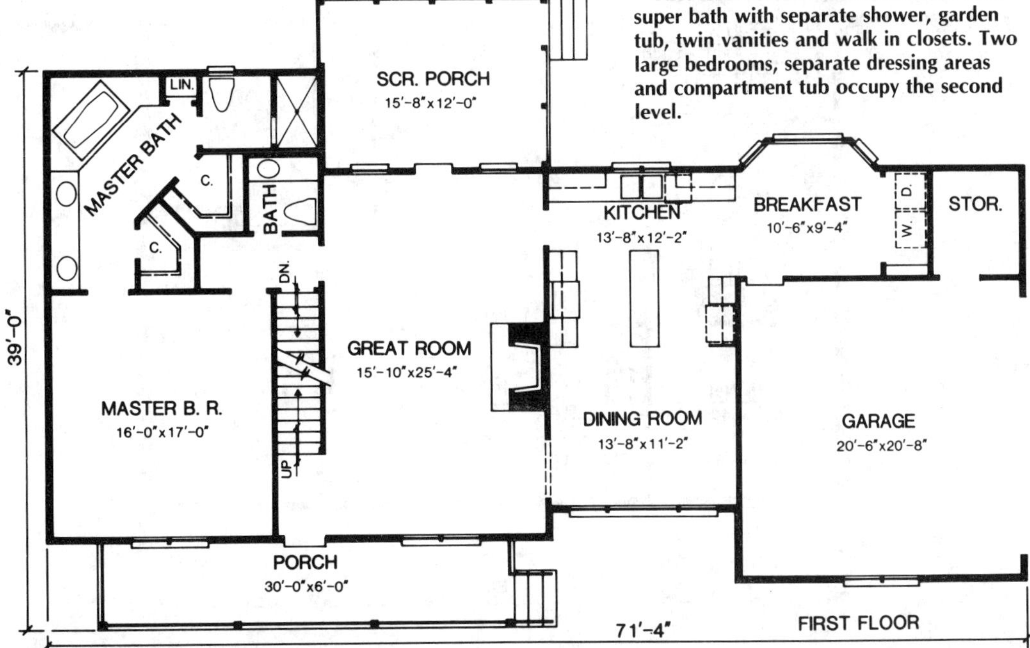

Blueprint Price Code C

Plan C-8535

TO ORDER THIS BLUEPRINT, CALL TOLL-FREE 1-800-547-5570
(prices and details on pp. 12-15.)

Master Wing is "Adult Retreat"

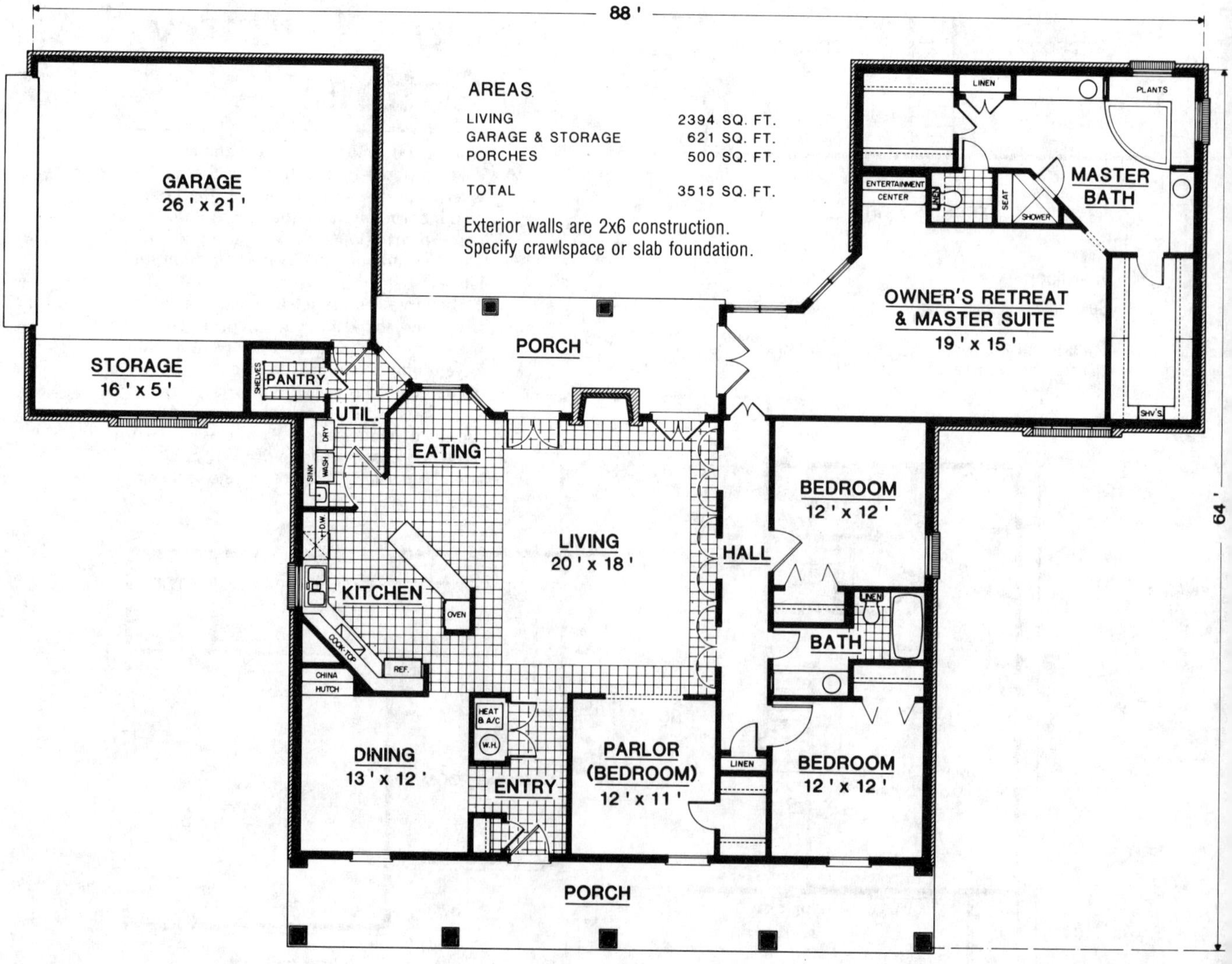

88'

AREAS

LIVING	2394 SQ. FT.
GARAGE & STORAGE	621 SQ. FT.
PORCHES	500 SQ. FT.
TOTAL	3515 SQ. FT.

Exterior walls are 2x6 construction.
Specify crawlspace or slab foundation.

GARAGE 26' x 21'

STORAGE 16' x 5'

SHELVES
PANTRY
UTIL.
DRY
WASH
SINK
PORCH
EATING
LIVING 20' x 18'
KITCHEN
D.W.
OVEN
COOK-TOP
REF.
CHINA HUTCH
DINING 13' x 12'
HEAT & A/C
W.H.
ENTRY
PARLOR (BEDROOM) 12' x 11'
LINEN
HALL
BEDROOM 12' x 12'
LINEN
BATH
BEDROOM 12' x 12'
PORCH
LINEN
PLANTS
ENTERTAINMENT CENTER
SEAT
SHOWER
MASTER BATH
OWNER'S RETREAT & MASTER SUITE 19' x 15'
SHV'S

64'

TO ORDER THIS BLUEPRINT, CALL TOLL-FREE 1-800-547-5570
(prices and details on pp. 12-15.)

Blueprint Price Code C

Plan E-2306

Plantation Charm

- Yesterday's plantation home has today's luxuries.
- A stand-alone fireplace separates the living room from the formal dining room and bayed breakfast nook, but still ensures easy traffic flow throughout.
- The well-equipped kitchen overlooks the nook and rear porch beyond, and has handy garage access through the utility room.
- The master suite offers a variety of pleasures, including a private bayed retreat with veranda access and a large bath with whirlpool tub and dressing seat.
- Three more nice-sized bedrooms are found upstairs.

Plan VL-2817	
Bedrooms: 4	**Baths:** 2 ½
Space:	
Upper floor	859 sq. ft.
Main floor	1,958 sq. ft.
Total Living Area	**2,817 sq. ft.**
Garage	488 sq. ft.
Exterior Wall Framing	2x4
Foundation options:	
Crawlspace	
Slab	
(Foundation & framing conversion diagram available—see order form.)	
Blueprint Price Code	D

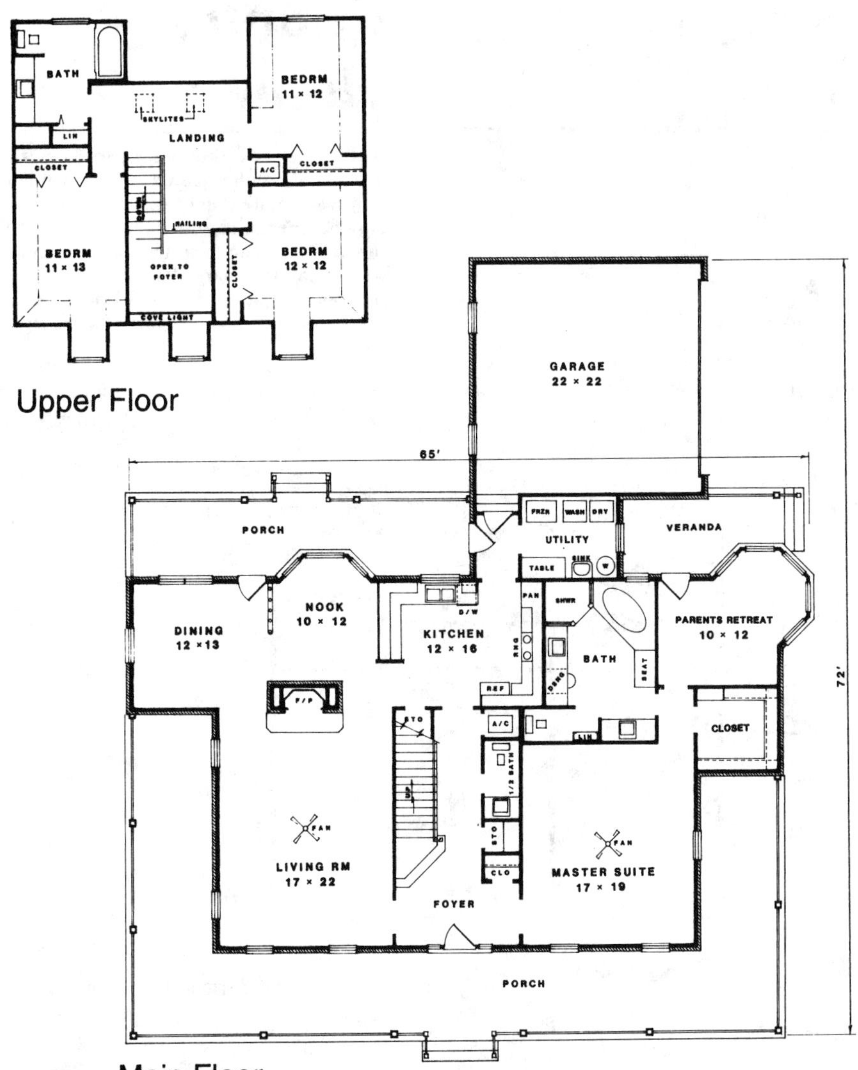

Upper Floor

Main Floor

Plan VL- 2817

TO ORDER THIS BLUEPRINT, CALL TOLL-FREE 1-800-547-5570
(prices and details on pp. 12-15.)

Bay Windows Enhance a Country Home

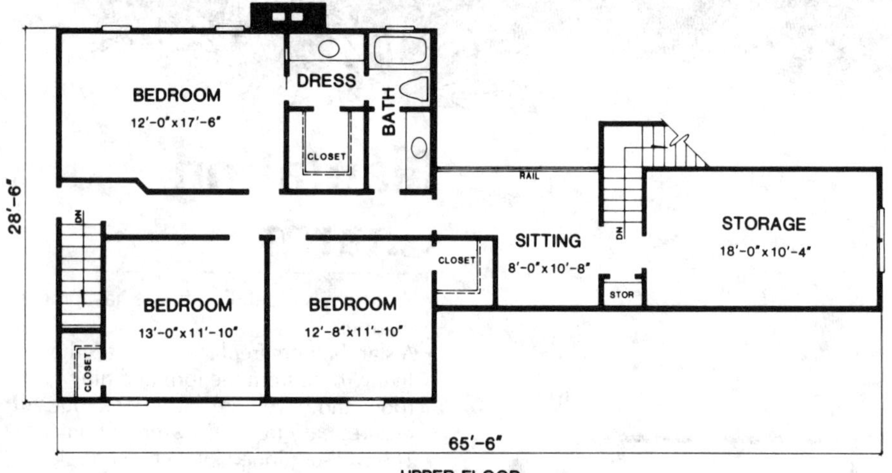

A large master bedroom suite includes a deluxe bath with separate shower, garden tub, twin vanities and two large walk-in closets. Kitchen has direct access to both the breakfast nook and the dining room, which features a large bay window. Three bedrooms, a sitting area and storage or bonus room combine to form the second level.

First floor:	2,005 sq. ft.
Second floor:	1,063 sq. ft.
Total living area: (Not counting basement or garage)	3,068 sq. ft.

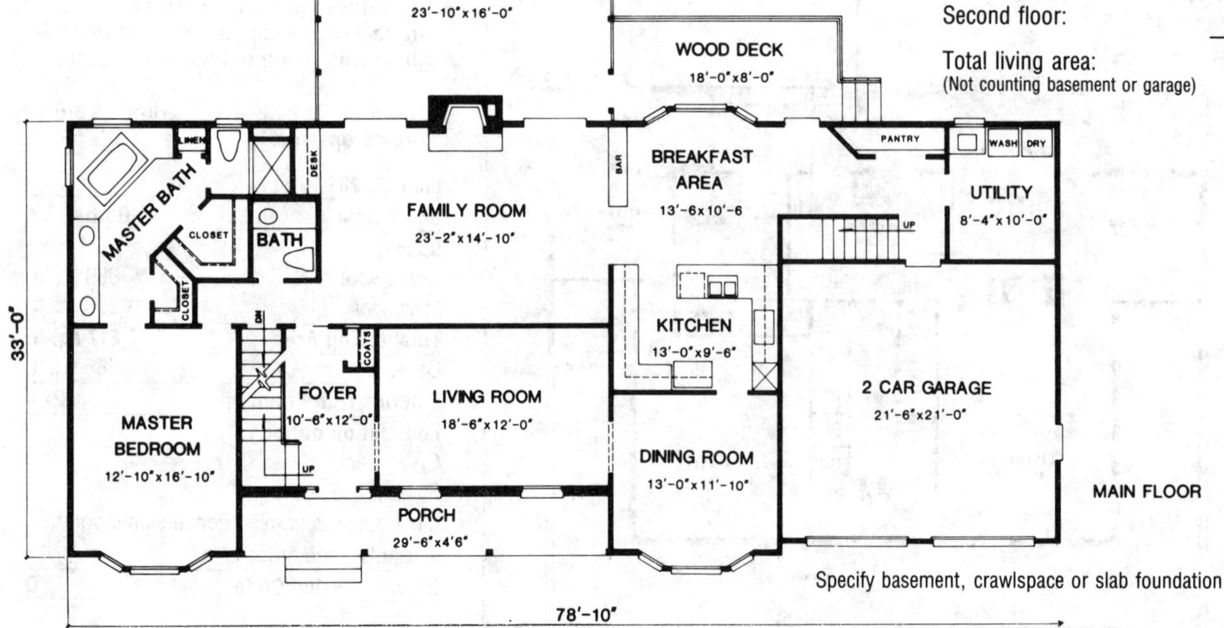

Specify basement, crawlspace or slab foundation.

TO ORDER THIS BLUEPRINT, CALL TOLL-FREE 1-800-547-5570 (prices and details on pp. 12-15.)

Blueprint Price Code E

Plan C-8409

Inviting Veranda Adds Look of Warm Welcome

- An exciting interior bridge overlooks the huge family room that stretches from the front of the home to the rear.
- Stairways in both the family room and foyer access the upper level.
- An open kitchen, breakfast room, and dining room stretch across the rear of the home.
- A luxurious master suite and bonus room highlight the upper level.

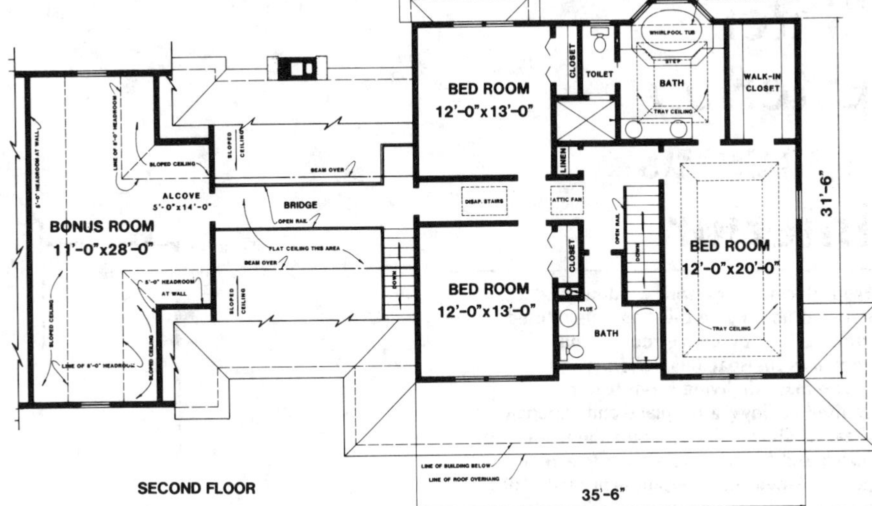

Plan W-3219

Bedrooms: 4-5	**Baths:** 3
Space:	
Upper floor:	1,120 sq. ft.
Main floor:	1,689 sq. ft.
Bonus room:	429 sq. ft.
Total living area:	3,238 sq. ft.
Basement:	1,130 sq. ft.
Garage and storage:	540 sq. ft.
Exterior Wall Framing:	2x4
Foundation options:	
Standard basement.	
(Foundation & framing conversion diagram available — see order form.)	
Blueprint Price Code:	E

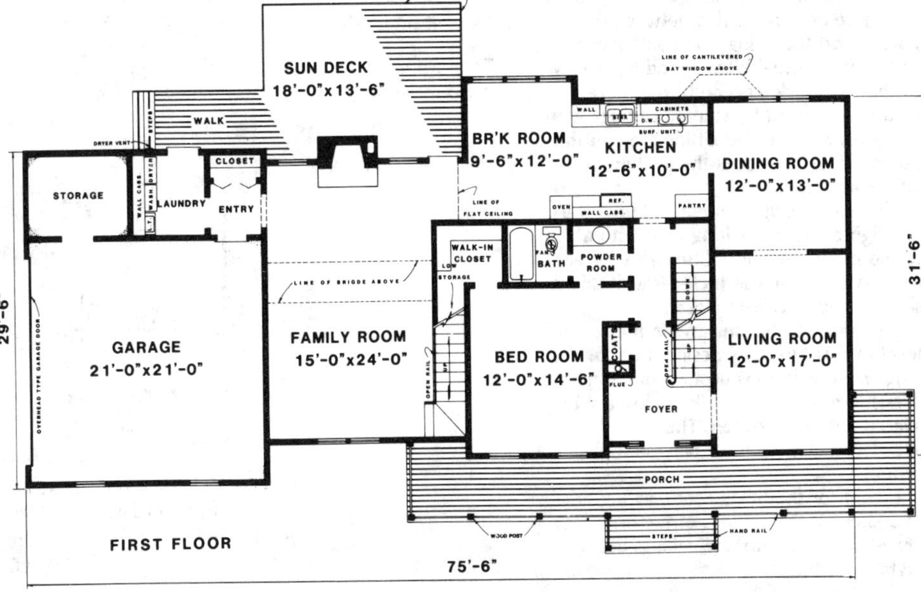

Plan W-3219

TO ORDER THIS BLUEPRINT, CALL TOLL-FREE 1-800-547-5570
(prices and details on pp. 12-15.)

Stately Exterior, Spacious Interior

Front dormers, transom windows and a covered porch give this home its refined look. Inside, a creative room layout enhances the spacious design.

The majestic living room features vaulted ceilings, a fireplace and expansive areas of glass. Windows face the front porch and French doors open to a rear porch. A built-in entertainment center fills a third wall, and divides the living room from the front entry and the eating nook.

A large deck is nestled between the porches off the living room and master suite. The unusual kitchen and nook view to the rear deck, and both rooms are further expanded by vaulted ceilings with skylights. A balconied sitting area on the second floor overlooks the kitchen, nook and living room.

The master suite is large and luxurious, highlighted by an inviting bath with a raised marble whirlpool tub. This his-and-hers bath design also includes a sit-down shower and a walk-in closet.

Two more bedrooms are on the second level of this 1½-story design. Each of the king-sized bedrooms upstairs has a private dressing room and a walk-in closet, with a shared bath in between. The sitting area/loft makes an ideal playroom or game room.

Except for the living room, eating area and kitchen, the ceilings of the first floor are 9′. The second-floor ceilings are 8′ high.

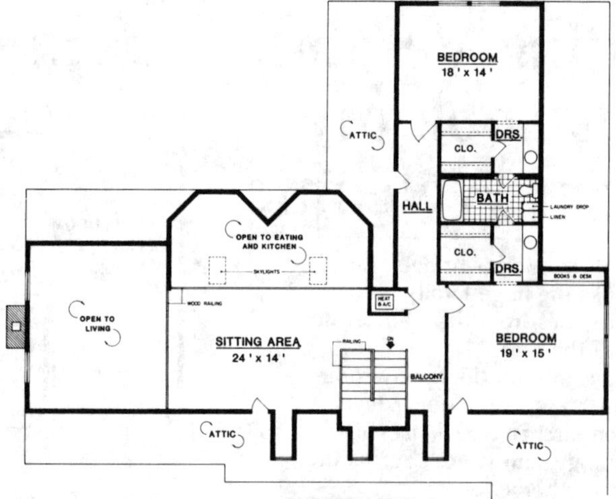

UPPER LEVEL

First floor:	2,045 sq. ft.
Second floor:	1,456 sq. ft.
Total living area: (Not counting garage)	3,501 sq. ft.

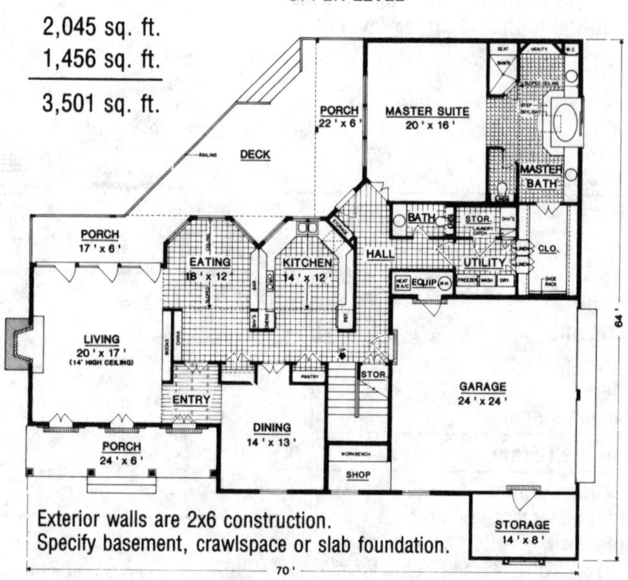

LOWER LEVEL

TO ORDER THIS BLUEPRINT, CALL TOLL-FREE 1-800-547-5570
(prices and details on pp. 12-15.)

Blueprint Price Code F

Plan E-3500

HomeStyles SOURCE 1 DESIGNERS' NETWORK

Floating Sunspace

Designed to take advantage of narrow and sometimes "left-over" lots, whether urban or rural, this compact dwelling is intended to attract the economy-minded small family. Though it boasts a private, traffic-directing entry hall, all other rooms, especially baths and kitchen, are scaled down to suit the more modest pocketbook. An exception is the beautiful passive sun room (every home should have at least one unique feature). Besides the practical advantage of collecting and storing the free heat of the sun, the room will act as a solarium, for relaxation, or a greenhouse for botanical buffs. In any case it will allow full enjoyment of nature's gifts in an otherwise limited location.

First floor:	1,075 sq. ft.
Sun room:	100 sq. ft.
Total living area: (Not counting basement or garage)	1,175 sq. ft.

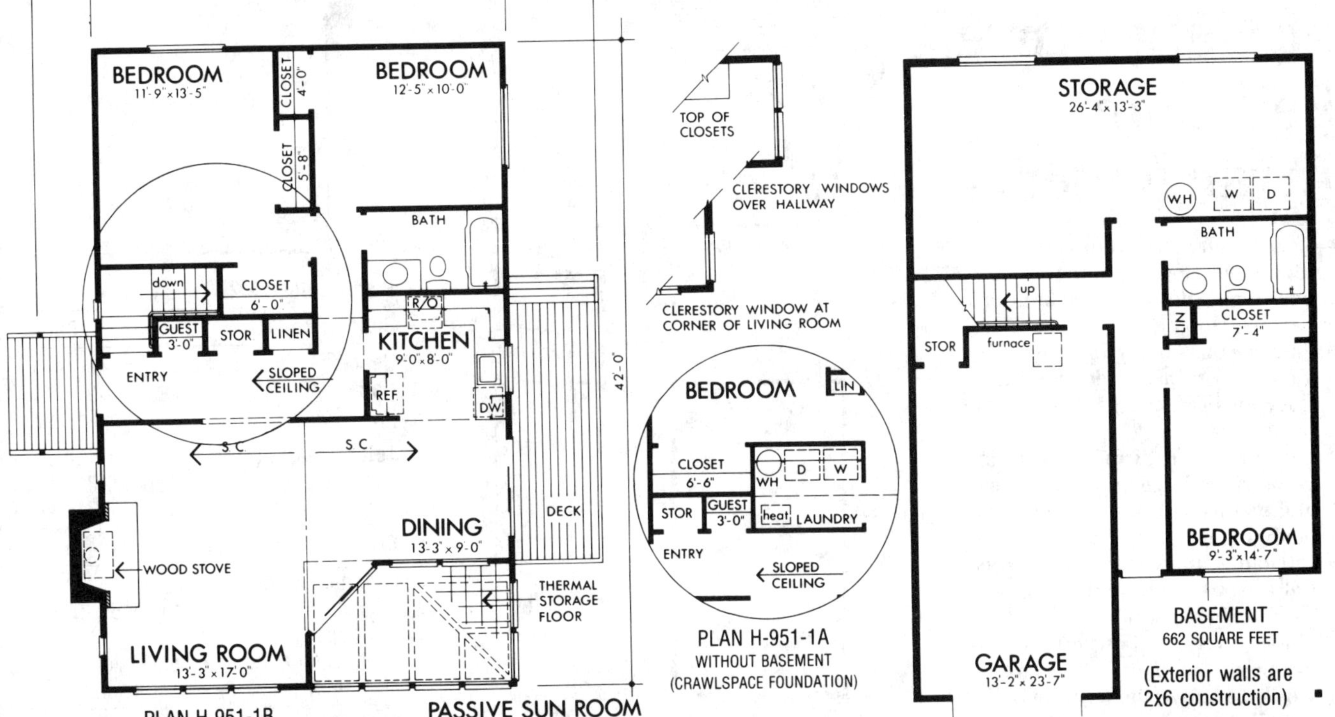

Blueprint Price Code A

Plans H-951-1A & H-951-1B

TO ORDER THIS BLUEPRINT, CALL TOLL-FREE 1-800-547-5570
(prices and details on pp. 12-15.)

Plans H-946-1A/1B

Bedrooms: 2	**Baths:** 2
Space:	
Upper floor:	381 sq. ft.
Main floor:	814 sq. ft.
Total living area:	1,195 sq. ft.
Basement	approx. 814 sq. ft.
Garage:	315 sq. ft.
Exterior Wall Framing:	2x6

Foundation options:
Daylight basement (Plan H-946-1B).
Crawlspace (Plan H-946-1A).
Foundation & framing conversion diagram available — see order form.)

Blueprint Price Code: A

Narrow Lot Solar Design Offers Choice of Upper-Level Bedroom Arrangements

- This design offers your choice of foundation and number of bedrooms, plus it can be built on a narrow, sloping lot.
- Passive solar dining room has windows on three sides and slate floor for heat storage; French door leads to rear deck.
- Living room features sloped ceiling, wood stove in ceiling-high masonry, and its own entrance to the adjoining deck.
- Kitchen is open to the dining room but separated from the living room by a 7½′ high wall.
- Upper level variations offer choice of one or two bedrooms. Clerestory windows above the balcony railing exist in both.

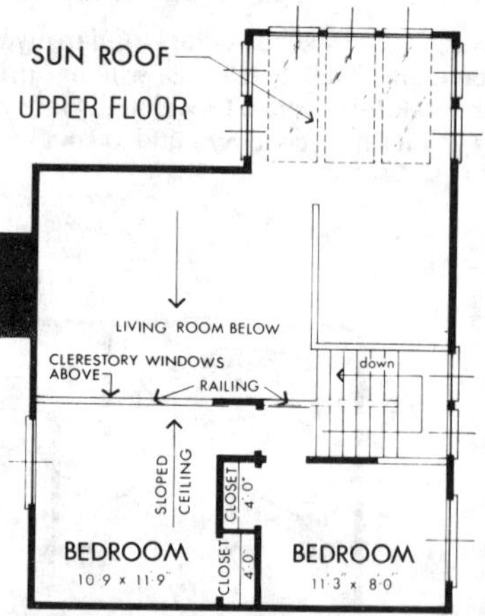

Plans H-946-2A/2B

Bedrooms: 3	**Baths:** 2
Space:	
Upper floor:	290 sq. ft.
Main floor:	814 sq. ft.
Total living area:	1,104 sq. ft.
Basement	approx. 814 sq. ft.
Garage:	315 sq. ft.
Exterior Wall Framing:	2x6

Foundation options:
Daylight basement (Plan H-946-2B).
Crawlspace (Plan H-946-2A).
Foundation & framing conversion diagram available — see order form.)

Blueprint Price Code: A

TO ORDER THIS BLUEPRINT, CALL TOLL-FREE 1-800-547-5570
(prices and details on pp. 12-15.)

Plans H-946-1A/1B & -2A/2B

More for Less

Big in function but small in footage, this two-story passive solar design puts every inch of space to valuable and efficient use. The house can be constructed either as a free-standing unit or as part of a condo development.

The plan flows visually from its entry, through its high-ceilinged great room, to a brilliant south-facing sun room where solar heat is collected and stored in the ceramic-tiled floor.

Thick insulation in exterior walls and ceilings minimizes heat loss during the cold season. In summer, air flow is created by convection while eave overhangs protect against over-exposure.

The first floor, excluding sun room, provides 915 sq. ft. of living area, while the second floor adds 397 sq. ft., for a total of 1,312 sq. ft. Garage is 427 sq. ft.; optional basement is 915 sq. ft.

First floor:	915 sq. ft.
Second floor:	397 sq. ft.
Total living area:	1,312 sq. ft.
Garage:	427 sq. ft.
Basement (Optional):	915 sq. ft.

(Slab-on-grade option included.)

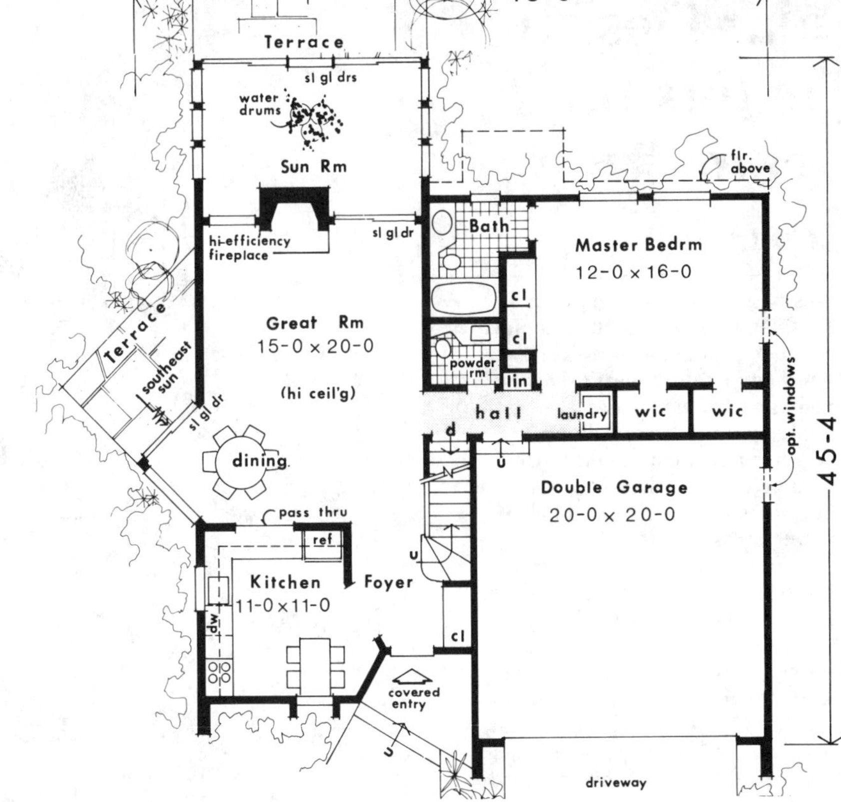

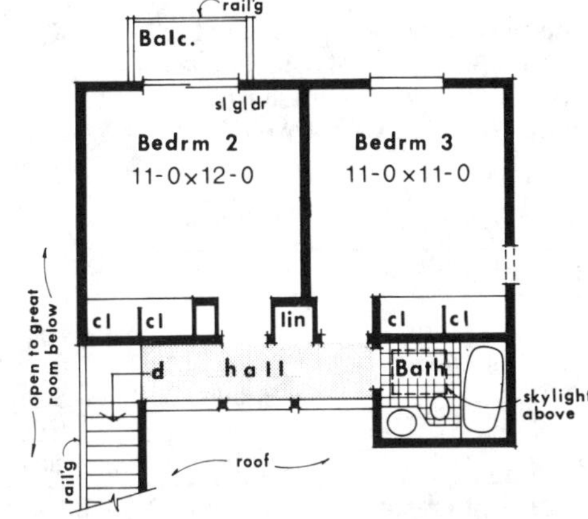

Solar Design Centers on Geometric Core

- This passive solar design, with a six-sided core, is angled to capture as much sunlight as possible.
- Finished in natural vertical cedar planks and stone veneer, this contemporary three-bedroom requires minimum maintenance.
- Double doors at the entry open into the spacious six-sided living-dining areas.
- The formal area, with its domed ceiling and free-standing fireplace, is enhanced by the two skylights overhead and the three sets of sliding glass doors, one of which leads to a glass-enclosed sunroom.
- The bright U-shaped kitchen is an extension of the den; sliding glass doors lead to one of the backyard terraces.
- The master bedoom, in a quiet sleeping wing, boasts ample closets, private terrace and a luxurious bath, complete with a whirlpool tub.

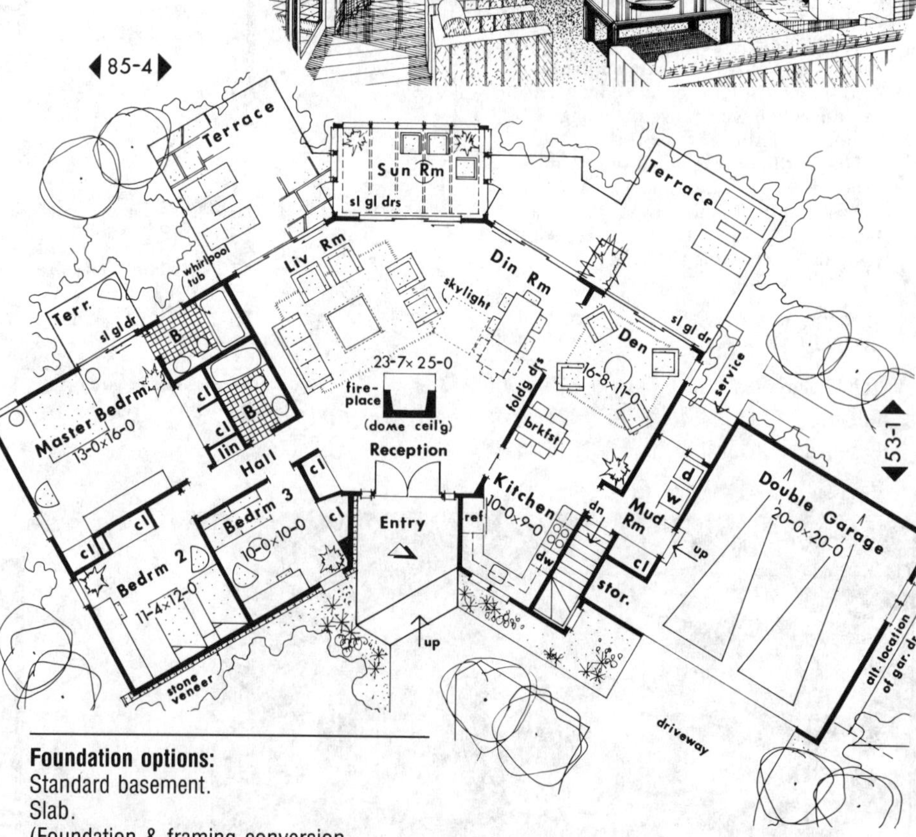

Plan K-534-L

Bedrooms: 3	**Baths:** 2
Space:	
Total living area:	1,495 sq. ft.
Basement:	1,505 sq. ft.
Garage:	400 sq. ft.
Mud room, etc.:	152 sq. ft.
Exterior Wall Framing:	2x4 or 2x6

Foundation options:
Standard basement.
Slab.
(Foundation & framing conversion diagram available — see order form)

Blueprint Price Code:	A

TO ORDER THIS BLUEPRINT, CALL TOLL-FREE 1-800-547-5570
(prices and details on pp. 12-15.)

Plan K-534-L

Low-Cost Comfort

Conceived to weather energy-tight times, this single-story passive solar home provides year-round comfort at much lower fuel costs. Inside, the open airy plan is a delight. In winter, the sun's warming rays penetrate deeply into the living spaces; warmth settles in the thermal stone wall and floors. After sundown, the floors and walls steadily radiate all the warmth saved during the day. Eave overhangs shade the interior during the summer; operable clerestory windows create a cooling air draft by convection.

The compact plan is suitable for many sites and conditions. With minor modifications, the design is also adaptable to a zero lot line or attached condominium developments. Living area is 1,495 sq. ft.; optional basement is 634 sq. ft.; garage, etc. is 504 sq. ft.

Living Area: 1,495 sq. ft.
Garage and Mud Room: 504 sq. ft.
Basement (Optional): 634 sq. ft.

(Alternate slab-on-grade foundation plan included.)

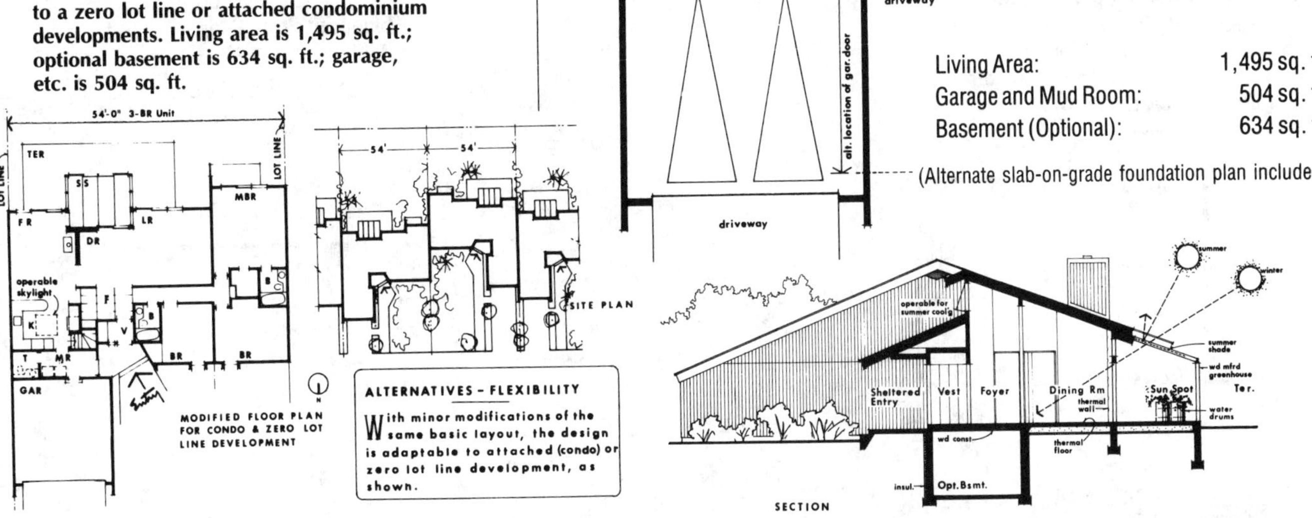

ALTERNATIVES – FLEXIBILITY

With minor modifications of the same basic layout, the design is adaptable to attached (condo) or zero lot line development, as shown.

Blueprint Price Code A

Plan K-392-T

TO ORDER THIS BLUEPRINT, CALL TOLL-FREE 1-800-547-5570

(prices and details on pp. 12-15.)

Unique, Dramatic Floor Plan

- An expansive and impressive Great Room, warmed by a wood stove, features an island kitchen that's completely open in design.
- A passive solar sun room is designed to collect and store heat from the sun, while also providing a good view of the surroundings.
- Upstairs, you'll see a glamorous master suite with a private bath and huge walk-in closet.
- The daylight basement adds a sunny sitting room, third bedroom and large recreation room.

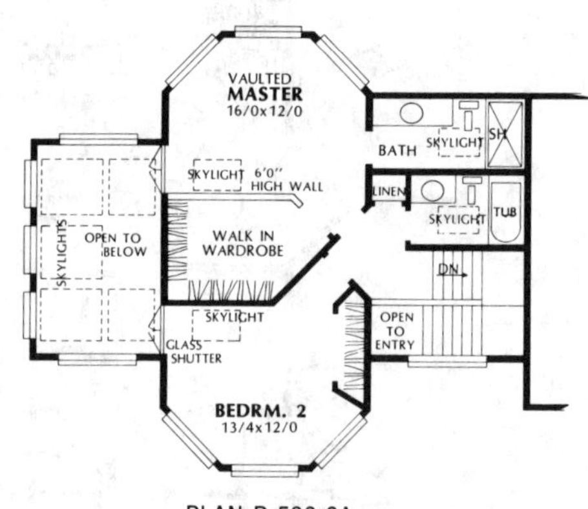

PLAN P-536-2A
WITHOUT BASEMENT

Plans P-536-2A & -2D

Bedrooms: 2-3	**Baths:** 2-3
Space:	
Upper floor:	642 sq. ft.
Main floor:	863 sq. ft.
Total living area:	1,505 sq. ft.
Basement:	863 sq. ft.
Garage:	445 sq. ft.
Exterior Wall Framing:	2x4

Foundation options:
Daylight basement (Plan P-536-2D).
Crawlspace (Plan P-536-2A).
(Foundation & framing conversion diagram available — see order form.)

Blueprint Price Code:

Without basement:	B
With basement:	C

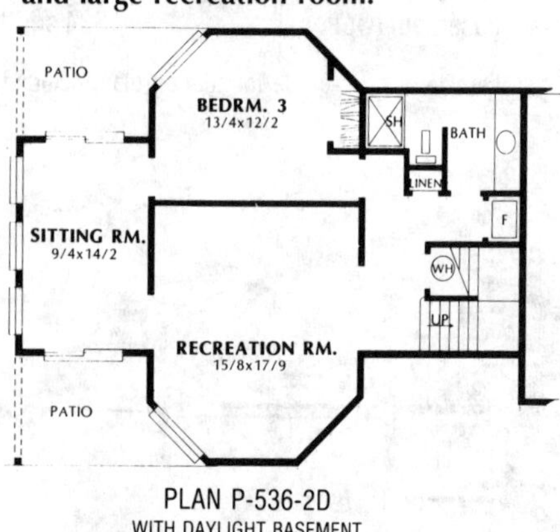

PLAN P-536-2D
WITH DAYLIGHT BASEMENT

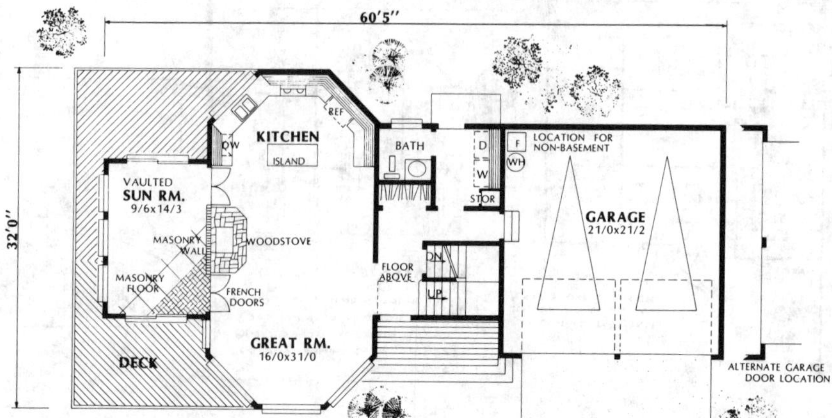

TO ORDER THIS BLUEPRINT, CALL TOLL-FREE 1-800-547-5570
(prices and details on pp. 12-15.)

Plans P-536-2A & -2D

SECOND FLOOR PLAN

SECTION
PASSIVE SOLAR AT WORK

FIRST FLOOR

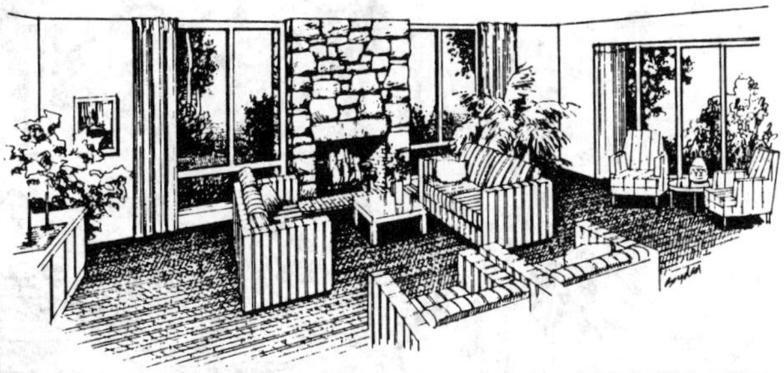

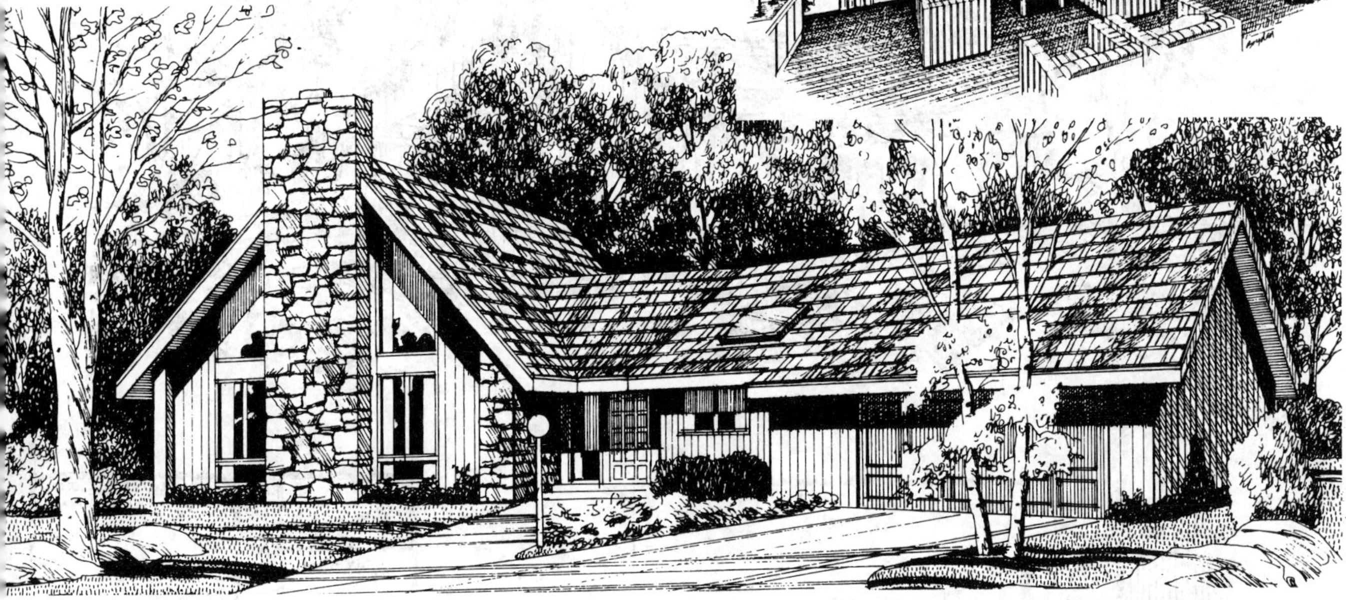

Passive Solar Home Meets Modern Demands

The exterior of this two-story plan is thoroughly contemporary. The layout is angled to give it added distinction in any neighborhood. Optional orientations in relation to the street allow this plan to adapt to a variety of plot shapes. Inside, the reception hall immediately presents a pleasing view of the rear terrace and solar room. To the left is the living room, which is graced by a stone fireplace.

In winter months, light and solar heat enter through the glass and heat is stored in the ceramic tiled floor of the solar room; after the sun sets, this warmth is released to the house. In summer months, the sun rises higher and its rays are blocked by adjustable shades built into glazed ceiling panels; automatic vent guards against heat buildup.

Generously sized, the master bedroom features extensive glass to the south side, a personal bath and sliding glass doors that lead out to a private terrace.

Total living area, excluding the solar room, is 1,132 sq. ft. on the first floor and 416 sq. ft. on the second. Optional basement is 1,176 sq. ft.; garage, mud room, etc., come to 560 sq. ft.
(Alternate slab-on-grade foundation plan is included.)

Total living area: 1,548 sq. ft.

Blueprint Price Code B

Plan K-513-A

(prices and details on pp. 12-15.)

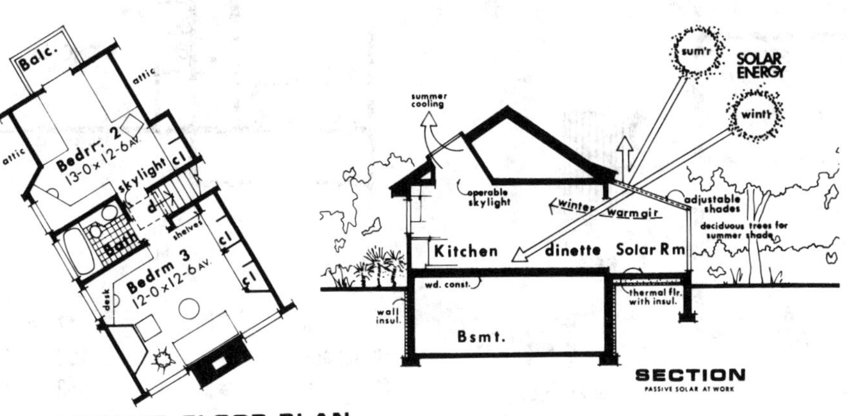

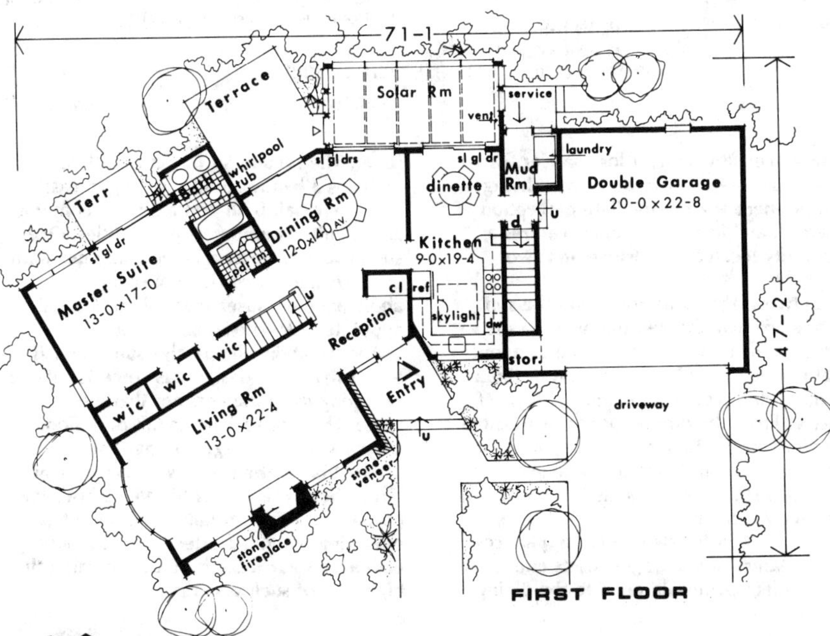

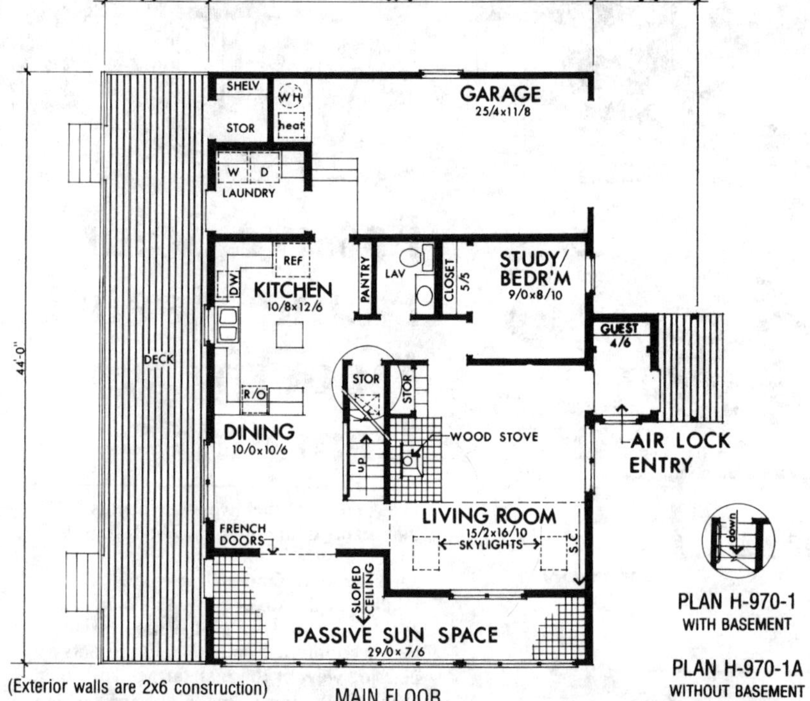

(Exterior walls are 2x6 construction)

MAIN FLOOR

PLAN H-970-1
WITH BASEMENT

PLAN H-970-1A
WITHOUT BASEMENT
(CRAWLSPACE FOUNDATION)

SECOND FLOOR

First floor:	817 sq. ft.
Sunspace:	192 sq. ft.
Second floor:	563 sq. ft.
Total living area: (Not counting basement or garage)	1,572 sq. ft.
Airlock entry:	40 sq. ft.
Garage:	288 sq. ft.

The Simple Life at Its Best in a Passive Solar Design

This home's rustic exterior is suggestive of Carpenter Gothic Style homes or early barn designs. The wood shake roof and "board-and-batten" style siding help to carry out this theme. An air-lock entry provides a protected place to remove outer garments as well as serving as an energy-conserving heat loss barrier. As you pass from the entry into the cozy living room, there is an immediate perception of warmth and light. This room features a centrally located woodstove and two skylights.

Between the living room and the sun space are two double-hung windows to provide heat circulation as well as admit natural light. Further inspection of the ground floor reveals a delightful flow of space. From the dining room it is possible to view the kitchen, the wider portion of the sun space and part of the living room. An open staircase connects this room with the second floor.

The kitchen boasts modern appliances, large pantry and storage closets and a convenient peninsula open to the dining room. The remainder of the first floor includes a handy laundry room, an easily accessible half-bath and a bonus room with an unlimited number of possibilities. One such use may be as a home computer/study area. Upstairs, two bedrooms with an abundance of closet space share the fully appointed, skylighted bathroom.

A word about the passive sun room: It seems that solar design has come full circle, returning us to the concept that less is more. This sun room uses masonry floor pavers as heat storage and natural convection as the primary means of heat circulation. This serves to reduce both the potential for system failures and the heavy operating workload often found in more elaborate solar designs, not to mention the high cost of such systems.

TO ORDER THIS BLUEPRINT, CALL TOLL-FREE 1-800-547-5570

 (prices and details on pp. 12-15.)

Blueprint Price Code B

Plans H-970-1 & H-970-1A

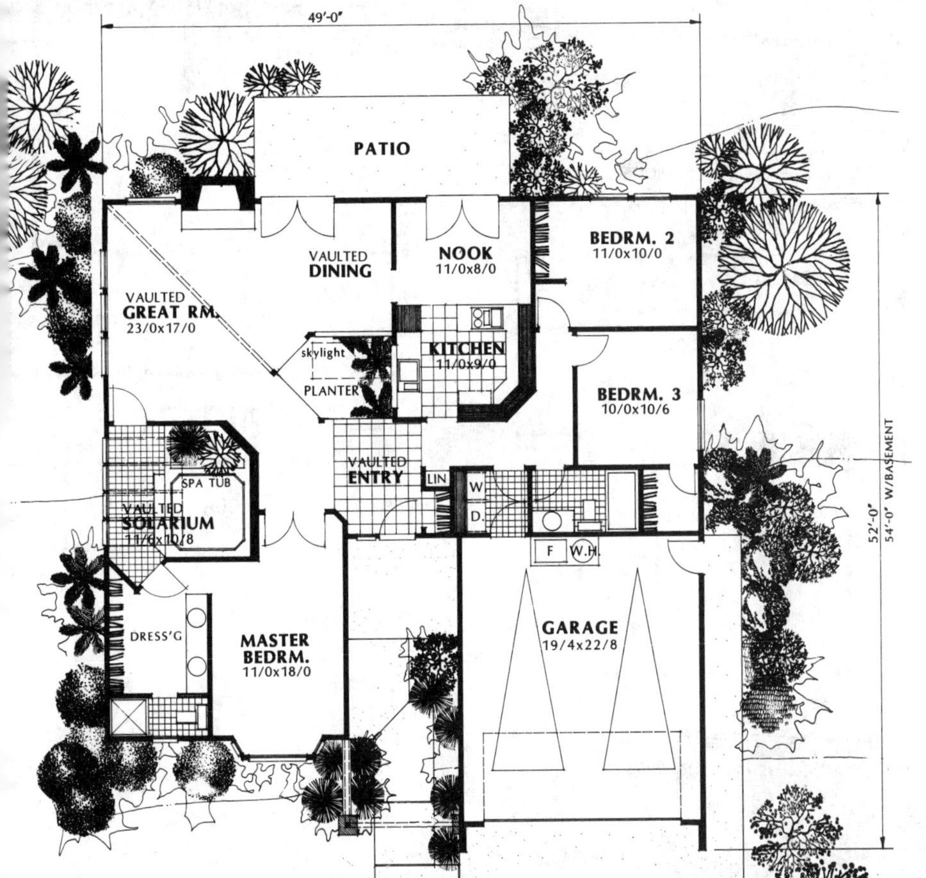

49'-0"

PATIO

VAULTED GREAT RM. 23/0x17/0

VAULTED DINING

NOOK 11/0x8/0

BEDRM. 2 11/0x10/0

skylight

PLANTER

KITCHEN 11/0x9/0

BEDRM. 3 10/0x10/6

SPA TUB

VAULTED SOLARIUM 11/6x10/8

VAULTED ENTRY

LIN

W

D.

F

W.H.

GARAGE 19/4x22/8

DRESS'G

MASTER BEDRM. 11/0x18/0

52'-0"

54'-0" W/BASEMENT

ENTRY

LINEN

BEDRM 2

DN

PLAT-FORM

GARAGE

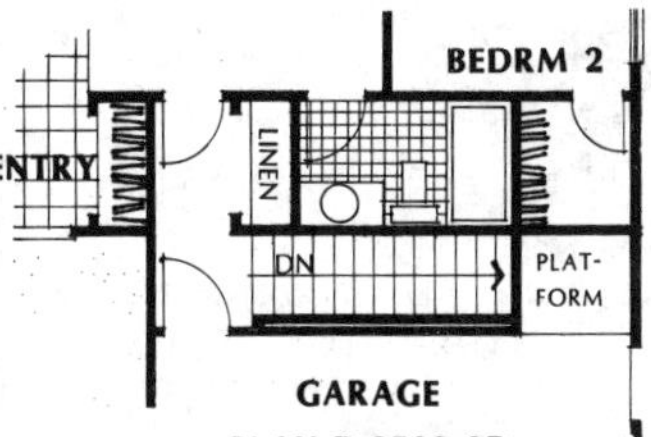

PLAN P-6562-3D
WITH DAYLIGHT BASEMENT

MAIN FLOOR

PLAN P-6562-3A
WITHOUT BASEMENT
(CRAWLSPACE FOUNDATION)

Master Suite Adjoins Spa Solarium

- This elegant mid-sized design includes all the amenities needed for gracious living.
- Especially note the luxurious spa tub located in the solarium conveniently between the master suite and the Great Room.
- The large, vaulted Great Room and dining room combine to create plenty of space for entertaining and family living alike.

Plans P-6562-3A & P-6562-3D

Bedrooms: 3 **Baths:** 2

Space:

Main floor (non-basement version):	1,639 sq. ft.
Main floor (basement version):	1,699 sq. ft.
(Both figures include 123 sq. ft. solarium.)	
Basement:	1,699 sq. ft.
Garage:	438 sq. ft.

Exterior Wall Framing: 2x4

Foundation options:
Daylight basement (P-6562-3D).
Crawlspace (P-6562-3A).
(Foundation & framing conversion diagram available — see order form.)

Blueprint Price Code: B

Plans P-6562-3A & -3D

TO ORDER THIS BLUEPRINT, CALL TOLL-FREE 1-800-547-5570

(prices and details on pp. 12-15.)

Sun Room Adds Warmth to "Switched-Level" Contemporary

Solar warmth abounds in this dining area sun room, bolstered by a nearby free-standing wood fireplace and heat-storing masonry. An unusual feature of this design is that the active areas are on the second floor for a better view, and the sleeping rooms on the lower floor.

The spacious entry hall, with a door in from the double garage, has stairs with an open balcony railing leading up to the living-dining-kitchen floor, or down to the bedrooms, for complete traffic separation.

The open-plan upper floor, with vaulted ceiling, has an eight-foot wall screening the dining area from the stairway and the half-bath that is adjacent to the kitchen.

The glass roof and windows over and around the dining area are passive solar collectors and a brick or slate floor provides a storage mass.

A sliding glass door in the living room window wall opens onto the large wood deck, enhancing the view orientation of the house. Another small deck is reached by a French door next to the woodstove.

Downstairs, a hallway from the stairs leads to the master bedroom, with its own bath and large closets, and to the other two bedrooms, second bath and utility room.

The upper floor has 886 sq. ft., and there are 790 sq. ft. downstairs. Ceilings have R-30 insulation and the 2x6 stud walls hold R-19 batts.

Upper floor:	886 sq. ft.
Lower floor:	790 sq. ft.
Total living area: (Not counting garage)	1,676 sq. ft.

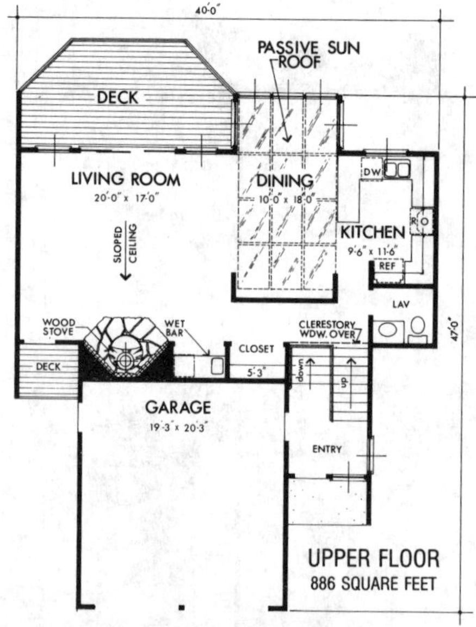

UPPER FLOOR
886 SQUARE FEET

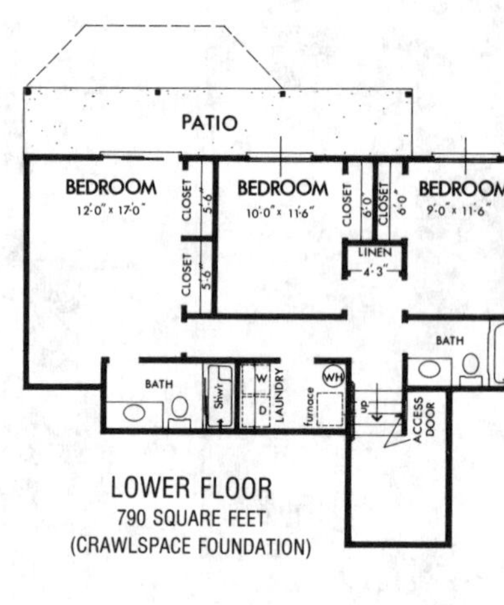

LOWER FLOOR
790 SQUARE FEET
(CRAWLSPACE FOUNDATION)

FRONT VIEW

Blueprint Price Code B

Plan H-945-1A

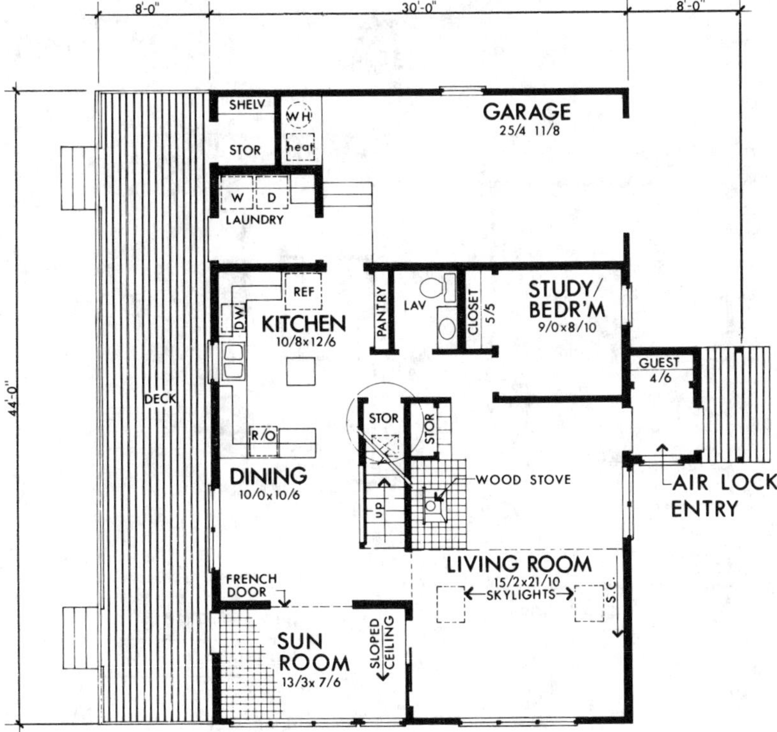

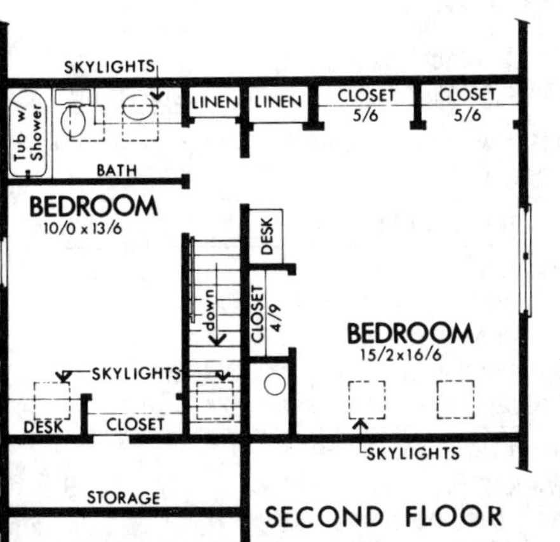

PLAN H-970-2A
WITHOUT BASEMENT
(CRAWLSPACE FOUNDATION)

Exterior walls are 2x6 construction.

PLAN H-970-2
WITH BASEMENT

Rustic Simplicity in a Passive Solar Design

Battened and barnlike, this rustic facade conceals a treasure of contemporary living. From the airlock entry which allows access without loss of heat, to the 100 sq. ft. passive sun room which collects heat without loss of money, each room contains its own surprises:

For example, the beautiful, efficient kitchen with its central work island and step saving pantry; or the skylighted living room with a tiled hearth which supports an old fashioned wood stove; or the aforementioned sun room, a joyous place to breakfast or keep one's green thumb in shape.

A small room on the first floor will serve many purposes from a guest bedroom to a hideaway den, study or even a small home office. The serious business of sleeping, however, will be accomplished in two spacious bedrooms on the second floor. These skylighted rooms include abundant closet space and built-in desks.

First floor:	1,009 sq. ft.
Second floor:	563 sq. ft.
Total living area: (Not counting basement or garage)	1,572 sq. ft.
Air lock entry:	40 sq. ft.
Garage:	288 sq. ft.

Blueprint Price Code B

Plans H-970-2 & H-970-2A

TO ORDER THIS BLUEPRINT, CALL TOLL-FREE 1-800-547-5570

(prices and details on pp. 12-15.)

Sunny Family Living

- Pleasant-looking and unassuming from the front, this plan breaks into striking, sun-catching angles at the rear.
- The living room sun roof gathers passive solar heat, which is stored in the tile floor and the two-story high masonry backdrop to the wood stove.
- A 516-square-foot master suite with private bath and balcony makes up the second floor.
- The main floor offers two more bedrooms and a full bath.

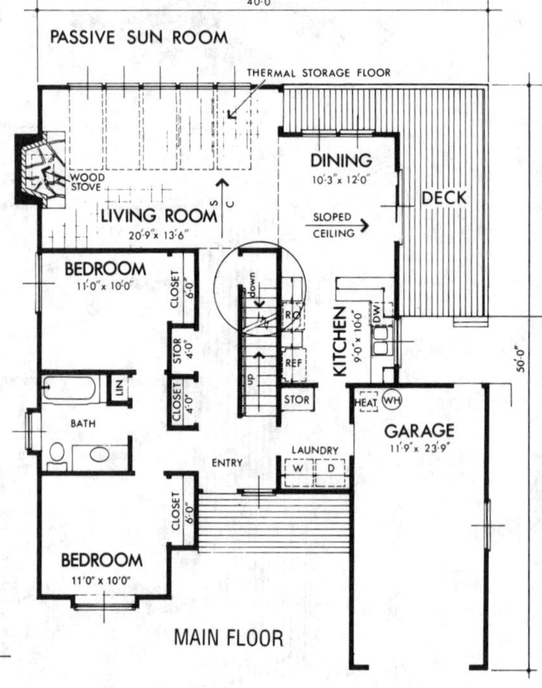

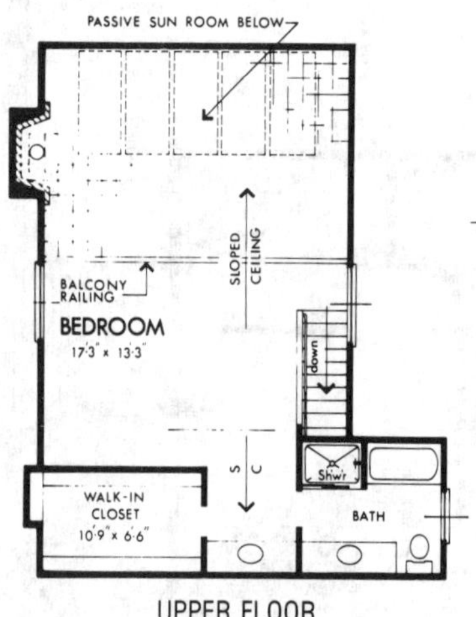

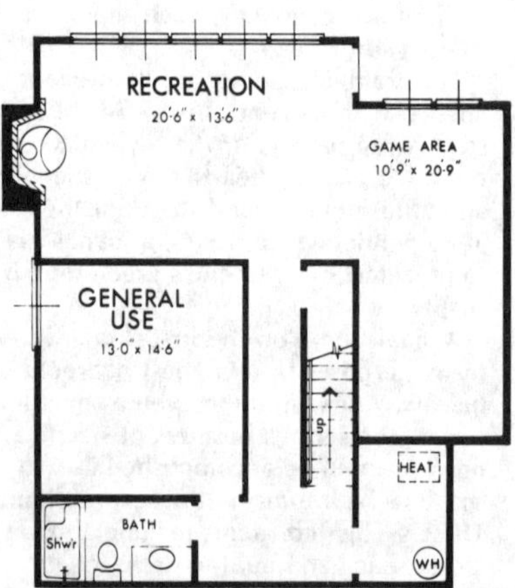

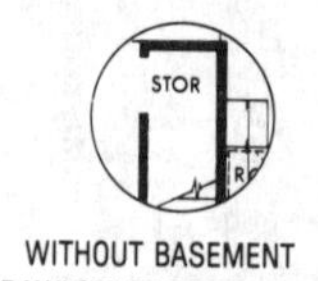

WITHOUT BASEMENT (CRAWLSPACE FOUNDATION)

Plans H-947-1A & -1B

Bedrooms: 3	**Baths:** 2-3
Space:	
Upper floor:	516 sq. ft.
Main floor:	1,162 sq. ft.
Total without basement:	1,678 sq. ft.
Daylight basement:	966 sq. ft.
Total with basement:	2,644 sq. ft.
Garage:	279 sq. ft.
Exterior Wall Framing:	2x6

Foundation options:
Daylight basement (H-947-1B).
Crawlspace (H-957-1A).
(Foundation & framing conversion diagram available — see order form.)

Blueprint Price Code:

Without basement:	B
With basement:	D

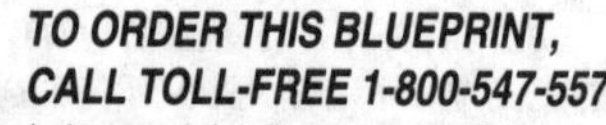

TO ORDER THIS BLUEPRINT, CALL TOLL-FREE 1-800-547-5570
(prices and details on pp. 12-15.)

Plans H-947-1A & -1B

Greenhouse Adds Extra Touch

Created for leisure living, this modern ranch design has 1,665 sq. ft. of living area, not counting the 165 sq. ft. in the greenhouse area. The living-dining area separates the large master bedroom suite from the other two bedrooms. A spacious family room, kitchen and greenhouse complete this floor plan.

Total living area: 1,830 sq. ft.
(Not counting garage)

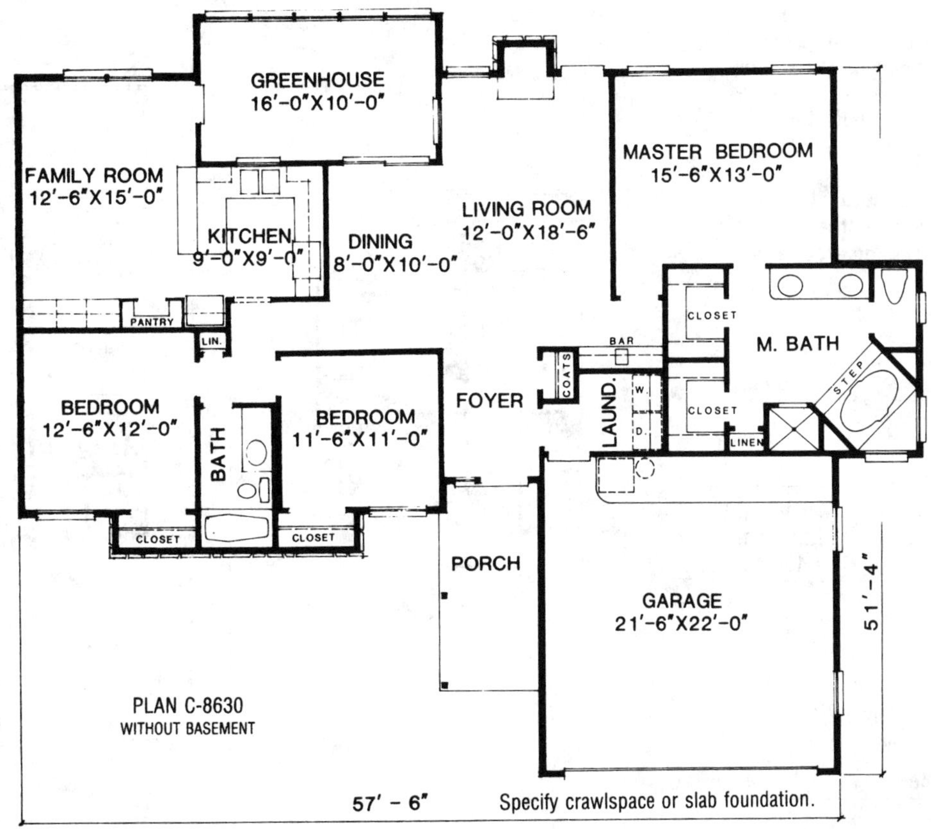

Blueprint Price Code B

Plan C-8630

TO ORDER THIS BLUEPRINT, CALL TOLL-FREE 1-800-547-5570
(prices and details on pp. 12-15.)

Soaring Spaces

- The soaring exterior rooflines and interior volumetrics give this contemporary home a dramatic appeal.
- The two-story rear sun room is a focal point of the design, adding interest to the Great Room and dining room on the main floor and the master bedroom on the upper floor.
- When properly oriented, the sun room will work well as a solar heat source.
- The private master suite also features a fireplace, cathedral ceiling , large dressing area, and private study.

Plan DG-149

Bedrooms: 3	**Baths:** 2
Space:	
Upper floor:	504 sq. ft.
Main floor:	1,340 sq. ft.
Total living area:	1,844 sq. ft.
Basement:	1,206 sq. ft.
Garage:	430 sq. ft.
Exterior Wall Framing:	2x4

Foundation options:
Standard basement.
Crawlspace.
(Foundation & framing conversion diagram available — see order form.)

Blueprint Price Code: B

REAR VIEW

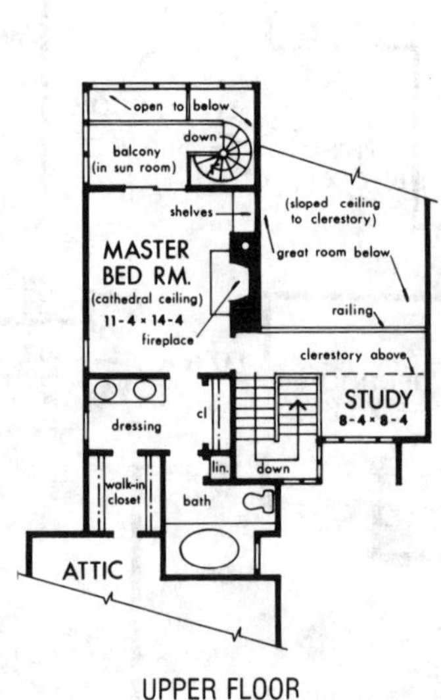

UPPER FLOOR

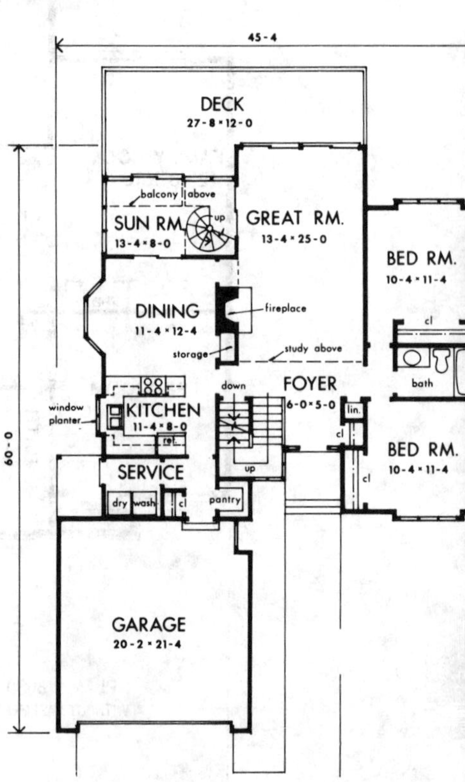

MAIN FLOOR

TO ORDER THIS BLUEPRINT, CALL TOLL-FREE 1-800-547-5570
(prices and details on pp. 12-15.)

Plan DG-149

Solar Flair

- Full window walls and a sun room with glass roof act as passive energy collectors in this popular floor plan.
- Expansive living room features wood stove and vaulted ceilings.
- Dining room shares a breakfast counter with the merging kitchen.
- Convenient laundry room is positioned near kitchen and garage entrance.
- Second level is devoted entirely to the private master suite, featuring vaulted ceiling and a balcony view to the living room below.

Plans H-877-5A & -5B

Bedrooms: 3-4	**Baths:** 2-3
Space:	
Upper floor:	382 sq. ft.
Main floor:	1,200 sq. ft.
Sun room:	162 sq. ft.
Total living area:	1,744 sq. ft.
Basement:	approx. 1,200 sq. ft.
Garage:	457 sq. ft.
Exterior Wall Framing:	2x6

Foundation options:
Daylight basement (Plan H-877-5B).
Crawlspace (Plan H-877-5A).
(Foundation & framing conversion diagram available — see order form.)

Blueprint Price Code:

Without finished basement:	B
With finished basement:	D

UPPER FLOOR

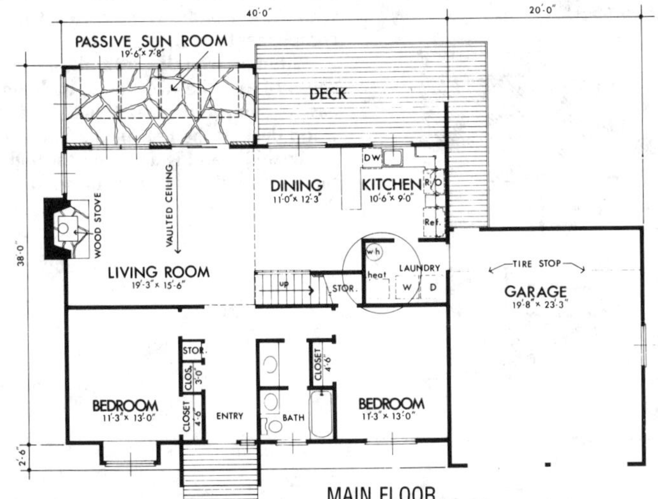

MAIN FLOOR

PLAN H-877-5B
WITH BASEMENT

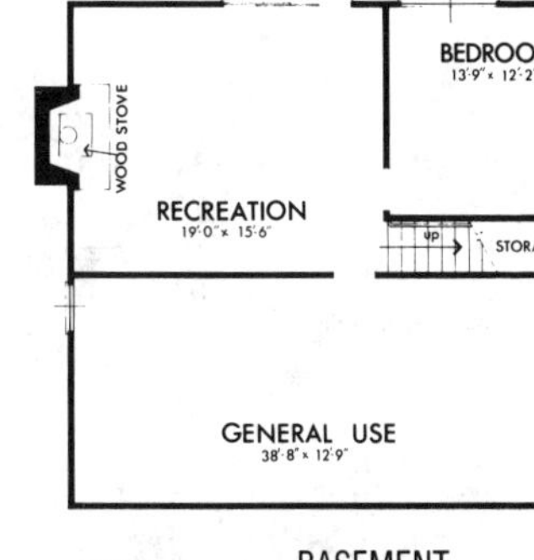

BASEMENT

Plans H-877-5A & -5B

TO ORDER THIS BLUEPRINT, CALL TOLL-FREE 1-800-547-5570
(prices and details on pp. 12-15.)

Contemporary Passive Solar

Energy-efficient housing is one of today's most important considerations, and this home is packed with many ideas that will help lower your utility bills. Utilizing many different elements, this plan will lend itself to your family's lifestyle with ease and comfort.

At the front door we see one of the first elements, the "air-lock" entry, which seals the heat, or cool air, inside. Notice also that the utility room and the passive sun room also act as "air-lock" entries, thus precluding a short circuit in the energy envelope. The passive sun room adjacent to the spacious living room features a trombe wall.

Exterior walls have 2x6 studs with R-19 batts in the stud cavities plus rigid foam sheathing for a total insulating value of nearly R-23. There is R-38 insulation in all ceilings and R-30 batts in the floors. All windows, which are sized and oriented for efficiency, are double-glazed.

This compact floor plan features good activity separation, with the two main-floor bedrooms isolated from the master bedroom on the second floor. A full bath with shower and a walk-in closet further complement the master bedroom.

Within an overall width of 54′ and a depth of 48′, the two floors, including the passive sun room, total 1,764 sq. ft. A wood deck at the rear of the home adds to the livability and is accessed through the sliding glass doors in the sun room.

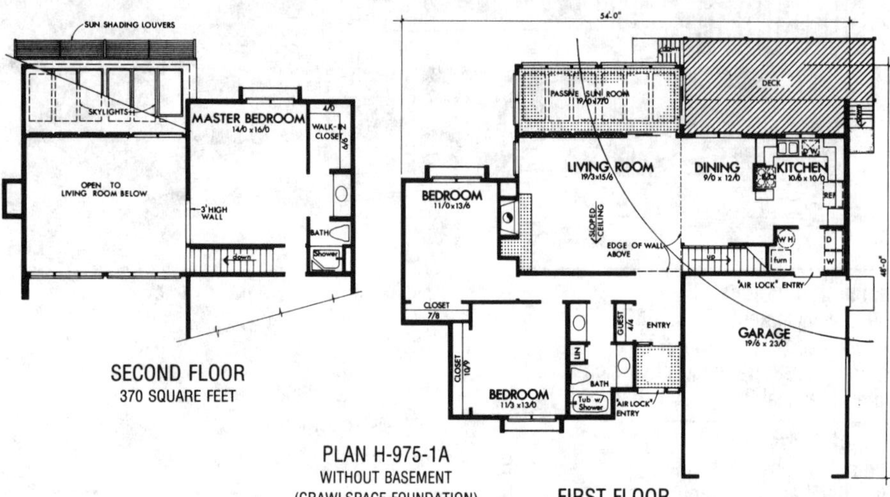

SECOND FLOOR
370 SQUARE FEET

PLAN H-975-1A
WITHOUT BASEMENT
(CRAWLSPACE FOUNDATION)

FIRST FLOOR
1252 SQUARE FEET (LIV. AREA)
142 SQUARE FEET (SUN RM.)

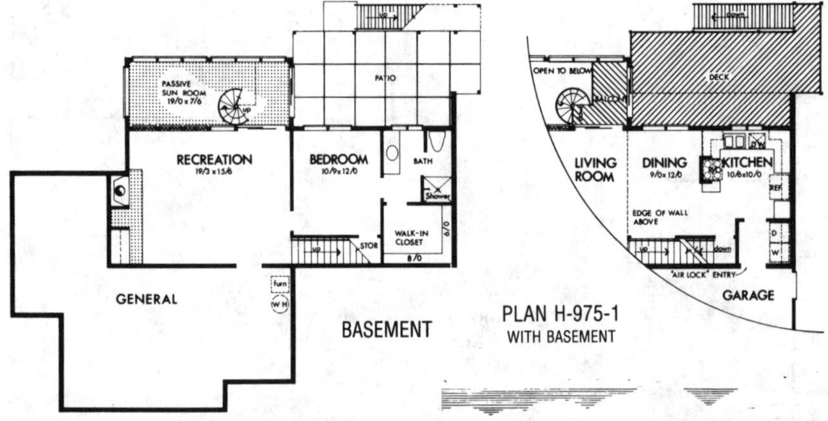

BASEMENT

PLAN H-975-1
WITH BASEMENT

First floor:	1,252 sq. ft.
Sun room:	142 sq. ft.
Second floor:	370 sq. ft.
Total living area: (Not counting basement or garage)	1,764 sq. ft.

Blueprint Price Code B

Plans H-975-1 & H-975-1A

The Warmth Of The Sun

- A rear-facing sun room serves both a functional and aesthetic role in this rustic contemporary home.
- When properly oriented, the sun room serves as a solar heat collector, saving on winter energy bills. With a hot tub and lounge chairs, the room also functions as a fun room.
- The vaulted Great Room with fireplace is the central room of the plan, with a study/play loft overlooking it from above.
- The spacious kitchen/dining area has plenty of light, including a window garden and deck access.
- The main floor master suite has a cathedral ceiling, fireplace, private bath and walk-in closet.

Plan DG-150

Bedrooms: 3	**Baths:** 2½
Space:	
Upper floor:	536 sq. ft.
Main floor:	1,345 sq. ft.
Total living area:	1,881 sq. ft.
Basement:	1,242 sq. ft.
Garage:	430 sq. ft.
Exterior Wall Framing:	2x4

Foundation options:
Standard basement.
Crawlspace.
(Foundation & framing conversion diagram available — see order form.)

Blueprint Price Code: B

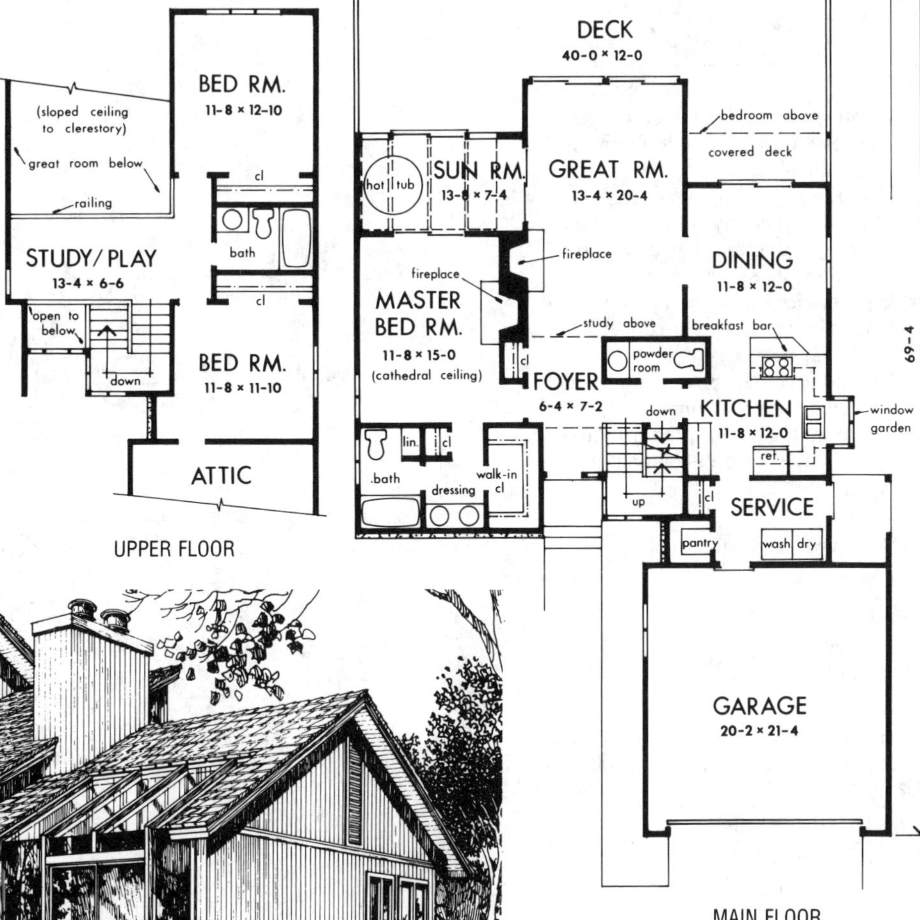

UPPER FLOOR

MAIN FLOOR

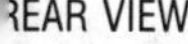

REAR VIEW

Plan DG-150

TO ORDER THIS BLUEPRINT, CALL TOLL-FREE 1-800-547-5570
(prices and details on pp. 12-15.)

Proven Plan Features Passive Sun Room

- A passive sun room, energy-efficient wood stove, and a panorama of windows make this design highly economical.
- Open living/dining room features attractive balcony railing, stone hearth, and adjoining sun room with durable stone floor.
- Well-equipped kitchen is separated from dining area by a convenient breakfast bar.
- Second level sleeping areas border a hallway and balcony.
- Optional basement plan provides extra space for entertaining or work.

Plans H-855-3A & -3B

Bedrooms: 3 **Baths:** 2-3

Space:

Upper floor:	586 sq. ft.
Main floor:	1,192 sq. ft.
Sun room:	132 sq. ft.
Total living area:	1,910 sq. ft.
Basement:	approx. 1,192 sq. ft.
Garage:	520 sq. ft.

Exterior Wall Framing: 2x6

Foundation options:
Daylight basement (Plan H-855-3B).
Crawlspace (Plan H-855-3A).
(Foundation & framing conversion diagram available — see order form.)

Blueprint Price Code:

Without basement	B
With basement	E

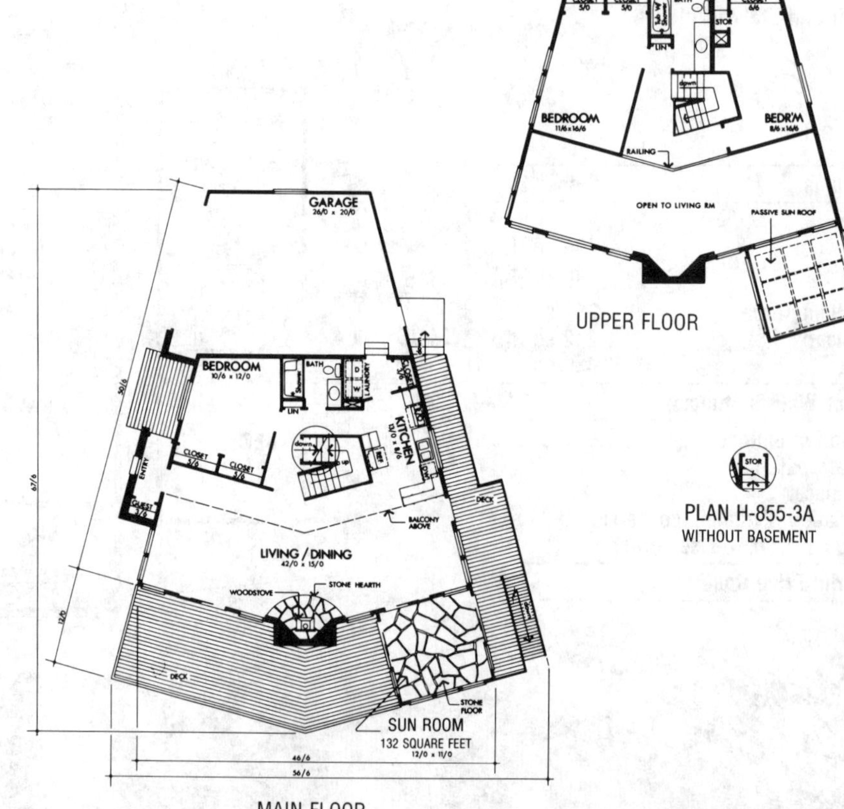

UPPER FLOOR

PLAN H-855-3A
WITHOUT BASEMENT

MAIN FLOOR
PLAN H-855-3B
WITH DAYLIGHT BASEMENT

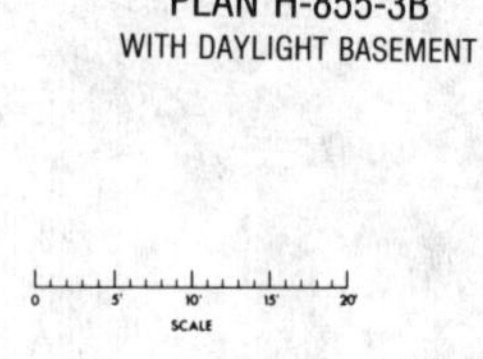

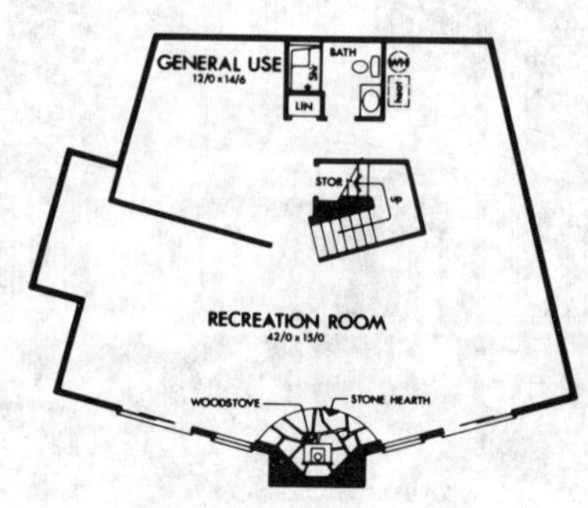

BASEMENT

TO ORDER THIS BLUEPRINT, CALL TOLL-FREE 1-800-547-5570
(prices and details on pp. 12-15.)

Plans H-855-3A & -3B

FRONT VIEW

Sun Chaser

\ passive sun room with two fully glazed valls and an all-glass roof offers leeway vhen siting this comfortable, contemporary eisure home. Orientation is towards the outh to capture maximum solar warmth. 'he window wall in the living room and a ank of clerestory windows high on the naster bedroom wall soak up the winter ays for direct heat gain, yet are shaded vith overhangs to block out the higher sun n the summer.

The 165 sq. ft. sun room is a focal point rom the living and family rooms, through vindows and sliding glass doors between hese rooms. A dining table in the family oom would command a sweeping view, r meals could be enjoyed in the sun room.

Sloping ceilings in the living and sun ooms allow balcony railings to open the naster bedroom partially for a view down o these rooms, and let warm air flow up rom the masonry storage floor of the sun oom.

Accent walls of solid board paneling add 'isual warmth and texture to the rooms. Vestern cedar bevel siding adds beauty nd individuality to the exterior. Exterior valls are of 2x6 construction.

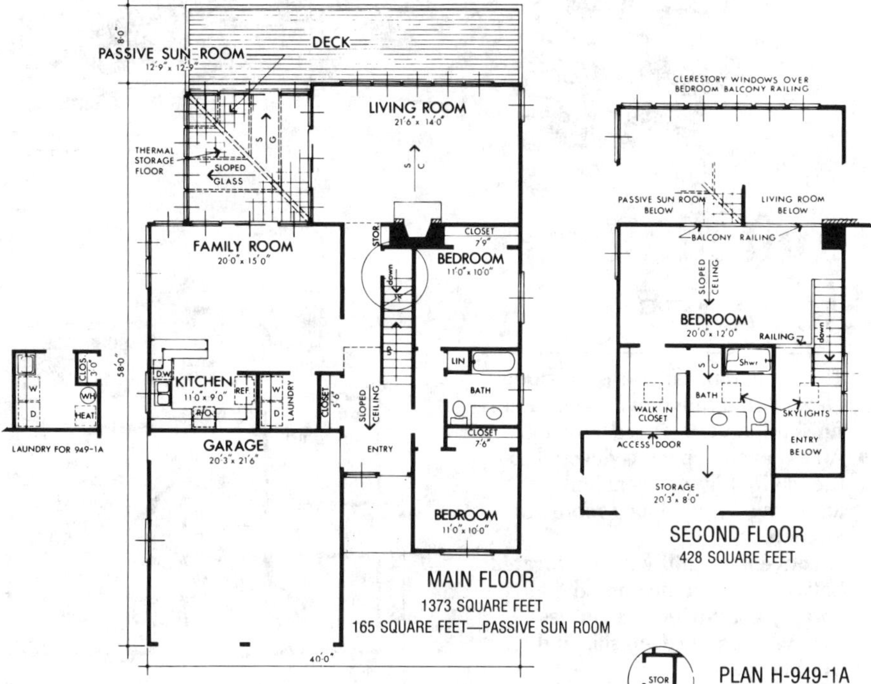

PLAN H-949-1A
WITHOUT BASEMENT
(CRAWLSPACE FOUNDATION)

PLAN H-949-1B
DAYLIGHT BASEMENT

PLAN H-949-1
STANDARD BASEMENT

First floor:	1,373 sq. ft.
Passive sun room:	165 sq. ft.
Second floor:	428 sq. ft.
Total living area:	1,966 sq. ft.

(Not counting basement or garage)

Blueprint Price Code B

Plans H-949-1, -1A & -1B

TO ORDER THIS BLUEPRINT, CALL TOLL-FREE 1-800-547-5570

(prices and details on pp. 12-15.)

Contemporary Elegance

- This contemporary design includes elegant traditional overtones, and is finished in vertical cedar siding.
- An expansive space is devoted to the vaulted living room and adjoining family/dining room and kitchen.
- A convenient utility area is located between the kitchen and the garage, and includes a clothes sorting counter, deep sink and ironing space.
- The master suite is spacious for a home of this size, and includes a sumptuous master bath and large walk-in closet.
- A loft area can be used for an additional bedroom, playroom, exercise area or hobby space.
- An optional sunroom can be added to the rear at any time.

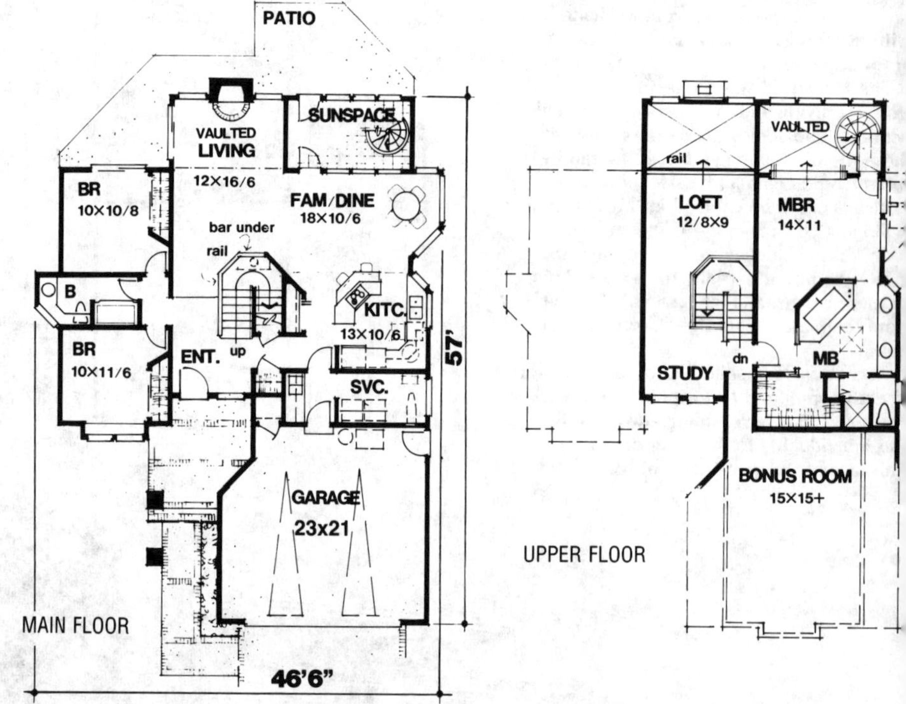

Plan S-1971

Bedrooms: 3-4	**Baths:** 2
Space:	
Upper floor:	723 sq. ft.
Main floor:	1,248 sq. ft.
Total living area:	1,971 sq. ft.
Bonus area:	225 sq. ft.
Basement:	approx. 1,248 sq. ft.
Garage:	483 sq. ft.

Exterior Wall Framing:	2x6

Foundation options:
Standard basement.
Crawlspace.
(Foundation & framing conversion diagram available — see order form.)

Blueprint Price Code:	B

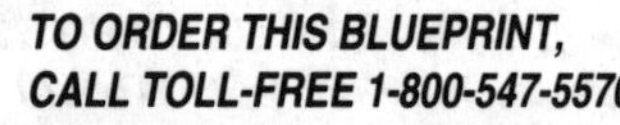
TO ORDER THIS BLUEPRINT, CALL TOLL-FREE 1-800-547-5570
(prices and details on pp. 12-15.)

Plan S-1971

Contemporary Minded

FRONT VIEW

- A handsome exterior combines with a functional interior to provide exciting design for the contemporary minded.
- When the two-story sun room is oriented to the south, the sun's heat is collected and stored in the concrete floor, saving energy.
- The dining and Great Room areas open to the sun room on the first floor through sliding glass doors, while the master bedroom has access on the second floor of the sun room.
- Access to the spacious deck is provided through sliding glass doors at the Great Room and sun room.
- A U-shaped kitchen with garden window provides ideal layout for food preparation.
- The Great Room ceiling, with exposed wood beams, slopes from the deck up to operable clerestory windows above balcony for natural ventilation.
- The master bedroom has a cathedral ceiling, fireplace, shelves for television and books, ample closet space, generous dressing and bath areas, and a whirlpool garden tub combo for the luxury minded.
- The other second level bedroom can act as a study or a nursery with or without the optional bath.
- Ample attic storage space over the garage has access through the master bedroom.

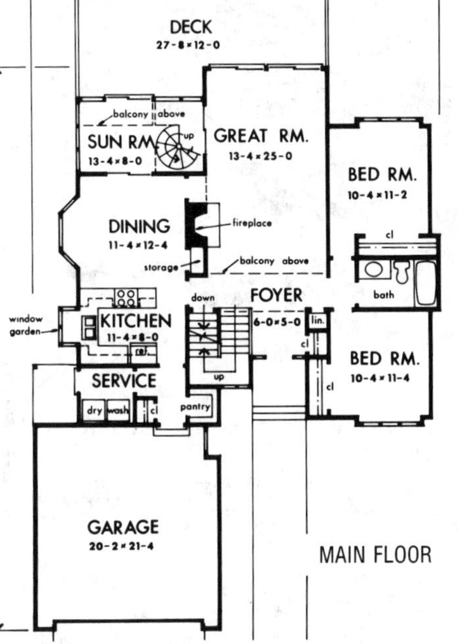

MAIN FLOOR

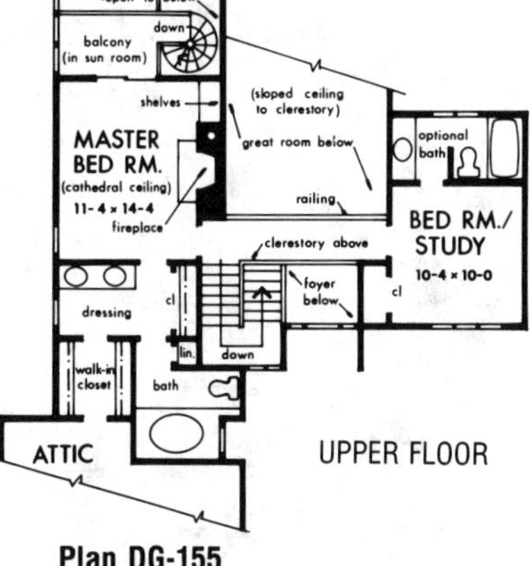

UPPER FLOOR

Plan DG-155

Bedrooms: 4	**Baths:** 3
Space:	
Upper floor:	651 sq. ft.
Main floor:	1,340 sq. ft.
Total living area:	1,991 sq. ft.
Basement:	1,224 sq. ft.
Garage:	430 sq. ft.
Exterior Wall Framing:	2x4

Foundation options:
Standard basement.
Crawlspace.
(Foundation & framing conversion diagram available — see order form.)

Blueprint Price Code: B

REAR VIEW

Plan DG-155

TO ORDER THIS BLUEPRINT, CALL TOLL-FREE 1-800-547-5570
(prices and details on pp. 12-15.)

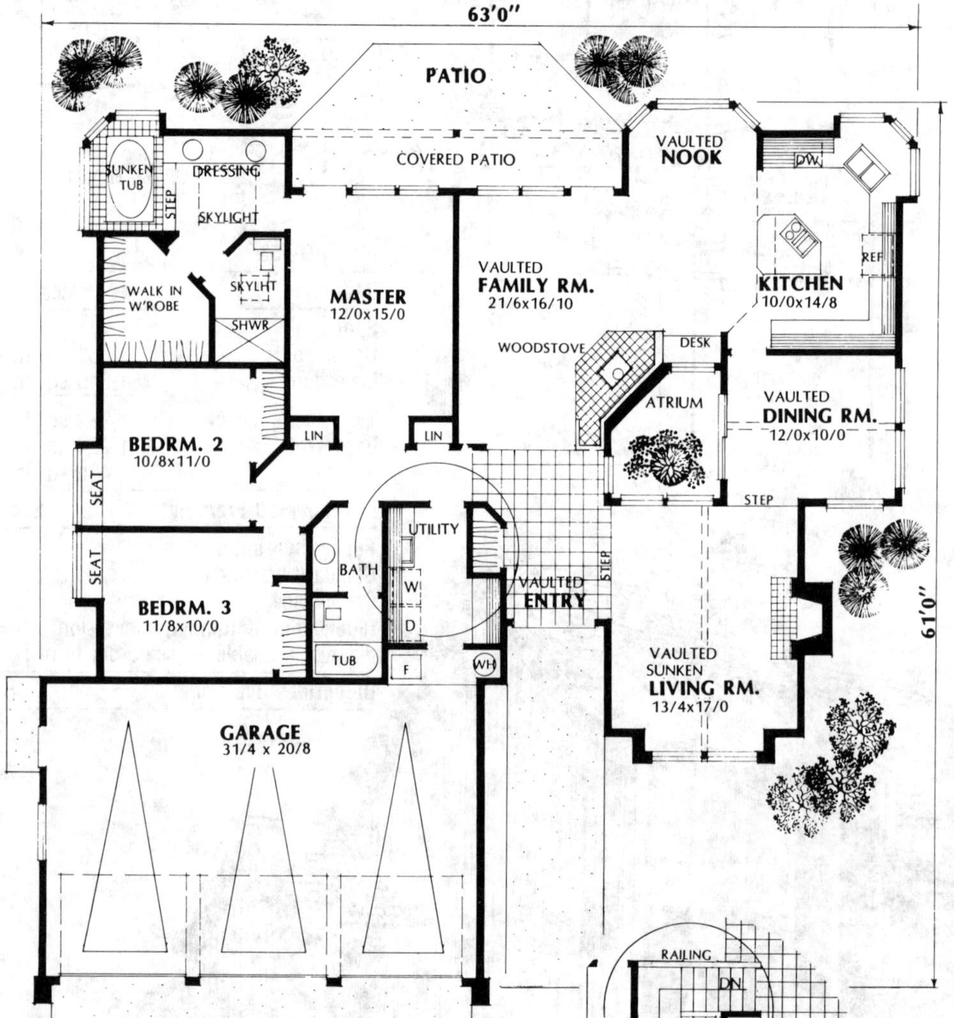

Soaring Spaces under Vaulted Ceilings

- A dignified exterior and a gracious, spacious interior combine to make this an outstanding plan for today's families.
- The living, dining, family rooms and breakfast nook all feature soaring vaulted ceilings.
- An interior atrium provides an extra touch of elegance, with its sunny space for growing plants and sunbathing.
- The master suite is first class all the way, with a spacious sleeping area, opulent bath, large skylight and enormous walk-in closet.
- A gorgeous kitchen includes a large work/cooktop island, corner sink with large corner windows and plenty of counter space.

63'0"

PATIO

COVERED PATIO

SUNKEN TUB

DRESSING

STEP

SKYLIGHT

WALK IN W'ROBE

SKYLHT

SHWR

MASTER 12/0x15/0

VAULTED FAMILY RM. 21/6x16/10

WOODSTOVE

VAULTED NOOK

DW

REF

KITCHEN 10/0x14/8

DESK

ATRIUM

VAULTED DINING RM. 12/0x10/0

STEP

BEDRM. 2 10/8x11/0

LIN

LIN

SEAT

SEAT

BEDRM. 3 11/8x10/0

BATH

UTILITY

W

D

TUB

F

WH

VAULTED ENTRY

STEP

VAULTED SUNKEN LIVING RM. 13/4x17/0

61'0"

GARAGE 31/4 x 20/8

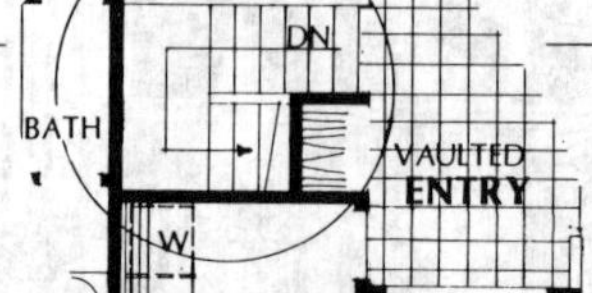

RAILING

DN

BATH

VAULTED ENTRY

W

D

PLAN P-7697-4D WITH DAYLIGHT BASEMENT

Plans P-7697-4A & -4D

Bedrooms: 3	**Baths:**

Space:

Main floor (crawlspace version):	2,003 sq. f
Main floor (basement version):	2,030 sq. f
Basement:	2,015 sq. f
Garage:	647 sq. f

Exterior Wall Framing:	2x

Foundation options:
Daylight basement (Plan P-7697-4D).
Crawlspace (Plan P-7697-4A).
(Foundation & framing conversion diagram available — see order form.)

Blueprint Price Code:

TO ORDER THIS BLUEPRINT, CALL TOLL-FREE 1-800-547-5570 (prices and details on pp. 12-15.)

Plans P-7697-4A & -4D

Striking Contemporary

- This striking contemporary home displays traditional flavor on the front exterior.
- The formal dining and Great Room areas open to the sun room, which has four skylights for passive solar heating purposes.
- The spacious kitchen allows for a breakfast bar or separate table.
- The sun room, Great Room, and master bedroom offer direct access to the deck, which provides space for a hot tub if preferred.
- A luxurious master bath has dual vanities, separate shower, and whirlpool tub.
- The second level has two spacious bedrooms sharing a full bath and a loft area overlooking the Great Room below.

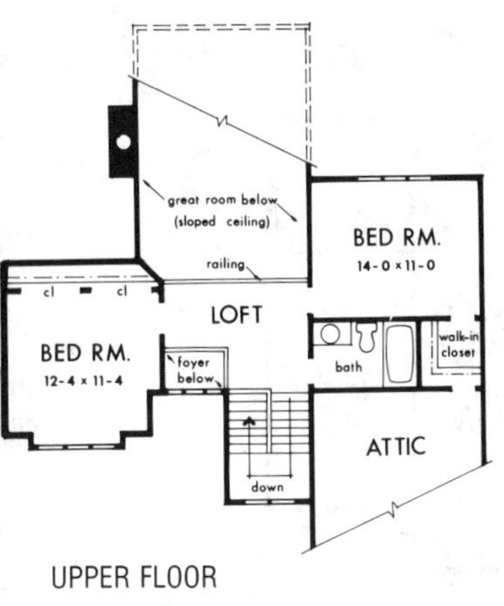

UPPER FLOOR

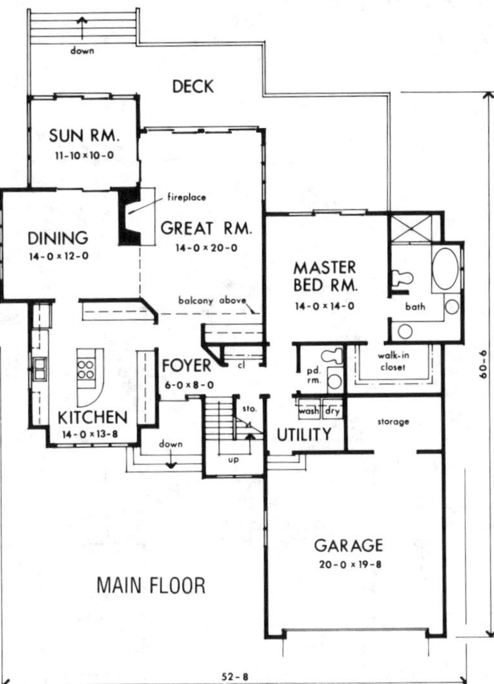

Plan DG-193	
Bedrooms: 3	Baths: 2½
Space:	
Upper floor:	576 sq. ft.
Main floor:	1,479 sq. ft.
Total living area:	2,055 sq. ft.
Garage:	393 sq. ft.
Storage area:	approx. 75 sq. ft.
Exterior Wall Framing:	2x4
Foundation options: Crawlspace. (Foundation & framing conversion diagram available — see order form.)	
Blueprint Price Code:	C

Plan DG-193

TO ORDER THIS BLUEPRINT, CALL TOLL-FREE 1-800-547-5570
(prices and details on pp. 12-15.)

Southern Comfort

- Winters will be warmer and energy bills lower with this passive solar home design.
- Sweeping rooflines with high transom windows give the north-facing front elevation a clean, contemporary look.
- The south-facing rear incorporates plenty of glass and a sun space to absorb the sun's energy for use in the winter months. Sliding doors allow many of the adjoining rooms to make use of this heat source when needed.
- The airlock entry vestibule opens to the dramatic living room with sloped ceiling, skylight, wood stove, and balcony overlooking the upper sun space.
- The kitchen serves the skylit breakfast room and the vaulted ceilinged formal dining room with clerestory windows high above.
- The main floor master suite offers a private bath and sliding glass doors opening to a dramatic balcony above the sun space.
- An optional loft and balcony can be incorporated upstairs, while two more bedrooms are located on the lower level.
- The partially finished lower level also includes a large family room with a second wood stove and the sun space opening to a rear patio.

Plan AX-98266

Bedrooms: 3	**Baths:** 2½
Space:	
Sunspace:	132 sq. ft.
Upper floor:	261 sq. ft.
Main floor:	1,192 sq. ft.
Lower floor (finished):	665 sq. ft.
Total living area:	2,250 sq. ft.
Lower floor (unfinished):	577 sq. ft.
Garage:	451 sq. ft.
Exterior Wall Framing:	2x4
Foundation options:	
Daylight basement. (Foundation & framing conversion diagram available — see order form.)	
Blueprint Price Code:	C

UPPER LIVING RM
LOFT 12'x11'
EXHAUST/RECIRCUL. FAN
DWARF PARTN.
BALCONY
UPPER DIN. RM
STOR

UPPER FLOOR

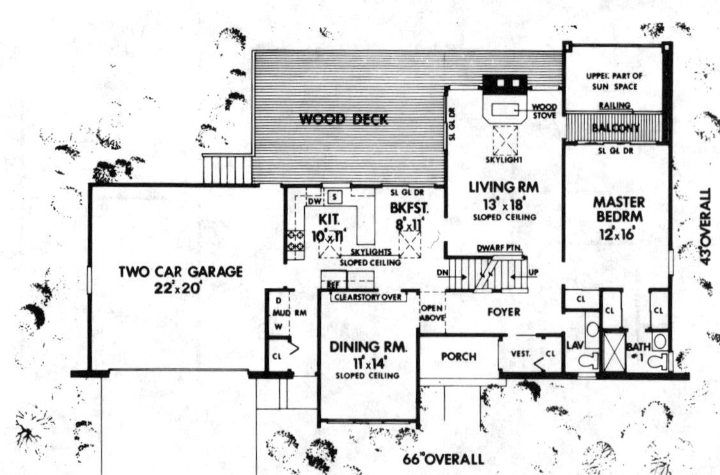

MAIN FLOOR

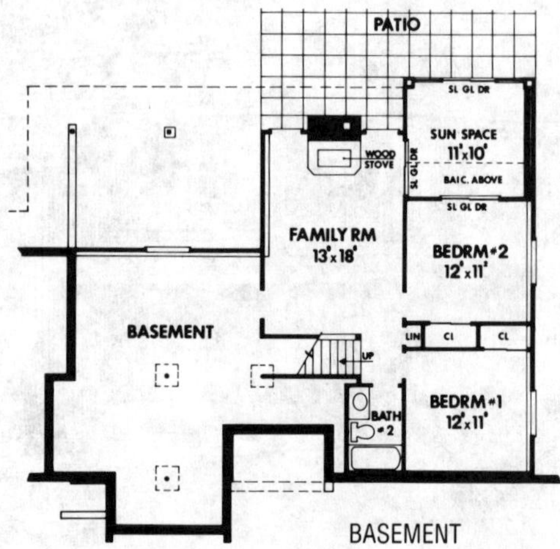

BASEMENT

TO ORDER THIS BLUEPRINT, CALL TOLL-FREE 1-800-547-5570
(prices and details on pp. 12-15.)

Plan AX-98266

FRONT VIEW

Sun Room Adds Warmth

At first glance this seems like just another very nice home, with crisp contemporary lines, a carefully conceived traffic flow and generous bedroom and living areas. What sets this home apart from most other houses is its passive sun room, a 13′ x 11′6″ solarium that collects, stores and distributes solar energy to warm the home, conserving fossil fuel and cutting energy costs. Adding to the energy efficiency of the design are 2x6 stud walls, allowing use of R-19 insulation batts, R-30 insulation in the ceiling, and an air-tight wood stove in the family room.

The passive sun room has glazing on three walls as it juts out from the home, and has a fully glazed ceiling to capture the maximum solar energy. A masonry tile floor stores the collected heat which is distributed to the family and living rooms through sliding glass doors. The wall adjoining the dining area also is glazed. With hanging plants, the sun room can be a visually stunning greenhouse extension of the vaulted-ceilinged living room. A French door from the sun room and sliding glass doors from the family room open onto a wood deck, for outdoor entertaining and relaxing.

First floor:	2,034 sq. ft.
Sun room:	159 sq. ft.
Total living area:	2,193 sq. ft.

(Not counting basement or garage)

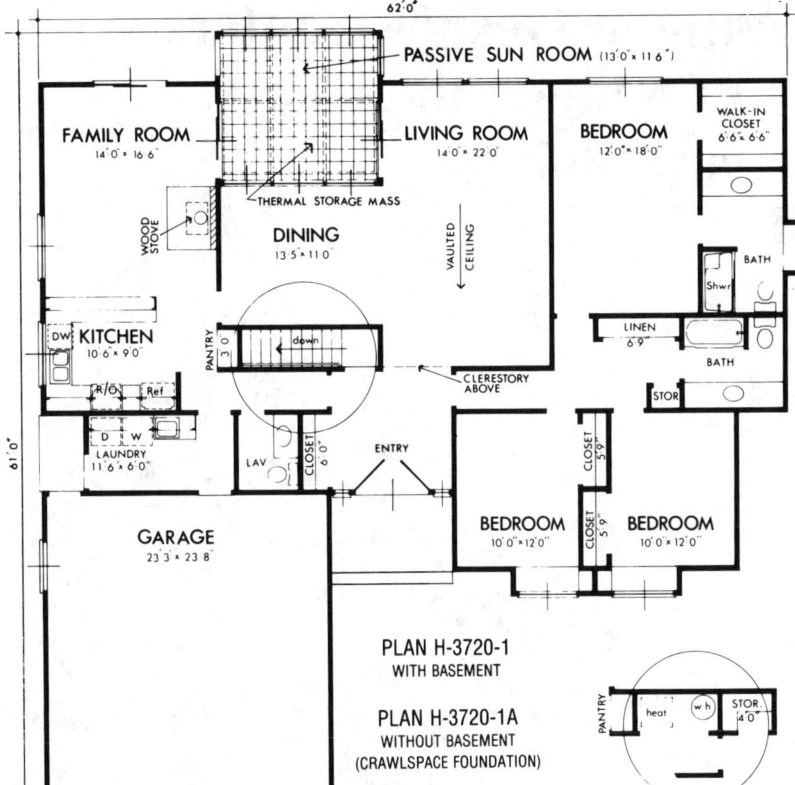

REAR VIEW

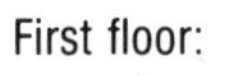

Blueprint Price Code C

Plans H-3720-1 & H-3720-1A

TO ORDER THIS BLUEPRINT, CALL TOLL-FREE 1-800-547-5570

(prices and details on pp. 12-15.)

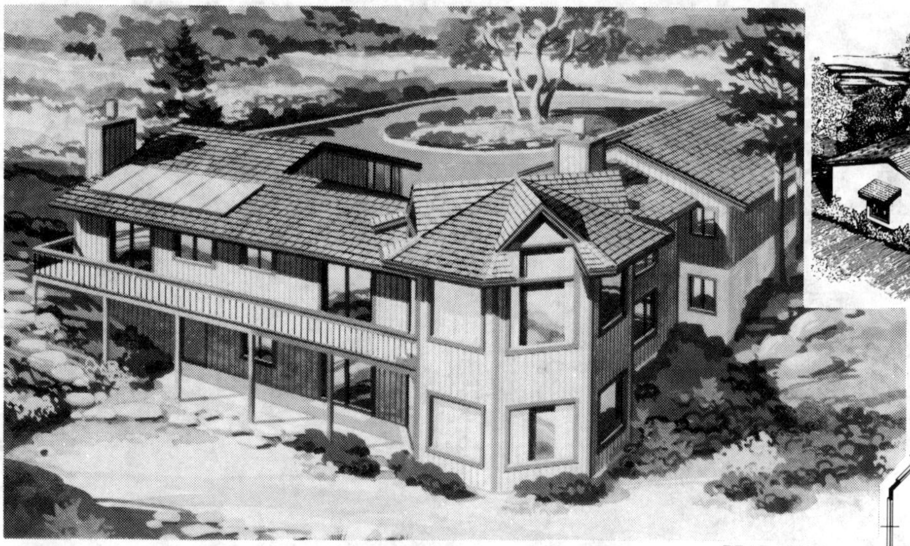

REAR VIEW

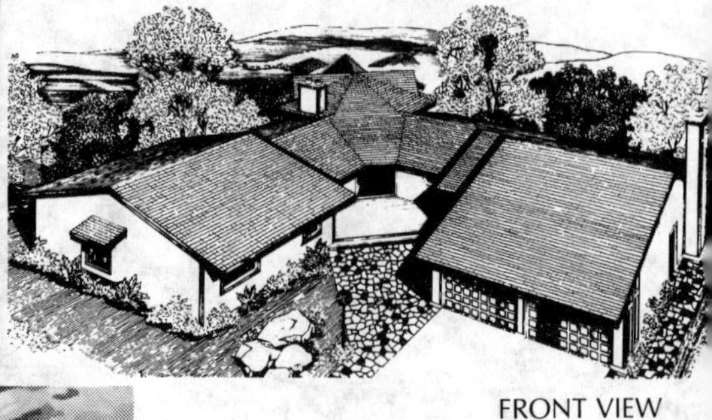

FRONT VIEW

Winged Design Centers on Octagonal Living Room

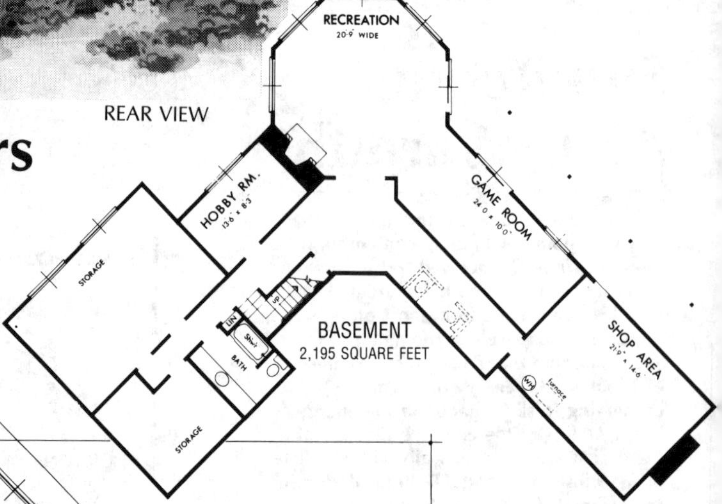

RECREATION 20'-9" WIDE
HOBBY RM. 13'-6" x 8'-3"
GAME ROOM 24'-0" x 10'-0"
STORAGE
SHOP AREA 21'-9" x 14'-6"
BASEMENT
2,195 SQUARE FEET

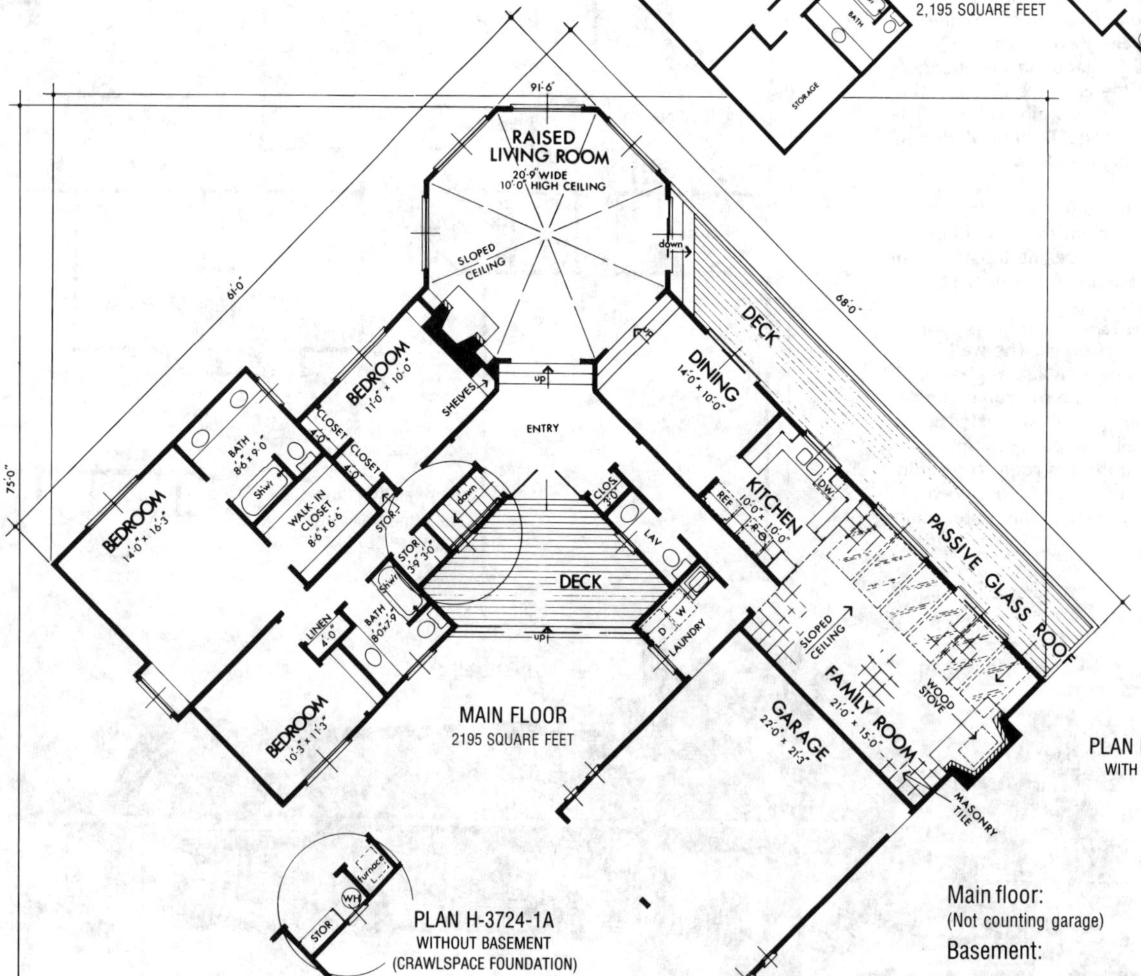

RAISED LIVING ROOM
20'-9" WIDE
10'-0" HIGH CEILING
SLOPED CEILING
BEDROOM 11'-0" x 10'-0"
DINING 14'-0" x 10'-0"
DECK
BATH 8'-6" x 9'-0"
BEDROOM 14'-0" x 16'-3"
WALK-IN CLOSET 8'-6" x 6'-6"
ENTRY
KITCHEN 10'-0" x 10'-0"
PASSIVE GLASS ROOF
DECK
BATH 8'-0" x 7'-9"
LAUNDRY
FAMILY ROOM 21'-0" x 15'-0"
WOOD STOVE
GARAGE 22'-0" x 21'-3"
BEDROOM 10'-3" x 11'-3"
MASONRY TILE

MAIN FLOOR
2195 SQUARE FEET

PLAN H-3724-1B
WITH BASEMENT

PLAN H-3724-1A
WITHOUT BASEMENT
(CRAWLSPACE FOUNDATION)

Main floor: (Not counting garage)	2,195 sq. ft.
Basement:	2,195 sq. ft.
Total with basement:	4,390 sq. ft.

Blueprint Price Code G With Basement
Blueprint Price Code C Without Basement

Plans H-3724-1A & -1B

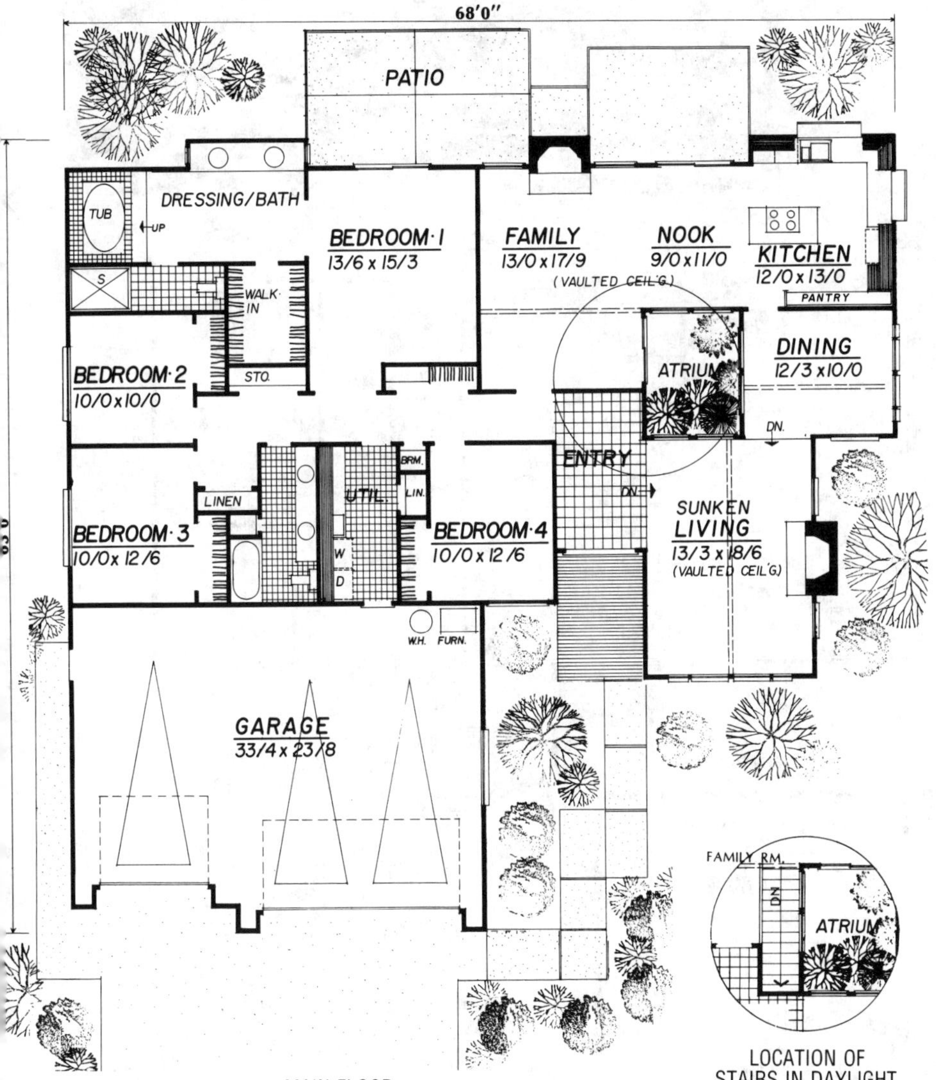

68'0"

PATIO

DRESSING/BATH

TUB

UP

S

WALK-IN

STO.

BEDROOM·1
13/6 x 15/3

FAMILY
13/0 x 17/9

NOOK
9/0 x 11/0

(VAULTED CEIL'G.)

KITCHEN
12/0 x 13/0

PANTRY

BEDROOM·2
10/0 x 10/0

ATRIUM

DINING
12/3 x 10/0

DN.

ENTRY

DN.

LINEN

BRM.

UTIL.

LIN.

BEDROOM·3
10/0 x 12/6

W

D

BEDROOM·4
10/0 x 12/6

SUNKEN
LIVING
13/3 x 18/6
(VAULTED CEIL'G.)

W.H.

FURN.

GARAGE
33/4 x 23/8

MAIN FLOOR

FAMILY RM.

DN

ATRIUM

LOCATION OF
STAIRS IN DAYLIGHT
BASEMENT VERSION

Atrium Attraction

- A central atrium allows each of the main living spaces to enjoy an oasis of color and light within this spacious contemporary home.
- The entry opens to a dramatic view of the atrium and the sunken living room with vaulted ceiling and fireplace.
- The vaulted dining room, with round-top windows, looks into the living room and the atrium and is conveniently located next to the kitchen.
- The kitchen has an island cooktop and overlooks the breakfast nook, family room with second fireplace, and the atrium.
- The sleeping wing of the plan incorporates four bedrooms, including a lavish master suite with walk-in closet, patio access and private bath with oversized tub.

Plans P-7581-2A, -2D

Bedrooms: 4	**Baths:** 2
Space:	
Main floor:	2,315 sq. ft.
Basement:	2,270 sq. ft.
Garage:	789 sq. ft.
Exterior Wall Framing:	2x4

Foundation options:
Daylight basement. (P-7581-2D)
Crawlspace. (P-7581-2A)
(Foundation & framing conversion diagram available — see order form.)

Blueprint Price Code:	C

Plans P-7581-2A, -2D

PLAN H-2107-1B

Solarium for Sloping Lots

PLAN H-2107-1

This plan is available in two versions. Plan H-2107-1B, shown above, is most suitable for a lot sloping upward from front to rear, providing a daylight front for the lower floor. The other version, Plan H-2107-1 (at right), is more suitable for a lot that slopes from side to side.

Either way, this moderately sized home has a number of interesting and imaginative features. Of these, the passive sun room will provoke the most comment. Spanning two floors between recreation and living rooms, this glass-enclosed space serves the practical purpose of collecting, storing and redistributing the sun's natural heat, while acting as a conservatory for exotic plants, an exercise room, or any number of other uses. A link between the formal atmosphere of the living room and the carefree activities of the recreation area is created by this two-story solarium by way of an open balcony railing. Living, dining, and entry blend together in one huge space made to seem even larger by the vaulted ceiling spanning the entire complex of rooms.

MAIN FLOOR
1505 SQUARE FEET

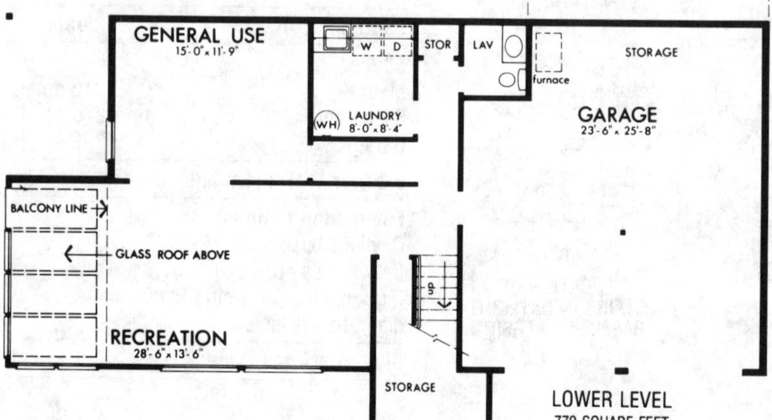

LOWER LEVEL
779 SQUARE FEET

PLAN H-2107-1B
DAYLIGHT BASEMENT

PLAN H-2107-1
WITH STANDARD BASEMENT
(BOTH VERSIONS INCLUDE
2X6 EXTERIOR WALL CONSTRUCTION)

Main floor:	1,505 sq. ft.
Lower level:	779 sq. ft.
Total living area: (Not counting garage)	2,284 sq. ft.

TO ORDER THIS BLUEPRINT, CALL TOLL-FREE 1-800-547-5570 (prices and details on pp. 12-15.)

Blueprint Price Code C

Plans H-2107-1 & H-2107-1B

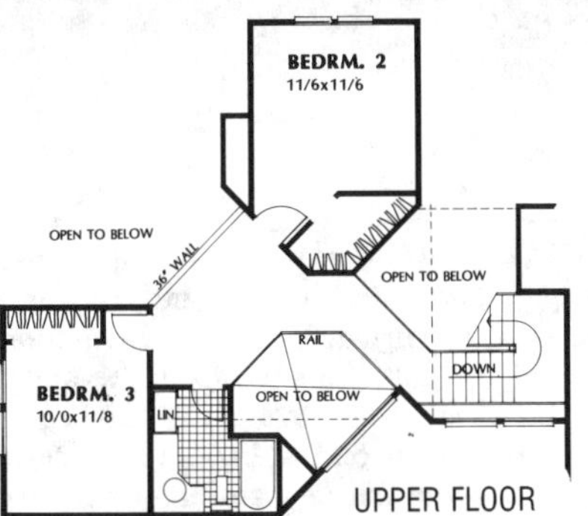

Convenience and Luxury

- Large roof planes and a modest exterior enclose a thoroughly modern, open floor plan.
- Entry hall, living/dining area and family room all have vaulted ceilings.
- Living room has floor-to-ceiling windows, fireplace and wall-length stone hearth.
- A sun room next to the spacious, angular kitchen offers passive solar heating and a bright look to the area.
- Main floor master suite includes a raised tub and separate shower, plus a large walk-in wardrobe.
- Upstairs, a bridge hallway overlooks the rooms below.
- The daylight basement version includes another 2,025 square feet of versatile space.

**NOTE: The above photographed home may have been modified by the homeowner. Please refer to floor plan and/or drawn elevation shown for actual blueprint details.

Plan P-7663-3D WITH BASEMENT

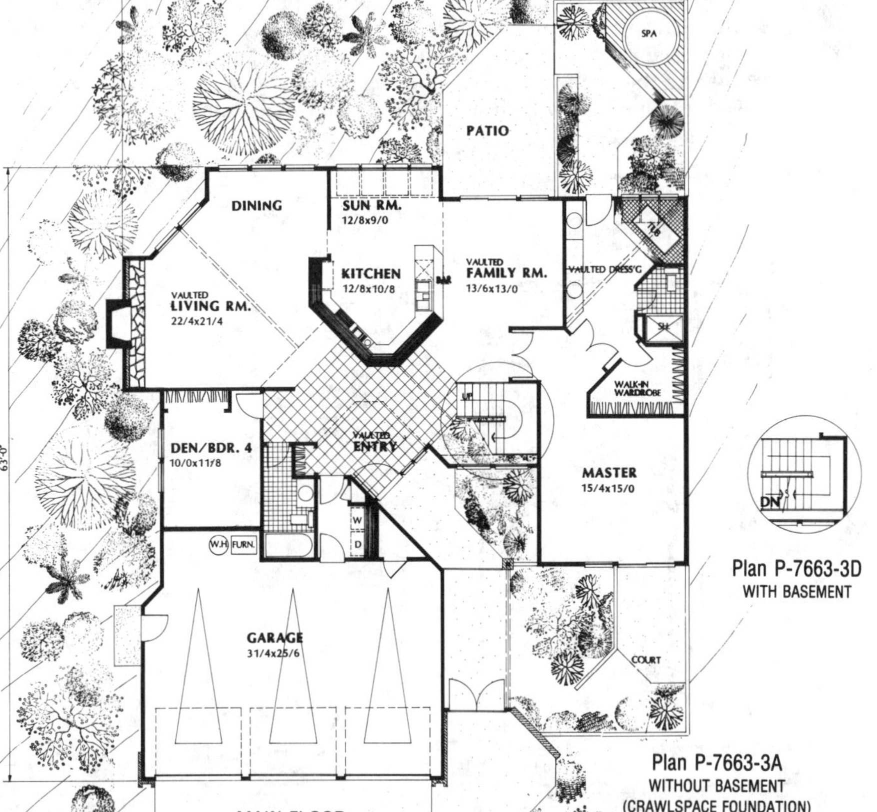

Plan P-7663-3A WITHOUT BASEMENT (CRAWLSPACE FOUNDATION)

Plans P-7663-3A & -3D	
Bedrooms: 3-4	**Baths:** 3
Space:	
Upper floor:	470 sq. ft.
Main floor:	2,025 sq. ft.
Total living area:	2,495 sq. ft.
Basement:	2,025 sq. ft.
Garage:	799 sq. ft.
Exterior Wall Framing:	2x4
Foundation options:	
Daylight basement (Plan P-7663-3D). Crawlspace (Plan P-7663-3A). (Foundation & framing conversion diagram available — see order form.)	
Blueprint Price Code:	C

Sunlit Elegance

- This elegant contemporary design offers just about all the amenities today's families expect in a home.
- The formal dining room is large enough for a good-sized dinner party.
- The living room is sunken and vaulted and includes a handsome fireplace.
- The spacious kitchen includes a large island and a pantry, and is open to the vaulted family room.
- Upstairs the master bedroom is impressive, with a private master bath, large closets and easy access to a private deck. (If the greenhouse is built, stairs go from the master bath down to the hot tub.)
- The second floor also includes a roomy library and large "bonus room."
- The plan also offers potential for an optional solar greenhouse which may contain a hot tub, or simply offer a great space for green plants and sunbathing.

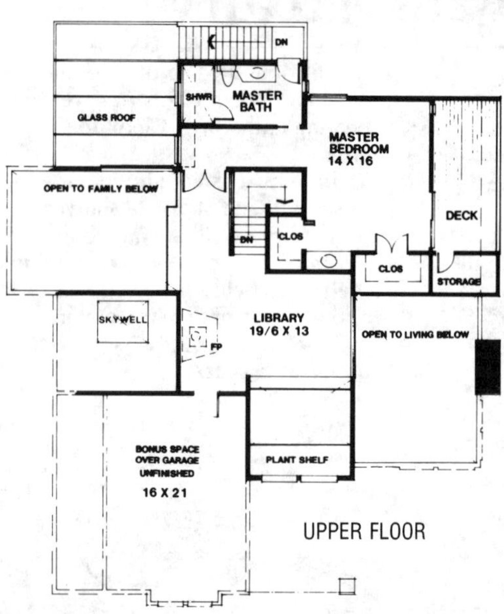

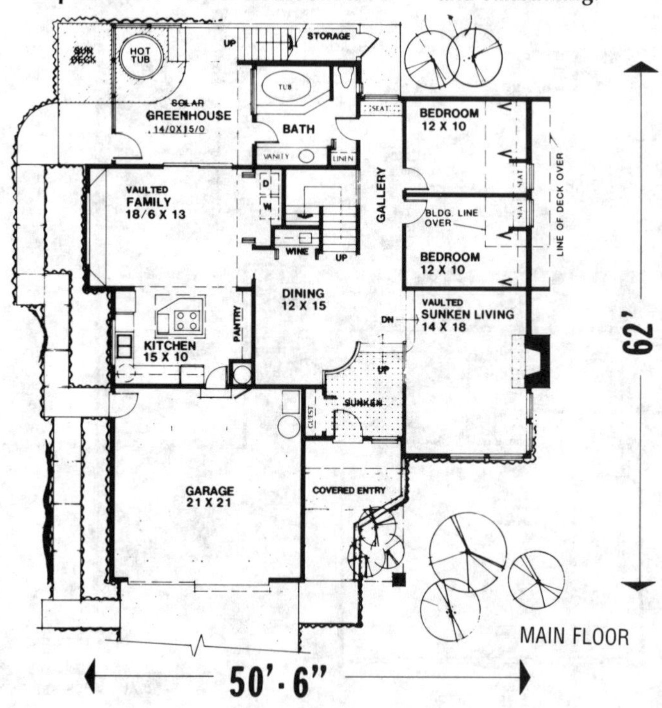

Plans S-8217 & -B	
Bedrooms: 3	**Baths:** 2
Space:	
Upper floor:	789 sq. ft.
Main floor:	1,709 sq. ft.
Total living area:	2,498 sq. ft.
Bonus area:	336 sq. ft.
Basement:	1,242 sq. ft.
Garage:	441 sq. ft.
Exterior Wall Framing:	2x6
Foundation options: Standard basement (Plan S-8217-B). Crawlspace (Plan S-8217). (Foundation & framing conversion diagram available — see order form.)	
Blueprint Price Code:	C

TO ORDER THIS BLUEPRINT, CALL TOLL-FREE 1-800-547-5570
(prices and details on pp. 12-15.)

Plan S-8217

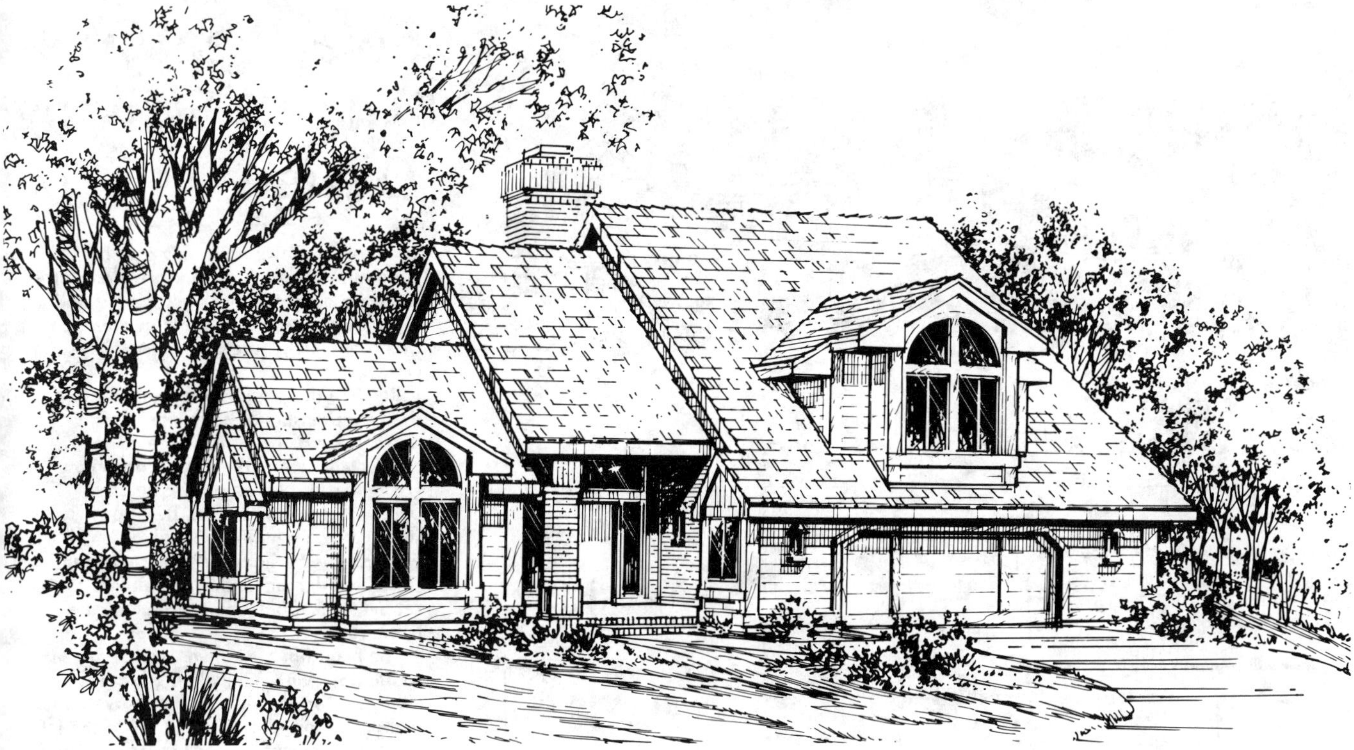

Spacious Great Room

This traditional home is designed for leisurely Great Room living. The main floor functions on an informal level for those enjoying entertaining without the fuss of maintaining a formal living room. The Great Room is partially vaulted to the balcony overhead. The home is planned along open space concepts to share light from adjacent rooms and areas.

Two generous bedrooms on the lower level are separated from the master suite which is located on the second level. The future bonus space can be finished as need arises.

The covered patio can be eliminated in favor of a two-story sunspace, accessible from the master bedroom and the lower level dining area.

This is a home for all seasons at a moderate size of 2,542 sq. ft. excluding the bonus space over the garage.

First floor:	1,632 sq. ft.
Second floor:	910 sq. ft.
Bonus space:	456 sq. ft.
Total living area: (Not counting garage or basement)	2,998 sq. ft.

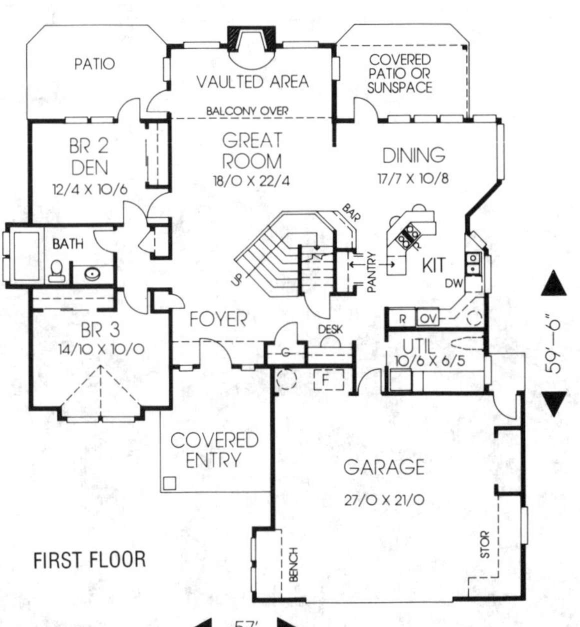

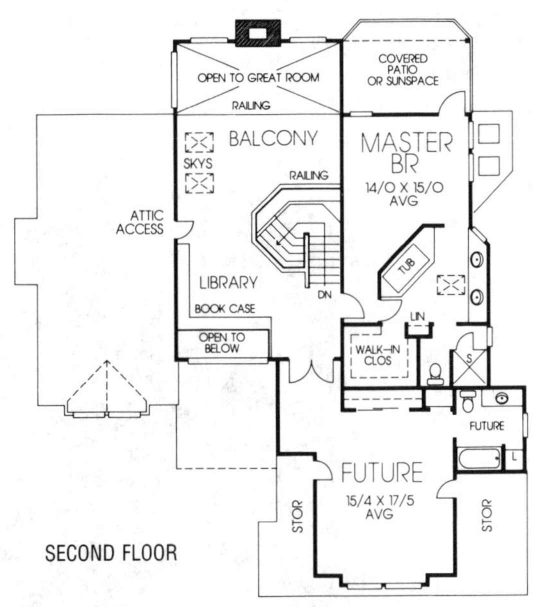

Exterior walls are 2x6 construction.
Specify basement or crawlspace foundation.

Blueprint Price Code D

Plan S-41389

TO ORDER THIS BLUEPRINT, CALL TOLL-FREE 1-800-547-5570
(prices and details on pp. 12-15.)

Solar Features Add to Striking Design

The passive sun room in this plan has a full window wall and glass roof oriented to the south for gathering the sun's energy, and a plank hardwood floor and large stone fireplace which store the heat for later release.

Because this area also is the living room, the windows should be equipped with moveable screens to make the room comfortable when the sun needs muting.

The master bedroom suite, in an upper-level loft of 757 sq. ft., also is warmed by a window wall aligned with the glass roof. An adjoining bath, closets and skylighted den make this a complete adult retreat, with a balcony overlooking the living room.

The main floor is zoned carefully for easy traffic flow, with family living areas and the kitchen off to the right of the entry and the bedroom wing on the left. Stairs to the loft and the basement are located at the center of the home.

Exterior walls feature 2x6 construction.

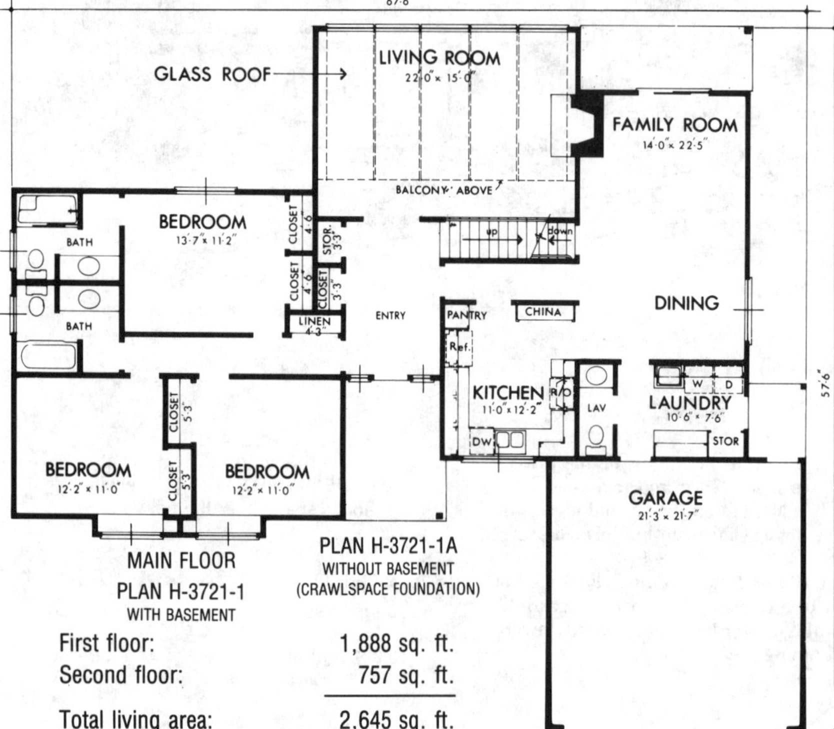

MAIN FLOOR
PLAN H-3721-1
WITH BASEMENT

PLAN H-3721-1A
WITHOUT BASEMENT
(CRAWLSPACE FOUNDATION)

First floor:	1,888 sq. ft.
Second floor:	757 sq. ft.
Total living area: (Not counting basement or garage)	2,645 sq. ft.

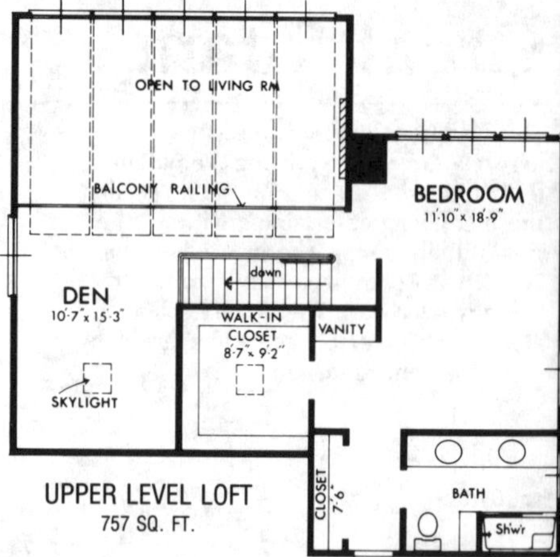

UPPER LEVEL LOFT
757 SQ. FT.

TO ORDER THIS BLUEPRINT, CALL TOLL-FREE 1-800-547-5570
(prices and details on pp. 12-15.)

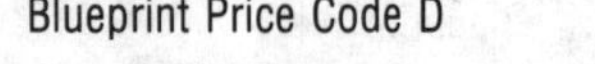

Blueprint Price Code D

Plans H-3721-1 & -1A

FRONT VIEW

Luxury on a Compact Foundation

Sky-lighted sloped ceilings, an intriguing stairway and overhead bridge and a carefully planned first floor arrangement combine to delight the senses as one explores this spacious 2737 sq. ft. home. A major element of the design is the luxurious master suite that is reached via the stairway and bridge. An abundance of closet space and an oversized bath are welcome features here.

Two bedrooms, generous bath facilities and a large family room provide lots of growing room for the younger members of the household.

All these features are available within a mere 36′ width which allows the house to be built on a 50′ wide lot — a real bonus these days.

Main floor:	1,044 sq. ft.
Upper level:	649 sq. ft.
Lower level:	1,044 sq. ft.
Total living area: (Not counting garage)	2,737 sq. ft.

(Exterior walls are 2x6 construction)

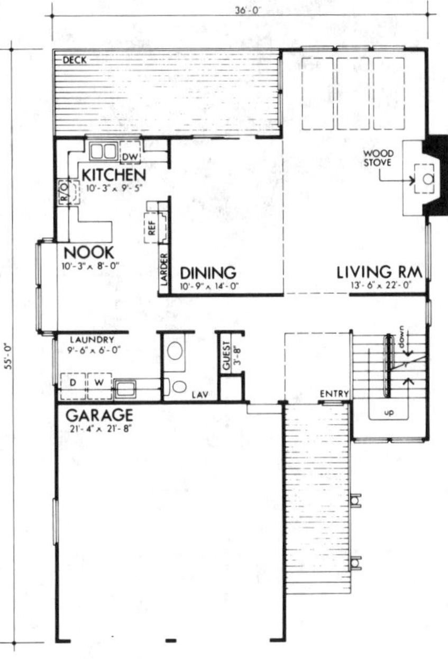

MAIN FLOOR
1044 SQUARE FEET

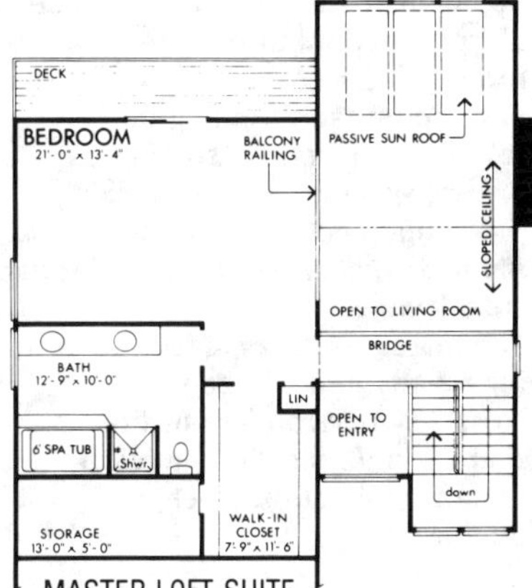

MASTER LOFT SUITE
649 SQUARE FEET

PATIO
FAMILY ROOM
13'-6" x 22'-0"
BEDROOM
10'-0" x 14'-0"
BEDROOM
10'-8" x 11'-8"
CLOSET 5'-0"
LIN
CLOSET 6'-6"
BATH
15'-6" x 5'-8"
WH
Tub w/ Shower
furnace
STORAGE
STOR
up

LOWER LEVEL
1044 SQUARE FEET

REAR VIEW

Blueprint Price Code D

Plan H-2110-1B

TO ORDER THIS BLUEPRINT, CALL TOLL-FREE 1-800-547-5570
(prices and details on pp. 12-15.)

Striking Octagonal Solarium

- The center of attraction in this dramatic design is the sunsoaking passive sun room. This 20′ diameter solarium reaches above the roofline to capture the most possible solar energy from any direction.
- For passive cooling, several of the vertical windows in the dome can be opened. The room also includes a "splash pool" to provide humidity in the winter.
- Then rooms surrounding the solarium are equally striking, as well as spacious and convenient, providing plenty of space for casual family living as well as more formal entertaining.
- The master suite includes a bath fit for royalty and a huge walk-in closet. Two secondary bedrooms share a large second bath with separate tub and shower and double sinks.

Plans H-3719-1 & -1A

Bedrooms: 3 **Baths:** 2½

Space:

Total living area: 3,166 sq. ft.
(Includes 324 sq. ft. sun room)
Basement (under bedrooms & family room): approx. 1,400 sq. ft.
Garage: 850 sq. ft.
Storage: 132 sq. ft.

Exterior Wall Framing: 2x6

Foundation options:
Partial basement (H-3719-1).
Crawlspace (H-3719-1A)
(Foundation & framing conversion diagram available — see order form.)

Blueprint Price Code: E

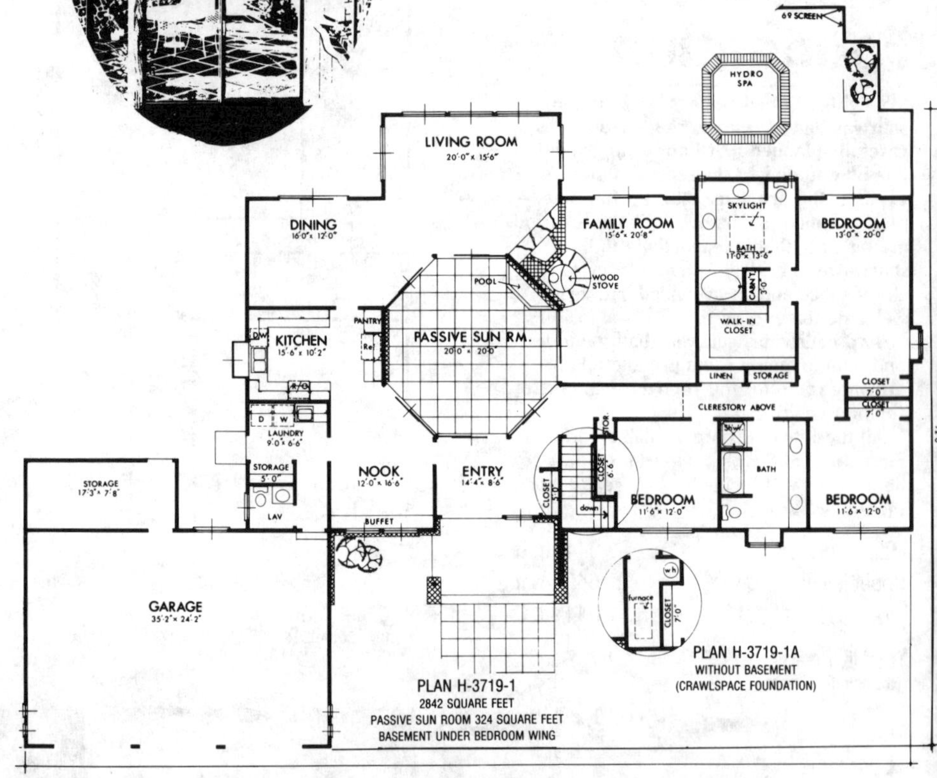

PLAN H-3719-1
2842 SQUARE FEET
PASSIVE SUN ROOM 324 SQUARE FEET
BASEMENT UNDER BEDROOM WING

PLAN H-3719-1A
WITHOUT BASEMENT
(CRAWLSPACE FOUNDATION)

Plans H-3719-1 & -1A

Versatile Garden/Sun Room

- A curved front-wrapping porch borders an octagonal dining area in this country home.
- Both the dining area and kitchen open to the Great Room, at the center of the floor plan; it features a rear fireplace, sloped ceiling and adjoining garden or sun room, also accessed through the garage.
- A generous-sized master bedroom is positioned at the rear of the home, with private luxury bath and walk-in closet.
- Two secondary bedrooms share a second full bath.
- Bonus attic space can be made into a game room, hobby area, study or additional bedrooms.

Plan DD-1852	
Bedrooms: 3	**Baths:** 2
Space:	
Main floor	1,852 sq. ft.
Total Living Area	**1,852 sq. ft.**
Basement	1,852 sq. ft.
Garage	528 sq. ft.
Exterior Wall Framing	2x4
Foundation options:	
Standard Basement	
Crawlspace	
Slab	
(Foundation & framing conversion diagram available—see order form.)	
Blueprint Price Code	B

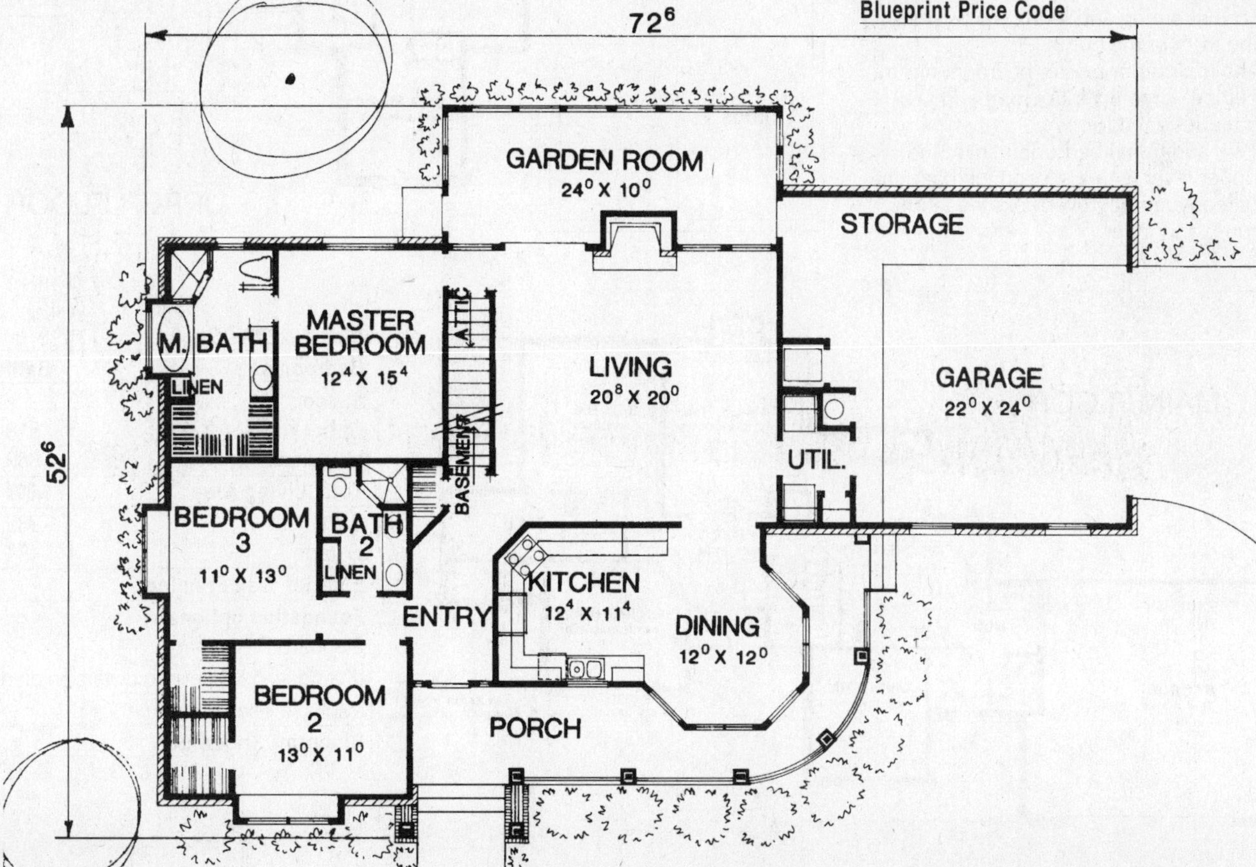

72^6
52^6
GARDEN ROOM 24^0 X 10^0
STORAGE
M. BATH
LINEN
MASTER BEDROOM 12^4 X 15^4
ATTIC
LIVING 20^8 X 20^0
GARAGE 22^0 X 24^0
UTIL.
BASEMENT
BEDROOM 3 11^0 X 13^0
BATH 2
LINEN
KITCHEN 12^4 X 11^4
ENTRY
DINING 12^0 X 12^0
BEDROOM 2 13^0 X 11^0
PORCH

NEW RELEASE

Plan DD-1852

TO ORDER THIS BLUEPRINT, CALL TOLL-FREE 1-800-547-5570
(prices and details on pp. 12-15.)

Spacious and Open

- A brilliant, sunken family room with rear fireplace, backyard access and vaulted ceiling is found at the center of this open floor plan.
- A cozy dinette with rear sliders and roomy island kitchen merge with the family room, creating a spacious, open atmosphere.
- Formal dining and living rooms share the front of the home.
- The main-floor master bedroom has tray ceiling, large walk-in closet and lavish bath designed for two.
- Two additional bedrooms share the upper level with a second full bath; the balcony landing overlooks the family room and foyer.

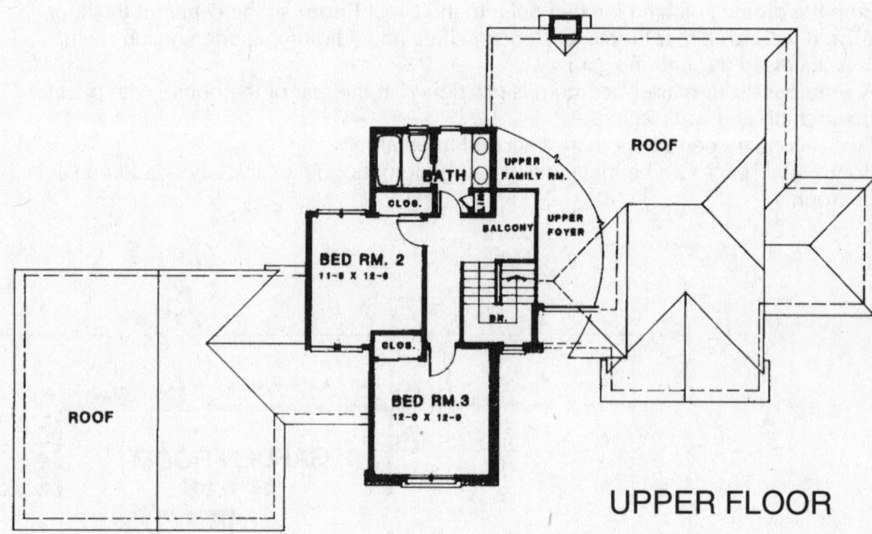

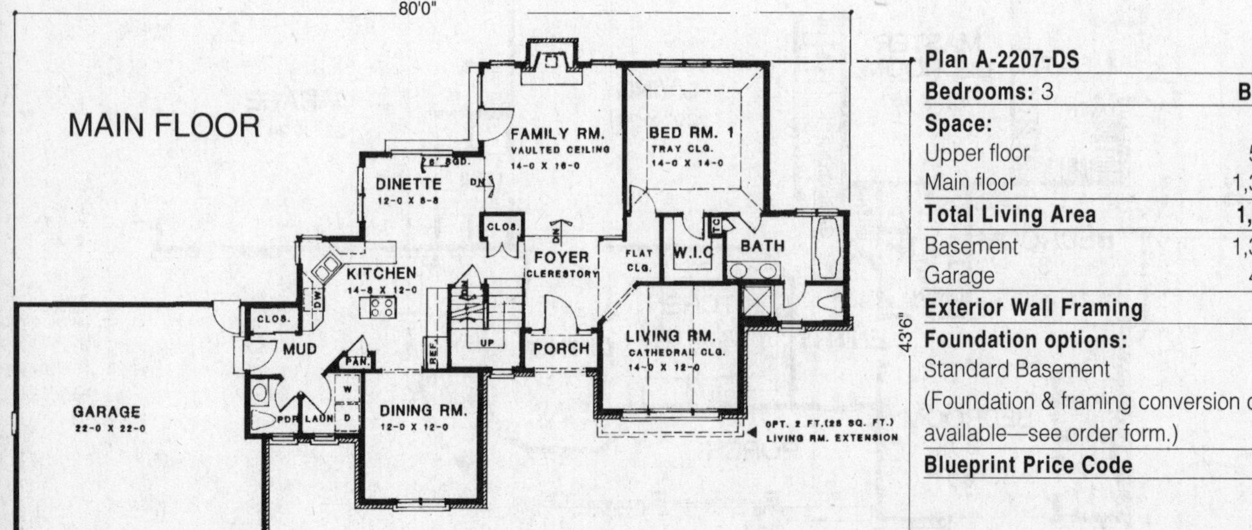

Plan A-2207-DS	
Bedrooms: 3	**Baths:** 2 ½
Space:	
Upper floor	518 sq. ft.
Main floor	1,389 sq. ft.
Total Living Area	**1,907 sq. ft.**
Basement	1,389 sq. ft.
Garage	484 sq. ft.
Exterior Wall Framing	2x6
Foundation options:	
Standard Basement	
(Foundation & framing conversion diagram available—see order form.)	
Blueprint Price Code	B

TO ORDER THIS BLUEPRINT, CALL TOLL-FREE 1-800-547-5570
(prices and details on pp. 12-15.)

Plan A-2207-DS

NEW RELEASE

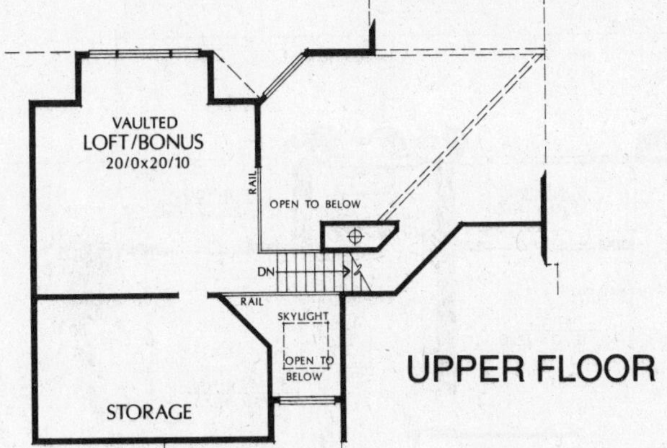

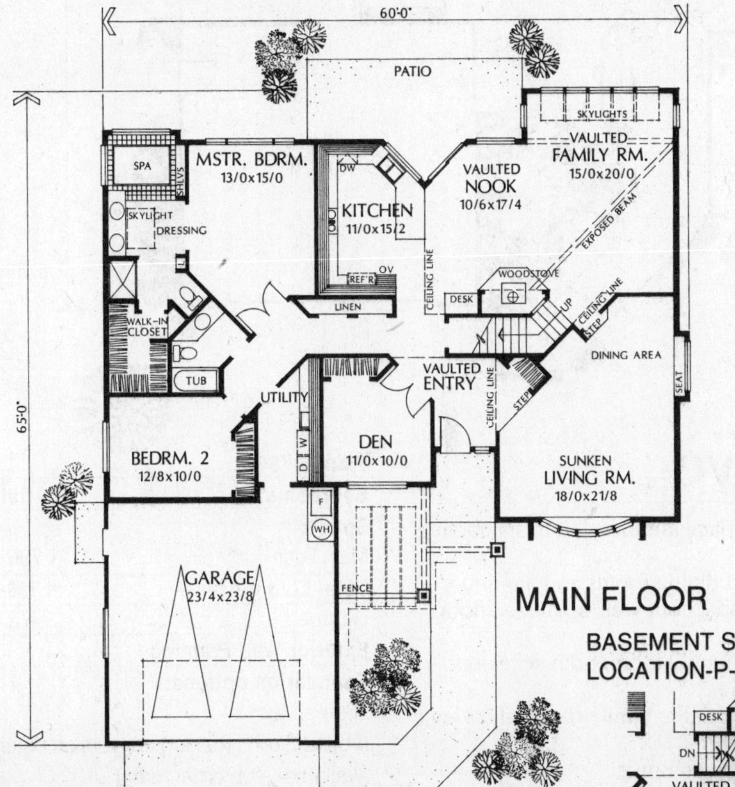

BASEMENT STAIR LOCATION-P-7721-4D

Versatile Contemporary

- Sleek and contemporary, this versatile design can accommodate two to four bedrooms.
- The upper level offers a large vaulted bonus area that overlooks the family room and nook; it could be used as a playroom, office or extra sleeping room.
- The main level begins with a vaulted, skylit entry; to the right is a sunken formal living room with dining area and window seat.
- The vaulted family room has wood stove, exposed beam, rear sun area and adjoining nook and kitchen.
- The master bedroom opens with double doors; it features a skylit dressing area with dual vanities, walk-in closet and garden spa tub.

Plan P-7721-4A and Plan P-7721-4D

Bedrooms: 2-4	**Baths:** 2
Space:	
Upper floor	415 sq. ft.
Main floor	2,175 sq. ft.
Storage	275 sq. ft.
Total Living Area	**2,865 sq. ft.**
Basement	2,175 sq. ft.
Garage	552 sq. ft.
Exterior Wall Framing	2x6
Foundation options:	Plan #
Daylight Basement	P-7721-4D
Crawlspace	P-7721-4A
(Foundation & framing conversion diagram available—see order form.)	
Blueprint Price Code	D

NEW RELEASE

Plans P-7721-4A and P-7721-4D

TO ORDER THIS BLUEPRINT, CALL TOLL-FREE 1-800-547-5570
(prices and details on pp. 12-15.)

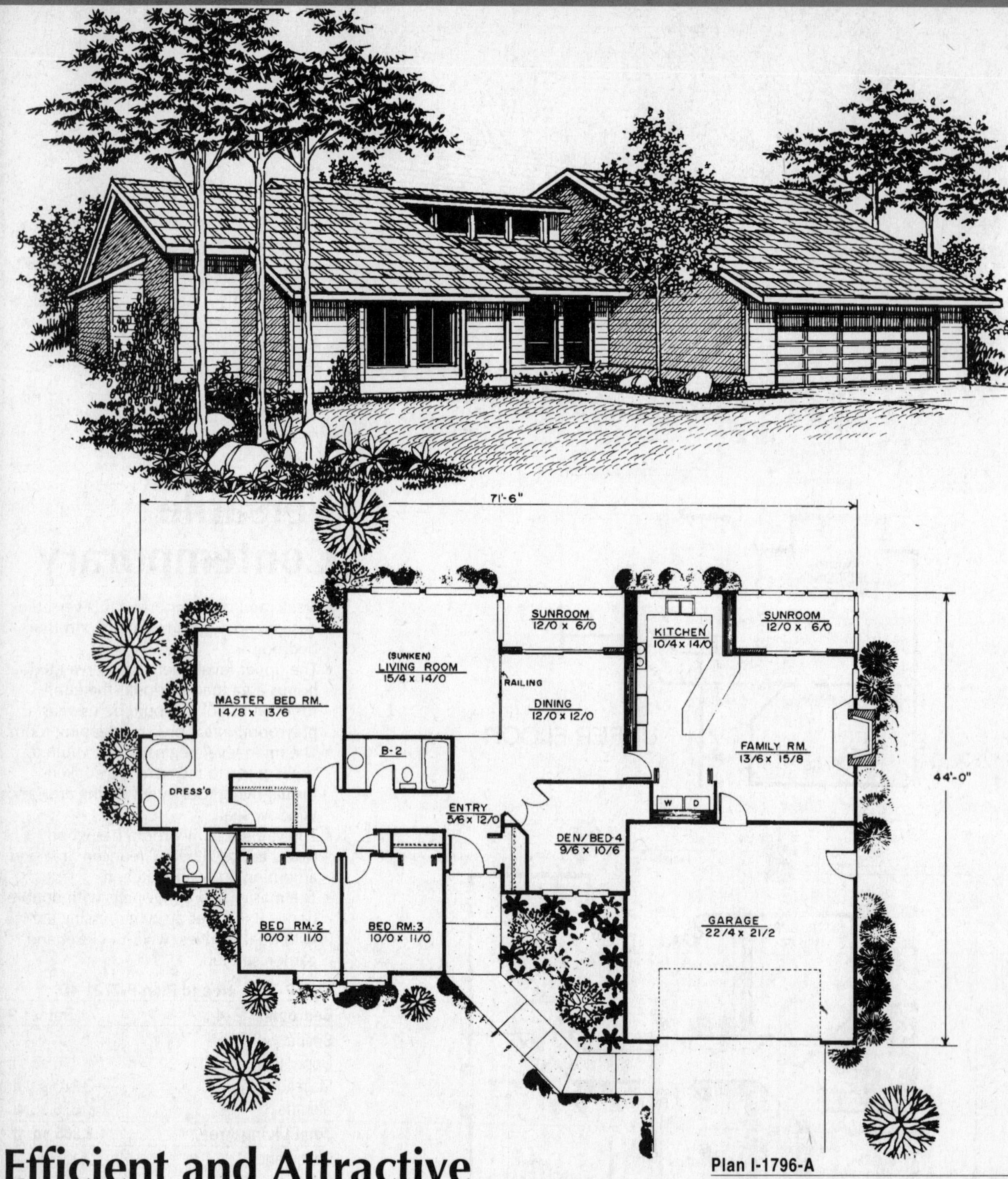

Efficient and Attractive

- Solar efficiency, practicality and economical use of space are found in this attractive ranch, and all under 1,800 square feet.
- A choice of three or four bedrooms, formal living and dining rooms and a unique combination kitchen and family room share this compact but well-organized floor plan.
- Sun rooms are attached to both the dining room and family room, both accessed through sliding doors.
- Only a functional counter bar separates the kitchen from the family room, allowing a view of the fireplace and on-going activities.
- A washer/dryer is convenient to the kitchen and garage entrance.

Plan I-1796-A	
Bedrooms: 3-4	**Baths:** 2
Space:	
Main floor	1,796 sq. ft.
Total Living Area	**1,796 sq. ft.**
Garage	473 sq. ft.
Exterior Wall Framing	2x6
Foundation options:	
Crawlspace	
(Foundation & framing conversion diagram available—see order form.)	
Blueprint Price Code	**B**

TO ORDER THIS BLUEPRINT, CALL TOLL-FREE 1-800-547-5570
(prices and details on pp. 12-15.)

Plan I-1796-A

NEW RELEASE

Interior Bridge Joins Loft

- Repeating front gables, a half-round transom, brick detailing and a covered front porch offer an inviting look to this 1 1/2 story home.
- The inside entry reveals a two-story, vaulted space and an interior bridge to the upper loft area that overlooks the entry and living room.
- Columns adorn the entrance to the adjoining dining room, which overlooks a large, side deck.
- The roomy kitchen opens to a sunny breakfast area with patio doors to the deck.
- Also on the main floor is the vaulted master bedroom with corner window, dual walk-in closets and a vaulted bath with twin vanities and garden tub.

Br2 12x11
Open to Living Rm
Loft
Br3 11x11-4
DN
Open to Entry
Plant Shelf

UPPER FLOOR

REAR VIEW

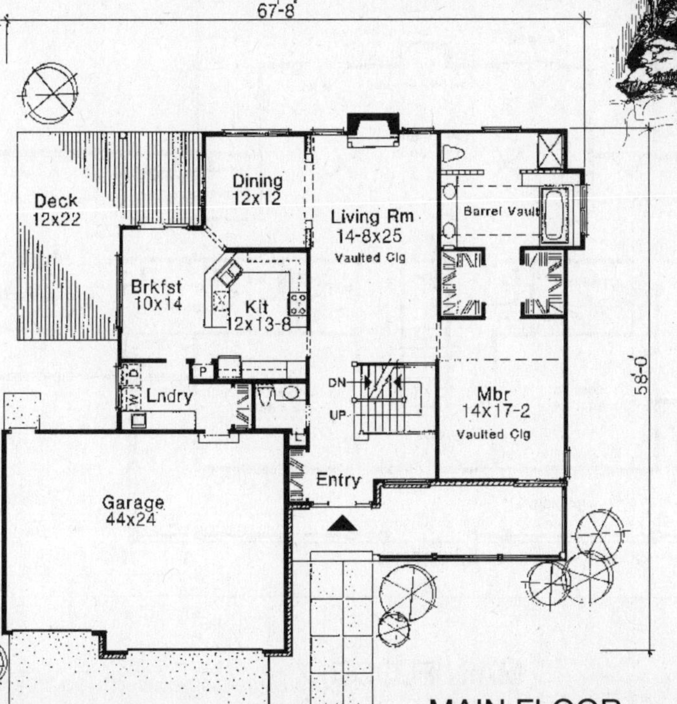

MAIN FLOOR

Plan UDG-91001	
Bedrooms: 3	**Baths:** 2 ½
Space:	
Upper floor	503 sq. ft.
Main floor	1,781 sq. ft.
Total Living Area	**2,284 sq. ft.**
Basement	1,781 sq. ft.
Garage	1,056 sq. ft.
Exterior Wall Framing	2x4
Foundation options:	
Standard Basement	
(Foundation & framing conversion diagram available—see order form.)	
Blueprint Price Code	**C**

NEW RELEASE

Plan UDG-91001

TO ORDER THIS BLUEPRINT, CALL TOLL-FREE 1-800-547-5570
(prices and details on pp. 12-15.)

Open Floor Plan Enjoys Outdoors

- Luxurious family living begins with a spectacular central Great Room; a fireplace is flanked by double doors that access the large wrapping rear porch.
- Casual dining can take place in the adjoining breakfast nook or island kitchen, with snack bar; access to a convenient laundry room, plus the front porch and rear veranda is also offered in the kitchen.
- Formal dining and living rooms flank the foyer.
- For privacy, you'll find the master suite on the main floor; it features a spacious walk-in closet and large bath with dual vanities, whirlpool tub and separate shower.
- Two extra bedrooms, each with personal dressing areas, share the upper level.

Plan VL-3038	
Bedrooms: 3	**Baths:** 2 ½
Space:	
Upper floor	836 sq. ft.
Main floor	2,202 sq. ft.
Total Living Area	**3,038 sq. ft.**
Exterior Wall Framing	2x4
Foundation options:	
Crawlspace	
Slab	
(Foundation & framing conversion diagram available—see order form.)	
Blueprint Price Code	**E**

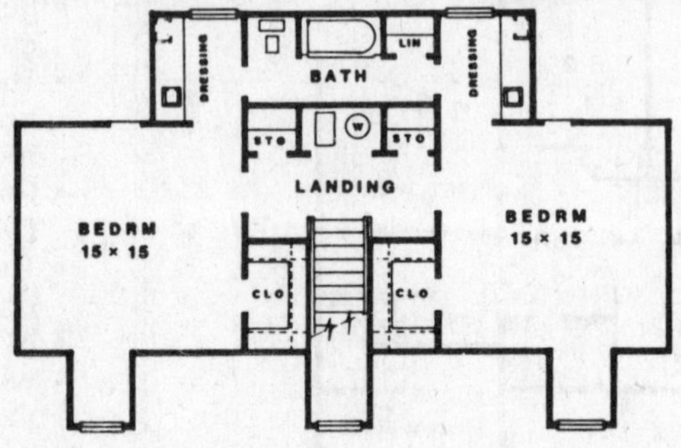

UPPER FLOOR

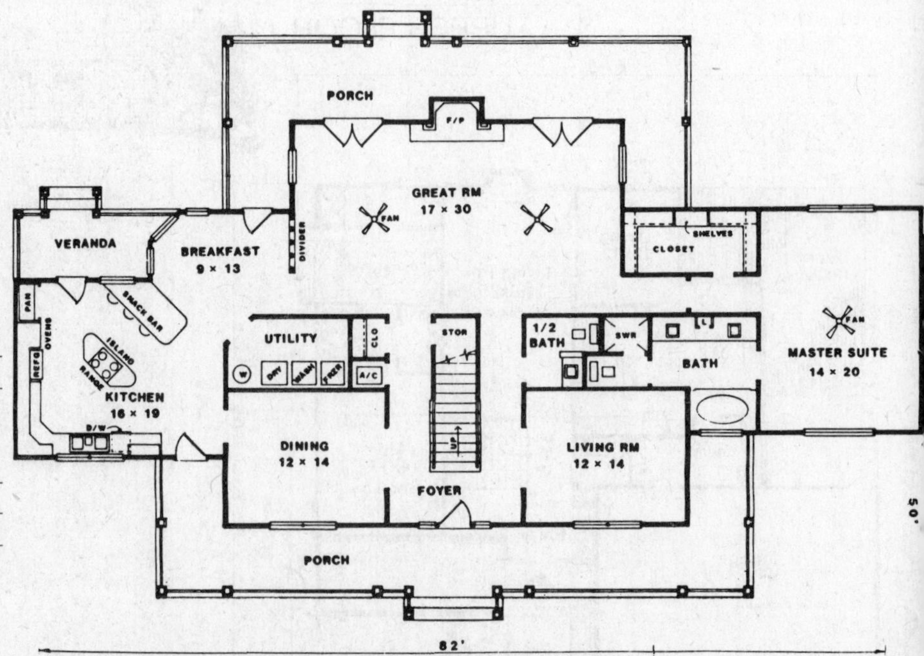

MAIN FLOOR

TO ORDER THIS BLUEPRINT,
CALL TOLL-FREE 1-800-547-5570
(prices and details on pp. 12-15.)

Plan VL-3038

NEW RELEASE

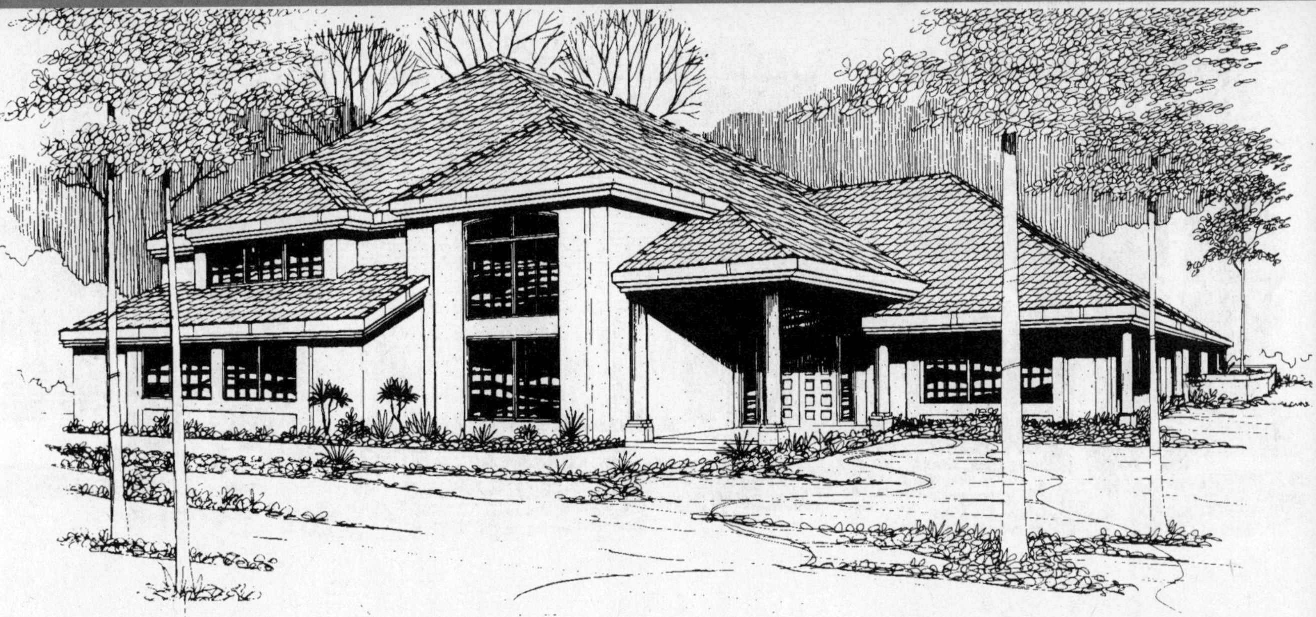

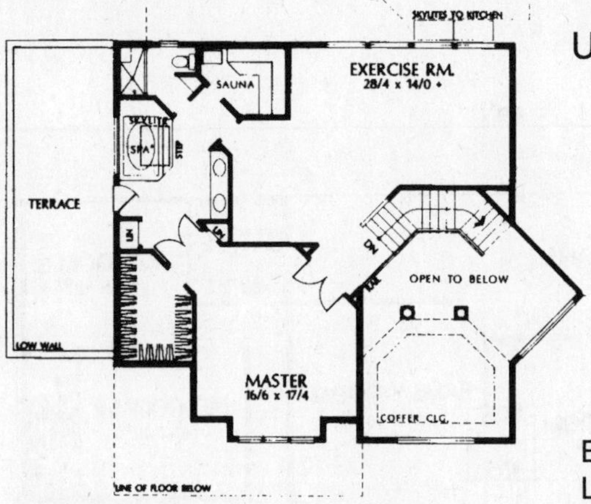

UPPER FLOOR

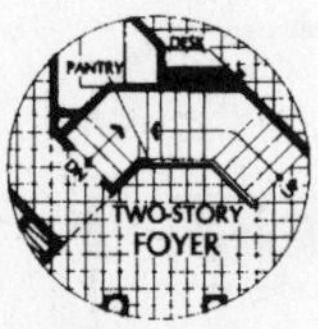

BASEMENT STAIR LOCATION-P-7723-3D

MAIN FLOOR

Southwestern Offers Two Master Suites

- Southwestern elegance is brought to mind in this stucco, four-bedroom villa.
- Two master suites are offered, one on the main level with private patio and garden spa tub, and the other on the upper level with personal exercise room, terrace and sauna.
- An informal family room with fireplace, a breakfast nook with eating bar, and a skylit kitchen with pantry and island cooktop overlook the rear covered patio.
- Formal sunken dining and living rooms flank the two-story foyer.
- Main-floor laundry facilities and a three-car garage are extras.

Plan P-7723-3A and P-7723-3D

Bedrooms: 4	**Baths:** 3 ½
Space:	
Upper floor	1,206 sq. ft.
Main floor	2,902 sq. ft.
Total Living Area	**4,108 sq. ft.**
Basement	2,902 sq. ft.
Garage	752 sq. ft.
Exterior Wall Framing	2x6
Foundation options:	**Plan #**
Daylight Basement	P-7723-3D
Crawlspace	P-7723-3A
(Foundation & framing conversion diagram available—see order form.)	
Blueprint Price Code	G

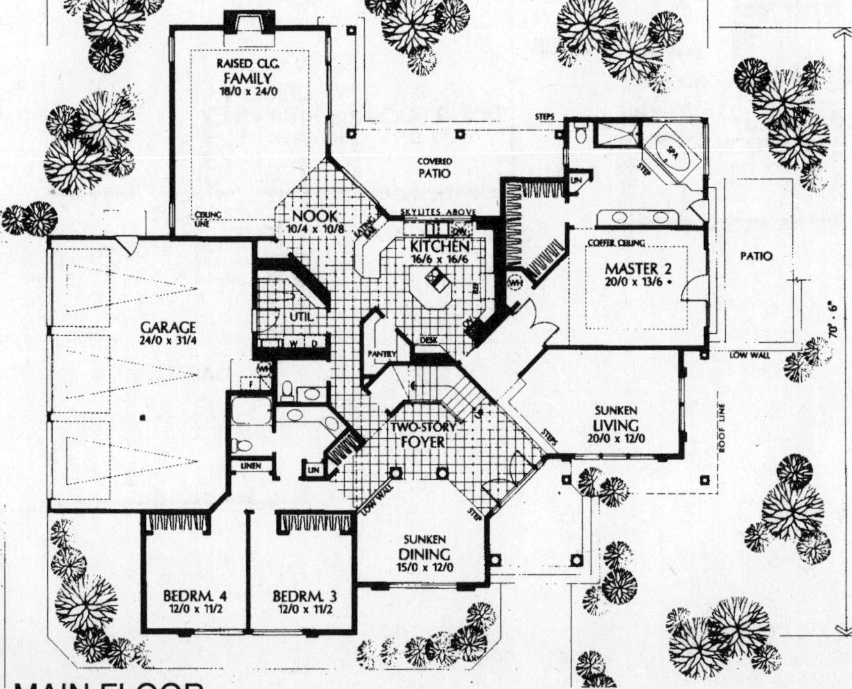

HomeStyles SOURCE 1 Designers Network

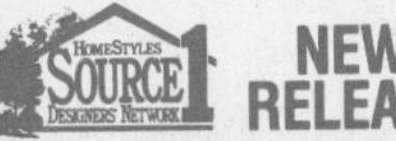

NEW RELEASE

Plans P-7723-3A and P-7723-3D

TO ORDER THIS BLUEPRINT, CALL TOLL-FREE 1-800-547-5570
(prices and details on pp. 12-15.)

Large Living, Family Room

- At the center of this elegant one-story is a large, open living and family area with see-thru fireplace, step-down entry, wet bar, rear window wall and exciting attached lanai.
- A sunny morning room and island kitchen join the family room on the opposite side; formal dining can take place in the dining room nearby.
- The sleeping rooms are split, with the master at the rear left; it offers a beautiful bay window, lavish private bath and huge walk-in closet.
- Two additional bedrooms are secluded to the rear right; an extra guest bedroom has a private bath.

Plan DD-3002	
Bedrooms: 4	**Baths:** 3
Space:	
Main floor	2,928 sq. ft.
Total Living Area	**2,928 sq. ft.**
Basement	2,280 sq. ft.
Garage and Storage	593 sq. ft.
Exterior Wall Framing	2x4
Foundation options:	
Partial Basement	
Crawlspace	
Slab	
(Foundation & framing conversion diagram available—see order form.)	
Blueprint Price Code	D

80 11

LANAI

BATH 2

BEDROOM 3
13 8 X 12 0

LINEN

MASTER SUITE
14 8 X 17 8

FAMILY ROOM
18 0 X 18 0

LIVING ROOM
18 4 X 18 0

BEDROOM 2
14 0 X 12 0

M. BATH

LINEN

MORNING
14 4 X 10 0

76 6

FOYER

PANTRY

G. BATH

DINING ROOM
14 8 X 12 6

ISLAND KITCHEN
14 0 X 12 6

GUEST BEDROOM
12 4 X 12 8

PORCH

UTILITY

STORAGE

GARAGE

TO ORDER THIS BLUEPRINT, CALL TOLL-FREE 1-800-547-5570
(prices and details on pp. 12-15.)

Plan DD-3002

NEW RELEASE

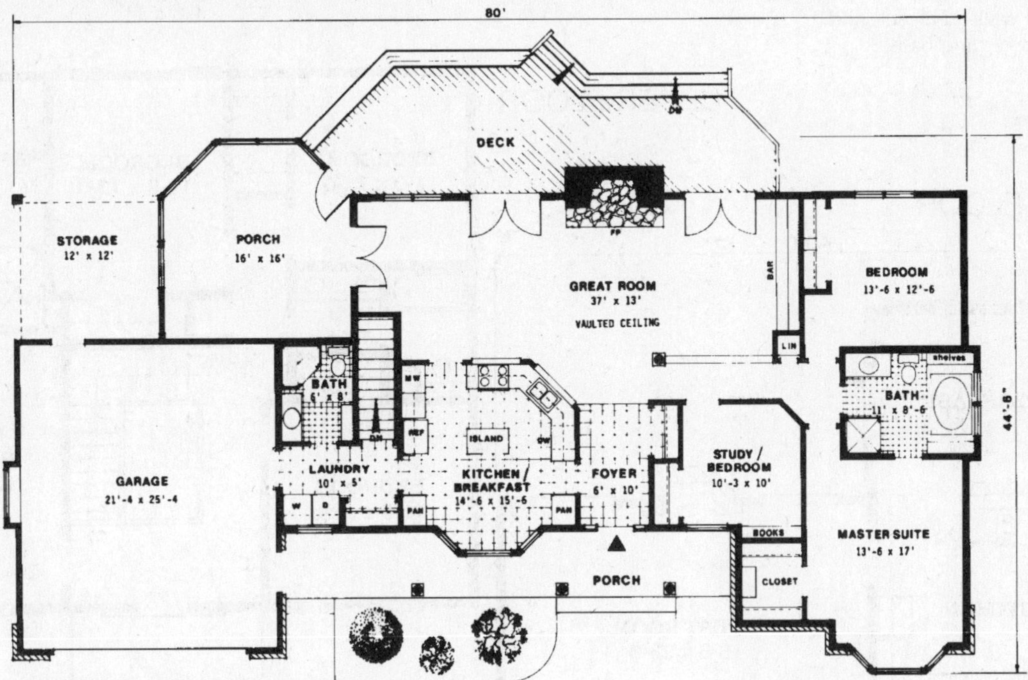

Spectacular Great Room Overlooks Rear Deck

- An inviting covered porch welcomes you inside this stylish ranch.
- Inside, your attention is drawn to a spectacular Great Room; nearly 500 square feet of relaxing, activity or entertaining space is offered, as is a stone fireplace flanked by French doors that open to a large, rear deck, an attached three-season porch and built-in bar.
- A bayed informal eating area, work island and dual pantries highlight the modern kitchen, also with nearby laundry room and bath.
- A bayed master suite, a second bedroom and a study or third bedroom complete the floor plan.

Plan CPS-1156	
Bedrooms: 2-3	**Baths:** 2
Space:	
Main floor	1,770 sq. ft.
Total Living Area	**1,770 sq. ft.**
Basement	1,770 sq. ft.
Garage	540 sq. ft.
Exterior Wall Framing	2x6
Foundation options:	
Standard Basement	
(Foundation & framing conversion diagram available—see order form.)	
Blueprint Price Code	B

NEW RELEASE

Plan CPS-1156

TO ORDER THIS BLUEPRINT, CALL TOLL-FREE 1-800-547-5570

(prices and details on pp.12-15.)

A Touch of Greece

- Modern additions update this Greek-styled two-story.
- Ten-foot ceilings are found throughout the home.
- The main floor offers a large central Great Room with fireplace; the open arrangement also features formal living and dining rooms that flank the foyer and stairway.
- A spacious kitchen with counter bar and sunny breakfast room joins the Great Room for efficient entertainment and casual dining occasions.
- All four bedrooms are found on the upper level, the master with generous, side-by-side walk-in closets and separate shower and bath.

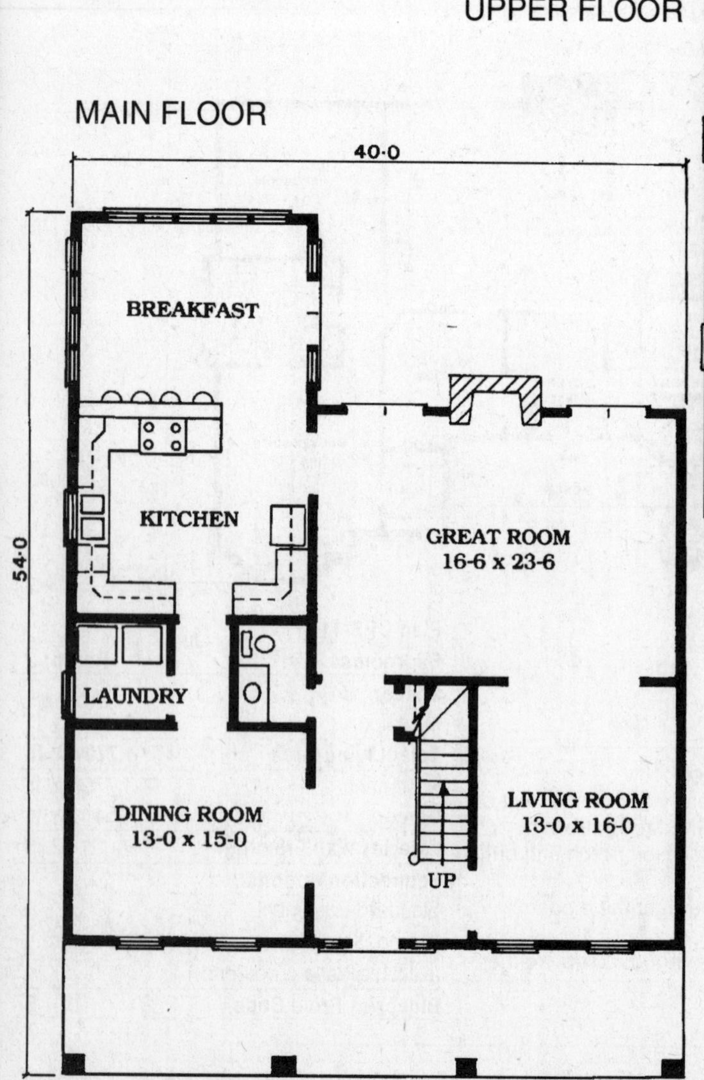

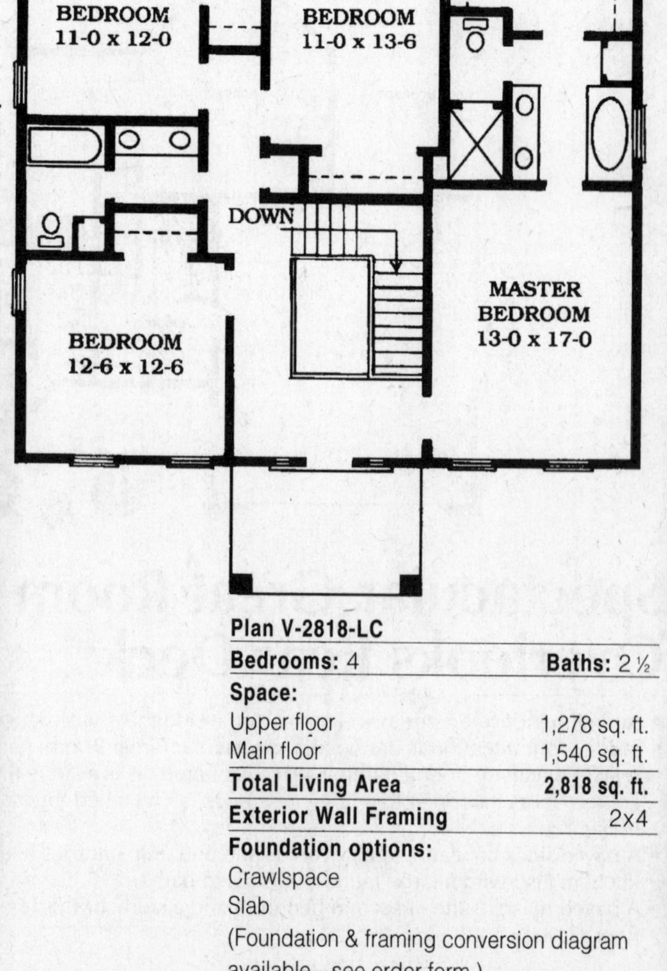

Plan V-2818-LC	
Bedrooms: 4	**Baths:** 2 ½
Space:	
Upper floor	1,278 sq. ft.
Main floor	1,540 sq. ft.
Total Living Area	**2,818 sq. ft.**
Exterior Wall Framing	2x4
Foundation options:	
Crawlspace	
Slab	
(Foundation & framing conversion diagram available—see order form.)	
Blueprint Price Code	D

TO ORDER THIS BLUEPRINT, CALL TOLL-FREE 1-800-547-5570
(prices and details on pp. 12-15.)

Plan V-2818-LC

NEW RELEASE

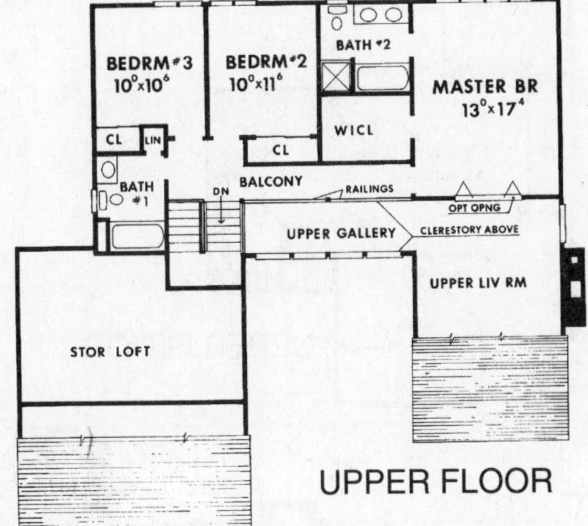

UPPER FLOOR

Rear-Oriented Contemporary

- This sleek contemporary design offers an open floor plan that complements the outdoors.
- A rustic exterior, clerestory windows above the entryway and rear-oriented rooms with views are other attractions.
- The spacious formal living room at the front of the home has a fireplace and cathedral ceiling.
- Laundry facilities are conveniently located near the garage entrance on the main floor.
- The upper level accommodates three bedrooms; the master has an optional balcony opening to view the living room below.

Plan AX-98381	
Bedrooms: 3	**Baths:** 2 ½
Space:	
Upper floor	800 sq. ft.
Main floor	1,120 sq. ft.
Total Living Area	**1,920 sq. ft.**
Basement	1,120 sq. ft.
Garage	400 sq. ft.
Exterior Wall Framing	2x4
Foundation options:	
Standard Basement	
Slab	
(Foundation & framing conversion diagram available—see order form.)	
Blueprint Price Code	B

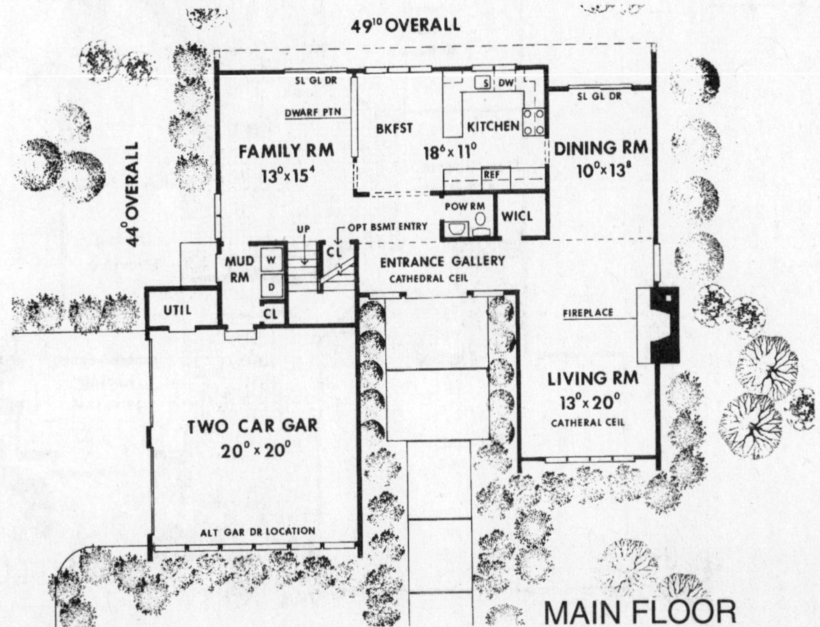

MAIN FLOOR

NEW RELEASE

Plan AX-98381

TO ORDER THIS BLUEPRINT, CALL TOLL-FREE 1-800-547-5570
(prices and details on pp. 12-15.)

Executive Flair

- Contemporary flair is found throughout this five-bedroom executive home.
- At the center of the main floor plan is a spacious island kitchen and nook with bayed eating area, corner window and convenient access on three sides.
- A sunken family room with fireplace is located at one end of the kitchen, the formal dining room and sunken living room with fireplace and vaulted ceiling, at the other.
- Three over-sized bedrooms, a large bonus room for a play room or media center and an extravagant master suite with windowed sitting area and private bath share the upper level.
- An optional fifth bedroom or den on the main floor has a nearby bath.

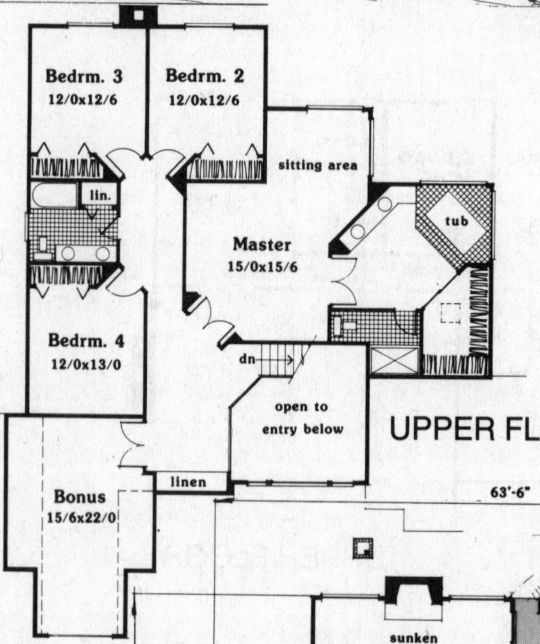

Plan R-2057	
Bedrooms: 4-5	**Baths:** 2½
Space:	
Upper floor	1,532 sq. ft.
Main floor	1,781 sq. ft.
Total Living Area	**3,313 sq. ft.**
Bonus	316 sq. ft.
Garage	740 sq. ft.
Exterior Wall Framing	2x4
Foundation options:	
Crawlspace	
(Foundation & framing conversion diagram available—see order form.)	
Blueprint Price Code	E

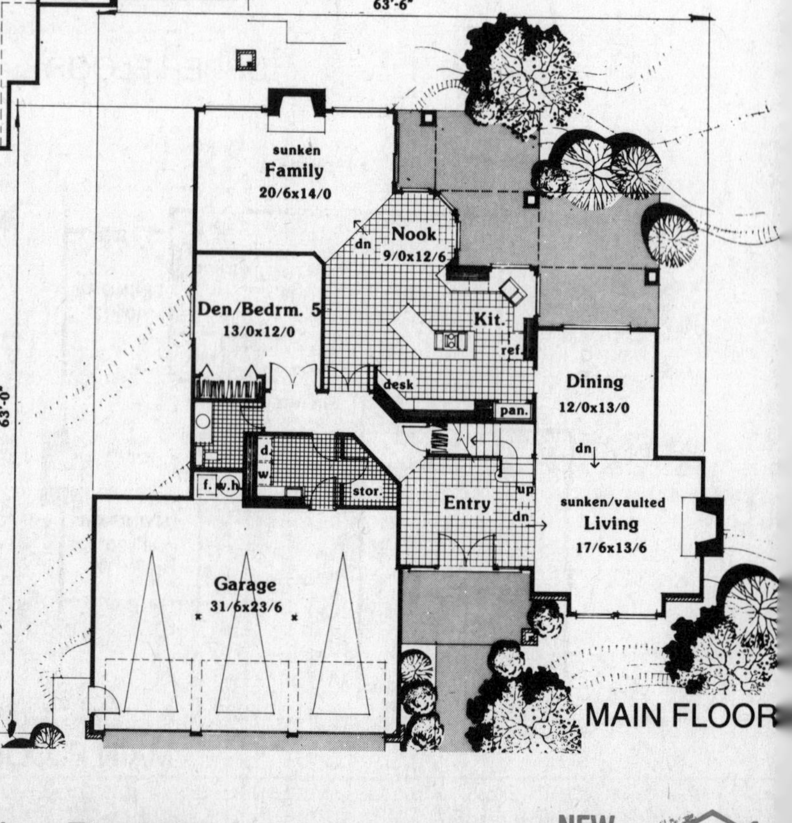

Bedrm. 3 12/0x12/6
Bedrm. 2 12/0x12/6
sitting area
lin.
tub
Master 15/0x15/6
Bedrm. 4 12/0x13/0
dn
open to entry below
Bonus 15/6x22/0
linen

UPPER FLOOR

63'-6"

sunken Family 20/6x14/0
Nook 9/0x12/6
dn
Den/Bedrm. 5 13/0x12/0
Kit.
ref.
desk
pan.
Dining 12/0x13/0
dn
d. w.
f. w.h.
stor.
Entry
up
dn
sunken/vaulted Living 17/6x13/6
Garage 31/6x23/6
63'-0"

MAIN FLOOR

TO ORDER THIS BLUEPRINT, CALL TOLL-FREE 1-800-547-5570
(prices and details on pp. 12-15.)

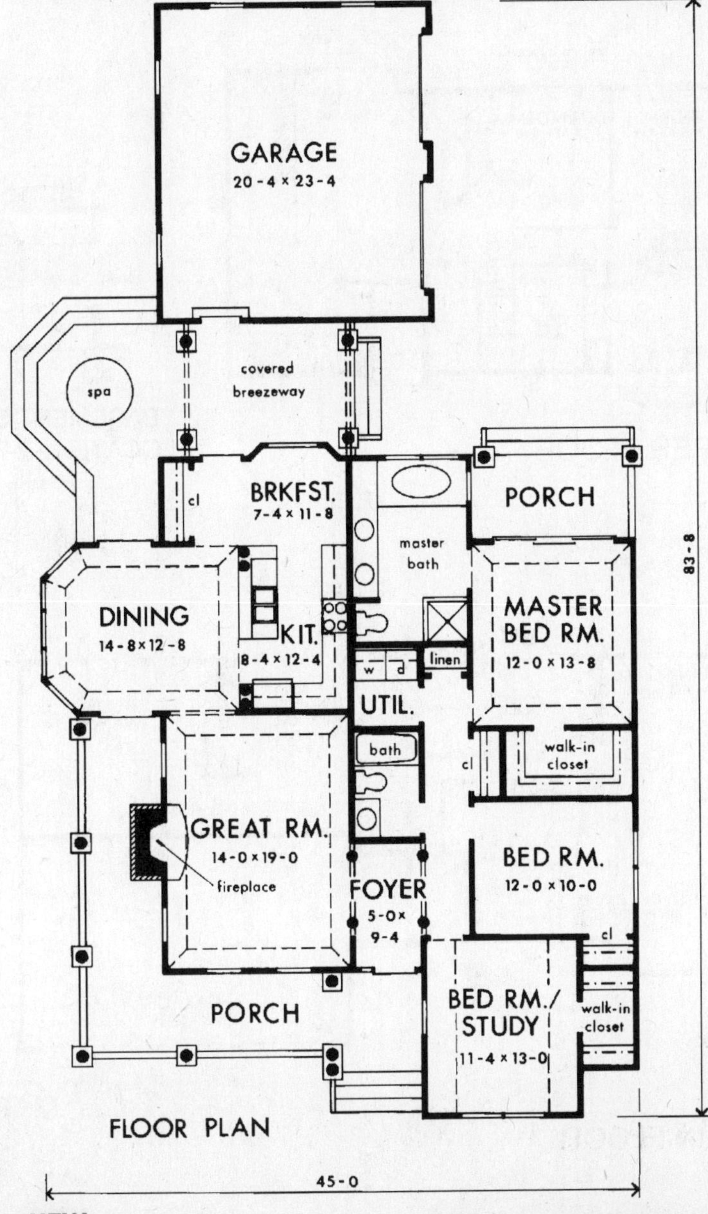

Narrow Home Goes Long Way

- This narrow three-bedroom home offers elegant round columns in the foyer and a two-sided porch and half-round windows on the exterior.
- Tray ceilings are found in the Great Room, dining room and master bedroom.
- The study or extra bedroom offers a vaulted ceiling to accentuate the large arched front window.
- The open kitchen layout conveniently services the breakfast area, dining room and attached deck.
- The secluded master bedroom has a private covered porch, walk-in closet and private bath with windowed whirlpool tub, double vanities and separate shower.

Plan DG-251

Bedrooms: 2-3 **Baths:** 2

Space:r

Main floor	1,608 sq. ft.
Total Living Area	**1,608 sq. ft.**
Garage	474 sq. ft.
Exterior Wall Framing	2x4

Foundation options:
Crawlspace
(Foundation & framing conversion diagram available—see order form.)

Blueprint Price Code B

TO ORDER THIS BLUEPRINT, CALL TOLL-FREE 1-800-547-5570
(prices and details on pp. 12-15.)

NEW RELEASE

Plan DG-251

Master Suite with Fireplace, Deck

- This brick-accented two-story has front stacked bay windows, a three-car garage and staggered rooflines.
- Inside you'll find large, open living areas oriented to the rear and fireplaces in the living room, sunken family room and master bedroom.
- Both the family room and study open out to a rear patio; the island kitchen and bayed nook join the family room, which also offers a wet bar.
- Room for two to three bedrooms plus the master suite with private deck and lavish, skylit spa bath is found on the upper level.

Plan P-7751-3A and P-7751-3D	
Bedrooms: 3-4	**Baths:** 2 ½
Space:	
Upper floor	1,411 sq. ft.
Main floor	1,737 sq. ft.
Total Living Area	**3,148 sq. ft.**
Basement	1,737 sq. ft.
Garage	677 sq. ft.
Exterior Wall Framing	2x6
Foundation options:	**Plan #**
Daylight Basement	P-7751-3D
Crawlspace	P-7751-3A
(Foundation & framing conversion diagram available—see order form.)	
Blueprint Price Code	E

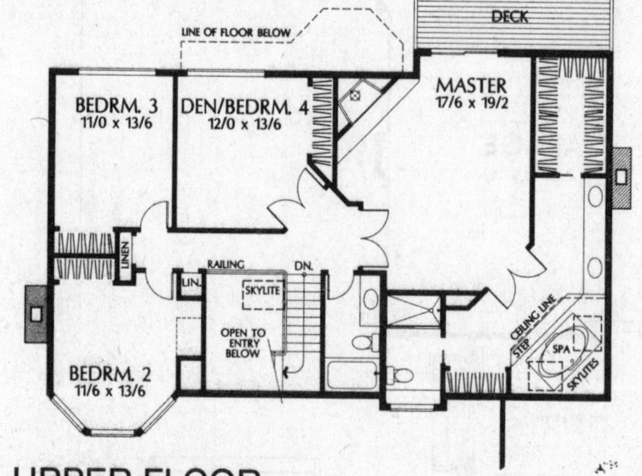

UPPER FLOOR

LIV.RM.
ENTRY
DESK
DN.
UP
W
D

BASEMENT STAIR LOCATION-P-7751-3D

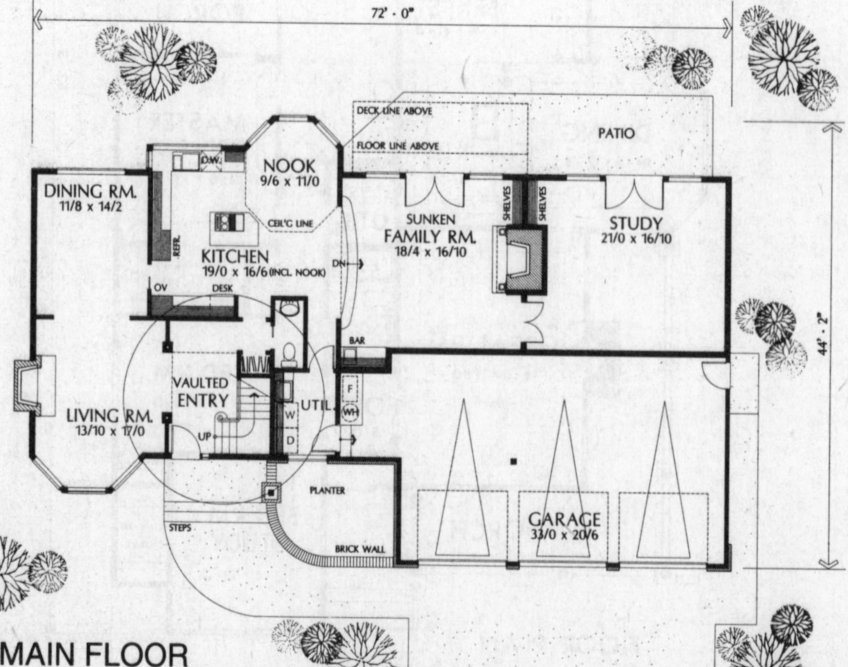

MAIN FLOOR

TO ORDER THIS BLUEPRINT, CALL TOLL-FREE 1-800-547-5570
(prices and details on pp. 12-15.)

Plans P-7751-3A and P-7751-3D

NEW RELEASE

Unique In and Out

- A variety of staggered rooflines give this transitional home an interesting and unique exterior.
- A huge family room, island kitchen and bayed nook combination share an open, sunny atmosphere with fireplace, wet bar and attached rear deck.
- Off the two-story foyer is a vaulted den or guest room; double doors, a closet and nearby half-bath are featured.
- A formal sunken living room with corner window and a dining room with private deck face one another off the foyer.
- Upper-level highlights include two conventional bedrooms, a large bonus area and a spectacular master bedroom with private deck, oversized spa tub in a bay window, and a dressing area.

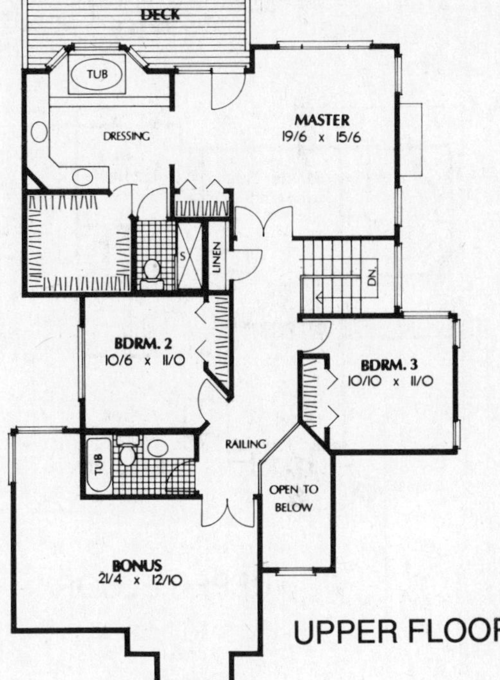

UPPER FLOOR

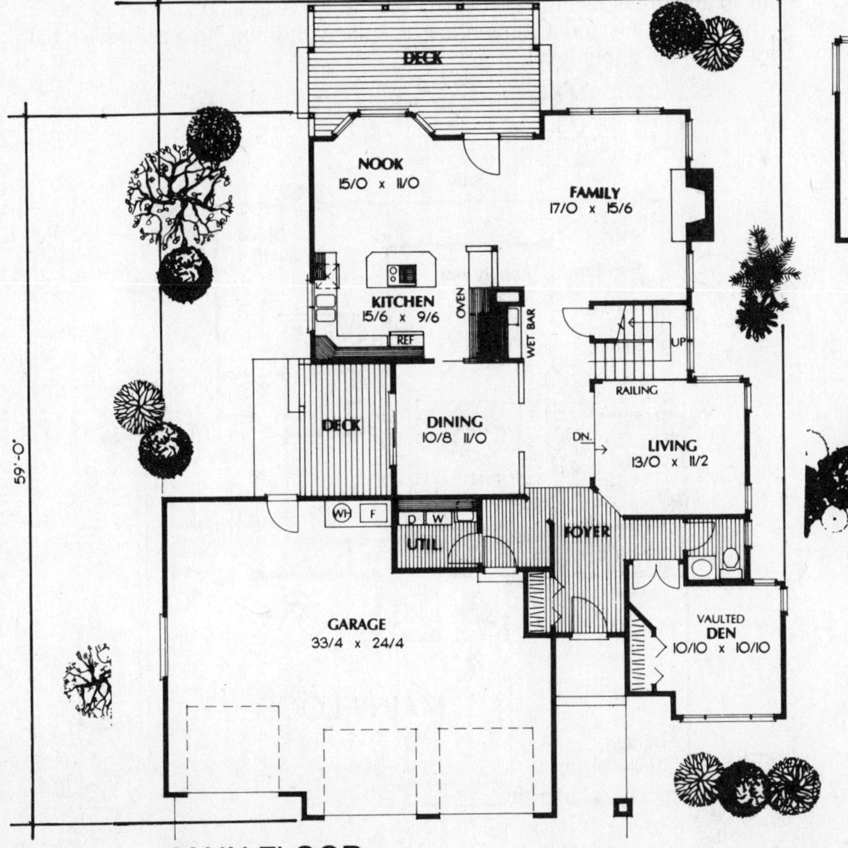

MAIN FLOOR

Plan U-89-208	
Bedrooms: 3-4	**Baths:** 2 ½
Space:	
Upper floor	1,149 sq. ft.
Bonus Room	274 sq. ft.
Main floor	1,414 sq. ft.
Total Living Area	**2,837 sq. ft.**
Basement	1,389 sq. ft.
Garage	811 sq. ft.
Exterior Wall Framing	2x4
Foundation options:	
Standard Basement	
Crawlspace	
Slab	
(Foundation & framing conversion diagram available—see order form.)	
Blueprint Price Code	**D**

TO ORDER THIS BLUEPRINT, CALL TOLL-FREE 1-800-547-5570

(prices and details on pp. 12-15.)

NEW RELEASE

Plan U-89-208

Homey Home Office

- This updated traditional has a variety of modern attractions.
- A unique parlor with decorative columns is perfect for greeting guests; a bayed breakfast room with wet bar can accommodate casual or entertaining refreshment needs.
- An open and functional kitchen offers an eating bar, nearby pantry and washer/dryer, plus handy service to the formal dining room.
- At the home's rear is a spacious, central family room, flanked by a relaxing sun room and versatile home office with fireplace and its own access to the main and upper levels, as well as a door to the rear patio.
- Three bedrooms and a vaulted master suite with sitting area and lavish bath make up the upper level.

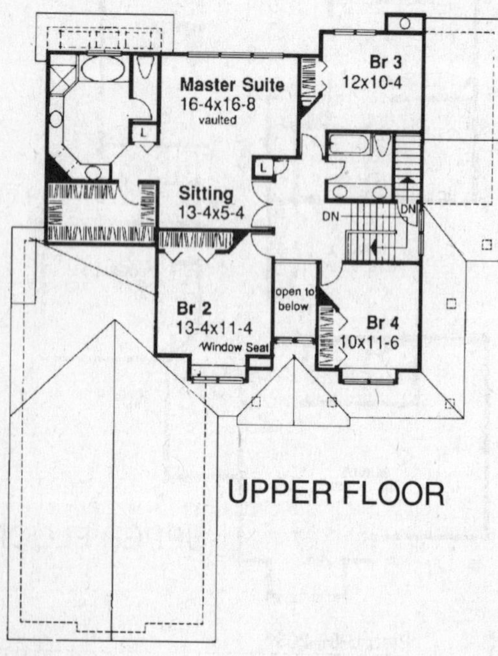

Plan B-90013	
Bedrooms: 4	**Baths:** 2 ½
Space:	
Upper floor	1,357 sq. ft.
Main floor	1,363 sq. ft.
Total Living Area	**2,720 sq. ft.**
Basement	1,363 sq. ft.
Garage	486 sq. ft.
Exterior Wall Framing	2x4
Foundation options:	
Standard Basement	
(Foundation & framing conversion diagram available—see order form.)	
Blueprint Price Code	**D**

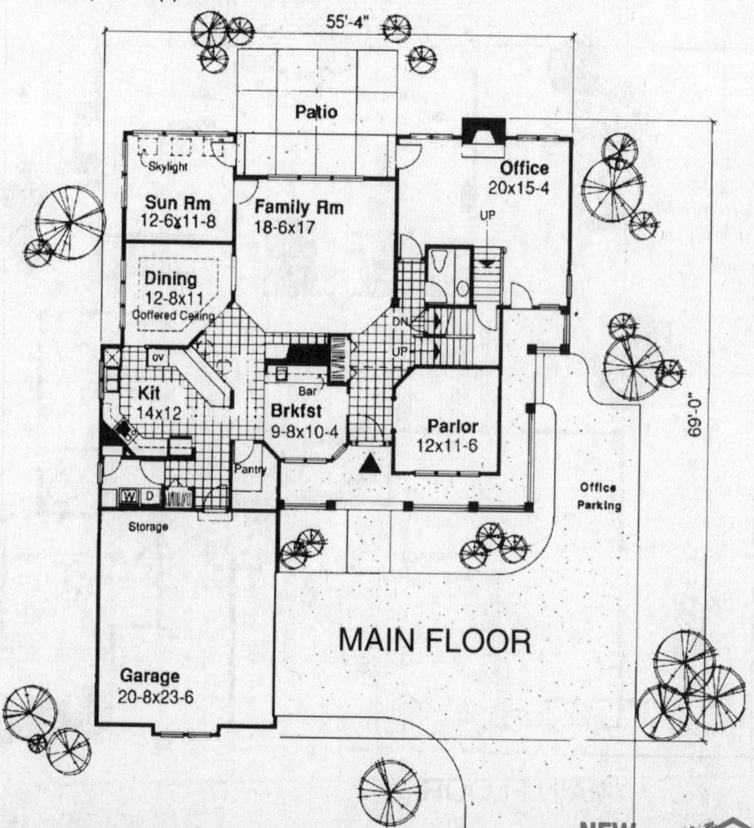

TO ORDER THIS BLUEPRINT,
CALL TOLL-FREE 1-800-547-5570
(prices and details on pp. 12-15.)

Plan B-90013

NEW RELEASE

Mediterranean Dream Home

- Brilliant columns and spectacular window treatments give a stately look to this impressive Mediterranean.
- The foyer, dining and living rooms share a 14' ceiling.
- The large, central family room ahead offers an entertainment center, fireplace and sliders to the rear patio.
- The generous kitchen and breakfast area also share a grand rear view.
- Three bedrooms are found on one wing with convenient laundry facilities and two baths, one also accessible from the patio.
- The master bedroom has private patio access, a huge walk-in closet and a luxury bath with step-up, corner tub and a separate walk-in shower.

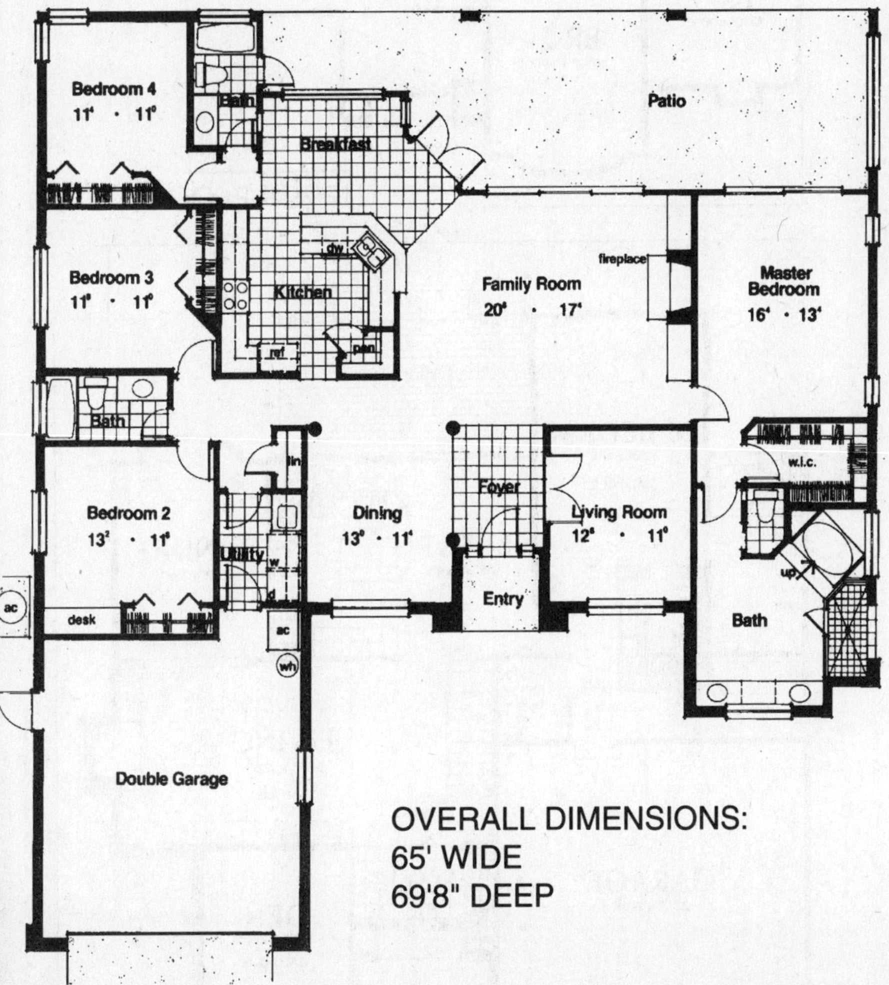

OVERALL DIMENSIONS:
65' WIDE
69'8" DEEP

Plan HDS-90-809	
Bedrooms: 4	**Baths:** 3
Space:	
Main floor	2,553 sq. ft.
Total Living Area	**2,553 sq. ft.**
Garage	476 sq. ft.
Exterior Wall Framing	2x4
Foundation options:	
Slab	
(Foundation & framing conversion diagram available—see order form.)	
Blueprint Price Code	**D**

NEW RELEASE

Plan HDS-90-809

TO ORDER THIS BLUEPRINT, CALL TOLL-FREE 1-800-547-5570
(prices and details on pp. 12-15.)

Volume Spaces

- Beautiful window treatments and a tall covered entry draw attention to this 1-1/2 story home.
- The open foyer reveals a den or home office with cathedral ceiling, a formal living room with 12' ceiling and fireplace, and the breakfast area beyond.
- The kitchen has a functional work island and a rear dining deck; it handily services the adjoining bayed dining room.
- A circle-top window, cathedral ceiling, walk-in closet and lavish private bath are luxuries in the master bedroom on the main floor.
- The upper level offers two additional bedrooms, a second full bath and a loft area above the living room.

Plan OH-107	
Bedrooms: 3	**Baths:** 2 ½
Space:	
Upper floor	484 sq. ft.
Main floor	1,509 sq. ft.
Total Living Area	**1,993 sq. ft.**
Basement	1,509 sq. ft.
Garage	440 sq. ft.
Exterior Wall Framing	2x4
Foundation options:	
Standard Basement	
(Foundation & framing conversion diagram available—see order form.)	
Blueprint Price Code	B

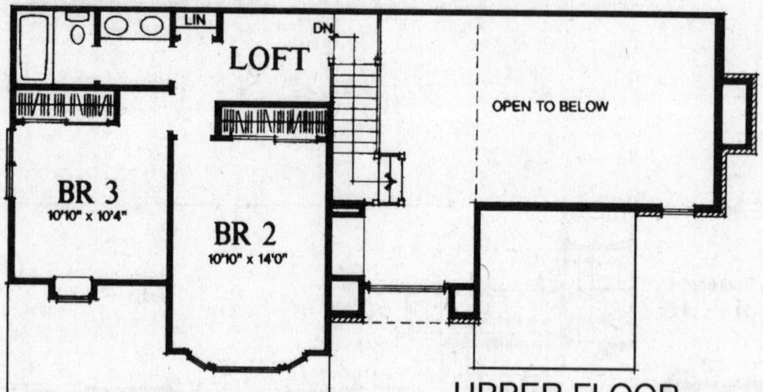

LIN
DN
LOFT
OPEN TO BELOW
BR 3
10'10" x 10'4"
BR 2
10'10" x 14'0"
UPPER FLOOR

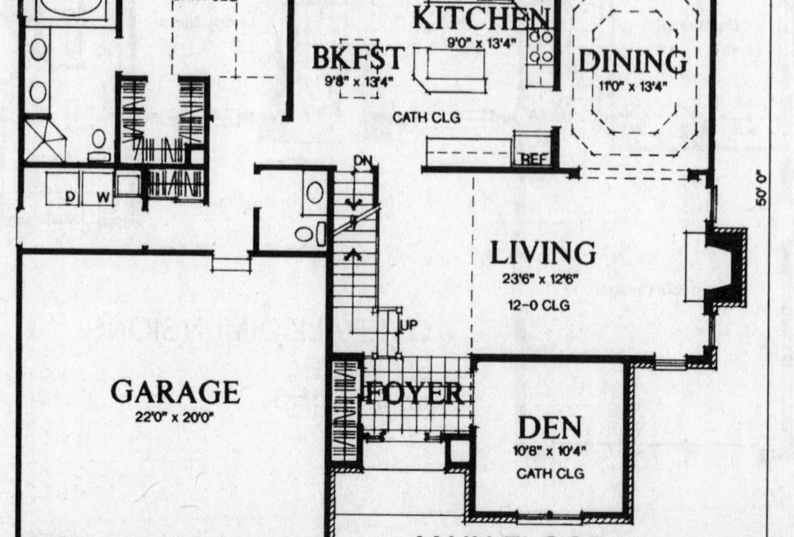

50' 0"
SEAT
DN
DN
DECK
M BEDRM
12'0" x 17'0"
CATH CLG
KITCHEN
9'0" x 13'4"
BKFST
9'8" x 13'4"
CATH CLG
DINING
11'0" x 13'4"
REF
D W
DN
LIVING
23'6" x 12'6"
12-0 CLG
UP
50' 0"
GARAGE
22'0" x 20'0"
FOYER
DEN
10'8" x 10'4"
CATH CLG
MAIN FLOOR

TO ORDER THIS BLUEPRINT, CALL TOLL-FREE 1-800-547-5570
(prices and details on pp. 12-15.)

Plan OH-107

NEW RELEASE

HomeStyles SOURCE 1 Designers Network

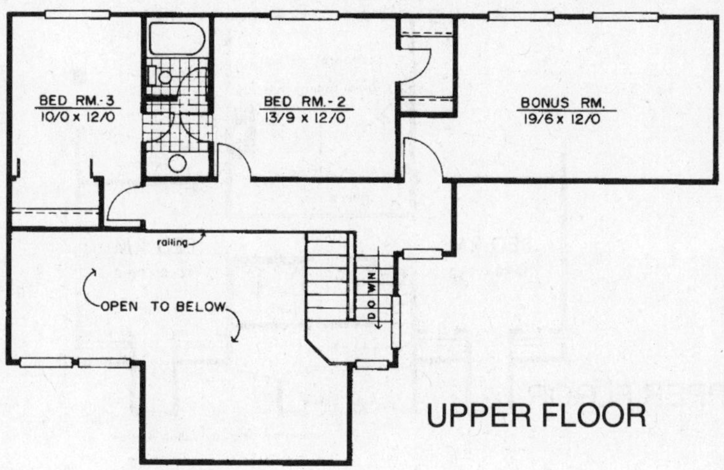

UPPER FLOOR

Economical Energy Features

- The energy features in this home should derive almost all of its heating needs. A concrete slab floor, greenhouse enclosure vented into the home, a woodstove, and clerestory windows with insulated shutters are some of these features.
- The vaulted ceiling in the living/dining room and the open stairs and loft hallway above let heat flow naturally to all rooms.
- The master bedroom is privately positioned on the main level.
- Convenient washer/dryer are also on the main level, hidden behind the kitchen.

Plan I-1586-A

Bedrooms: 3-4	**Baths:** 2
Space:	
Upper floor (Does not include bonus room)	541 sq. ft.
Main floor	1,017 sq. ft.
Total Living Area	**1,558 sq. ft.**
Bonus Room	275 sq. ft.
Garage	439 sq. ft.
Exterior Wall Framing	2x6
Foundation options:	
Crawlspace	
(Foundation & framing conversion diagram available—see order form.)	
Blueprint Price Code	B

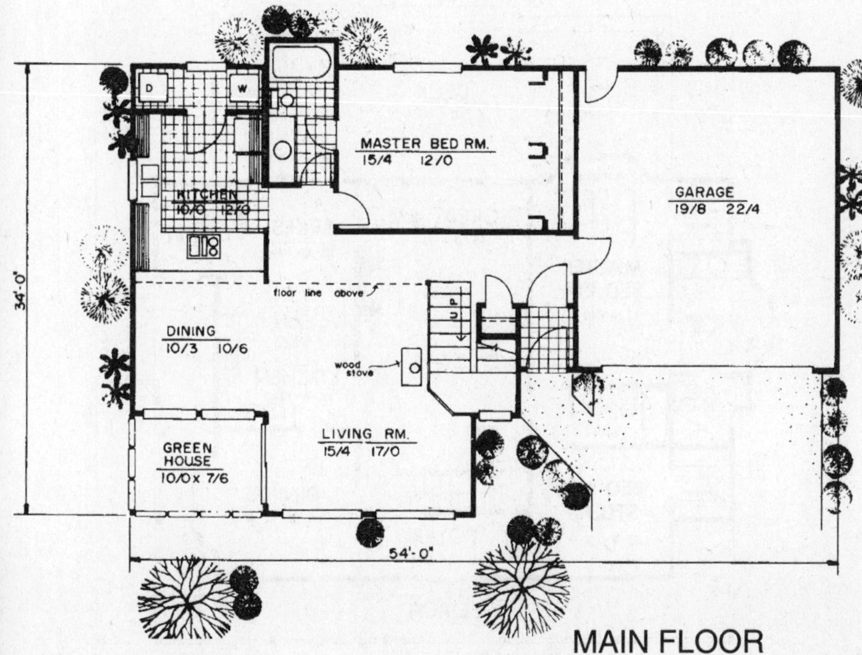

MAIN FLOOR

Plan I-1586-A

(prices and details on pp.12-15.)

Indoor and Outdoor Excitement

- A front wraparound, covered porch and open deck with spa and seating at the rear provides alternative outdoor living.
- The foyer is open to the upper level and has a clerestory Palladian window to let natural light in.
- At the center of the floor plan is a spacious Great Room with fireplace, cathedral ceiling and clerestory with arched window; the second-floor balcony overlooks the room.
- The large island kitchen handily serves the formal bayed dining room, bayed breakfast area with skylights and the Great Room.
- A fabulous master bedroom has bayed deck overlook with skylights and a private bath with garden tub and separate shower.

Plan DG-256	
Bedrooms: 3-4	**Baths:** 3
Space:	
Upper floor	565 sq. ft.
Main floor	1,756 sq. ft.
Total Living Area	**2,321 sq. ft.**
Exterior Wall Framing	2x4
Foundation options:	
Crawlspace	
(Foundation & framing conversion diagram available—see order form.)	
Blueprint Price Code	**C**

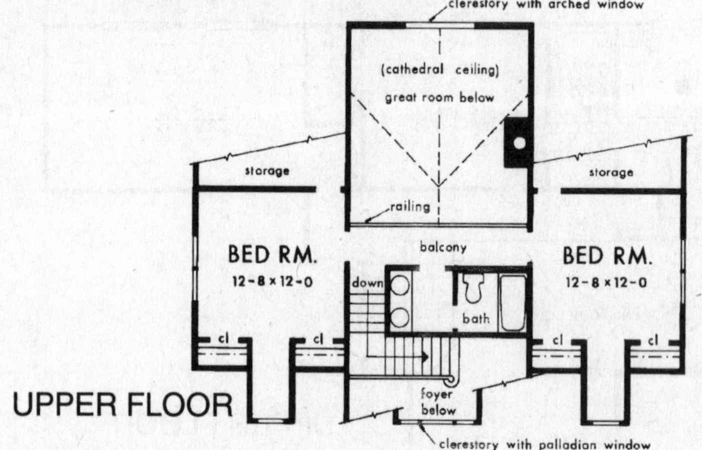

UPPER FLOOR

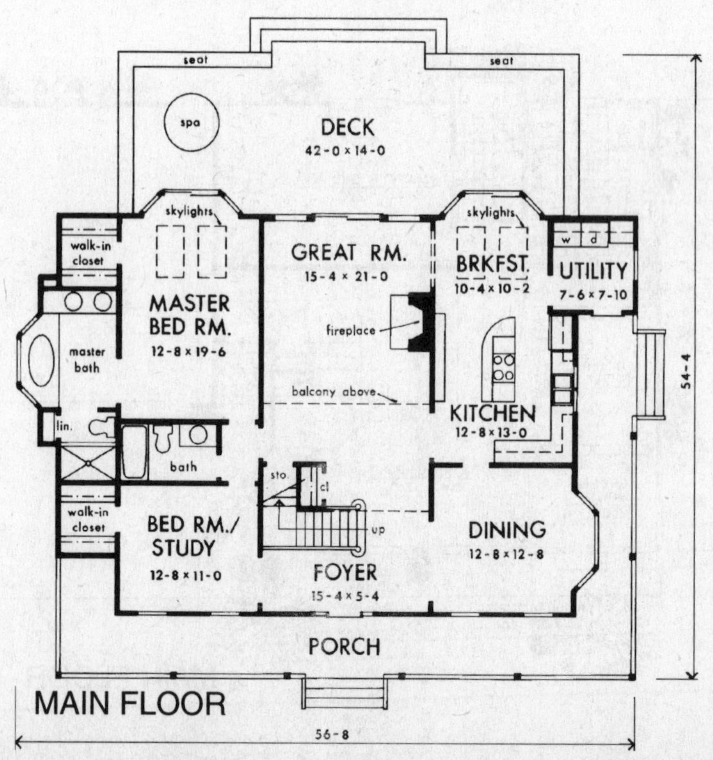

MAIN FLOOR

TO ORDER THIS BLUEPRINT,
CALL TOLL-FREE 1-800-547-5570
(prices and details on pp. 12-15.)

Plan DG-256

NEW RELEASE

Contemporary Farmhouse

- A contemporary farmhouse describes this elegant five-bedroom two-story.
- Over 4,000 square feet of family living space is offered, including formal living and dining rooms, a main-floor guest room, a versatile library or home office, and an informal vaulted family room with fireplace, brilliant corner windows and an adjoining rear patio.
- An island kitchen and breakfast area have nearby half-bath, washer/dryer, pantry and wet bar.
- Three additional bedrooms and an elegant master suite with corner fireplace, sunny sitting area and luxury bath share the upper level.

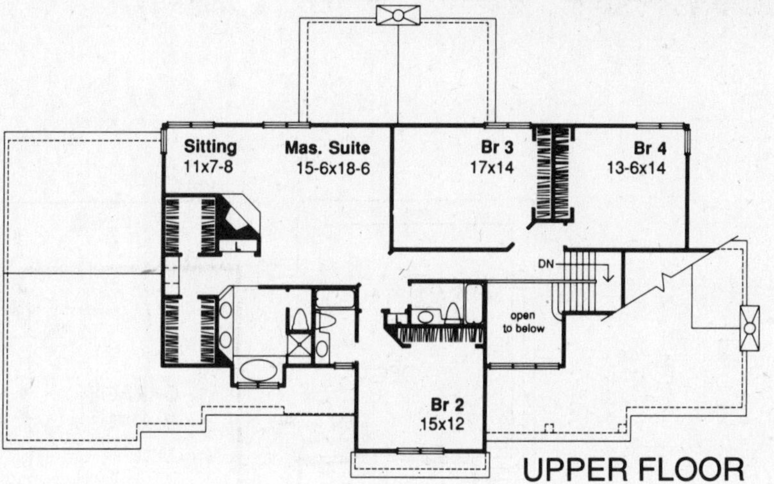

UPPER FLOOR

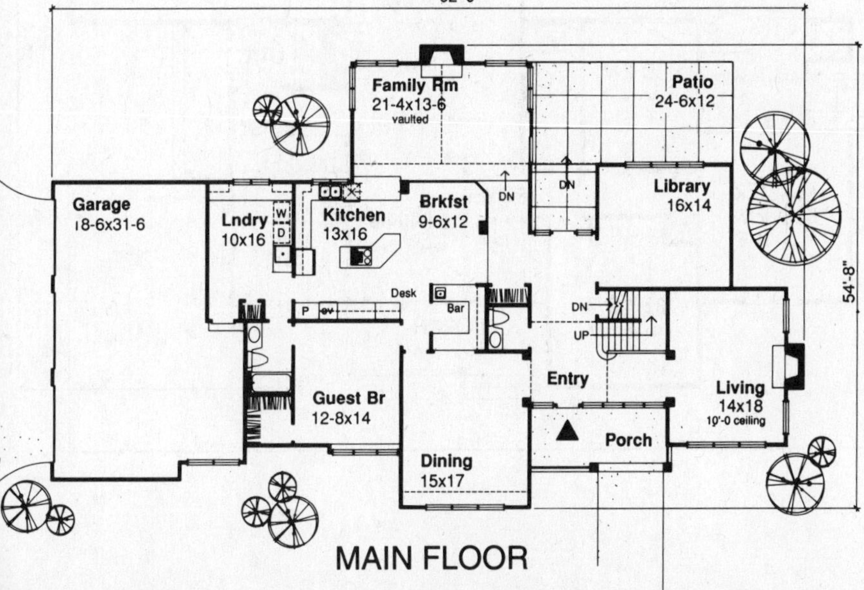

MAIN FLOOR

Plan B-90501-LHP	
Bedrooms: 5	**Baths:** 3 ½
Space:	
Upper floor	1,712 sq. ft.
Main floor	2,424 sq. ft.
Total Living Area	**4,136 sq. ft.**
Basement	2,424 sq. ft.
Garage	583 sq. ft.
Exterior Wall Framing	2x4
Foundation options:	
Standard Basement	
(Foundation & framing conversion diagram available—see order form.)	
Blueprint Price Code	**G**

NEW RELEASE

Plan B-90501-LHP

TO ORDER THIS BLUEPRINT, CALL TOLL-FREE 1-800-547-5570

(prices and details on pp. 12-15.)

A Larger Impression

- This three-bedroom traditional with front and side porches, dormer and half-round windows projects the appearance of a much larger home.
- Inside, elegant round columns define the dining room and generate visual excitement but promote an open, contemporary floor plan.
- The adjoining Great Room has cathedral ceiling, fireplace and arched window above the sliding glass door to the rear spa deck.
- The open kitchen has a location convenient to all living areas.
- A generous master bedroom has private lavish bath; two additional bedrooms share a second bath designed for two.

Plan DG-254	
Bedrooms: 3	**Baths:** 2
Space:	
Main floor	1,541 sq. ft.
Total Living Area	**1,541 sq. ft.**
Garage	418 sq. ft.
Exterior Wall Framing	2x4
Foundation options:	
Crawlspace	
(Foundation & framing conversion diagram available—see order form.)	
Blueprint Price Code	B

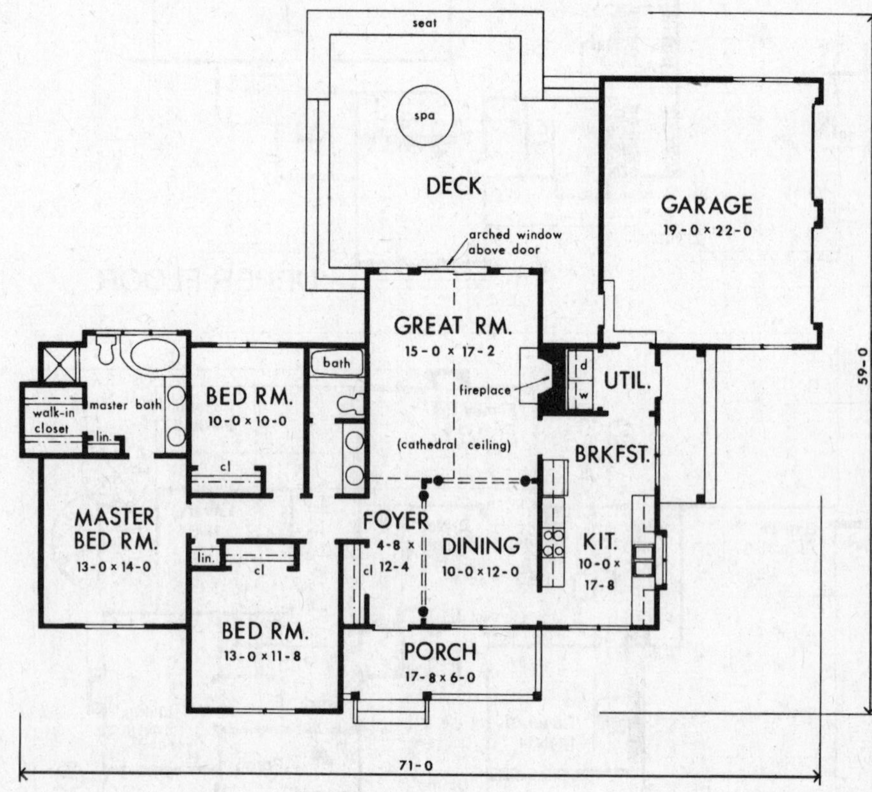

TO ORDER THIS BLUEPRINT, CALL TOLL-FREE 1-800-547-5570
(prices and details on pp. 12-15.)

Plan DG-254

NEW RELEASE

French Farmhouse

- An optional game room or fifth bedroom is offered in this classic French-styled farmhouse. The upper level also features a balcony that overlooks the Great Room.
- Bay windows are found throughout the main level, including the formal dining room, versatile studio, the nook and the secluded master suite and bath.
- At the center of the home, the Great Room has a vaulted ceiling, massive corner fireplace and access to the rear porch.
- A convenient utility room houses extra freezer, storage space and washer/dryer.

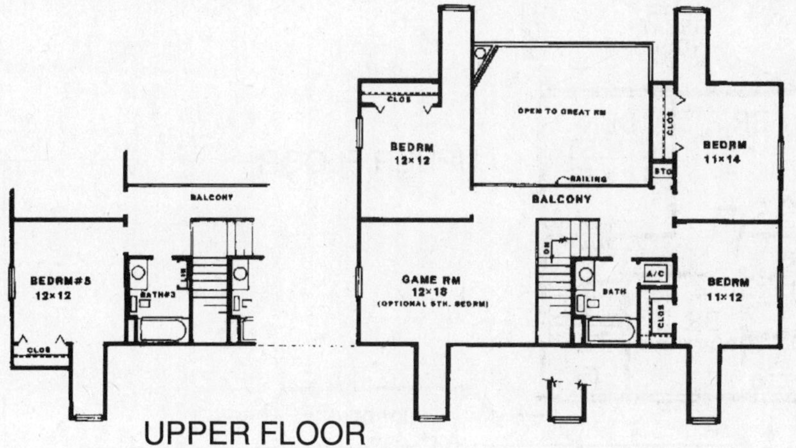

UPPER FLOOR

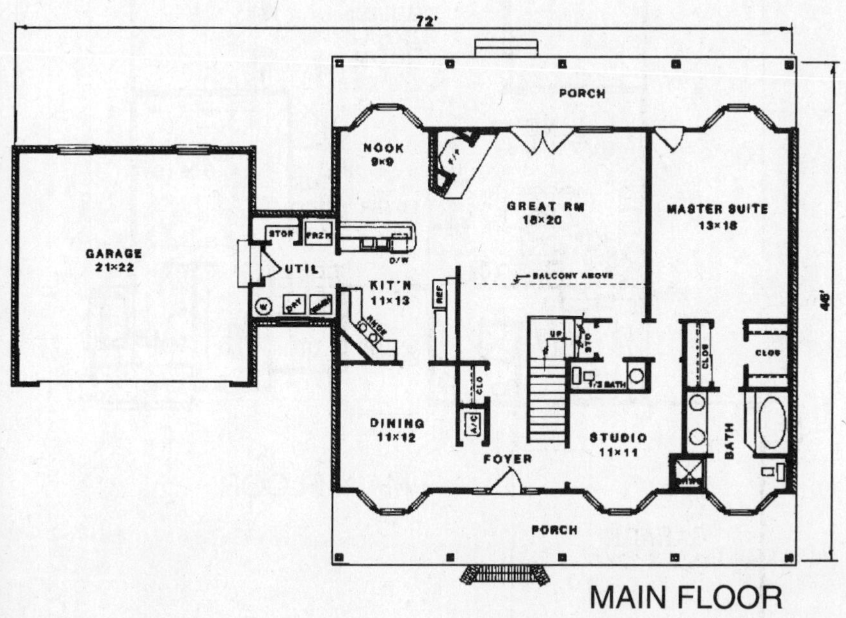

MAIN FLOOR

Plan VL-2716	
Bedrooms: 4-5	**Baths:** 2 ½-3 ½
Space:	
Upper floor	1,127 sq. ft.
Main floor	1,589 sq. ft.
Total Living Area	**2,716 sq. ft.**
Garage	469 sq. ft.
Exterior Wall Framing	2x4
Foundation options:	
Crawlspace	
Slab	
(Foundation & framing conversion diagram available—see order form.)	
Blueprint Price Code	D

A Custom Contemporary

- Clean lines and custom design touches are found throughout this contemporary home.
- A spectacular vaulted Great Room enclosed in windows offers a fireplace and a wraparound deck.
- Open to the Great Room is a cozy dining area and kitchen with island cooktop/eating bar, pantry and view of the adjoining deck.
- The secluded master suite has a coved ceiling, large walk-in closet and private bath with dual vanities, garden tub and separate shower.
- Two additional bedrooms, plus a guest room or den that can be enclosed or informally open, are found on the upper level.

Plan S-51391	
Bedrooms: 3-4	**Baths:** 3
Space:	
Upper floor	550 sq. ft.
Main floor	1,671 sq. ft.
Total Living Area	**2,221 sq. ft.**
Basement	1,671 sq. ft.
Garage	552 sq. ft.
Exterior Wall Framing	2x6
Foundation options:	
Standard Basement	
Crawlspace	
(Foundation & framing conversion diagram available—see order form.)	
Blueprint Price Code	C

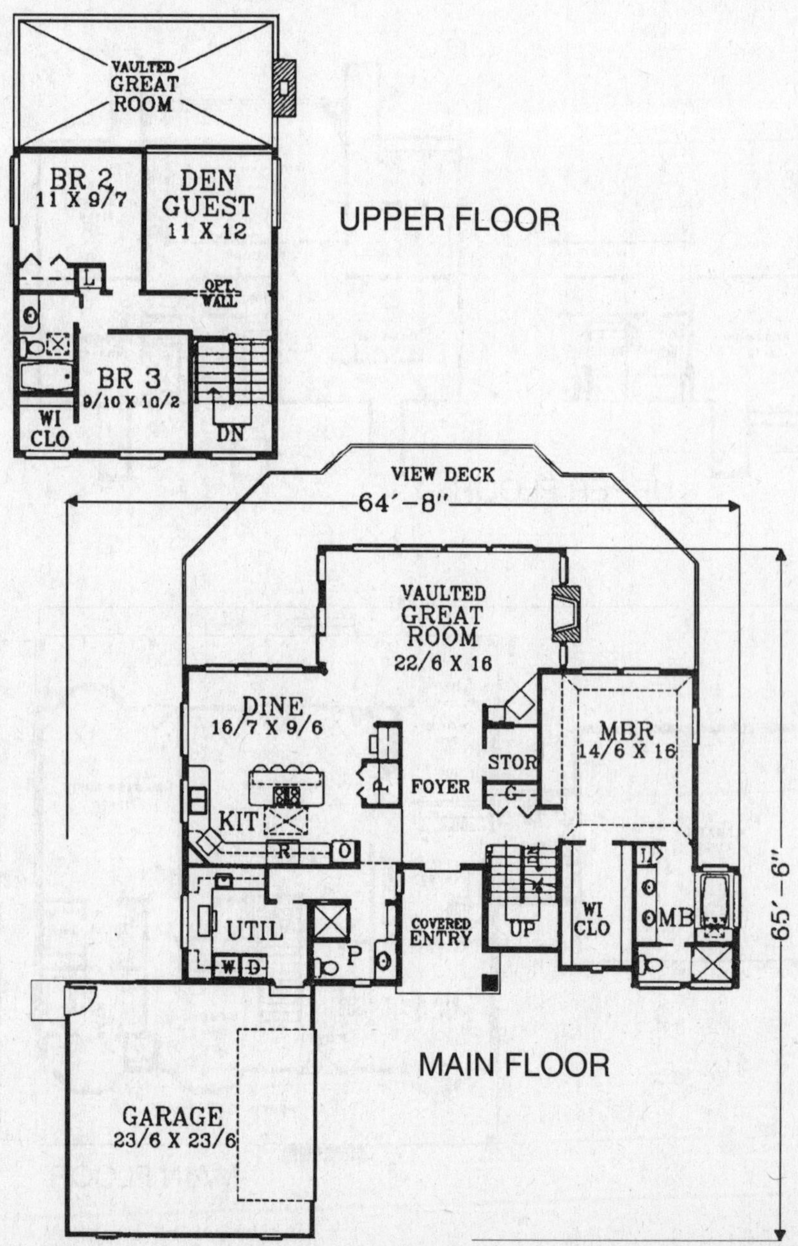

Plan S-51391

TO ORDER THIS BLUEPRINT, CALL TOLL-FREE 1-800-547-5570
(prices and details on pp. 12-15.)

NEW RELEASE

A Horizontal Emphasis

- A metal roof with 4' overhangs offer this unique home energy savings and distinction; a horizontal emphasis is created with the use of blocks.
- The foyer opens to a spacious living and dining room arrangement with see-thru fireplace.
- The family room, on the other side, has vaulted ceiling and rear window wall overlooking the patio.
- The island kitchen is open to the family room and breakfast nook, which offers a second fireplace.
- The main-floor master suite features his 'n her walk-in closets, access to the adjoining patio and a luxury bath.
- Two additional bedrooms share the upper level.

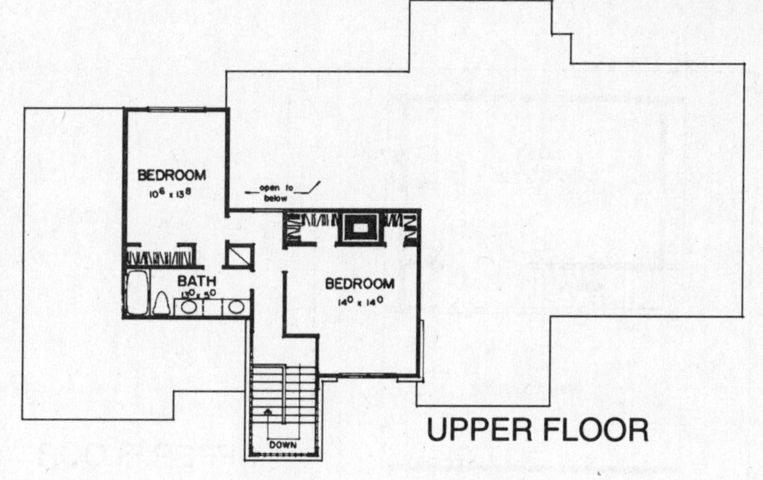

UPPER FLOOR

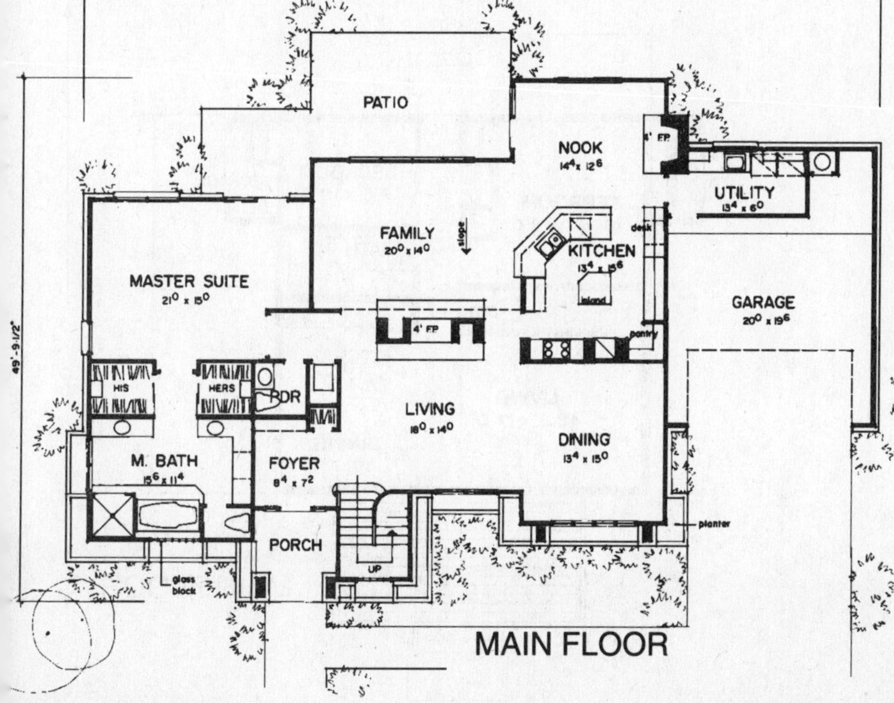

MAIN FLOOR

Plan DW-2394	
Bedrooms: 3	**Baths:** 2 ½
Space:	
Upper floor	501 sq. ft.
Main floor	1,893 sq. ft.
Total Living Area	**2,394 sq. ft.**
Basement	1,893 sq. ft.
Garage	390 sq. ft.
Exterior Wall Framing	2x4
Foundation options:	
Standard Basement	
Crawlspace	
Slab	
(Foundation & framing conversion diagram available—see order form.)	
Blueprint Price Code	C

NEW RELEASE

Plan DW-2394

TO ORDER THIS BLUEPRINT, CALL TOLL-FREE 1-800-547-5570
(prices and details on pp. 12-15.)

Open Living for Weekend or Forever

- This cozy, 1 1/2 story home is perfect for a weekend retreat, summer home, or casual permanent residence.
- A large, open living area on the first level combines the kitchen, dining area and living room for a spacious setting; sliding doors to the front offer an outdoor relaxing or dining alternative.
- Two bedrooms and a full bath are located at the rear, both with closet space.
- The upper loft would be ideal for a private master bedroom or quiet study area.

Plan CPS-1095	
Bedrooms: 2-3	**Baths:** 1
Space:	
Upper floor	320 sq. ft.
Main floor	784 sq. ft.
Total Living Area	**1,104 sq. ft.**
Basement	784 sq. ft.
Exterior Wall Framing	2x6
Foundation options:	
Standard Basement	
(Foundation & framing conversion diagram available—see order form.)	
Blueprint Price Code	A

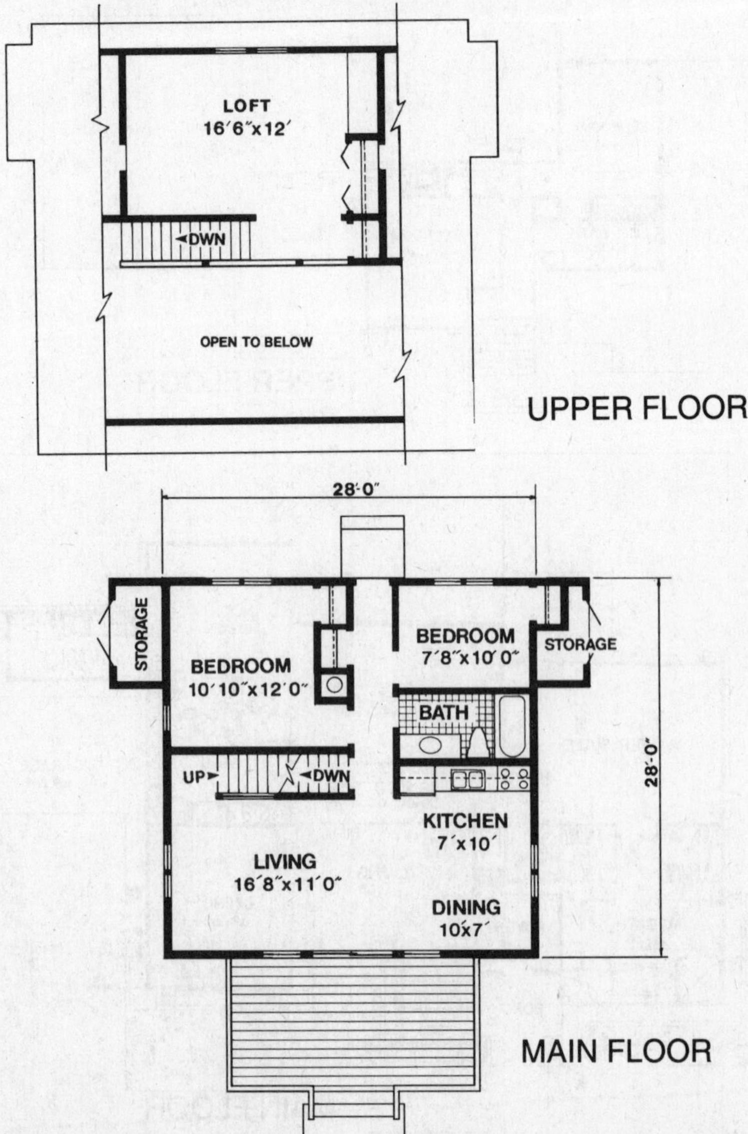

Plan CPS-1095

NEW RELEASE

HomeStyles SOURCE Designers Network

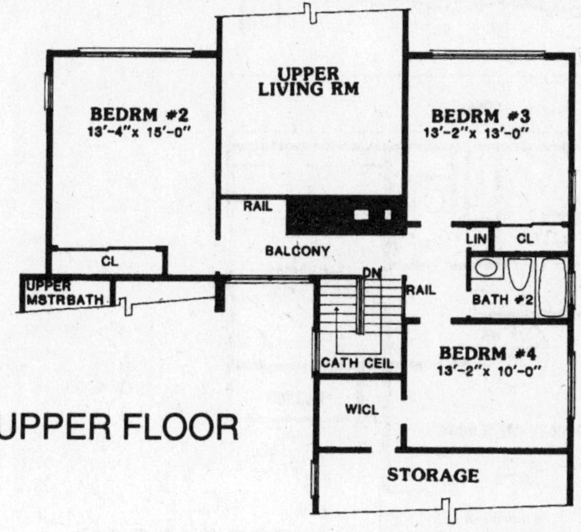

UPPER FLOOR

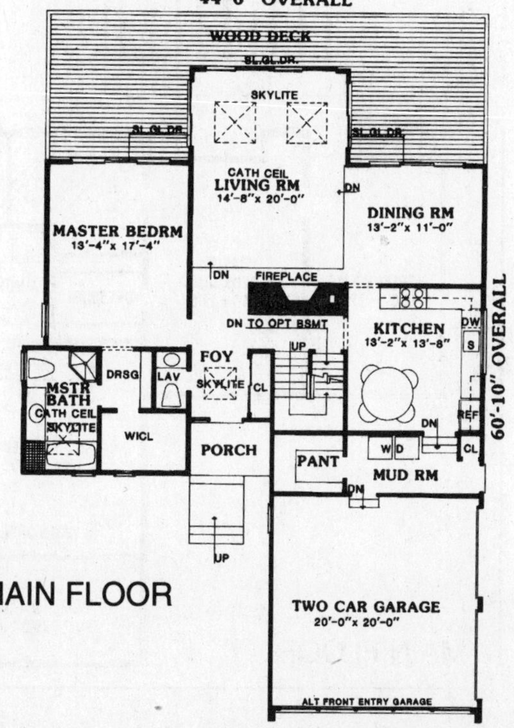

MAIN FLOOR

Dramatic Contemporary

- A dramatic roofline and a combination of vertical and horizontal siding give an interesting look to this contemporary.
- Drama continues to the large, sunken living room at the center of the home where you'll find a fireplace, cathedral ceiling open to the upper level, skylights and a rear attached deck accessed through sliding glass doors on three sides.
- The adjoining dining room also has a view of the fireplace and deck.
- A generous kitchen steps down to a utility area with handy washer/dryer and pantry before reaching the garage.
- Secluded to the rear is also a main-floor master bedroom with private access to the deck and a skylit bath with cathedral ceiling, dressing area and walk-in closet.

Plan AX-98712	
Bedrooms: 4	**Baths:** 2 ½
Space:	
Upper floor	815 sq. ft.
Main floor	1,343 sq. ft.
Total Living Area	**2,158 sq. ft.**
Basement	1,298 sq. ft.
Garage	400 sq. ft.
Exterior Wall Framing	2x4
Foundation options:	
Standard Basement	
Slab	
(Foundation & framing conversion diagram available—see order form.)	
Blueprint Price Code	C

NEW RELEASE

Plan AX-98712

TO ORDER THIS BLUEPRINT, CALL TOLL-FREE 1-800-547-5570
(prices and details on pp. 12-15.)

Cabin with Solar Gain

- Direct solar gain is offered in this 1 1/2 story indoor/outdoor retreat.
- An attached greenhouse off the master bedroom and a solarium adjoining the Great Room at the rear provide drama and warmth.
- A unique spiral stairway is at the center of the Great Room, also with fireplace and cathedral ceiling with clerestory windows.
- The merging dining room is open to the kitchen as well; it features a private deck.
- Besides the greenhouse, the master bedroom also has a large, convenient bath with dual vanities and generous corner tub.

Plan PH-1802	
Bedrooms: 3	**Baths:** 2
Space:	
Upper floor	534 sq. ft.
Main floor	1,268 sq. ft.
Total Living Area	**1,802 sq. ft.**
Exterior Wall Framing	2x6
Foundation options:	
Crawlspace	
Slab	
(Foundation & framing conversion diagram available—see order form.)	
Blueprint Price Code	**B**

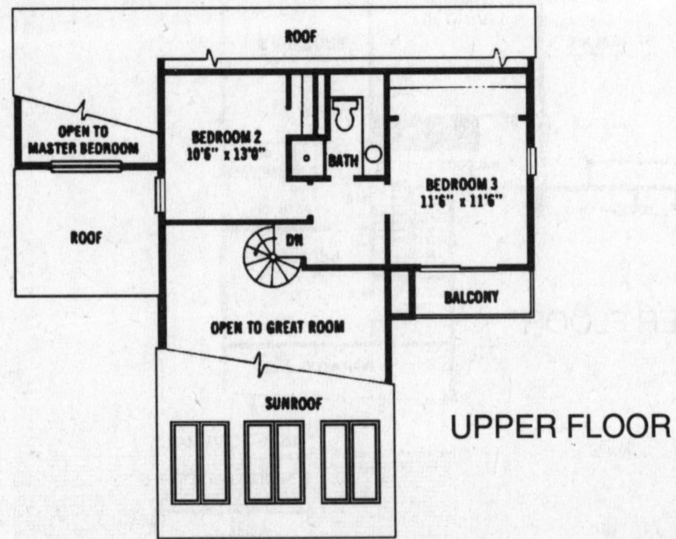

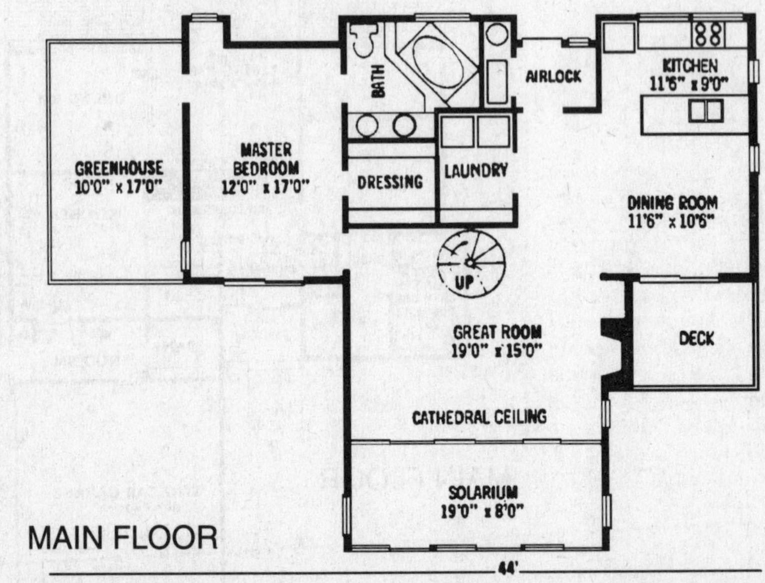

TO ORDER THIS BLUEPRINT, CALL TOLL-FREE 1-800-547-5570
(prices and details on pp. 12-15.)

Plan PH-1802

NEW RELEASE

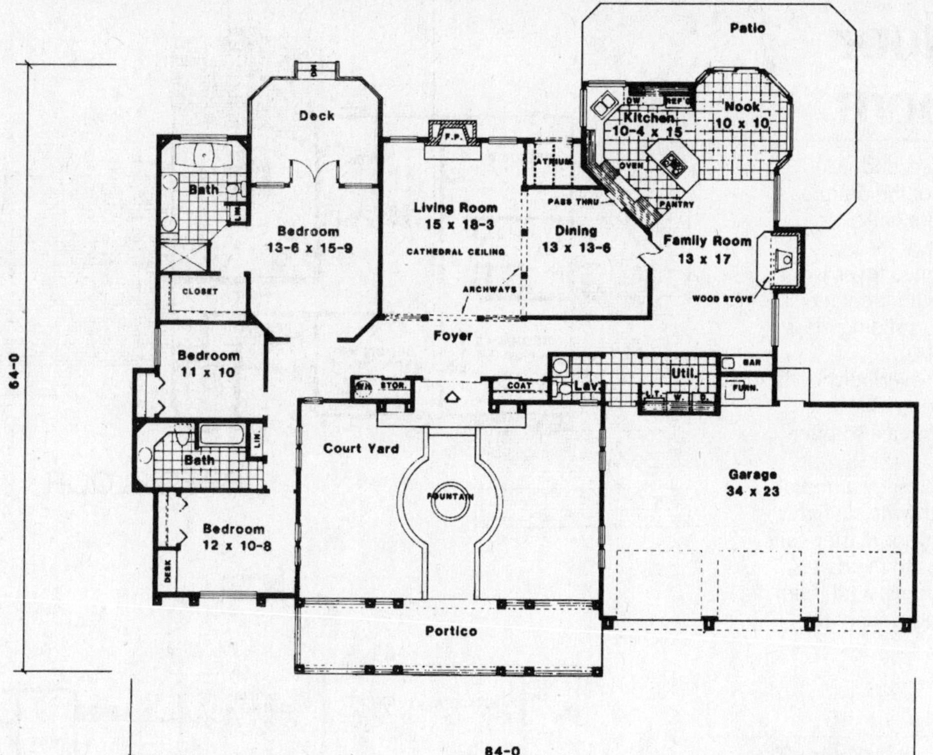

Southwestern Flavor

A spectacular fountain courtyard, eye-catching portico and tile roof display a unique Southwestern flavor.

The U-shaped interior and three-car garage surround the courtyard; three bedrooms along one side include the master with double doors to the entrance and private deck, plus a large bath with dual vanities, luxury bath and separate shower.

Columned archways adorn entrances to the central living room with cathedral ceiling, fireplace and adjoining atrium and the dining room with pass-thru to the kitchen.

The kitchen also offers a lovely corner sink window, pantry, merging, bayed nook with surrounding patio and adjacent family room with wood stove and wet bar.

Plan NW-391-M	
Bedrooms: 3	**Baths:** 2 ½
Space:	
Main floor	2,207 sq. ft.
Total Living Area	**2,207 sq. ft.**
Garage	782 sq. ft
Exterior Wall Framing	2x6
Foundation options:	
Crawlspace	
(Foundation & framing conversion diagram available—see order form.)	
Blueprint Price Code	C

NEW RELEASE

Plan NW-391-M

TO ORDER THIS BLUEPRINT, CALL TOLL-FREE 1-800-547-5570
(prices and details on pp. 12-15.)

Second-Floor Family Room

- An interior bridge and second-floor family room are some of the unique features found in this dramatic contemporary.
- Off the cathedral ceilinged foyer is a spacious living room with fireplace flanked by windows and sliding glass doors on opposite walls.
- The upper-level bridge overlooks both the foyer and living room.
- The den and breakfast area also offer outdoor access.
- An oversized walk-in closet, cathedral ceiling, and luxury bath with skylights are found in the main-floor master suite, also with private access to the den.
- Three additional bedrooms, a full bath and the skylit family room share the upper level.

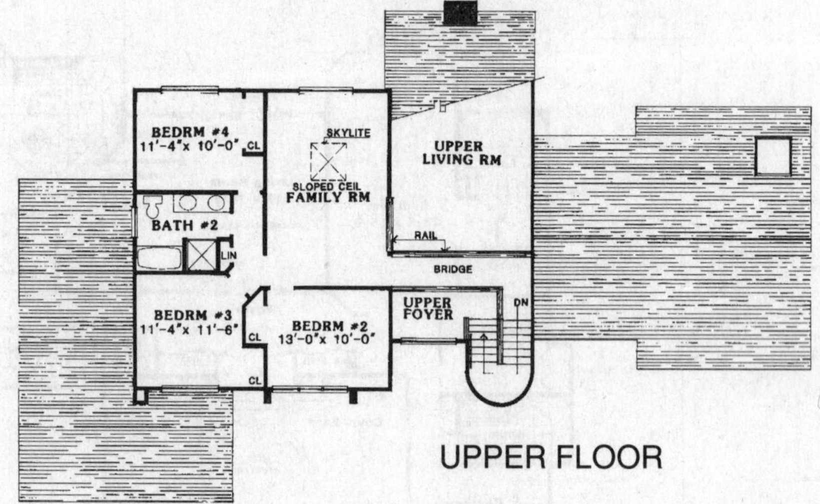

UPPER FLOOR

Plan AX-989308

Bedrooms: 4	**Baths:** 2 ½
Space:	
Upper floor	923 sq. ft.
Main floor	1,890 sq. ft.
Total Living Area	**2,813 sq. ft.**
Basement	1,890 sq. ft.
Garage	600 sq. ft.
Exterior Wall Framing	2x4
Foundation options:	
Standard Basement	
(Foundation & framing conversion diagram available—see order form.)	
Blueprint Price Code	**D**

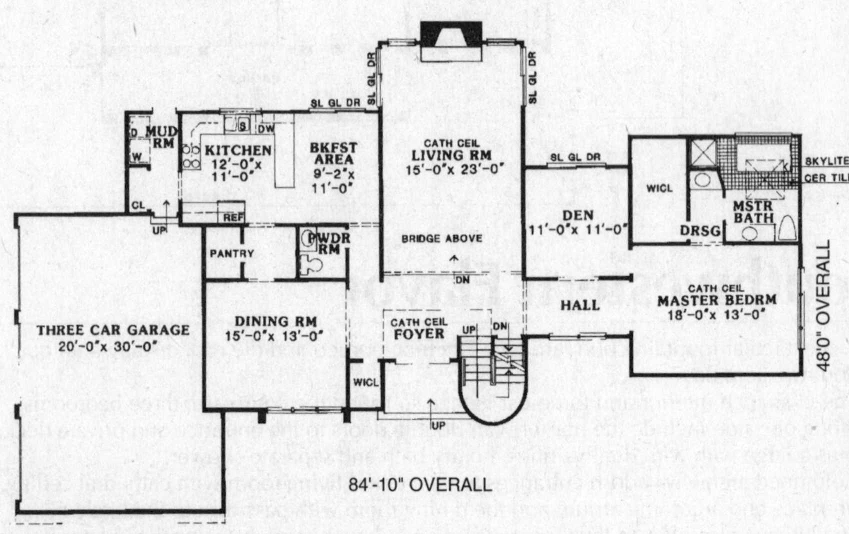

MAIN FLOOR

TO ORDER THIS BLUEPRINT, CALL TOLL-FREE 1-800-547-5570
(prices and details on pp. 12-15.)

Plan AX-989308

NEW RELEASE

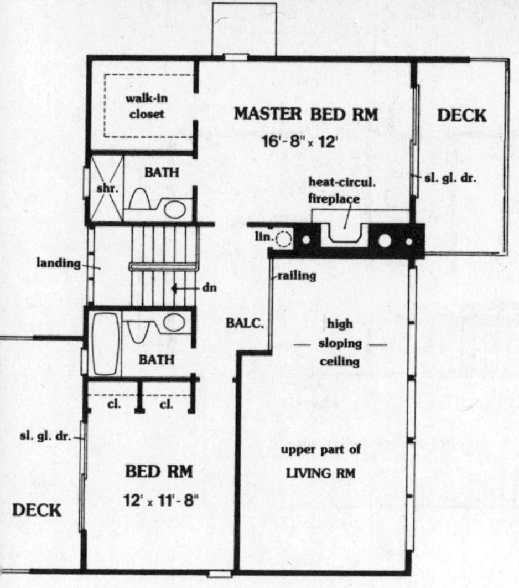

UPPER FLOOR

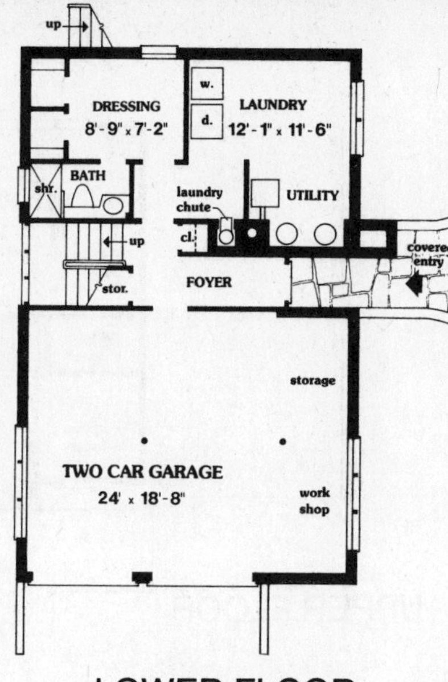

LOWER FLOOR

A Deck for each Room

- Exciting outdoor living is possible in this three-level contemporary design.
- The front entrance and garage are located on the lower level, along with a dressing room, full bath and laundry facilities.
- The main level offers a spectacular two-story living room overlooked by an upper-level balcony; highlights include a massive stone wall with heat-circulating fireplace and two sets of sliding glass doors that offer entrance to the front deck that stretches to the kitchen.
- Outdoor dining can take place off the kitchen deck with barbecue or off the formal dining/family area.
- The main-level bedroom and pair of upper-level bedrooms each offer private decks.

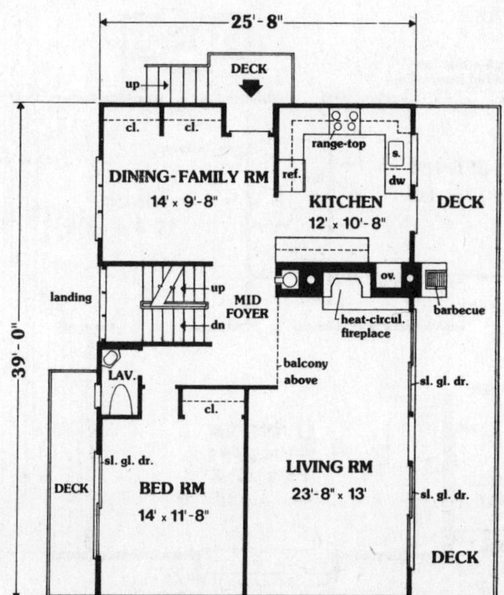

MAIN FLOOR

Plan HFL-2176

Bedrooms: 3	**Baths:** 3½
Space:	
Upper floor	712 sq. ft.
Main floor	1,001 sq. ft.
Lower floor	463 sq. ft.
Total Living Area	**2,176 sq. ft.**
Garage and storage	448 sq. ft.
Exterior Wall Framing	2x6

Foundation options:
Slab
(Foundation & framing conversion diagram available—see order form.)

Blueprint Price Code	C

NEW RELEASE

Plan HFL-2176

TO ORDER THIS BLUEPRINT, CALL TOLL-FREE 1-800-547-5570
(prices and details on pp. 12-15.)

Simple, but Dramatic

- A dramatic sloped roof exterior and interior living room with sloped ceiling, floor-to-ceiling windows, an adjoining deck and wood stove give this home an interesting, but easy and affordable structure under 1,500 square feet.
- The attached kitchen and dining area also has access to the deck, for an outdoor dining alternative; a pantry and convenient laundry room is secluded to the rear.
- The main-level bedroom could ideally be used as the master; it offers dual closets and nearby bath.
- Off the two-story foyer is the stairway to the second level which ends in a balcony area that overlooks the living room. Two good-sized bedrooms, one with unique dressing vanity, share the upper level with a second bath.

Plan HFL-1382	
Bedrooms: 3	**Baths:** 2
Space:	
Upper floor	465 sq. ft.
Main floor (Without mudroom)	917 sq. ft.
Total Living Area	**1,382 sq. ft.**
Basement	811 sq. ft.
Garage	220 sq. ft.
Exterior Wall Framing	2x6
Foundation options:	
Standard Basement	
Slab	
(Foundation & framing conversion diagram available—see order form.)	
Blueprint Price Code	**A**

UPPER FLOOR

roof
BED RM 14' x 11'
BATH
BED RM 12'-4" x 12'
louver above
w.i.c.
dn.
lin.
cl.
vanity
louver above
upper foyer
upper part of living room

MAIN FLOOR

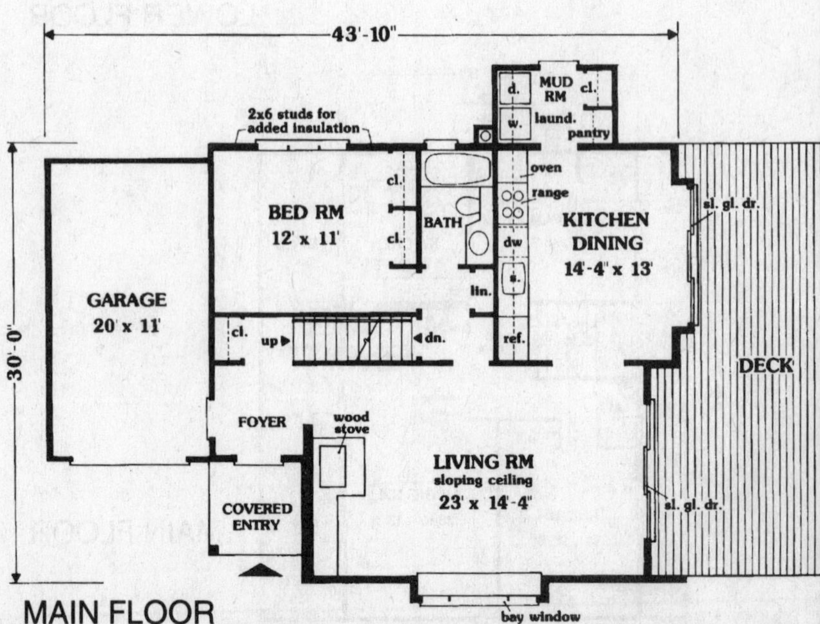

TO ORDER THIS BLUEPRINT, CALL TOLL-FREE 1-800-547-5570
(prices and details on pp. 12-15.)

Plan HFL-1382

NEW RELEASE

INDOOR/OUTDOOR DECKS AND MORE DECKS

Photo by: Karl Bischoff

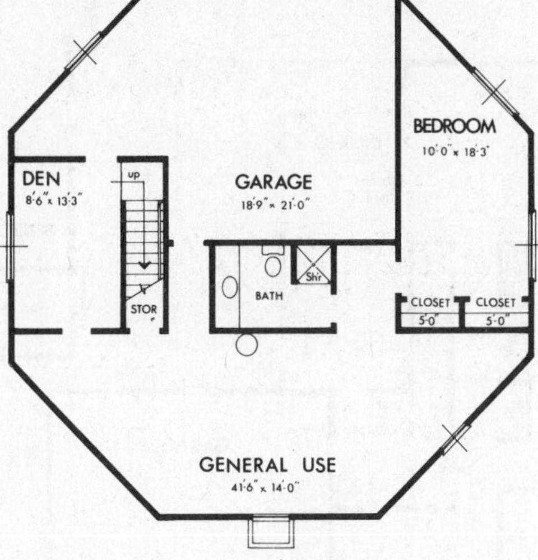

BASEMENT

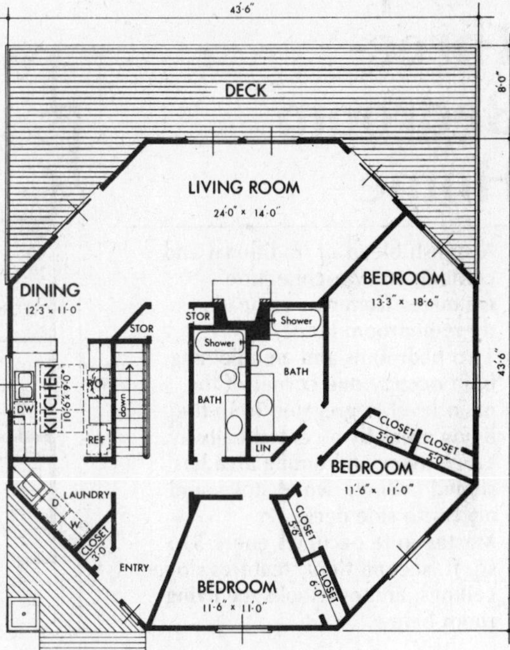

MAIN FLOOR

1/16" = 1'

Unique Octagon Design

- Irregularly shaped rooms are oriented around an entrance hall paralleling the octagonal exterior.
- Short directional hallways eliminate cross-room traffic and provide independent room access to the front door.
- Spacious living and dining rooms form a continuous area more than 38' wide.
- Oversized bathroom serves a large master suite which features a deck view and dual closets.
- This plan is also available with a stucco exterior (Plans H-942-2, with daylight basement, and H-942-2A, without basement).

Plans H-942-1, -1A, -2, & -2A (Stucco)

Bedrooms: 3-4	**Baths:** 2-3
Space:	
Main floor:	1,564 sq. ft.
Basement:	approx. 1,170 sq. ft.
Total with basement:	2,734 sq. ft.
Garage:	394 sq. ft.
Exterior Wall Framing:	2x6

Foundation options:
Daylight basement (Plans H-942-1 & -2).
Crawlspace (Plans H-942-1A & -2A).
(Foundation & framing conversion diagram available — see order form.)

Blueprint Price Code:	
Without basement:	B
With basement:	D

Plans H-942-1/1A & -2/2A

TO ORDER THIS BLUEPRINT, CALL TOLL-FREE 1-800-547-5570

(prices and details on pp. 12-15.)

Compact Three-Bedroom Home

- A stylish blend of traditional and contemporary architecture emanates from this compact, three-bedroom home.
- Two bedrooms and an adjoining bath occupy one corner of the main level, segregated from the living areas by a central hallway.
- Large living and dining area has sloped ceilings, wood stove, and access to side deck.
- Master suite occupies entire 516 sq. ft. second floor, features sloped ceilings, and overlooks the living room below.

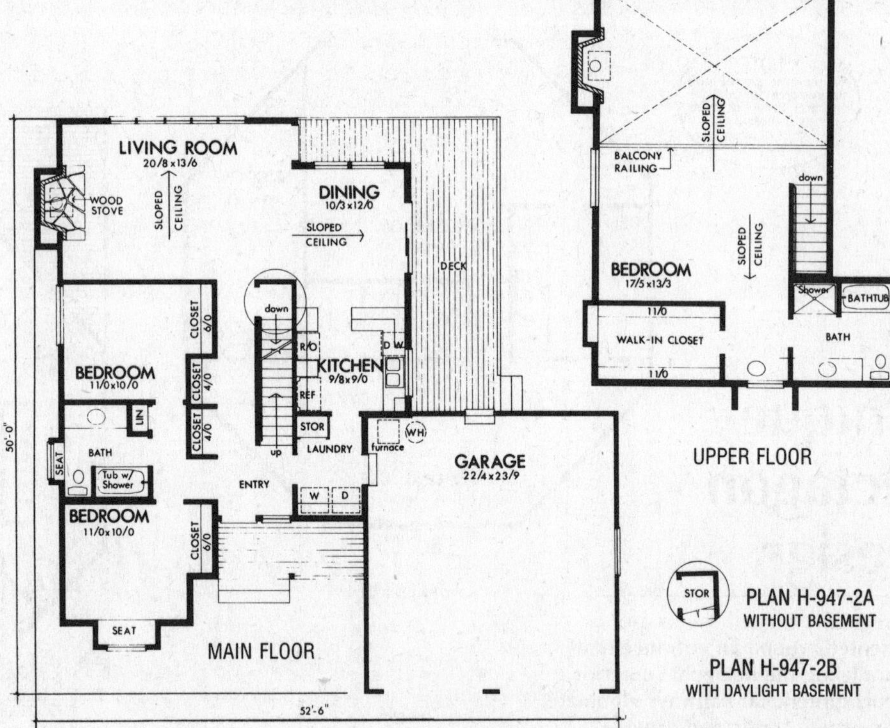

Plans H-947-2A & -2B

Bedrooms: 3	**Baths:** 2
Space:	
Upper floor:	516 sq. ft.
Main floor:	1,162 sq. ft.
Total living area:	1,678 sq. ft.
Basement:	approx. 1,162 sq. ft.
Garage:	530 sq. ft.

Exterior Wall Framing: 2x6

Foundation options:
Daylight basement (Plan H-947-2B).
Crawlspace (Plan H-947-2A).
(Foundation & framing conversion diagram available — see order form.)

Blueprint Price Code: B

TO ORDER THIS BLUEPRINT, CALL TOLL-FREE 1-800-547-5570
(prices and details on pp. 12-15.)

Plans H-947-2A & -2B

Photo by James Erickson

Rustic Styling, Comfortable Interior

- Front-to-back split level with large decks lends itself to steep sloping site, particularly in a scenic area.
- Compact, space-efficient design makes for economical construction.
- Great Room design concept utilizes the entire 36′ width of home for the kitchen/dining/living area.
- Two bedrooms and a bath are up three steps, on the entry level.
- Upper level bedroom includes a compact bath and a private deck.

**NOTE: The above photographed home may have been modified by the homeowner. Please refer to floor plan and/or drawn elevation shown for actual blueprint details.

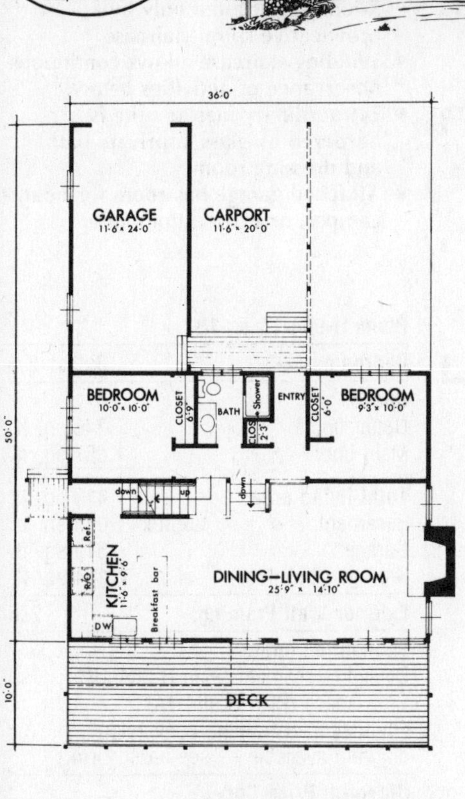

MAIN FLOOR

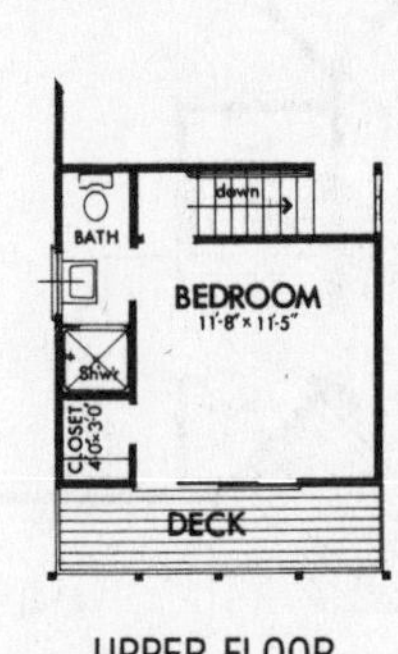

UPPER FLOOR

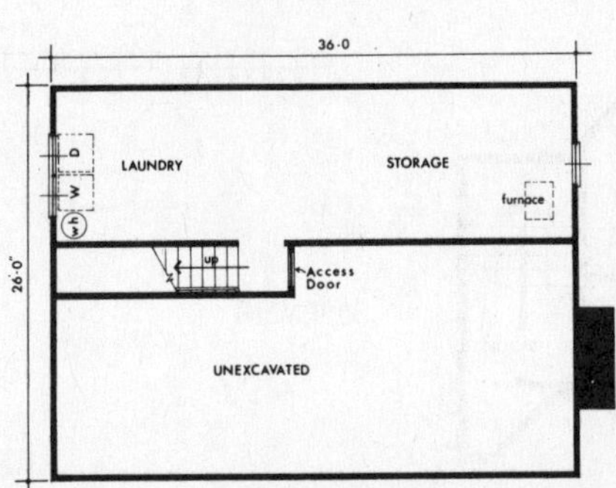

BASEMENT

Plan H-25-C

Bedrooms: 3	**Baths:** 2
Space:	
Upper floor:	222 sq. ft.
Main floor:	936 sq. ft.
Basement:	365 sq. ft.
Total living area:	1,523 sq. ft.
Garage:	276 sq. ft.
Exterior Wall Framing:	2x4

Foundation options:
Daylight basement only.
(Foundation & framing conversion diagram available — see order form.)

Blueprint Price Code: B

Plan H-25-C

TO ORDER THIS BLUEPRINT, CALL TOLL-FREE 1-800-547-5570
(prices and details on pp. 12-15.)

Octagonal Vacation Retreat

- Octagonal shape offers a view on all sides.
- Living, dining, and meal preparation are combined in a single Great Room, interrupted only by a provocative spiral staircase.
- Winding staircase allows continuous observance of activities below.
- Extraordinary master suite is bordered by glass, a private bath, and dressing room.
- Attached garage has room for boat, camper, or extra automobile.

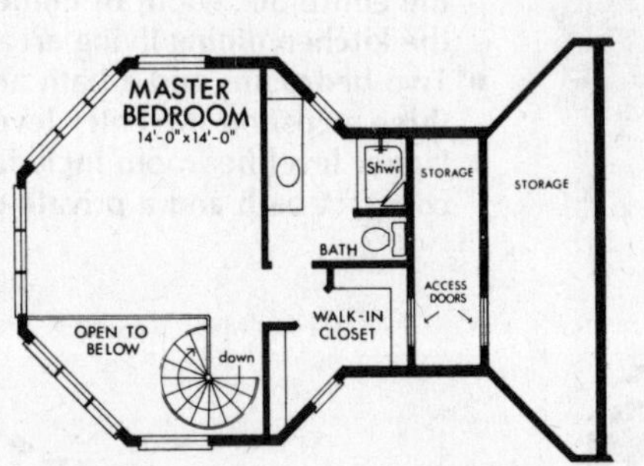

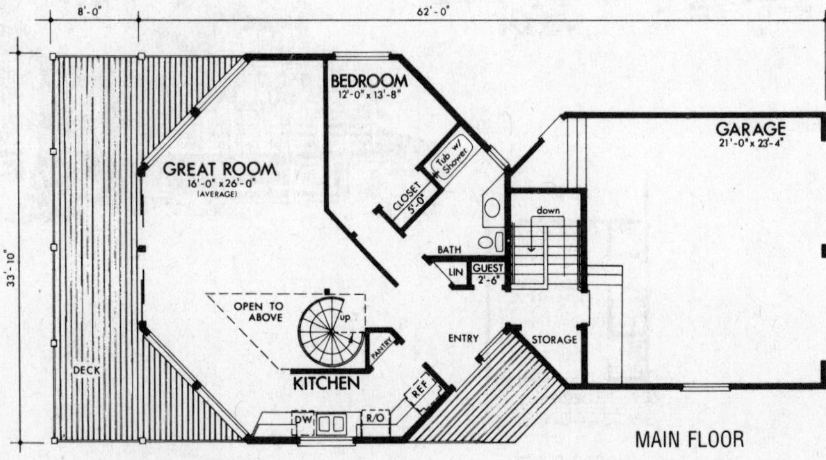

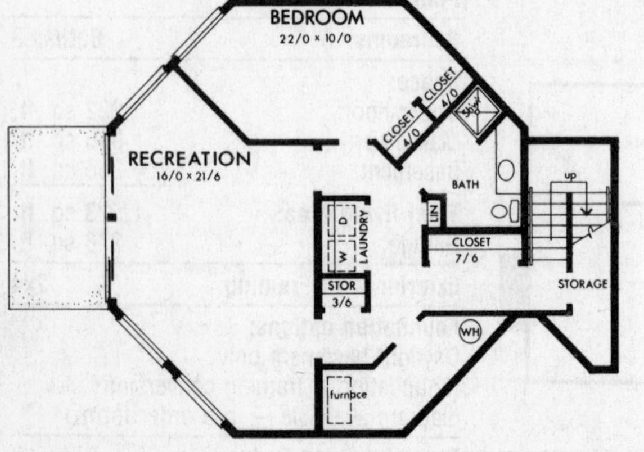

SCALE 0 1 2 3 4 5 6 7 8 9 10 15 20

Plans H-964-1A & -1B

Bedrooms: 2-3	**Baths:** 2-3
Space:	
Upper floor:	346 sq. ft.
Main floor:	1,067 sq. ft.
Total living area:	1,413 sq. ft.
Basement:	approx. 1,045 sq. ft.
Garage:	512 sq. ft.
Storage (2nd floor)	134 sq. ft.
Exterior Wall Framing:	2x6

Foundation options:
Daylight basement (Plan H-964-1B).
Crawlspace (Plan H-964-1A).
Foundation & framing conversion diagram available — see order form.)

Blueprint Price Code:

Without basement:	A
With basement:	C

TO ORDER THIS BLUEPRINT, CALL TOLL-FREE 1-800-547-5570
(prices and details on pp. 12-15.)

Plans H-964-1A & -1B

Spacious Octagon

- Highly functional main floor plan makes traffic easy and minimizes wasted hall space.
- Double-sized entry opens to spacious octagonal living room with central fireplace and access to all rooms.
- U-shaped kitchen and attached dining area allow for both informal and formal occasions.
- Contiguous bedrooms each have independent deck entrances.
- Exciting deck borders entire home.

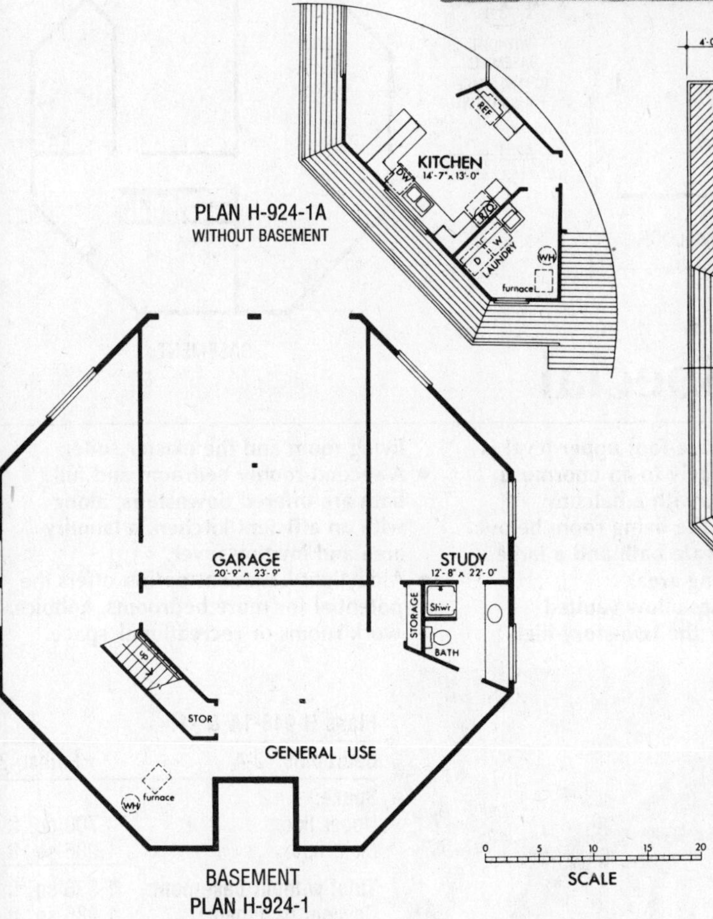

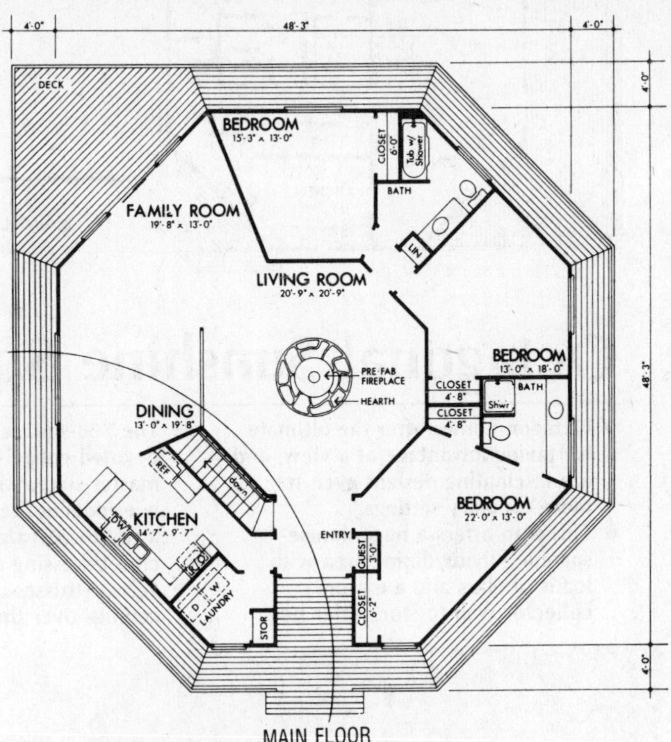

SCALE 0 5 10 15 20

Plans H-924-1 & -1A

Bedrooms: 3-4	**Baths:** 2-3
Space:	
Main floor:	1,888 sq. ft.
Total without basement:	1,888 sq. ft.
Basement:	1,395 sq. ft.
Total with basement:	3,283 sq. ft.
Garage:	493 sq. ft.
Exterior Wall Framing:	2x4

Foundation options:
Daylight basement (Plan H-924-1).
Crawlspace (Plan H-924-1A).
(Foundation & framing conversion diagram available — see order form.)

Blueprint Price Code:

Without basement:	B
With basement:	E

Plans H-924-1 & -1A

TO ORDER THIS BLUEPRINT, CALL TOLL-FREE 1-800-547-5570
(prices and details on pp. 12-15.)

FRONT VIEW

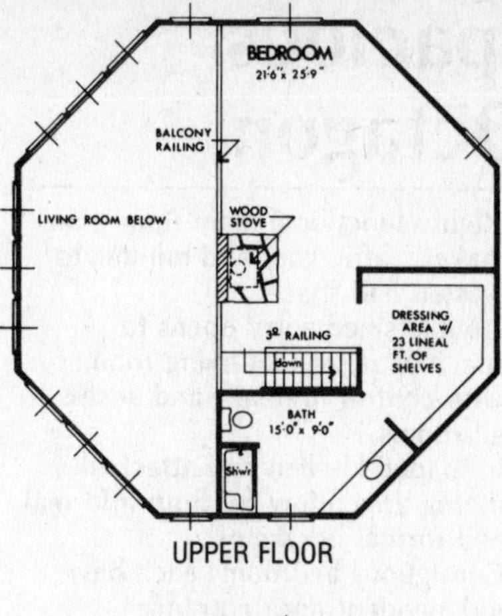

UPPER FLOOR

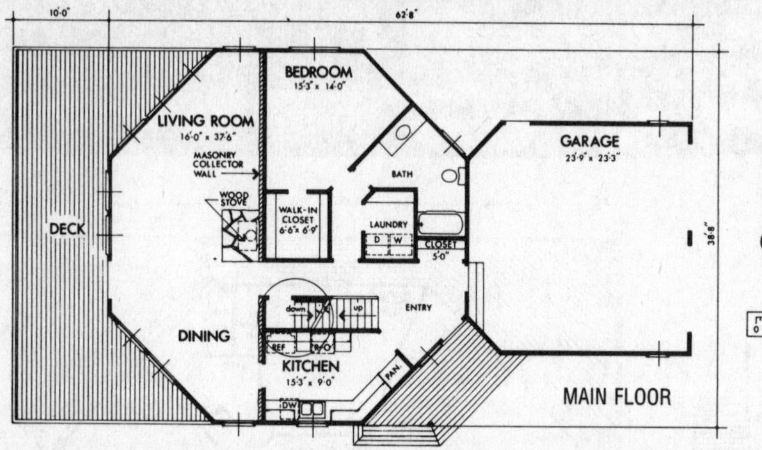

MAIN FLOOR

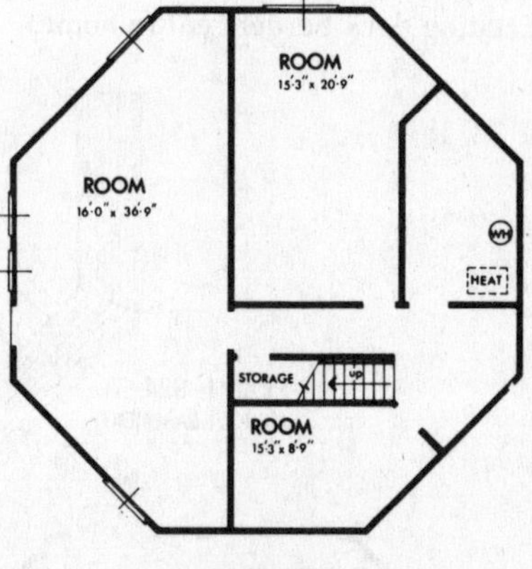

BASEMENT

Octagonal Sunshine Special

- Octagon homes offer the ultimate for taking advantage of a view, and are fascinating designs even for more ordinary settings.
- This plan offers a huge, house-spanning living/dining area with loads of glass and a masonry collector wall to store solar heat.
- The 700-square-foot upper level is devoted entirely to an enormous master suite, with a balcony overlooking the living room below, a roomy private bath and a large closet/dressing area.
- Scissor-trusses allow vaulted ceilings over the two-story-high living room and the master suite.
- A second roomy bedroom and full bath are offered downstairs, along with an efficient kitchen, a laundry area and inviting foyer.
- A daylight basement option offers the potential for more bedrooms, hobbies, work rooms or recreational space.

REAR VIEW

Plans H-948-1A & -1B

Bedrooms: 2-4	**Baths:** 2
Space:	
Upper floor:	700 sq. ft.
Main floor:	1,236 sq. ft.
Total without basement:	1,936 sq. ft.
Daylight basement:	1,236 sq. ft.
Total with basement:	3,172 sq. ft.
Garage:	550 sq. ft.
Exterior Wall Framing:	2x6

Foundation options:
Daylight basement (H-948-1B).
Crawlspace (H-948-1A).
(Foundation & framing conversion diagram available — see order form.)

Blueprint Price Code:

Without basement:	B
With basement:	E

TO ORDER THIS BLUEPRINT, CALL TOLL-FREE 1-800-547-5570
(prices and details on pp. 12-15.)

Plans H-948-1A & -1B

Excellent Family Design

- Long sloping rooflines and bold design features make this home attractive for any neighborhood.
- Inside, a vaulted entry takes visitors into an impressive vaulted Great Room with a wood stove and window-wall facing the house-spanning rear deck.
- Clerestory windows flanking the stove area and large windows front and rear flood the Great Room with natural light.
- The magnificent kitchen includes a stylish island and opens to the informal dining area which in turn flows into the Great Room.
- Two bedrooms on the main floor share a full bath, and bedroom #2 boasts easy access to the rear deck which spans the width of the house.
- The upstairs comprises an "adult retreat," with a roomy master suite, luxurious bath with double sinks, and a large walk-in closet.
- A daylight basement version adds another 1,410 sq. ft. of space for entertaining and recreation, plus a fourth bedroom and a large shop/storage area.

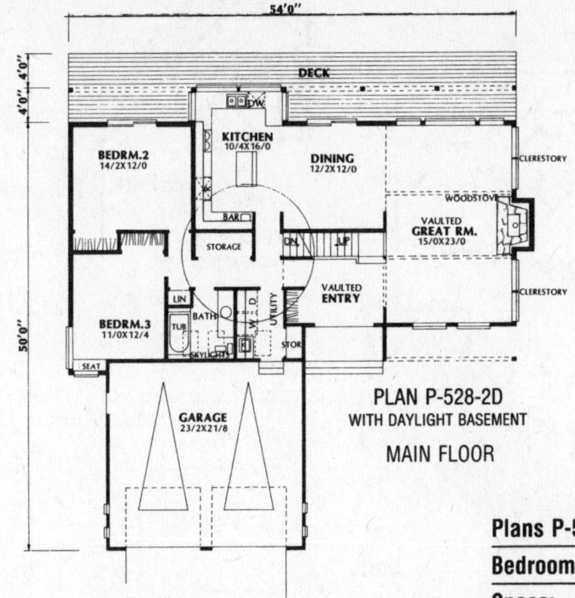

PLAN P-528-2D
WITH DAYLIGHT BASEMENT

MAIN FLOOR

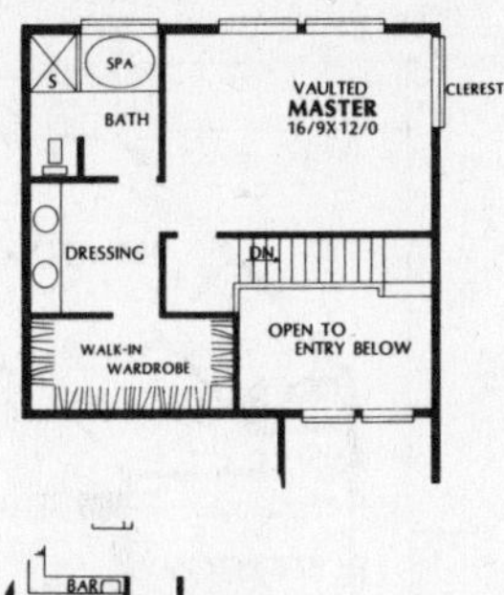

UPPER FLOOR
PLAN P-528-2A
WITHOUT BASEMENT
(CRAWLSPACE FOUNDATION)

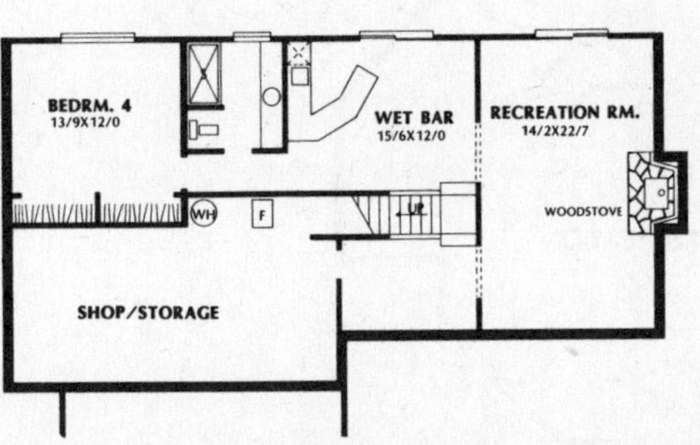

Plans P-528-2A & -2D

Bedrooms: 3-4 | **Baths:** 2-3

Space:
Upper floor: 498 sq. ft.
Main floor: 1,456 sq. ft.

Total living area: 1,954 sq. ft.
Basement: 1,410 sq. ft.
Garage: 502 sq. ft.

Exterior Wall Framing: 2x4

Foundation options:
Daylight basement (Plan P-528-2D).
Crawlspace (Plan P-528-2A).
(Foundation & framing conversion diagram available — see order form.)

Blueprint Price Code:
Without basement: B
With basement: E

Plans P-528-2A & -2D

TO ORDER THIS BLUEPRINT, CALL TOLL-FREE 1-800-547-5570
(prices and details on pp. 12-15.)

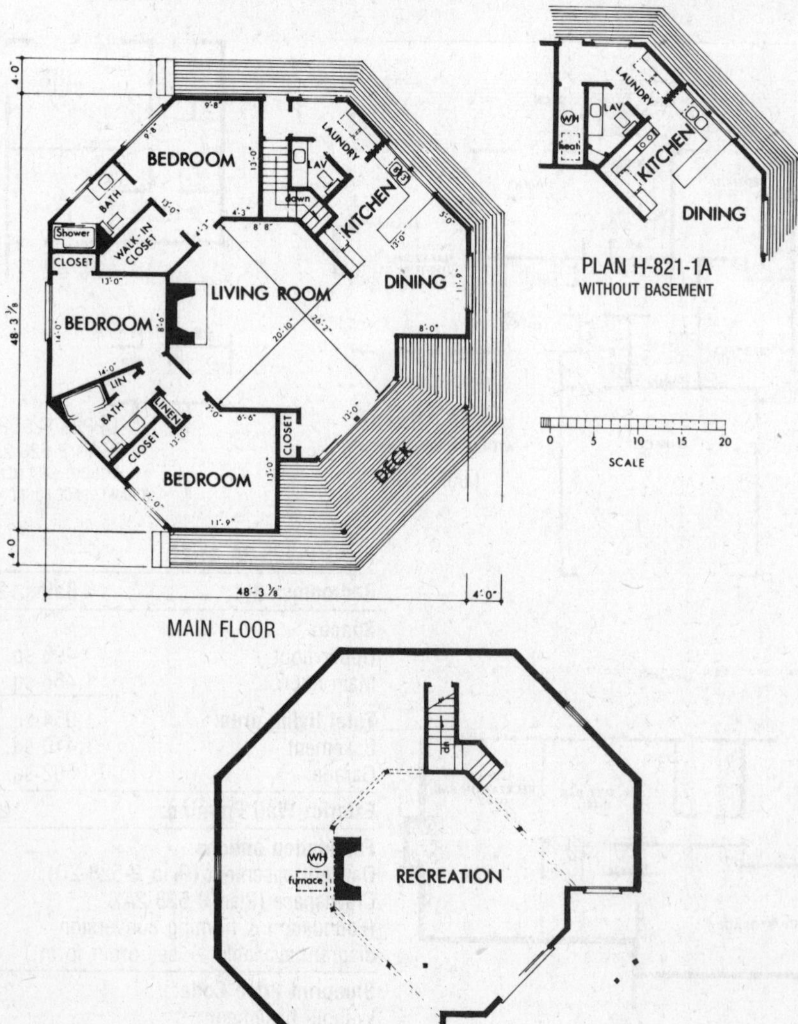

Versatile Octagon

- Popular octagonal design features a secondary raised roof to allow light into the 500 sq. ft. living room.
- Unique framing design allows you to divide the living space any way you choose: left open, with 3 or more bedrooms, a den, library or other options.
- Large, winding deck can accommodate outdoor parties and guests.
- Optional basement expands recreational opportunities.

Plans H-821-1 & -1A

Bedrooms: 3 **Baths:** 2½

Space:

Main floor:	1,699 sq. ft.
Total living area:	1,699 sq. ft.
Basement:	approx. 1,699 sq. ft.

Exterior Wall Framing: 2x4

Foundation options:
Daylight basement (Plan H-821-1).
Crawlspace (Plan H-821-1A).
(Foundation & framing conversion diagram available — see order form.)

Blueprint Price Code:

Without basement	B
With basement	E

TO ORDER THIS BLUEPRINT, CALL TOLL-FREE 1-800-547-5570 (prices and details on pp. 12-15.)

Plans H-821-1 & -1A

Economical Design

FRONT VIEW

- Uninterrupted glass and a full, rear deck afford a sweeping view of the outdoors.
- Rear orientation provides a seclusion from street and neighbors.
- Open, flexible family living areas allow for efficient traffic flow.
- Optional daylight basement plan offers recreation room, additional bedroom and third bath.

Plans H-868-1 & -1A

Bedrooms: 3-4	**Baths:** 2-3
Space:	
Main floor:	1,525 sq. ft.
Total living area:	1,525 sq. ft.
Basement:	1,420 sq. ft.
Garage:	426 sq. ft.
Exterior Wall Framing:	2x4

Foundation options:
Daylight basement (Plan H-868-1).
Crawlspace (Plan H-868-1A).
(Foundation & framing conversion diagram available — see order form.)

Blueprint Price Code:

Without basement	B
With basement	D

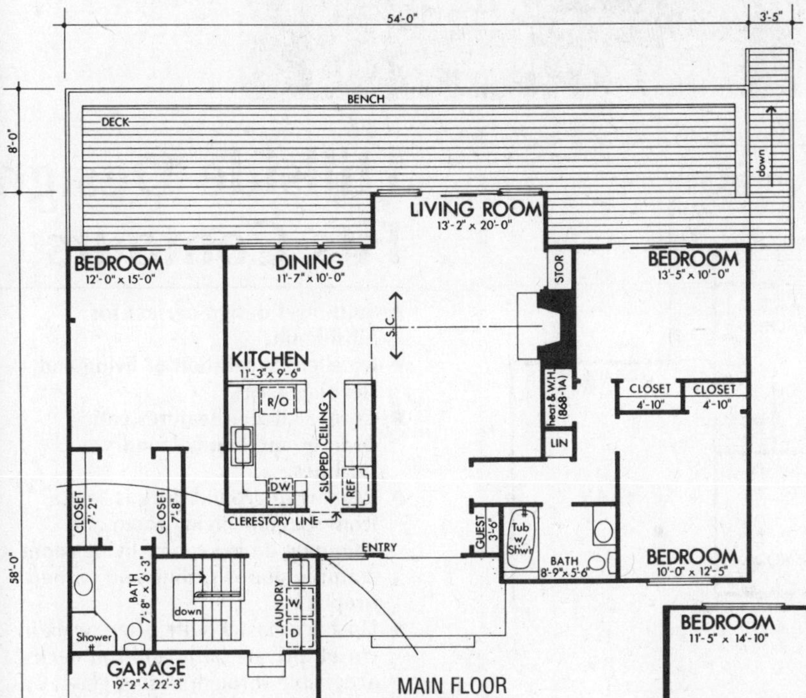

CLOSET 7'-2"
CLOSET 7'-2"
BATH 6'-3" x 8'-6"
Sh'wr
D
W
LAUNDRY
GARAGE 19'-2" x 23'-7"

MAIN FLOOR
PLAN H-868-1A
WITHOUT BASEMENT

54'-0"
3'-5"
8'-0"
58'-0"
BENCH
DECK
down
LIVING ROOM 13'-2" x 20'-0"
BEDROOM 12'-0" x 15'-0"
DINING 11'-7" x 10'-0"
STOR
BEDROOM 13'-5" x 10'-0"
S.C.
KITCHEN 11'-3" x 9'-6"
R/O
SLOPED CEILING
heat & W.H. (868-1A)
CLOSET 4'-10"
CLOSET 4'-10"
LIN
DW
REF
CLOSET 7'-2"
CLOSET 7'-8"
CLERESTORY LINE
ENTRY
GUEST 3'-6"
Tub w/ Sh'wr
BATH 8'-9" x 5'-6"
BEDROOM 10'-0" x 12'-5"
BATH 7'-8" x 6'-3"
down
LAUNDRY
W
D
Shower
GARAGE 19'-2" x 22'-3"

MAIN FLOOR
PLAN H-868-1
WITH DAYLIGHT BASEMENT

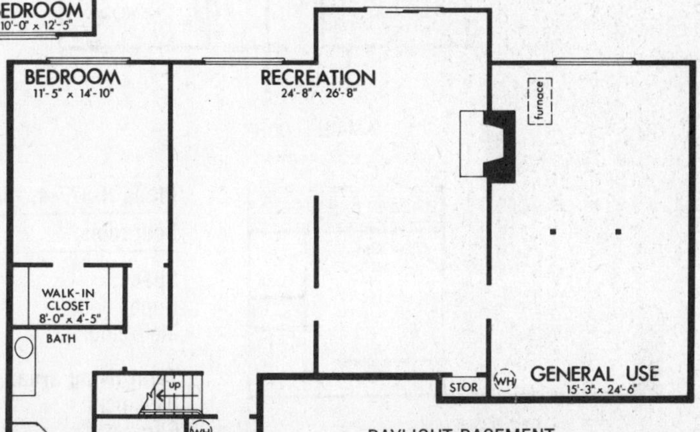

CLERESTORY WINDOW OVER KITCHEN

BEDROOM 11'-5" x 14'-10"
RECREATION 24'-8" x 26'-8"
furnace
WALK-IN CLOSET 8'-0" x 4'-5"
BATH
up
STOR
WH
GENERAL USE 15'-3" x 24'-6"
Shower
WH

DAYLIGHT BASEMENT

Plans H-868-1 & -1A

REAR VIEW

PLAN H-877-4
WITH BASEMENT

PLAN H-877-4A
WITHOUT BASEMENT

PLAN H-877-4B
WITH DAYLIGHT BASEMENT

MAIN FLOOR

Hillside Design Fits Contours

- **Split-level design perfect for hillside lot.**
- **Excellent separation of living and sleeping areas.**
- **Corner kitchen features eating counter and handy laundry facilities.**
- **Rear wrap-around deck is seen from spacious living room and adjoining dining room; living room features sloped ceiling and corner fireplace.**
- **Upstairs master suite offers walk-in closet, private bath, and sun deck accessible through sliding glass doors.**

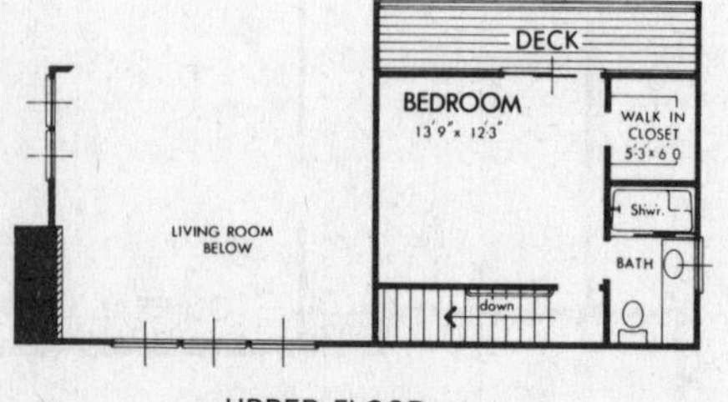

UPPER FLOOR

Plans H-877-4, -4A & -4B

Bedrooms: 3	**Baths:** 2
Space:	
Upper floor:	333 sq. ft.
Main floor:	1,200 sq. ft.
Total living area:	1,533 sq. ft.
Basement:	741 sq. ft.
Garage:	459 sq. ft.

Exterior Wall Framing:	2x6

Foundation options:
Daylight basement (Plan H-877-4B).
Standard basement (Plan H-877-4).
Crawlspace (Plan H-877-4A).
(Foundation & framing conversion diagram available — see order form.)

Blueprint Price Code:	B

TO ORDER THIS BLUEPRINT, CALL TOLL-FREE 1-800-547-5570
(prices and details on pp. 12-15.)

Plans H-877-4, -4A & -4B

Dramatic Contemporary Takes Advantage of Slope

- Popular plan puts problem building site to work by taking advantage of the slope to create a dramatic and pleasant home.
- Spacious vaulted living/dining area is bathed in natural light from cathedral windows facing the front and clerestory windows at the peak.
- Big kitchen includes pantry and abundant counter space.
- Three main-level bedrooms are isolated for more peace and quiet.
- Lower level includes large recreation room, a fourth bedroom, third bath, laundry area and extra space for a multitude of other uses.

Photo courtesy of HomeStyles Plan Service

**NOTE: The above photographed home may have been modified by the homeowner. Please refer to floor plan and/or drawn elevation shown for actual blueprint details.

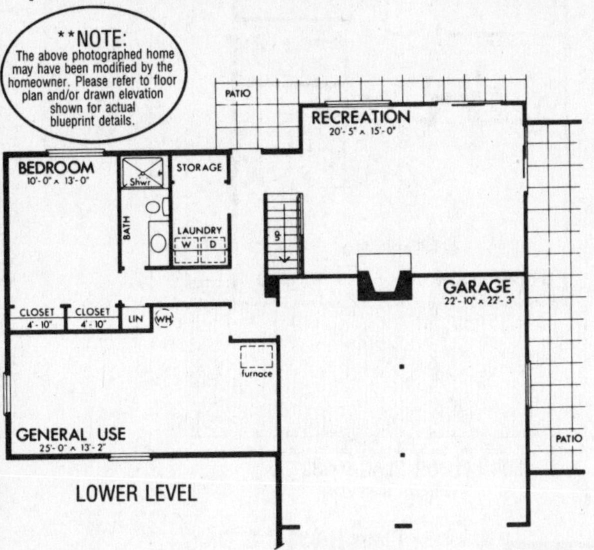

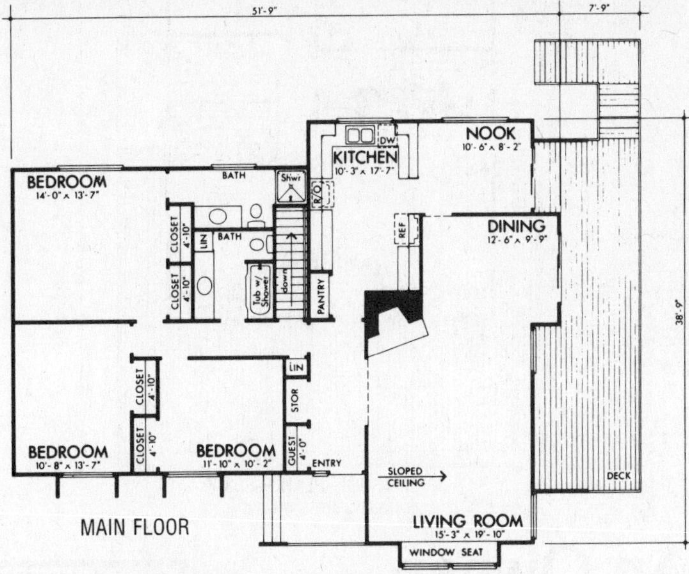

Plan H-2045-5	
Bedrooms: 4	**Baths:** 3
Space:	
Main floor:	1,602 sq. ft.
Lower floor:	1,133 sq. ft.
Total living area:	2,735 sq. ft.
Garage:	508 sq. ft.
Exterior Wall Framing:	2x4
Foundation options: Daylight basement only. (Foundation & framing conversion diagram available — see order form.).	
Blueprint Price Code:	D

Plans H-2045-5

(prices and details on pp. 12-15.)

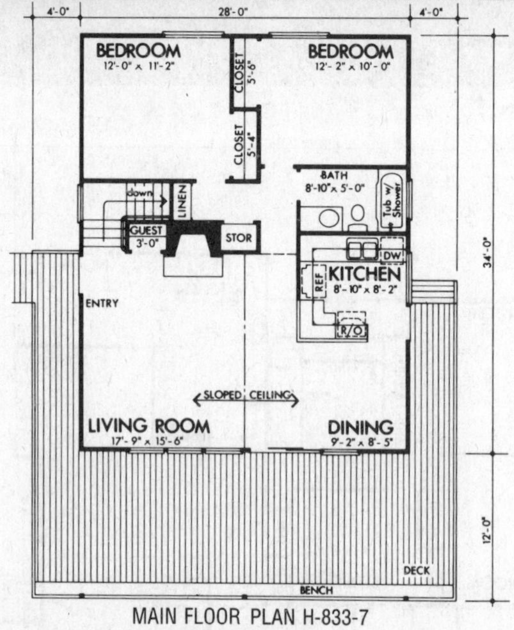

MAIN FLOOR PLAN H-833-7
WITH DAYLIGHT BASEMENT

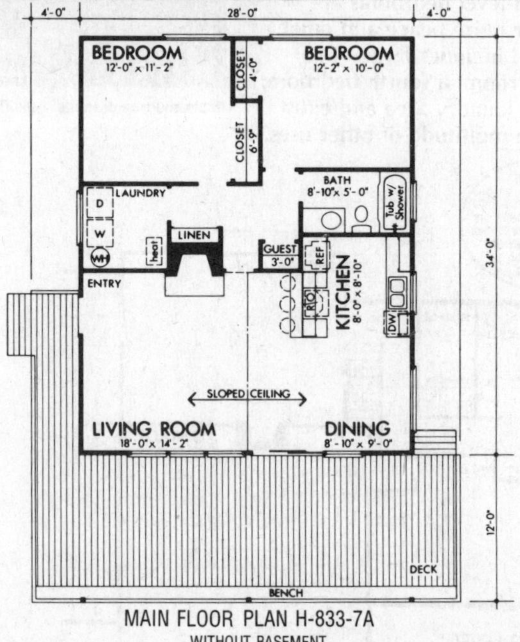

MAIN FLOOR PLAN H-833-7A
WITHOUT BASEMENT

An Owner-Builder Special

- Everything you need for a leisure or retirement retreat is neatly packaged in just 952 square feet.
- Basic rectangular design features unique wrap-around deck entirely covered by the projecting roof line.
- Vaulted ceilings and central fireplace visually enhances the cozy living-dining room.
- Daylight basement option is suitable for building on a sloping lot.

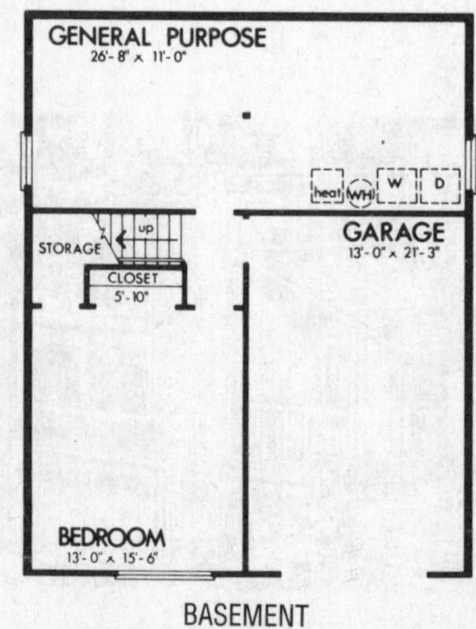

BASEMENT

Plans H-833-7 & -7A

Bedrooms: 2-3 **Baths:** 1

Space:
Main floor: 952 sq. ft.

Total living area: 952 sq. ft.
Basement: approx. 952 sq. ft.
Garage: (included in basement) 276 sq. ft.

Exterior Wall Framing: 2x6

Foundation options:
Daylight basement (Plan H-833-7).
Crawlspace (Plan H-833-7A).
(Foundation & framing conversion diagram available — see order form.)

Blueprint Price Code:
Without basement A
With basement B

Plans H-833-7 & -7A

Build It On Weekends

- The basic design and use of truss roof framing promote easy and speedy erection.
- See-through kitchen allows a look into the living or dining rooms.
- Living room reveals the outdoors and surrounding deck through sliding glass doors.
- Separate bedroom/bathroom area eliminates cross-room traffic and wasted hall space.
- Plan H-921-2A utilizes the sealed crawlspace as an air distribution chamber for a Plen-Wood heating system.
- Plan H-921-1A has a standard crawlspace foundation and optional solar heating system.

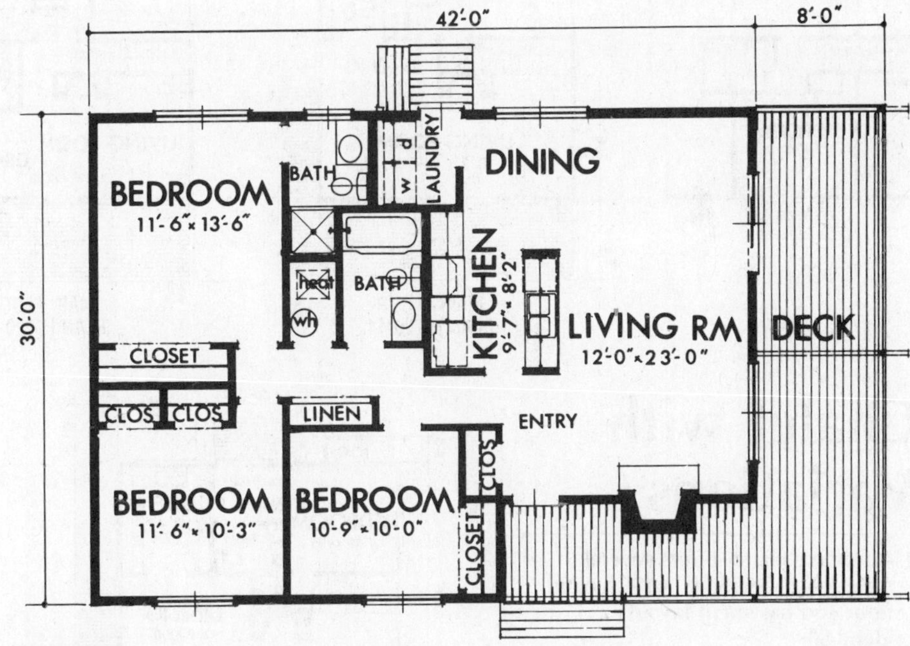

Plans H-921-1A & -2A

Bedrooms: 3 **Baths:** 2

Space:
Main floor: 1,164 sq. ft.
Total living area: 1,164 sq. ft.

Exterior Wall Framing: 2x6

Foundation options:
Plen-Wood crawlspace system (Plan H-921-2A).
Standard crawlspace (Plan H-921-1A).
Foundation & framing conversion diagram available — see order form.)

Blueprint Price Code: A

Plans H-921-1A & -2A

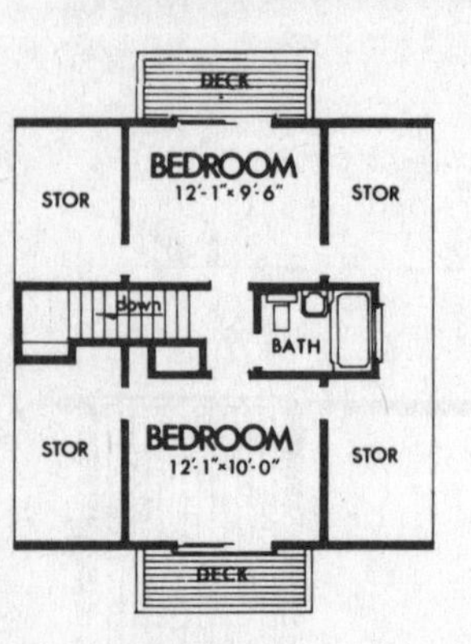

UPPER FLOOR

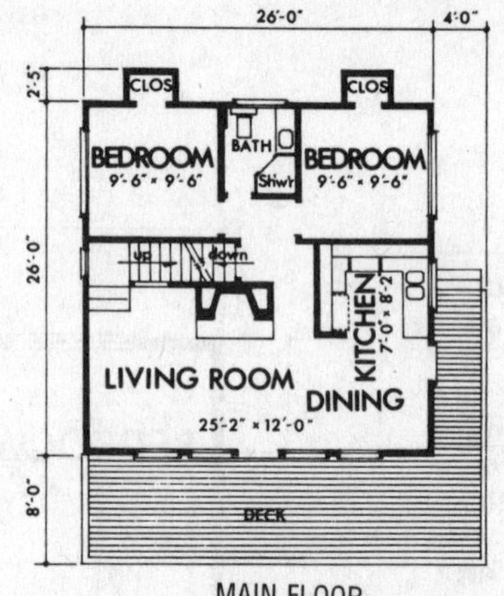

MAIN FLOOR
PLAN H-720-11

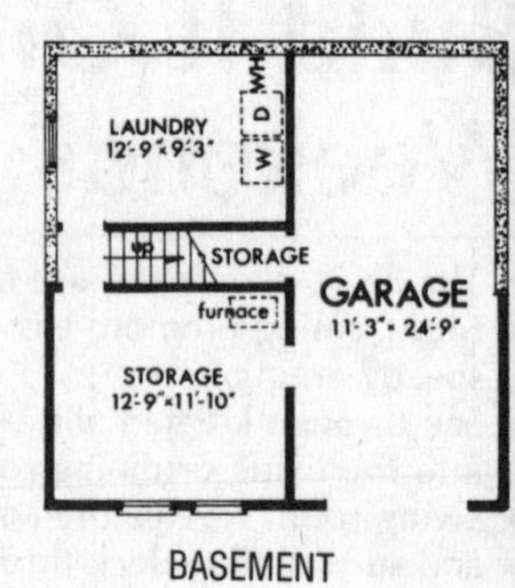

MAIN FLOOR
PLAN H-720-10

BASEMENT

Chalet with Variations

- Attractive chalet offers several main level variations, with second floor and basement layouts identical.
- All versions feature well-arranged kitchen, attached dining area, and large living room.
- Second-floor amenities include private decks off each bedroom and storage space in every corner!

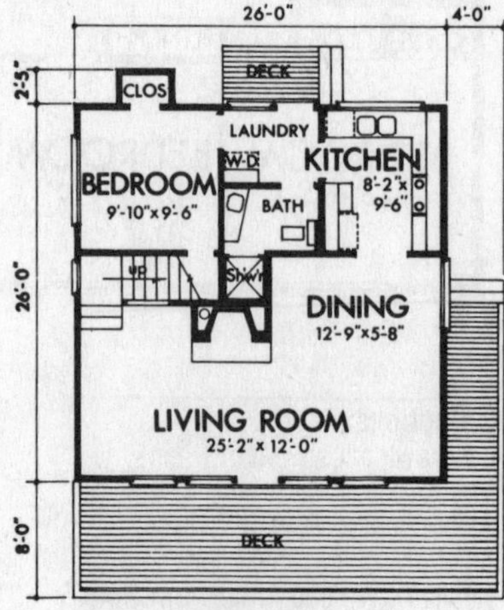

MAIN FLOOR
PLAN H-720-12A
WITHOUT BASEMENT

Plans H-720-10, -11 & -12A

Bedrooms: 3-4	**Baths:** 2
Space:	
Upper floor:	328 sq. ft.
Main floor:	686 sq. ft.
Total living area:	1,014 sq. ft.
Basement:	approx. 686 sq. ft.
Garage: (incl. in basement)	278 sq. ft.
Exterior Wall Framing:	2x4

Foundation options:
Daylight basement
(Plans H-720-10 or -11).
Crawlspace (Plan H-720-12A)
(Foundation & framing conversion diagram available — see order form.)

Blueprint Price Code:

Without basement:	A
With basement:	B

TO ORDER THIS BLUEPRINT,
CALL TOLL-FREE 1-800-547-5570
 (prices and details on pp. 12-15.)

Five-Bedroom Chalet

ealizing that there are situations that equire the maximum number of bedrooms, e have created this modest-sized home ontaining five bedrooms. One of these, specially the one over the garage, would erve very well as a private den, card oom or library. The plan is available with or without basement.

This is an excellent example of the classic chalet. Close study will reveal how hall space has been kept at an absolute minimum. As a result, a modest first floor area of 952 sq. ft. and a compact second floor plan of 767 sq. ft. make the five bedrooms possible.

Also notice the abundance of storage space and built-ins with many other conveniences. Plumbing is provided in two complete bathrooms, and a washer and dryer has been tucked into one corner of the central hall on the main floor.

A clever technique has been used in the design of the staircase as it progresses halfway up to a landing midway between the two floors. From here it branches in two directions to a bedroom over the garage and to a hallway common to other rooms.

First floor:	952 sq. ft.
Second floor:	767 sq. ft.
Total living area:	1,719 sq. ft.

(Not counting basement or garage)

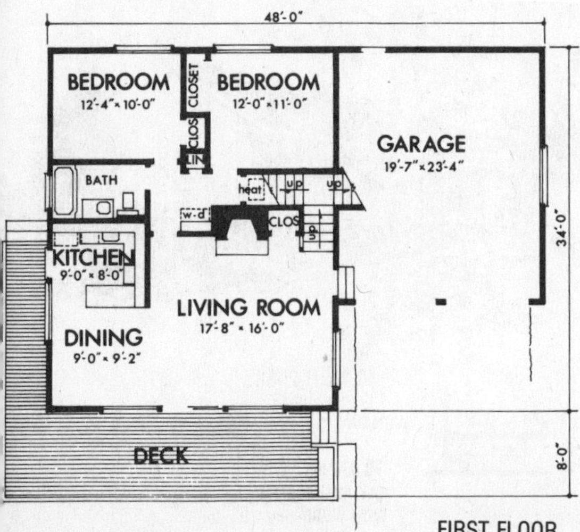

FIRST FLOOR
952 SQUARE FEET

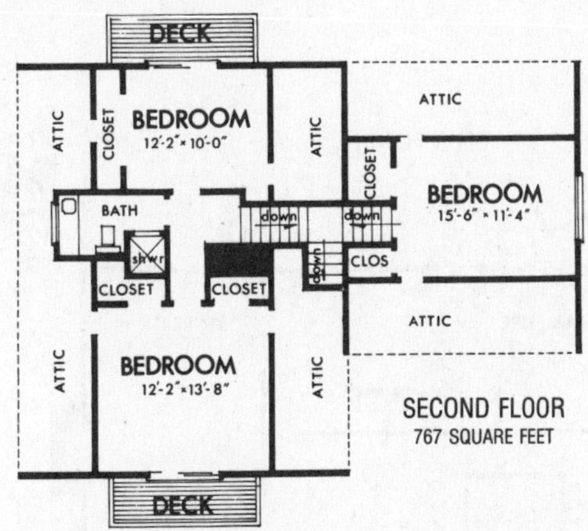

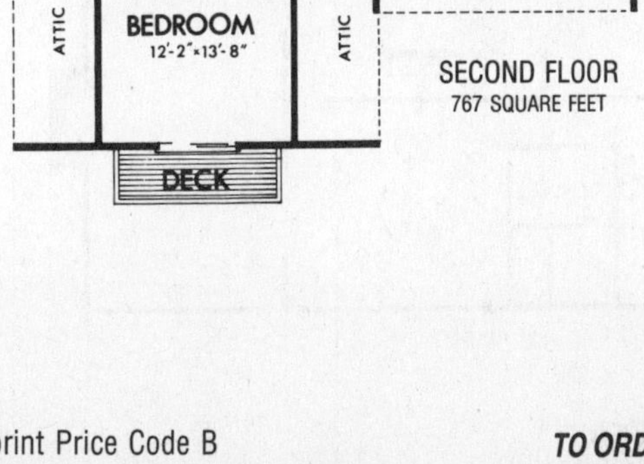

SECOND FLOOR
767 SQUARE FEET

PLAN H-804-2
WITH BASEMENT
PLAN H-804-2A
WITHOUT BASEMENT
(CRAWLSPACE FOUNDATION)

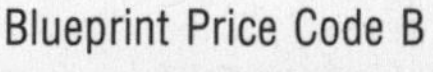

Blueprint Price Code B

Plans H-804-2 & -2A

TO ORDER THIS BLUEPRINT, CALL TOLL-FREE 1-800-547-5570

(prices and details on pp. 12-15.)

Surrounded by Decks

- Wrap-around deck offers a panoramic view of the surroundings as well as space for outdoor living and relaxation.
- Angular arrangement of garage, breezeway, and home provides front-yard privacy and a visual barrier to front bedrooms from street traffic.
- Exciting L-shaped dining room, attached sunken living room, and deck create a perfect atmosphere for entertaining.
- Basement is available with either a concrete floor (Plan H-2083), a framed floor for steep sloping sites (Plan H-2083-B), or on a crawlspace (Plan H-2083-A).

DECK
BEDROOM 12'-0" × 15'-10"
BATH
NOOK 7'-0" × 12'-6"
KITCHEN 9'-0" × 9'-2"
WALK-IN CLOSET
DINING 10'-0" × 12'-6"
HALL
BEDROOM 11'-0" × 11'-0"
BATH
LAUNDRY
BEDROOM 10'-0" × 11'-0"
ENTRY
SUNKEN LIVING ROOM 14'-3" × 27'-3"
ENTRY BRIDGE
GARAGE 23'-3" × 23'-3"

MAIN FLOOR

GENERAL USE
RECREATION ROOM 14'-3" × 26'-6"
BATH

BASEMENT

Plans H-2083, -A & -B

Bedrooms: 3	**Baths:** 2-3
Space:	
Main floor:	1,660 sq. ft.
Basement:	1,660 sq. ft.
Total living area with basement:	3,320 sq. ft.
Garage:	541 sq. ft.
Exterior Wall Framing:	2x4

Foundation options:
Daylight basement (Plans H-2083 & H-2083-B).
Crawlspace (Plan H-2083-A).
(Foundation & framing conversion diagram available — see order form.)

Blueprint Price Code:

Without basement:	B
With basement:	E

(Seeing facing page for alternate floor plan).

PLAN H-2083
(CONCRETE)
WITH DAYLIGHT BASEMENT

PLAN H-2083-B
DAYLIGHT BASEMENT
WITH WOOD-FRAMED
LOWER LEVEL

TO ORDER THIS BLUEPRINT, CALL TOLL-FREE 1-800-547-5570

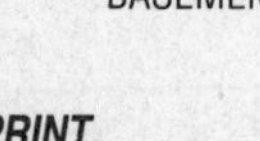

 (prices and details on pp. 12-15.)

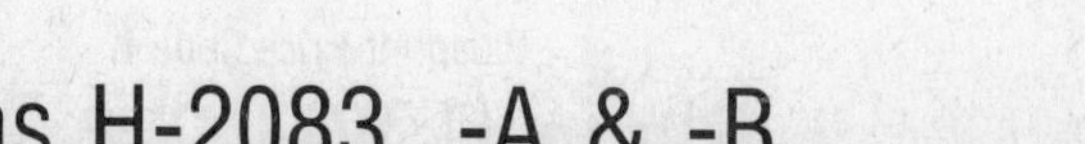

Plans H-2083, -A & -B

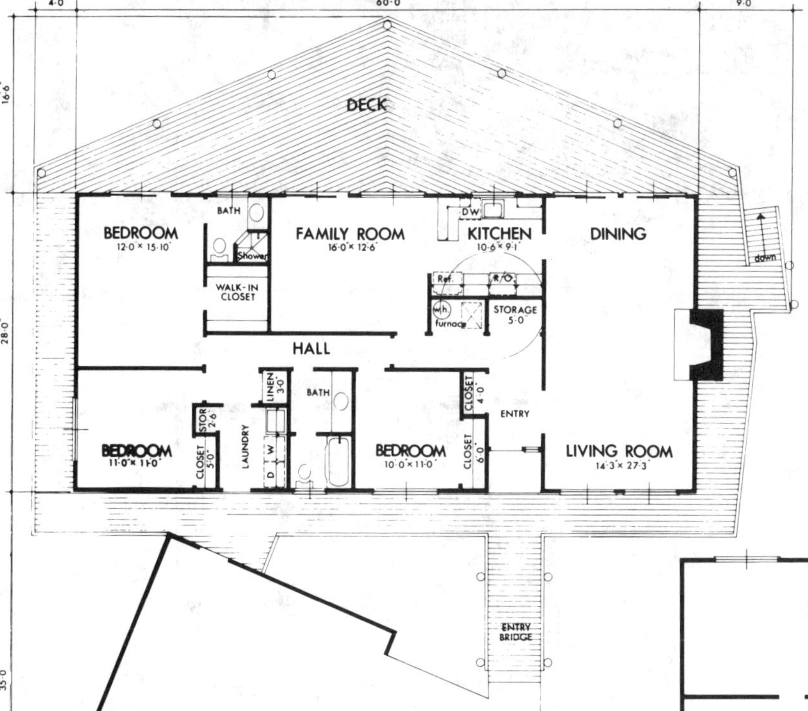

Gracious Indoor/ Outdoor Living

- A clean design makes this plan adaptable to almost any climate or setting.
- Perfect for a scenic, hillside lot, the structure and wrap-around deck offers a spanning view.
- Kitchen is flanked by family and dining rooms, allowing easy entrance from both.
- Foundation options include a daylight basement on concrete slab (H-2083-1), a wood-framed lower level (H-2083-1B), and a crawlspace (H-2083-1A).

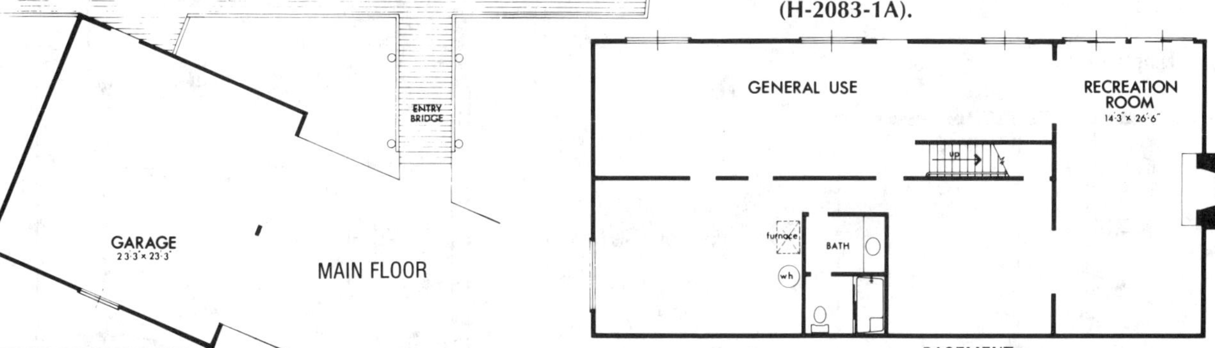

Ref. R/O STOR down

PLAN H-2083-1
WITH DAYLIGHT BASEMENT
(ON CONCRETE SLAB)

PLAN H-2083-1B
(WITH WOOD-FRAMED LOWER LEVEL)

(See facing page for both rear view and alternate floor plan.)

Plans H-2083-1, -1A & -1B

Bedrooms: 3	**Baths:** 2-3
Space:	
Main floor:	1,660 sq. ft.
Basement:	1,660 sq. ft.
Total living area: with basement:	3,320 sq. ft.
Garage:	541 sq. ft.

Exterior Wall Framing:	2x4
Foundation options: Daylight basement (Plan H-2083-1 or -1B). Crawlspace (Plan H-2083-1A). (Foundation & framing conversion diagram available — see order form.)	
Blueprint Price Code:	
Without basement:	B
With basement:	E

TO ORDER THIS BLUEPRINT, CALL TOLL-FREE 1-800-547-5570

Week-End Retreat

For those whose goal is a small, affordable retreat at the shore or in the mountains, this plan may be the answer. Although it measures less than 400 sq. ft. of living space on the main floor, it lacks nothing in comfort and convenience. A sizeable living room boasts a masonry hearth on which to mount your choice of wood stove or pre-fab fireplace. There is plenty of room for furniture, including a dining table.

The galley type kitchen is a small marvel of compact convenience and utility, even boasting a dishwasher and space for a stackable washer and dryer. The wide open nature of the first floor guarantees that even the person working in the kitchen area will still be included in the party. On the floor plan, a dashed line across the living room indicates the limits of the balcony bedroom above. In front of this line, the A-frame shape of the living room soars from floor boards to the ridge beam high above. Clerestory windows lend a further note of spaciousness and unity with nature's outdoors. A huge planked deck adds to the indoor-outdoor relationship.

A modest sized bedroom on the second floor is approached by a standard stairway, not an awkward ladder or heavy pull-down stairway as is often the case in small A-frames. The view over the balcony rail to the living room below adds a note of distinction. The unique framing pattern allows a window at either end of the bedroom, improving both outlook and ventilation.

A compact bathroom serves both levels and enjoys natural daylight through a skylight window.

First floor:	391 sq. ft.
Upper level:	144 sq. ft.
Total living area:	535 sq. ft.

FRONT VIEW

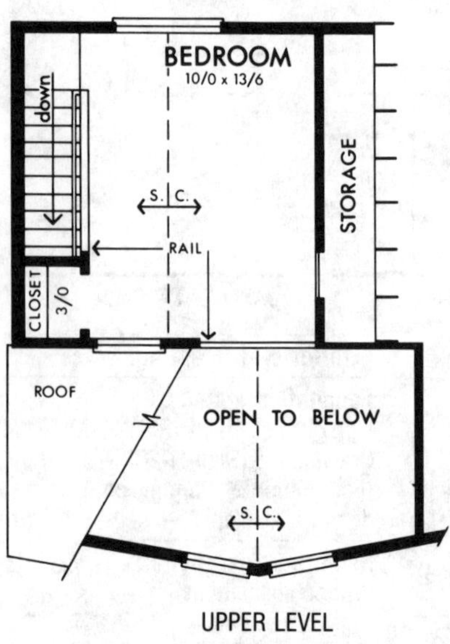

UPPER LEVEL
144 SQUARE FEET

(Exterior walls are 2x6 construction)

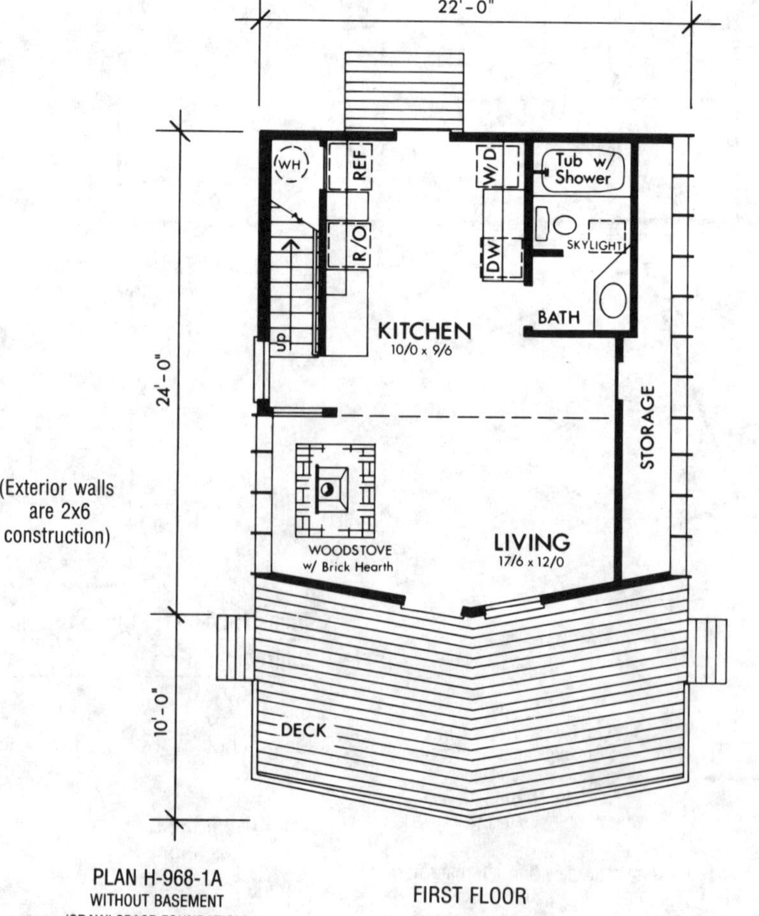

PLAN H-968-1A
WITHOUT BASEMENT
(CRAWLSPACE FOUNDATION)

FIRST FLOOR
391 SQUARE FEET

TO ORDER THIS BLUEPRINT, CALL TOLL-FREE 1-800-547-5570
(prices and details on pp. 12-15.)

Blueprint Price Code A

Plan H-968-1A

A Plan for Weekends or Permanent Retirement

Some recreation homes are more suited than others to eventual retirement living. Plan H-786-3 is one of these. Simplicity of design keeps the cost in line. Careful attention to appearance and arrangement make this plan suitable for almost any neighborhood and livable for any time of life. Revolving around a central entry hall, the design provides a traffic pattern superior to most small recreation homes.

Although the small family will probably use the breakfast bar for most meals, ample space for a dining table is provided at one end of the 24′ living room.

The convenience of a U-shaped kitchen makes this by far the most desirable type for most homemakers.

A more than adequate sized bath serves the two large bedrooms and a 3′ x 4′-6″ hall storage closet is a most unusual bonus feature. The central location of the furnace provides for economical and effective heating.

Vaulted ceilings with exposed beams are specified in all but the hall, bath and bedrooms. Insulation for these vaulted areas is easily accomplished by use of a rigid fiberglass board laid between sheathing and roofing. The nearly 300 sq. ft. deck provides the final touch for this excellent home.

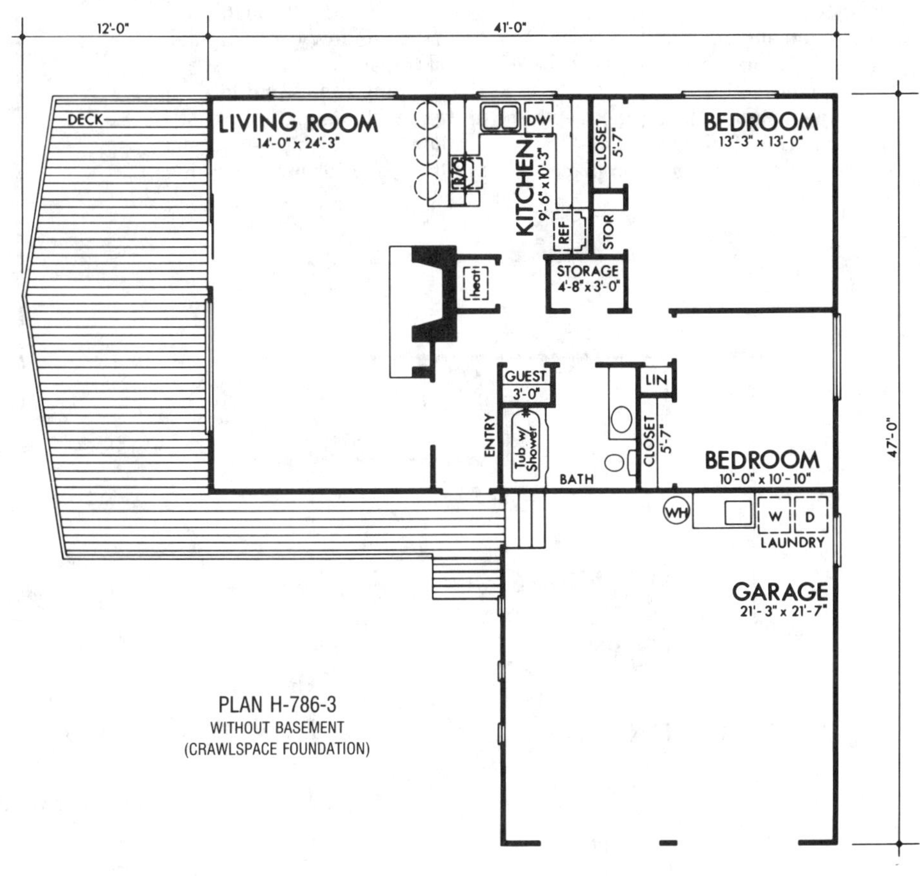

Total living area: 1,025 sq. ft.
(Not counting garage)

Blueprint Price Code A

Plan H-786-3

(prices and details on pp. 12-15.)

Casual Flexibility

- This beautifully designed vacation or year-round suite incorporates flexibility in its space and style of living.
- The abundance of windows offers stained glass opportunities as well as a bright interior.
- The open, vaulted living room boasts a central fireplace that makes a great conversation place or a cozy spot for cold winter evenings.
- The kitchen opens to the dining room and beyond through the dramatic window-wall with half-round transom.
- The sleeping rooms and loft upstairs will adequately accommodate eight, or you may use the space for other activities.

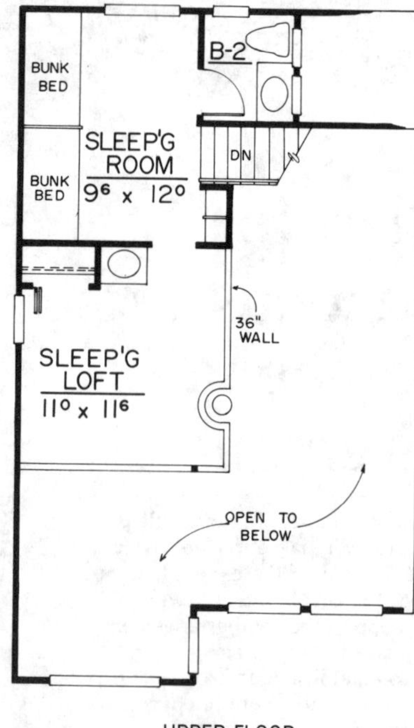

UPPER FLOOR

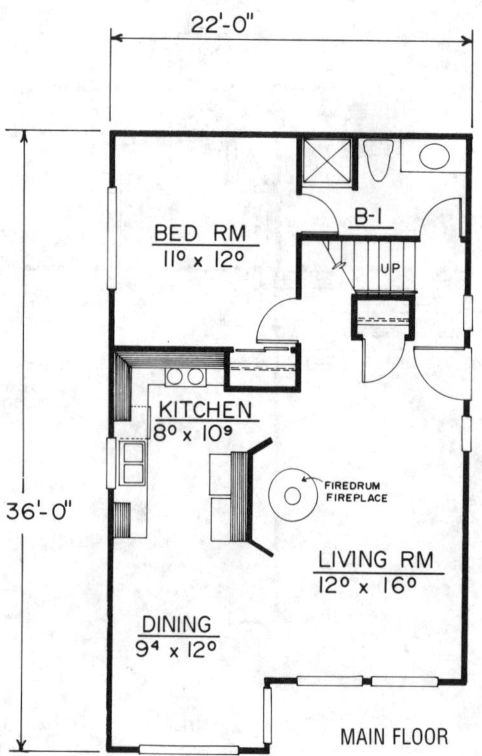

MAIN FLOOR

Plan I-1032-A

Bedrooms: 2-3	**Baths:** 1½
Space:	
Upper floor:	288 sq. ft.
Main floor:	744 sq. ft.
Total living area:	1,032 sq. ft.
Exterior Wall Framing:	2x6

Foundation options:
Partial basement.
(Foundation & framing conversion diagram available — see order form.)

Blueprint Price Code: A

TO ORDER THIS BLUEPRINT, CALL TOLL-FREE 1-800-547-5570

 (prices and details on pp. 12-15.)

Plan I-1032-A

Contemporary Chalet

- Vertical wood siding, angled transom windows, and a steeply pitched roof give a contemporary chalet character to this recreation home.
- The spacious, open-feeling interior blends the living and dining rooms together under a sloped two-story ceiling with loft overlook above.
- The living room also offers a fireplace and sliders to an angled deck.
- Sleeping quarters include a main floor bedroom and one or two additional bedrooms upstairs.

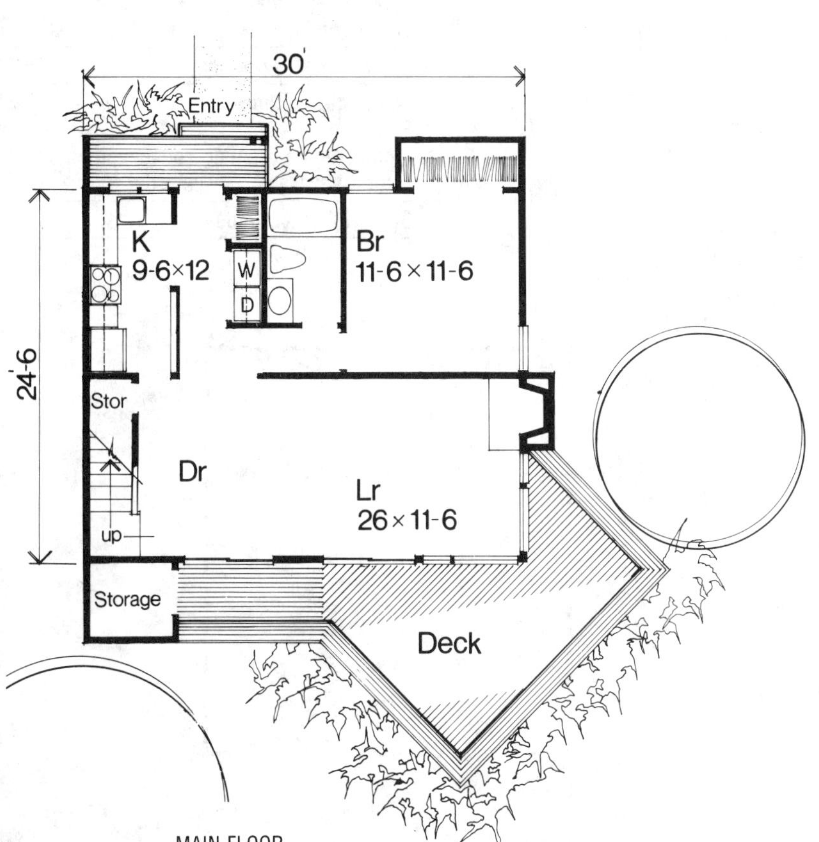

MAIN FLOOR

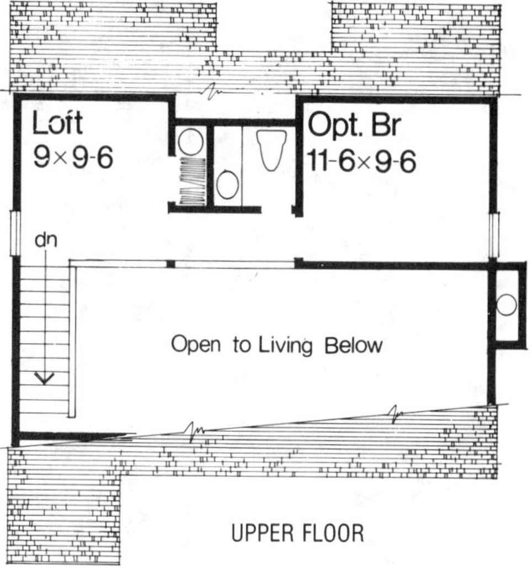

UPPER FLOOR

Plan B-7807

Bedrooms: 2-3	**Baths:** 1½
Space:	
Upper floor	270 sq. ft.
Main floor:	769 sq. ft.
Total living area:	1,039 sq. ft.
Storage area:	approx. 40 sq. ft.
Exterior Wall Framing:	2x4
Foundation options:	
Crawlspace.	
(Foundation & framing conversion diagram available — see order form.)	
Blueprint Price Code:	A

Plan B-7807

TO ORDER THIS BLUEPRINT, CALL TOLL-FREE 1-800-547-5570
(prices and details on pp. 12-15.)

The Simple & Economical Housing Solution

- This compact plan could serve as a second home or a primary residence for a small family.
- Spacious Great Room features woodstove and a large adjoining deck.
- Efficent kitchen is close to storage and laundry area.
- Large, overlooking loft offers infinite possibilities, such as extra sleeping quarters, a home office, art studio, or recreation room.
- Clerestory window arrangement and sloped-ceilings top the loft for added light.

Plan H-963-2A

Bedrooms: 1	**Baths:** 1
Space:	
Loft:	432 sq. ft.
Main floor:	728 sq. ft.
Total living area:	1,160 sq. ft.
Lower level/garage:	728 sq. ft.
Exterior Wall Framing:	2x4
Foundation options:	
Slab.	
(Foundation & framing conversion diagram available — see order form.)	
Blueprint Price Code:	A

SLOPED CEILING
LOFT
25'-3" x 16'-2"
down
RAILING
S.C.
CLERESTORY LINE
S.C.
OPEN TO GREAT ROOM
SKYLIGHTS

LOFT

CLERESTORY WINDOWS OVER LOFT AND STAIRS

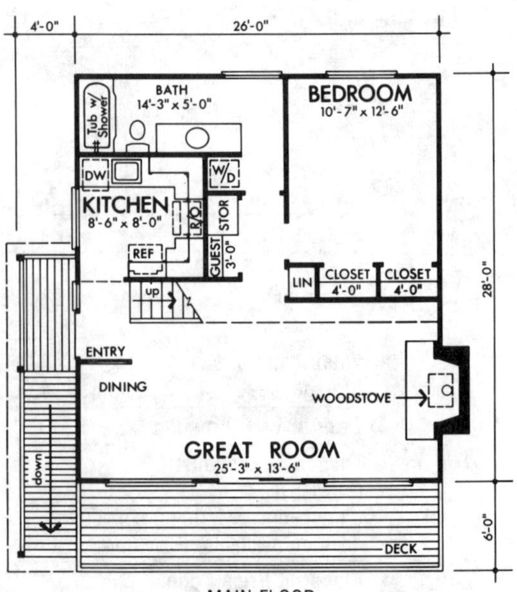

MAIN FLOOR

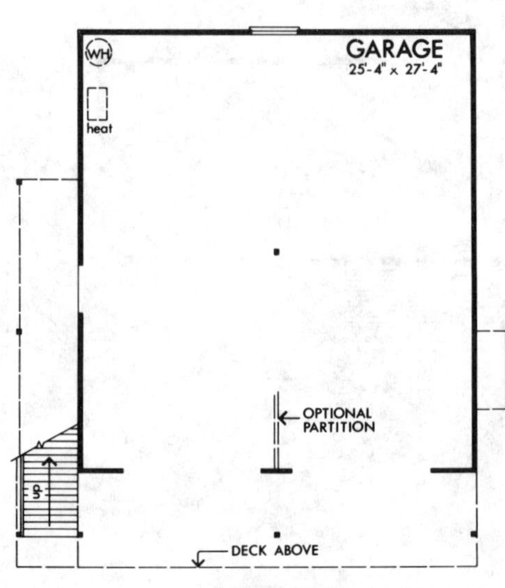

LOWER LEVEL

TO ORDER THIS BLUEPRINT, CALL TOLL-FREE 1-800-547-5570
(prices and details on pp. 12-15.)

Plan H-963-2A

HomeStyles SOURCE 1 DESIGNERS' NETWORK

Spectacular Sloping Design

- For the lake or mountain-view sloping lot, this spectacular design hugs the hill and takes full advantage of the views.
- A three-sided wrap-around deck makes indoor-outdoor living a pleasure.
- The sunken living room, with cathedral ceiling, skylight, fireplace, and glass galore, is the heart of the plan.
- The formal dining room and the kitchen/breakfast room both overlook the living room and deck views beyond.
- The main-floor master bedroom has private access to the deck and the bath.
- Two more bedrooms upstairs share a skylit bath and flank a dramatic balcony sitting area overlooking the living room below.

Plan AX-98607

Bedrooms: 3	**Baths:** 2
Space:	
Upper floor:	531 sq. ft.
Main floor:	1,098 sq. ft.
Total living area:	1,629 sq. ft.
Basement:	894 sq. ft.
Garage:	327 sq. ft.
Exterior Wall Framing:	2x4

Foundation options:
Standard basement.
Slab.
(Foundation & framing conversion diagram available — see order form.)

Blueprint Price Code: B

MAIN FLOOR

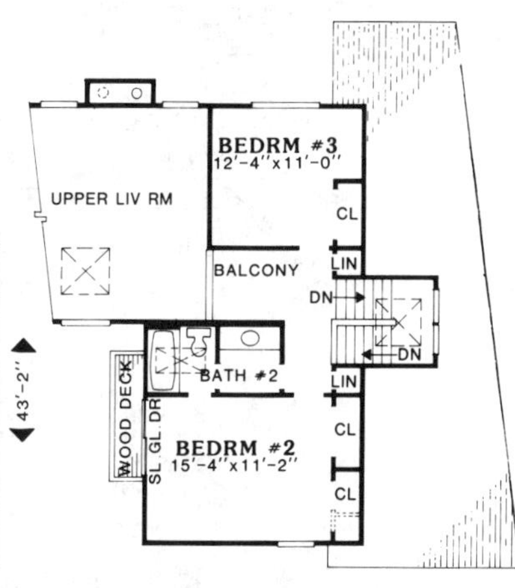

UPPER FLOOR

Plan AX-98607

Multi-Level Contemporary

- Multiple levels in this exciting contemporary home allow it to step down the side of a mountain or sloping lakeside site.
- A wooden deck skirts three sides of the home to maximize views outside while an abundance of windows and glass doors allow enjoyment of the views while inside.
- The entry opens to a view of the sunken living room with a dramatic 21-foot ceiling.
- The U-shaped kitchen flows into the spacious dining area with sliders to the deck.
- A main-level bedroom has handy access to a bath with a large shower.
- The upper level includes two more bedrooms, a bath with a tub, and a balcony overlooking the living room below.

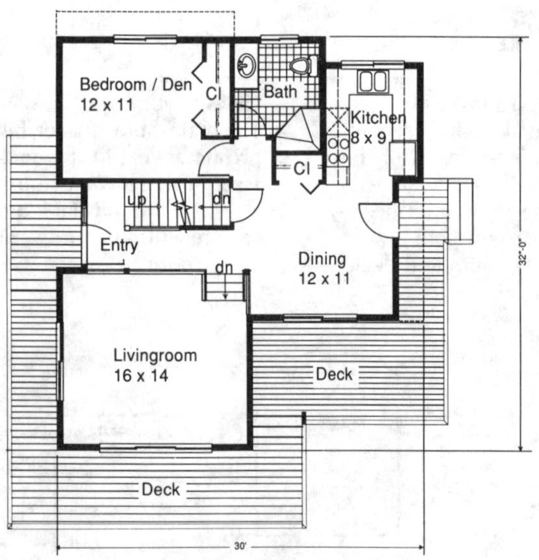

MAIN FLOOR

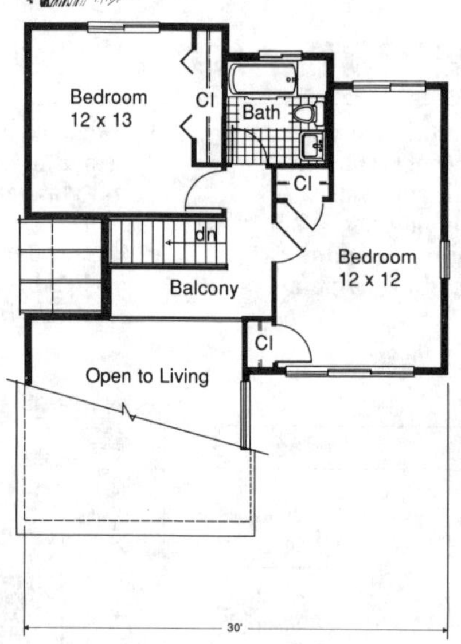

UPPER FLOOR

Plan CAR-78019

Bedrooms: 3	**Baths:** 2
Space:	
Upper floor:	572 sq. ft.
Main floor:	769 sq. ft.
Total living area:	1,341 sq. ft.
Basement:	540 sq. ft.

Exterior Wall Framing: 2x6

Foundation options:
Standard basement.
Slab.
(Foundation & framing conversion diagram available — see order form.)

Blueprint Price Code: A

TO ORDER THIS BLUEPRINT, CALL TOLL-FREE 1-800-547-5570

 (prices and details on pp. 12-15.)

Plan CAR-78019

Loaded With Options

- This rustic A-frame offers an optional solar heating system and attached screened porch; other exciting features include a large rear deck, an attached outdoor shower, and a second floor balcony off the upper level bedrooms.
- The dramatic living/dining area below boasts a heat-circulating fireplace with opposite-facing barbecue, sliding glass doors on four sides and a snack bar off the kitchen; it is open to the second floor balcony.
- A whirlpool tub is located in the main floor bath, shared by both the master and secondary bedrooms.
- Two additional bedrooms and a second bath are found on the upper level.

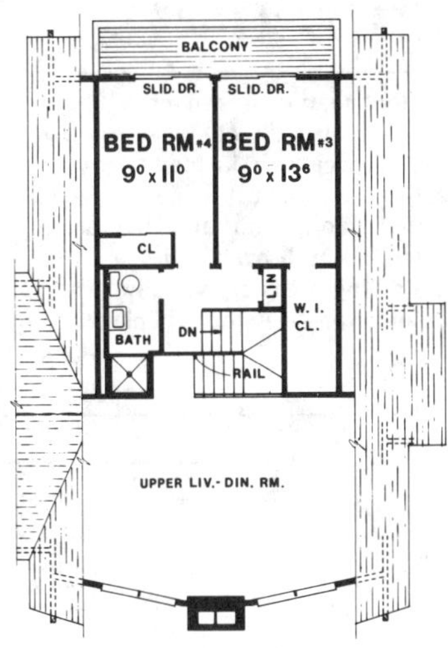

UPPER FLOOR

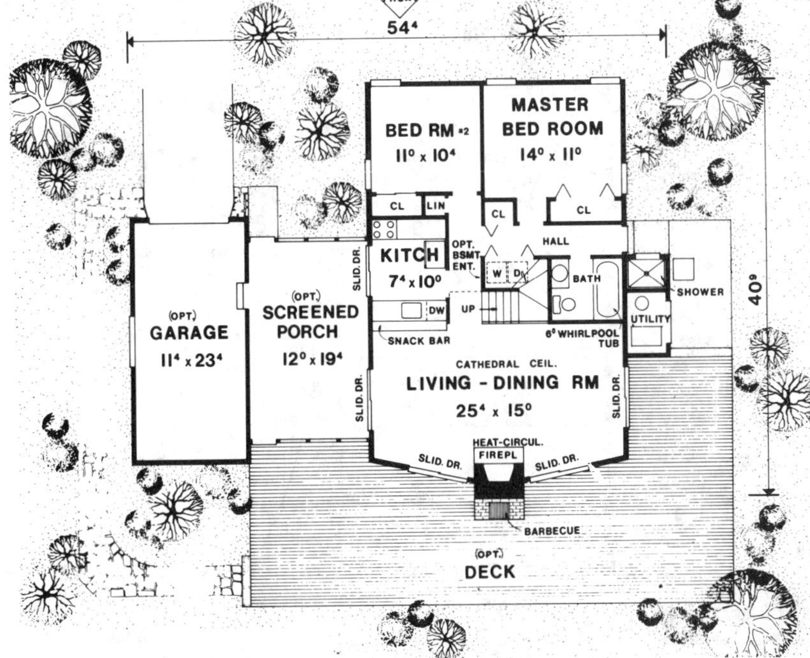

MAIN FLOOR

Plan AX-97729

Bedrooms: 4 — **Baths:** 2

Space:

Upper floor:	450 sq. ft.
Main floor:	988 sq. ft.
Total living area:	1,438 sq. ft.
Basement:	905 sq. ft.
Garage:	264 sq. ft.

Exterior Wall Framing: 2x4

Foundation options:
Standard basement.
Slab.
(Foundation & framing conversion diagram available — see order form.)

Blueprint Price Code: B

Plan AX-97729

TO ORDER THIS BLUEPRINT, CALL TOLL-FREE 1-800-547-5570

(prices and details on pp. 12-15.)

Cathedral Ceiling Featured

The open floor plan of this modified A-Frame design virtually eliminates wasted hall space. The centrally located Great Room features a 15′4″ cathedral ceiling with exposed wood beams and large areas of fixed glass on both front and rear. Living and dining areas are visually separated by a massive stone fireplace.

The isolated master suite features a walk-in closet and sliding glass doors opening onto the front deck.

A walk-thru utility room provides easy access from the carport and outside storage area to the compact kitchen. On the opposite side of the Great Room are two additional bedrooms and a second full bath. All this takes up only 1,454 square feet of heated living area. A full length deck and vertical wood siding with stone accents on the corners provide a rustic yet contemporary exterior.

Total living area: 1,454 sq. ft.
(Not counting basement or garage)

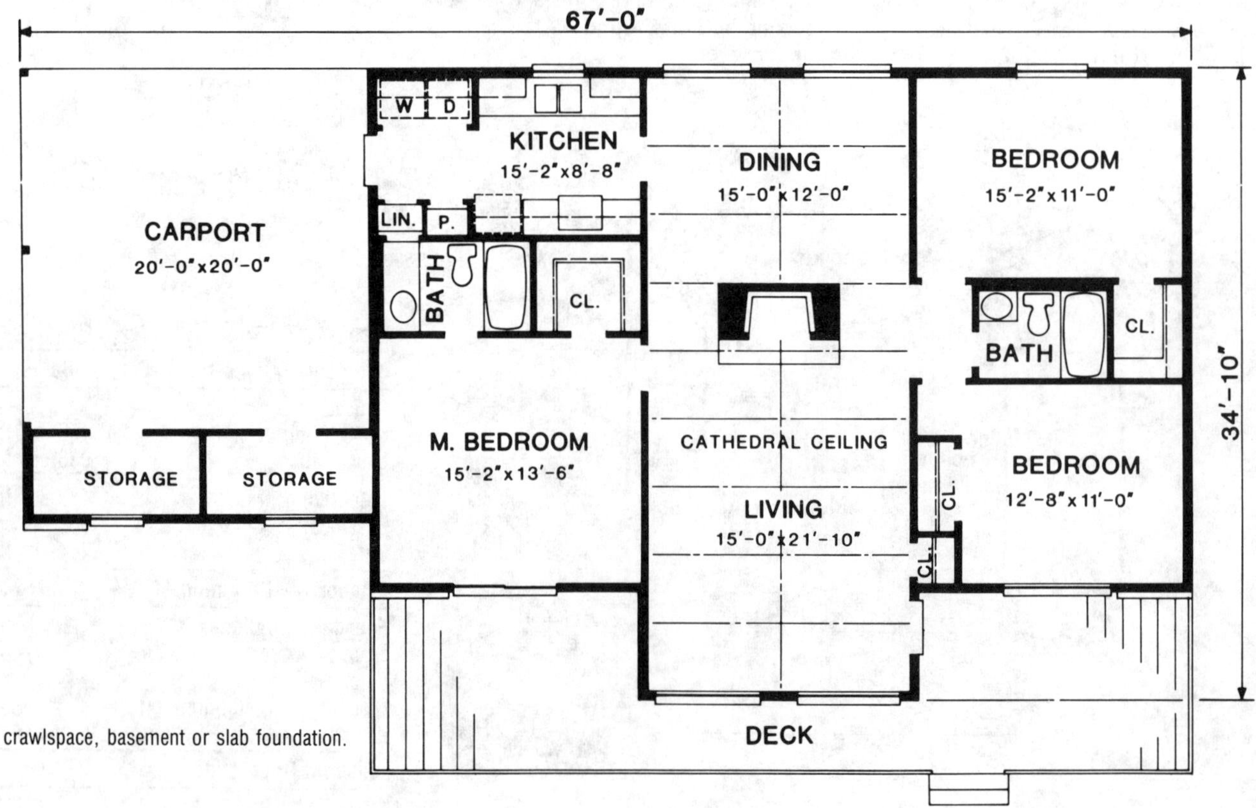

Specify crawlspace, basement or slab foundation.

TO ORDER THIS BLUEPRINT, CALL TOLL-FREE 1-800-547-5570
(prices and details on pp. 12-15.)

Blueprint Price Code A

Plan C-7360

Private Decks Abound

- With two bedrooms opening to their own private deck, and another deck extending the full length of the living room, the scenic views can be fully enjoyed, both inside and out.
- The sunken living room features a fireplace, a dramatic 19-foot ceiling with skylights, and three sliding glass doors opening to the deck.
- The efficient kitchen overlooks the front yard and the rear view over the breakfast bar and dining room with opening to the living room.

Plan CAR-81007

Bedroom: 3	**Baths:** 1½
Space:	
Upper floor:	560 sq. ft.
Main floor:	911 sq. ft.
Total living area:	1,471 sq. ft.
Basement:	911 sq. ft.
Exterior Wall Framing:	2x6

Foundation options:
Standard basement.
(Foundation & framing conversion diagram available — see order form.)

Blueprint Price Code:	A

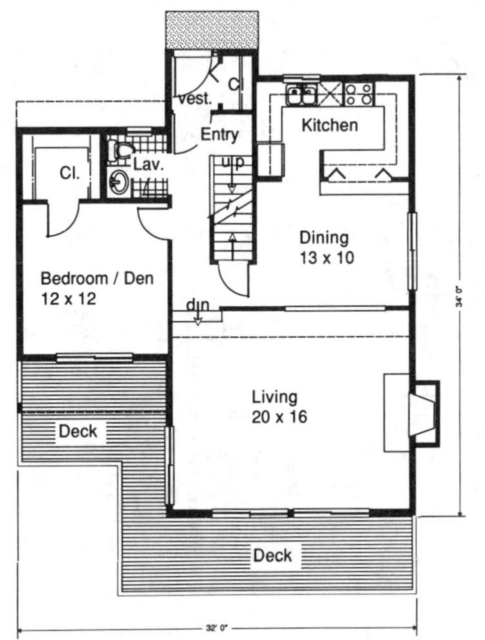

MAIN FLOOR

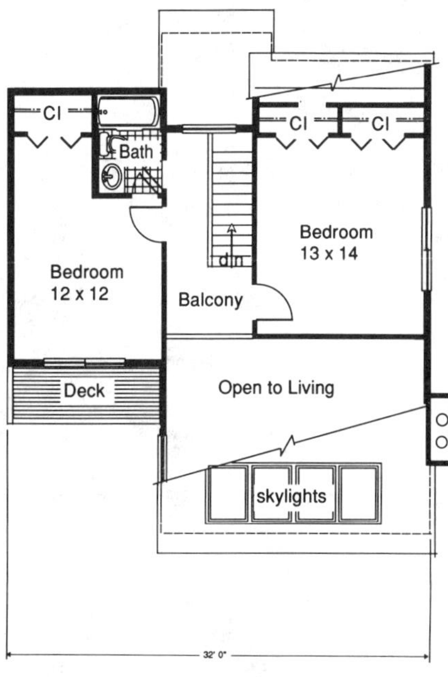

UPPER FLOOR

Plan CAR-81007

TO ORDER THIS BLUEPRINT, CALL TOLL-FREE 1-800-547-5570
(prices and details on pp. 12-15.)

Hexagon Home Maximizes Scenic Settings

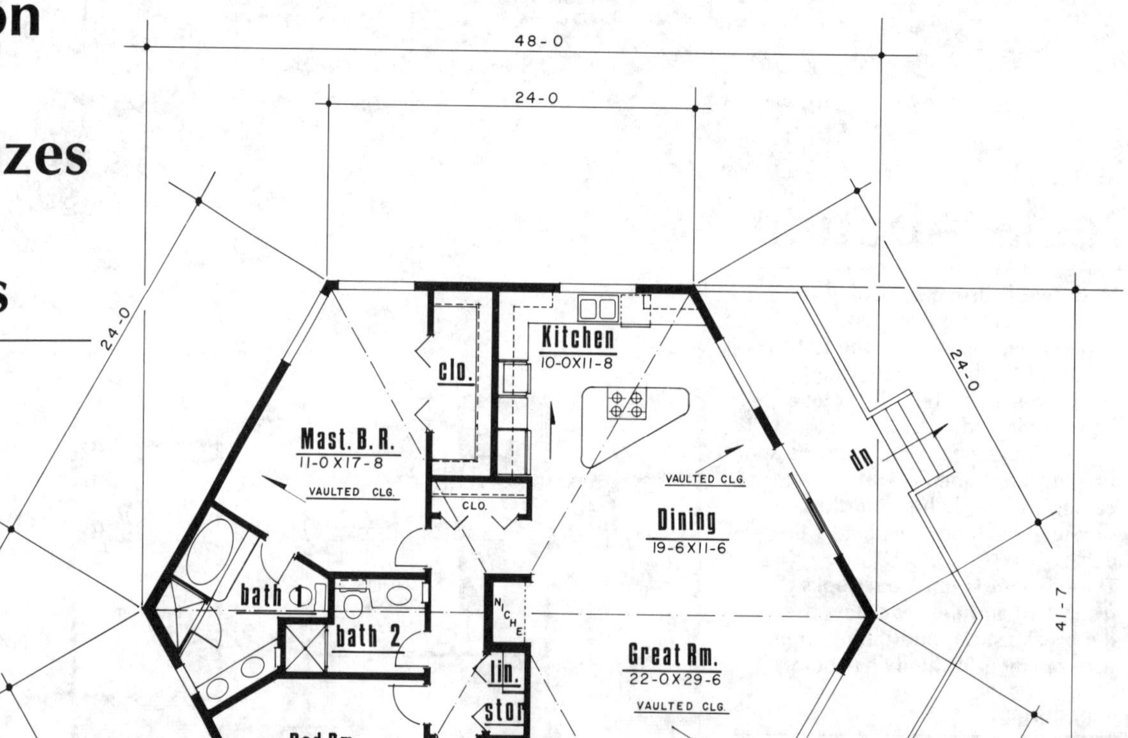

48-0
24-0
24-0
24-0
24-0
24-0
41-7

Kitchen
10-0X11-8

clo.

Mast. B. R.
11-0X17-8
VAULTED CLG.

CLO.

VAULTED CLG.

Dining
19-6X11-6

dn

bath 1

bath 2

NICHE

Great Rm.
22-0X29-6
VAULTED CLG.

lin.

stor

Bed Rm.
12-0X16-0
VAULTED CLG.

utility

VAULTED CLG.

CABINET

WH

Entry

clo.

dn

deck

Plan Q-1475-1A
WITHOUT BASEMENT
(CRAWLSPACE FOUNDATION)

Total living area: 1,475 sq. ft.
(Not counting garage)

TO ORDER THIS BLUEPRINT,
CALL TOLL-FREE 1-800-547-5570

 (prices and details on pp. 12-15.)

Blueprint Price Code A

Plan Q-1475-1A

Eye-Catching Prow-Shaped Chalet

- Steep pitched roof lines and wide cornices give this chalet a distinct alpine appearance.
- Prowed shape, large windows, and 10′ deck provide view and enhancement of indoor/outdoor living.
- Functional division of living and sleeping areas by hallway and first floor full bath.
- Laundry facilities conveniently located near bedroom wing.
- U-shaped kitchen and spacious dining/living areas make the main floor perfect for entertaining.

UPPER FLOOR

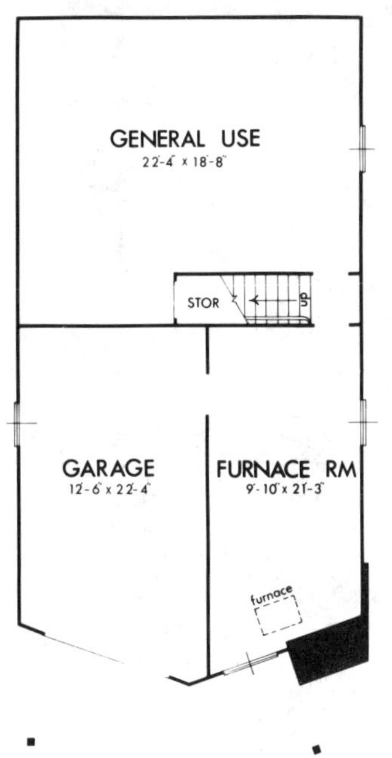

BASEMENT

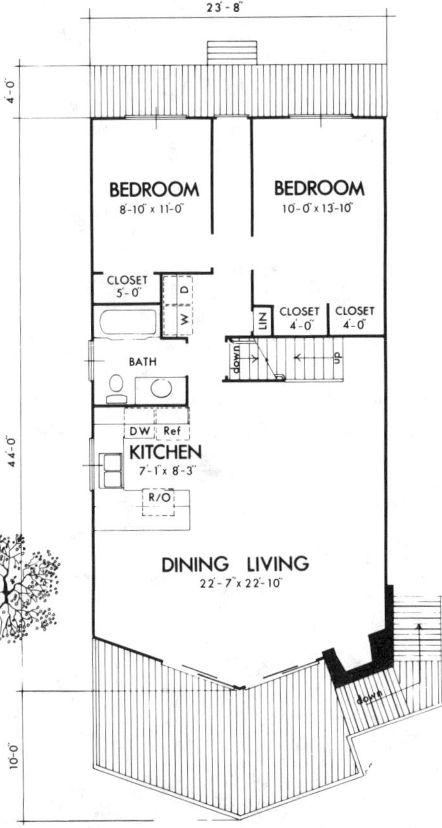

MAIN FLOOR

Plans H-886-3 & -3A

Bedrooms: 3	**Baths:** 2
Space:	
Upper floor:	486 sq. ft.
Main floor:	994 sq. ft.
Total without basement:	1,480 sq. ft.
Basement:	approx. 715 sq. ft.
Total with basement:	2,195 sq. ft.
Garage:	279 sq. ft.
Exterior Wall Framing:	2x6

Foundation options:
Daylight basement (Plan H-886-3).
Crawlspace (Plan H-886-3A).
(Foundation & framing conversion diagram available — see order form.)

Blueprint Price Code:	
Without basement:	A
With basement:	C

Plans H-886-3 & -3A

TO ORDER THIS BLUEPRINT, CALL TOLL-FREE 1-800-547-5570
(prices and details on pp. 12-15.)

For Casual Holiday Living

More than 500 sq. ft. of deck area sets the theme of casual holiday living for this design. The living-dining-kitchen combination is enclosed in one huge beamed and vaulted 15′ x 39′ room. Unusual interest and dramatic effect is achieved by dropping this room several steps below the entry level, so that one's first impression of the living area is that of a lovely stage setting.

Two large bedrooms and bath are also on the main floor, along with the convenient laundry room near the kitchen.

The real feature of the home is the completely private master suite. Reached from the entry hall by a few steps up, this lovely room has an individual bath, a walk-in wardrobe and a private deck.

Exterior walls are framed in 2x6 studs for energy efficiency.

First floor:	1,200 sq. ft.
Second floor:	320 sq. ft.
Total living area: (Not counting basement or garage)	1,520 sq. ft.

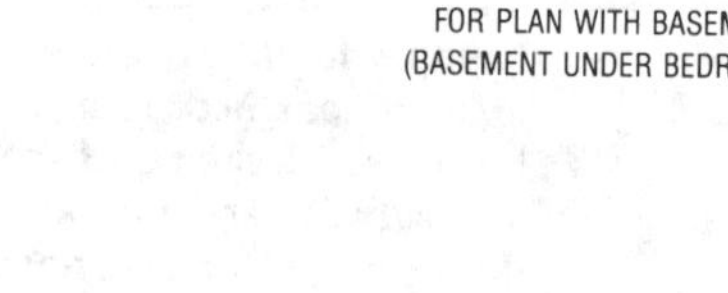

STAIRWAY ARRANGEMENT FOR PLAN WITH BASEMENT (BASEMENT UNDER BEDROOMS)

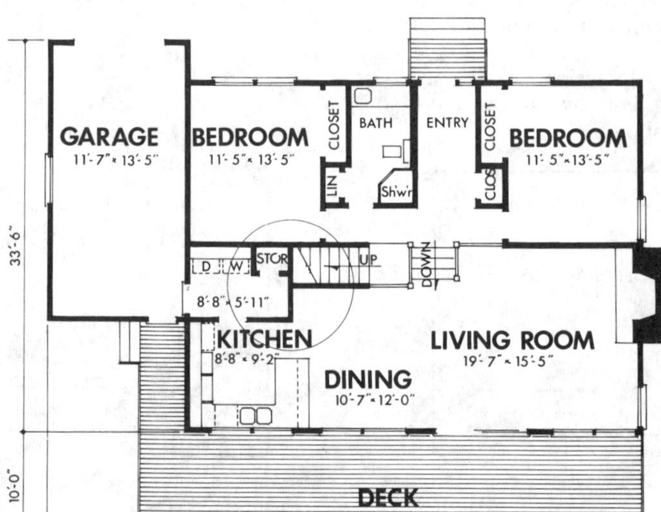

MAIN FLOOR
1200 SQUARE FEET

PLAN H-877-1A
WITHOUT BASEMENT
(CRAWLSPACE FOUNDATION)

PLAN H-877-1
WITH BASEMENT

UPPER LEVEL
320 SQUARE FEET

Blueprint Price Code B

Plans H-877-1 & H-877-1A

Open Floor Plan

The open floor plan of this modified A-Frame design virtually eliminates wasted hall space. The centrally located great room features a 15'4" cathedral ceiling with exposed wood beams and large areas of fixed glass on both front and rear. Living and dining areas are visually separated by a massive stone fireplace. The isolated master suite features a walk-in closet and sliding glass doors opening onto the front deck.

A walk-thru utility room provides easy access from the carport and outside storage areas to the compact kitchen. On the opposite side of the great room are two additional bedrooms and a second full bath. All this in only 1,669 sq. ft. of heated living area. A full length deck and vertical wood siding with stone accents on the corners provide a rustic yet contemporary exterior.

Total living area: 1,669 sq. ft.
(Not counting basement or carport)

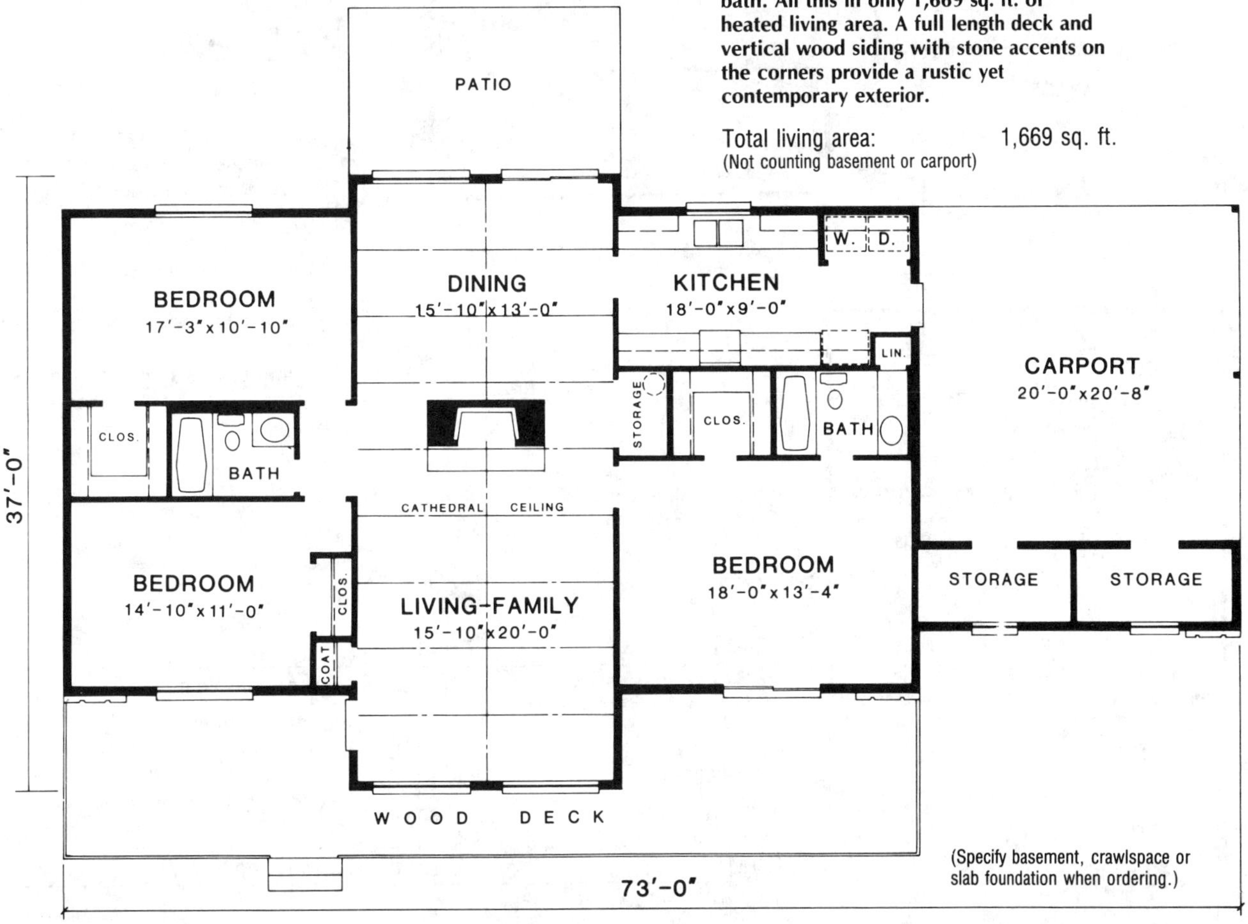

PATIO

BEDROOM 17'-3" x 10'-10"

DINING 15'-10" x 13'-0"

KITCHEN 18'-0" x 9'-0"

W. D.

LIN.

CARPORT 20'-0" x 20'-8"

CLOS.

BATH

STORAGE

CLOS.

BATH

CATHEDRAL CEILING

37'-0"

BEDROOM 14'-10" x 11'-0"

CLOS.

COAT

LIVING-FAMILY 15'-10" x 20'-0"

BEDROOM 18'-0" x 13'-4"

STORAGE

STORAGE

WOOD DECK

73'-0"

(Specify basement, crawlspace or slab foundation when ordering.)

Blueprint Price Code B

Plan C-8160

TO ORDER THIS BLUEPRINT, CALL TOLL-FREE 1-800-547-5570
(prices and details on pp. 12-15.)

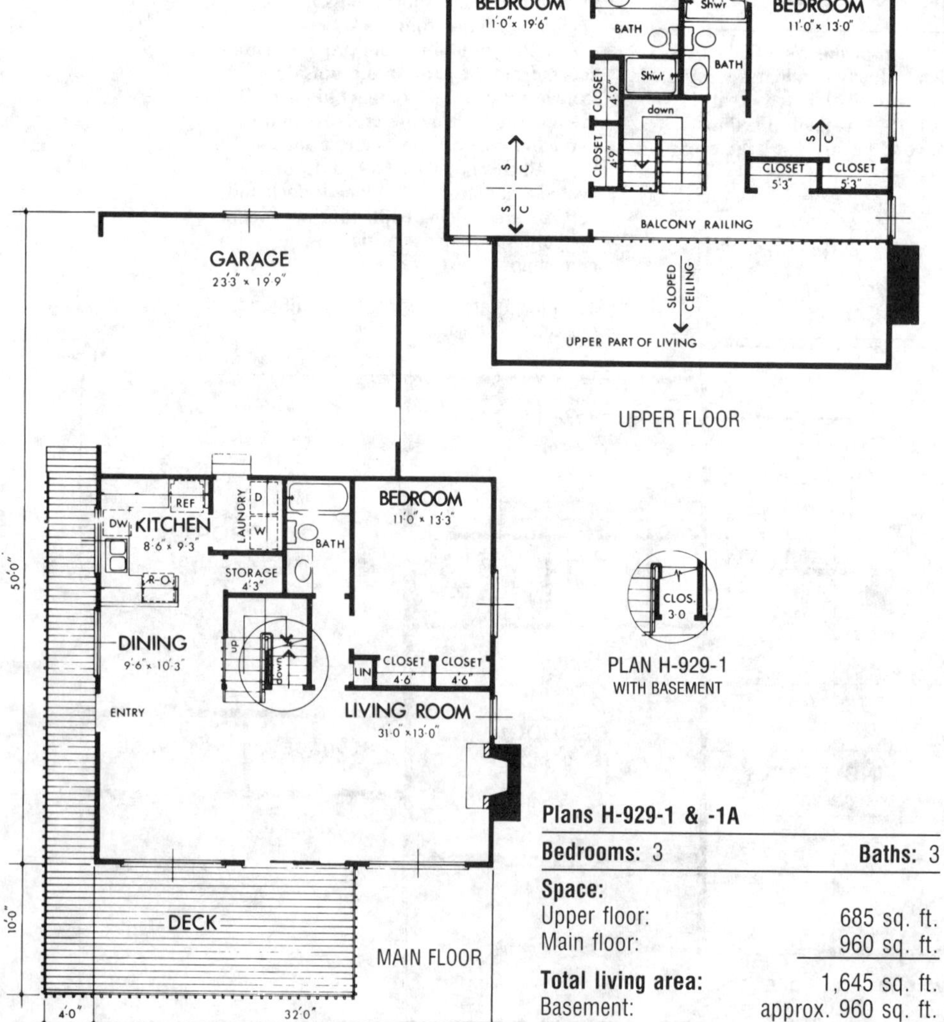

Contemporary Retreat

- Main floor plan revolves around an open, centrally located stairway.
- Spaciousness prevails throughout entire home with open kitchen and combination dining/living room.
- Living room features a great-sized fireplace and access to two-sided deck.
- Separate baths accommodate each bedroom.
- Upstairs hallway reveals an open balcony railing to oversee activities below.

Plans H-929-1 & -1A

Bedroom: 3	**Baths:** 3
Space:	
Upper floor:	685 sq. ft.
Main floor:	960 sq. ft.
Total living area:	1,645 sq. ft.
Basement:	approx. 960 sq. ft.
Garage:	459 sq. ft.

Exterior Wall Framing: 2x6

Foundation options:
Daylight basement (Plan H-929-1).
Crawlspace (Plan H-929-1A).
(Foundation & framing conversion diagram available — see order form.)

Blueprint Price Code: B

TO ORDER THIS BLUEPRINT, CALL TOLL-FREE 1-800-547-5570
(prices and details on pp. 12-15.)

Plans H-929-1 & -1A

Panoramic Prow View

- A glass-filled prow gable design is almost as spectacular as the panoramic view from inside. The two-story window-wall floods the living room with light and views.
- The open-feeling corner kitchen has the right angle to enjoy the dining room and the family room, including views of the front and rear decks.
- Two main level bedrooms share a full bath.
- The entire upper floor is a private master bedroom suite with large bath, dressing area and balcony opening to the two-story glass wall, a real "good morning" view.

Plan NW-196

Bedrooms: 3	**Baths:** 2
Space:	
Upper floor	394 sq. ft.
Main floor:	1,317 sq. ft.
Total living area:	1,711 sq. ft.
Exterior Wall Framing:	2x6

Foundation options:
Crawlspace.
(Foundation & framing conversion diagram available — see order form.)

Blueprint Price Code: B

48'-0"

27'-0"

Deck DN

Br #2 11-6 x 11

Br #3 11 x 11-3

Util.

Family 15-4 x 13-6

L.

DN UP

Dining 12 x 10-6

Kit.

Living Rm. 25-8 x 14-6

DN

Deck

MAIN FLOOR

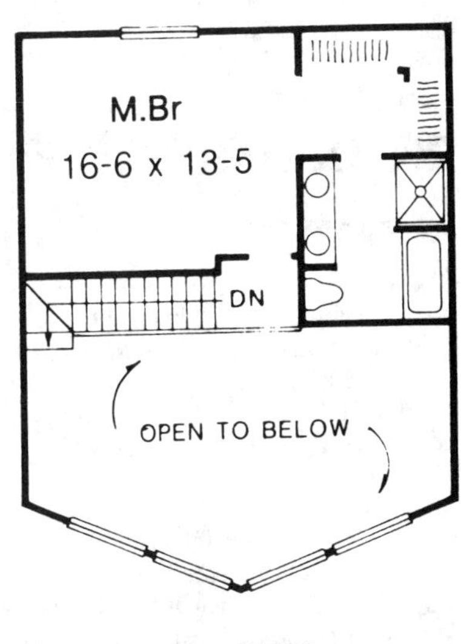

UPPER FLOOR

Plan NW-196

TO ORDER THIS BLUEPRINT, CALL TOLL-FREE 1-800-547-5570
(prices and details on pp. 12-15.)

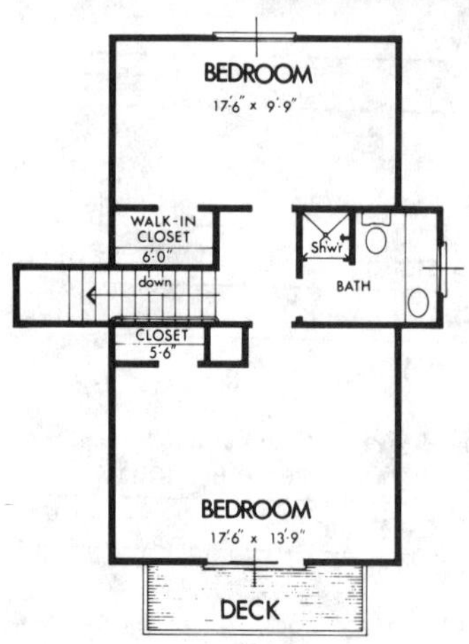

UPPER FLOOR

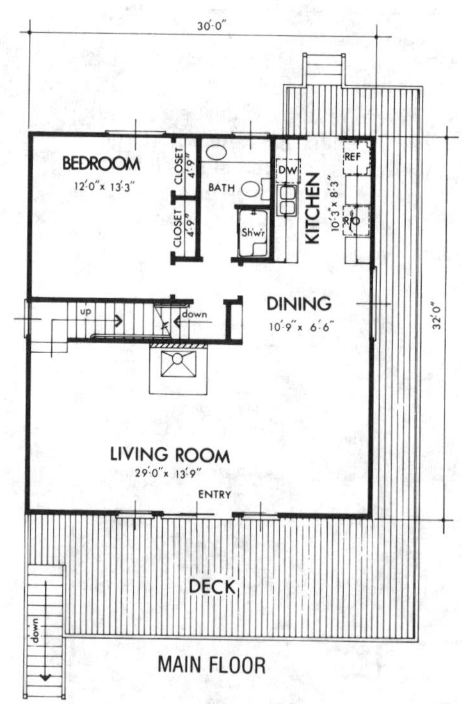

MAIN FLOOR

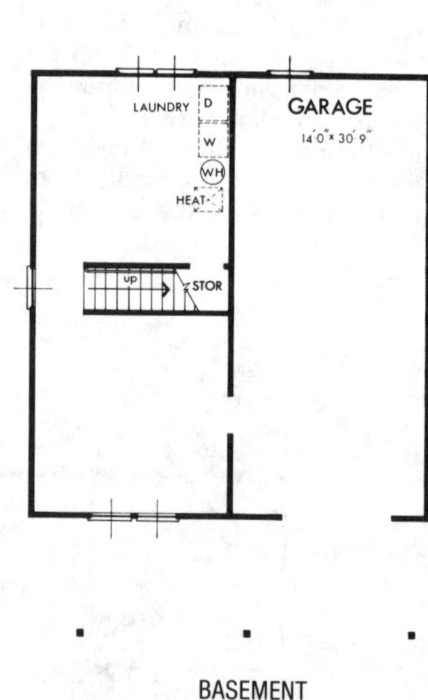

BASEMENT

Chalet for All Seasons

- Rustic exterior makes this design suitable for a lakefront, beach, or wooded setting.
- Patterned railing and wood deck edge the front and side main level, while a smaller deck assumes a balcony role.
- Designed for relaxed, leisure living, the main level features a large L-shaped Great Room warmed by a central free-standing fireplace.
- Upper level offers a second bath and added sleeping accommodations.

Plans H-858-2

Bedrooms: 3	**Baths:** 2
Space:	
Upper floor:	576 sq. ft.
Main floor:	960 sq. ft.
Total without basement:	1,536 sq. ft.
Basement:	530 sq. ft.
Total with basement:	2,066 sq. ft.
Garage: (included in basement)	430 sq. ft.

Exterior Wall Framing: 2x6

Foundation options:
Daylight basement.
(Foundation & framing conversion diagram available — see order form.)

Blueprint Price Code: C

TO ORDER THIS BLUEPRINT, CALL TOLL-FREE 1-800-547-5570

 (prices and details on pp. 12-15.)

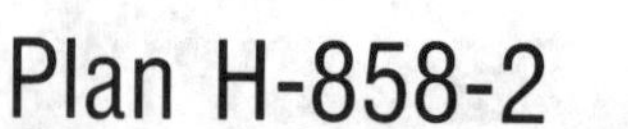

Contrasting Rustic and Contemporary

- In this design, contemporary styling is combined with the rustic atmosphere of a country lodge, for a home that will serve equally well for year-round or recreational living.
- A studio-type master bedroom is isolated upstairs, and includes a private bath, a balcony overlooking the living room below and a private outdoor deck.
- Interior touches include diagonal paneling, an open-beamed, cathedral ceiling and a massive stone fireplace with raised hearth.
- The main floor offers easy access to three large decks.
- Three foundation options include a daylight basement with recreation room, standard basement or crawlspace.

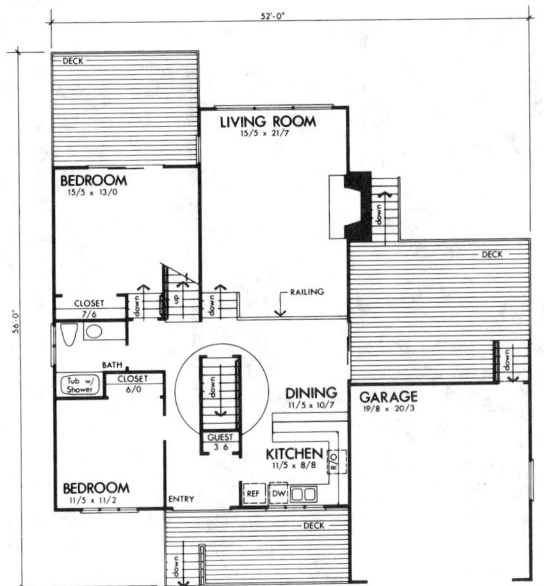

MAIN FLOOR

UPPER FLOOR

WITHOUT BASEMENT
(CRAWLSPACE FOUNDATION)

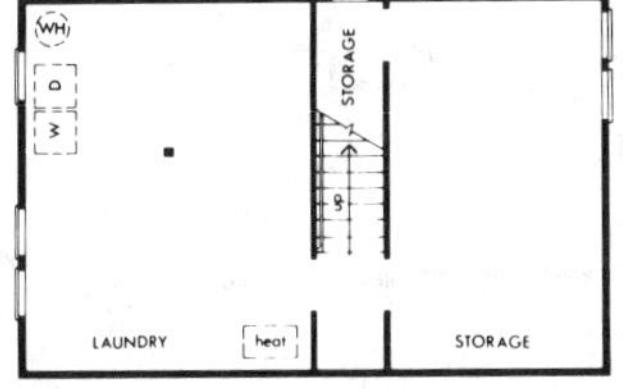

STANDARD BASEMENT

DAYLIGHT BASEMENT

Plans H-834-5, -5A & -5B

Bedrooms: 3	**Baths:** 2
Space:	
Upper floor:	399 sq. ft.
Main floor:	1,249 sq. ft.
Total without basement:	1,648 sq. ft.
Daylight basement:	1,249 sq. ft.
Total with basement:	2,897 sq. ft.
Standard basement:	640 sq. ft.
Garage:	398 sq. ft.

Exterior Wall Framing:	2x4

Foundation options:
Daylight basement (H-834-5B).
Standard basement (H-834-5).
Crawlspace (H-834-5A).
(Foundation & framing conversion diagram available — see order form.)

Blueprint Price Code:	
Without basement:	B
With standard basement:	C
With daylight basement:	D

Plans H-834-5, -5A & -5B

TO ORDER THIS BLUEPRINT, CALL TOLL-FREE 1-800-547-5570
(prices and details on pp. 12-15.)

California Style

- Open, versatile living is the key to this California styled two-story.
- The high, spacious foyer reveals the massive Great Room which spans almost the entire length of the home; it features a dramatic vaulted ceiling open to the master bedroom balcony and skylights.
- A counter bar separates the Great Room from the adjoining kitchen.
- Laundry facilities are conveniently located near the sleeping rooms on the upper level, along with storage space and two full baths.

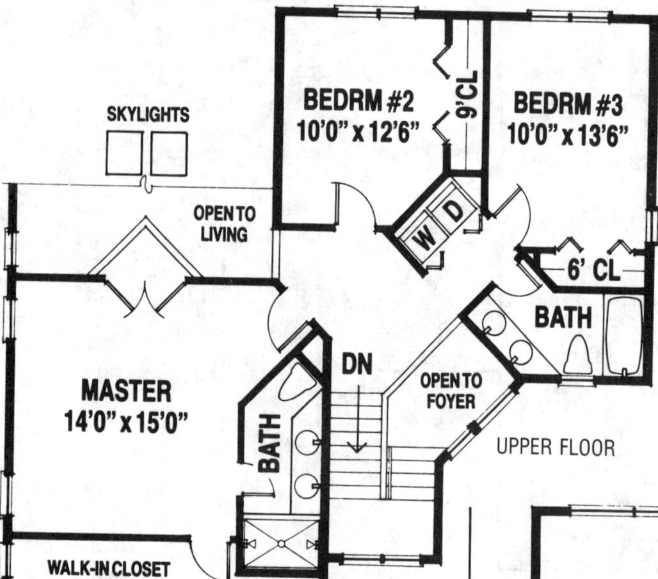

UPPER FLOOR

LIVING
15'8" x 15'8"
VAULTED

DINING
12'0" x 11'0"

KITCHEN
11'0" x 15'8"

DECK

CL

P

FOYER

PR

DN UP

GARAGE
19'4" x 23'0"

40'

40'

MAIN FLOOR

Plan PH-1839	
Bedrooms: 3	**Baths:** 2 ½
Space:	
Upper floor	970 sq. ft.
Main floor	869 sq. ft.
Total Living Area	**1,839 sq. ft.**
Basement	869 sq. ft.
Garage	437 sq. ft.
Exterior Wall Framing	2x6
Foundation options:	
Daylight Basement	
Standard Basement	
Crawlspace	
Slab	
(Foundation & framing conversion diagram available—see order form.)	
Blueprint Price Code	B

TO ORDER THIS BLUEPRINT, CALL TOLL-FREE 1-800-547-5570
(prices and details on pp. 12-15.)

Plan PH-1839

An Octagonal Home with a Lofty View

- There's no better way to avoid the ordinary than by building an octagonal home and escaping from square corners and rigid rooms.
- The roomy main floor offers plenty of space for full-time family living or for a comfortable second home retreat.
- The vaulted entry hall leads to the bedrooms on the right or down the hall to the Great Room.
- Warmed by a wood stove, the Great Room offers a panoramic view of the surrounding scenery.
- The center core of the main floor houses two baths, one of which contains a spa tub and is private to the master bedroom.
- This plan also includes a roomy kitchen and handy utility area.
- A large loft is planned as a recreation room, also with a wood stove.
- The daylight basement version adds another bedroom, bath, garage and large storage area.

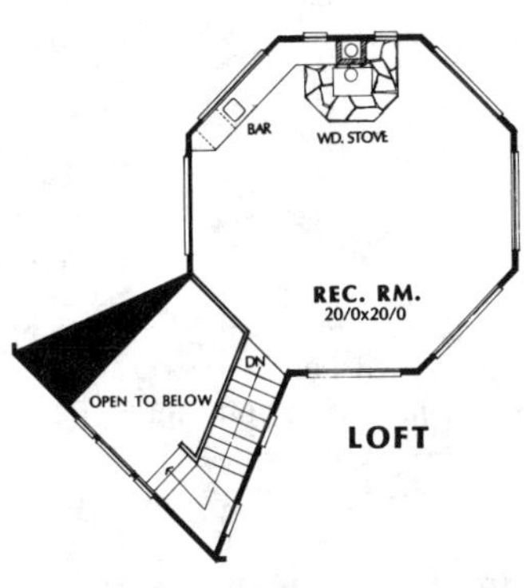

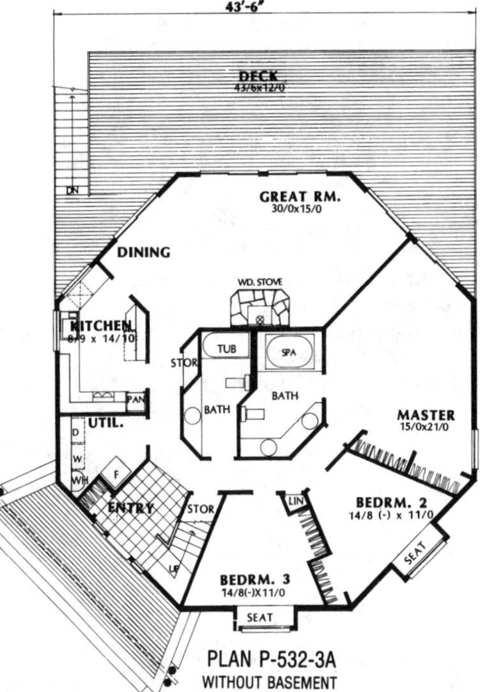

PLAN P-532-3A
WITHOUT BASEMENT

Plans P-532-3A & -3D

Bedrooms: 3-4	**Baths:** 2-3
Space:	
Upper floor:	355 sq. ft.
Main floor:	1,567 sq. ft.
Total living area:	1,922 sq. ft.
Basement living area:	430 sq. ft.
Garage (included in basement):	approx. 735 sq. ft.
Storage:	approx. 482 sq. ft.

Exterior Wall Framing:	2x6

Foundation options:
Daylight basement (Plan P-532-3D).
Crawlspace (Plan P-532-3A).
(Foundation & framing conversion diagram available — see order form.)

Blueprint Price Code:	
Without basement:	B
With basement:	C

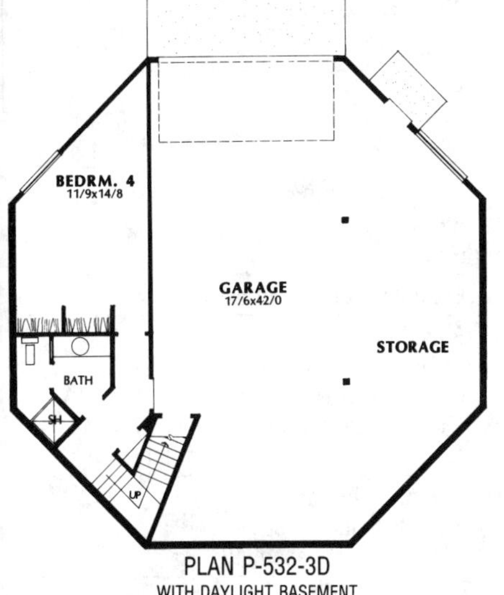

PLAN P-532-3D
WITH DAYLIGHT BASEMENT

Plans P-532-3A & -3D

TO ORDER THIS BLUEPRINT, CALL TOLL-FREE 1-800-547-5570
(prices and details on pp. 12-15.)

Decked-Out for Fun

- Spacious deck surrounds this comfortable cabin/chalet.
- Sliding glass doors and windows blanket the living-dining area, indulged with raised hearth and a breathtaking view.
- Dining area and compact kitchen separated by breakfast bar.
- Master bedroom, laundry room and bath complete first floor; two additional bedrooms located on second floor.
- Upper level also features impressive balcony room with exposed beams

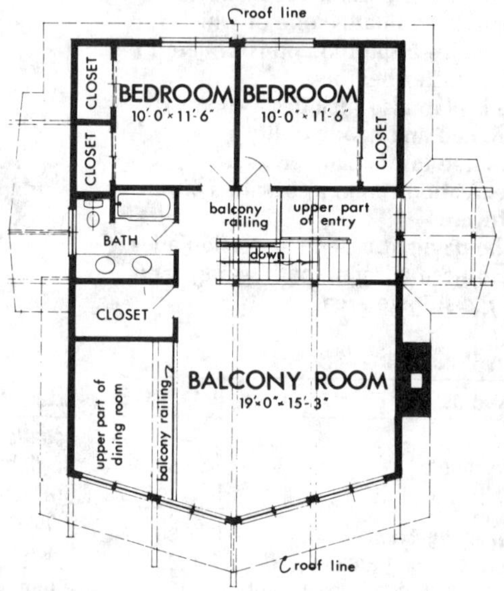

UPPER FLOOR

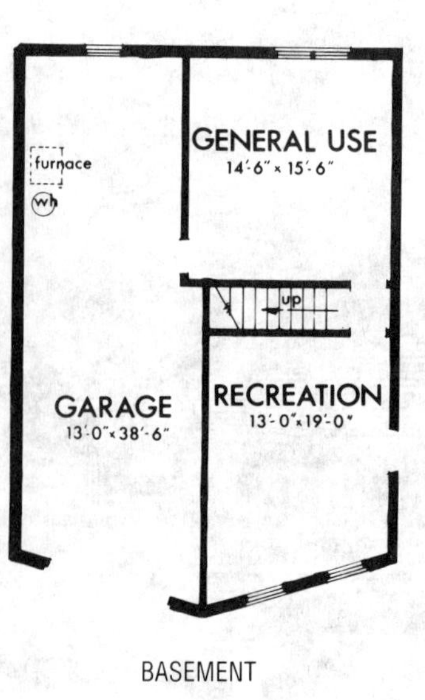

BASEMENT

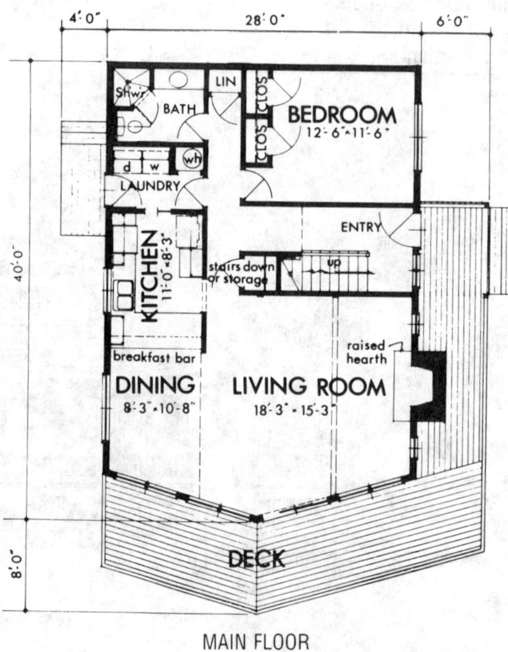

MAIN FLOOR

Plans H-919-1 & -1A

Bedrooms: 3	**Baths:** 2
Space:	
Upper floor:	869 sq. ft.
Main floor:	1,064 sq. ft.
Total living area:	1,933 sq. ft.
Basement:	475 sq. ft.
Garage:	501 sq. ft.
Exterior Wall Framing:	2x6

Foundation options:
Daylight basement (Plan H-919-1).
Crawlspace (Plan H-919-1A).
(Foundation & framing conversion diagram available — see order form.)

Blueprint Price Code:

Without finished basement:	B
With finished basement:	C

TO ORDER THIS BLUEPRINT, CALL TOLL-FREE 1-800-547-5570

 (prices and details on pp. 12-15.)

Plans H-919-1 & -1A

Indoor/Outdoor Living on A Sloping Lot

- The wood siding, the front deck, and the multi-paned exterior of this Northwest contemporary will beckon you up to the entry stairs and inside.
- The two-story entry opens up to a vaulted living room with tall windows, exposed beam ceiling and adjoining dining area which accesses the hand-railed deck.
- An updated kitchen offers a walk-in pantry, eating bar and breakfast nook with sliders to a rear deck.
- A fireplace and rear patio highlight the attached family room.
- A washer/dryer in the upper level bath is convenient to all three bedrooms, making laundry a breeze.

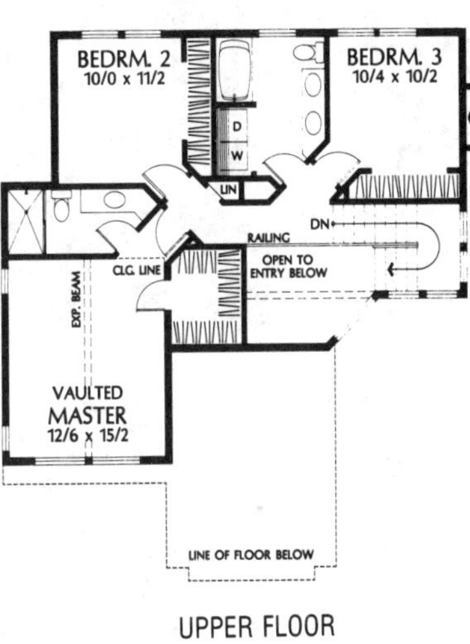

UPPER FLOOR

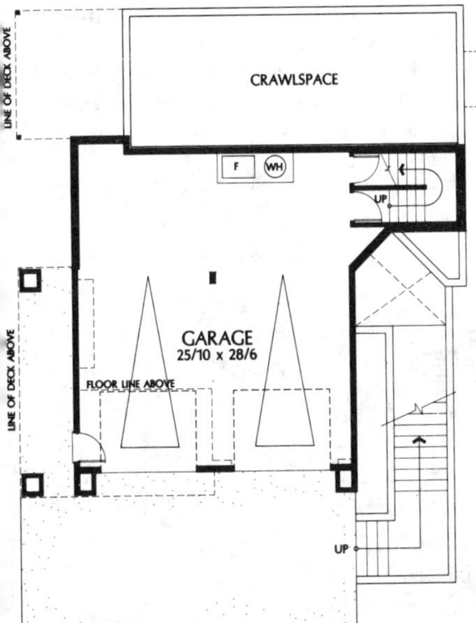

CRAWLSPACE

F WH

UP

GARAGE 25/10 x 28/6

FLOOR LINE ABOVE

LINE OF DECK ABOVE

BASEMENT

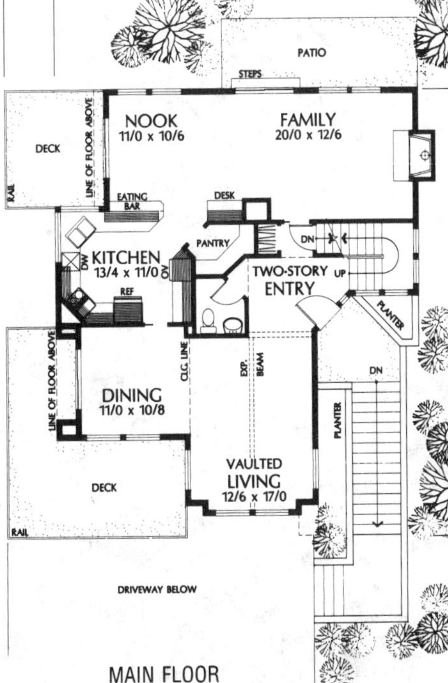

MAIN FLOOR

Plan P-7737-4D

Bedrooms: 3	**Baths:** 2½
Space:	
Upper floor:	802 sq. ft.
Main floor:	1,158 sq. ft.
Total living area:	1,960 sq. ft.
Garage/basement:	736 sq. ft.
Exterior Wall Framing:	2x6

Foundation options:
Crawlspace.
(Foundation & framing conversion diagram available — see order form.)

Blueprint Price Code:	B

Plan P-7737-4D

TO ORDER THIS BLUEPRINT, CALL TOLL-FREE 1-800-547-5570

(prices and details on pp. 12-15.)

Visual Excitement

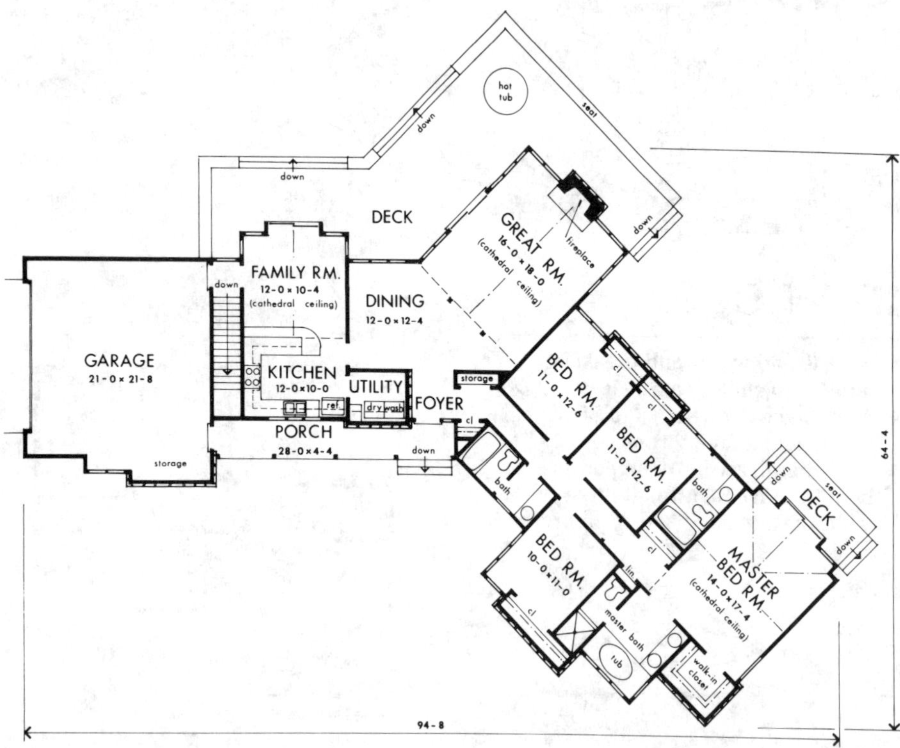

- This country-style ranch generates visual excitement through its combination of exterior building materials and shapes, including stone, board & batton siding and a covered front porch with timber supports.
- The angled ranch plan offers flexibility in design, with the ability to lengthen the Great Room and/or the family room to suit individual family space requirements.
- The master bedroom has a cathedral ceiling, walk-in closet, private deck and spacious master bath with whirlpool tub. There are three (3) other bedrooms with two sharing a full bath and the other having a private bath.
- The expansive deck area with hot tub wraps around interior family gathering areas for outdoor living.
- Both the family room and Great Room have cathedral ceilings, with the Great Room having a fireplace as well.

Plan DG-172

Bedrooms: 4	**Baths:** 3
Space:	
Total living area:	1,988 sq. ft.
Basement:	853 sq. ft.
Garage:	455 sq. ft.
Exterior Wall Framing:	2x4
Foundation options: Partial basement. Crawlspace. (Foundation & framing conversion diagram available — see order form.)	
Blueprint Price Code:	B

TO ORDER THIS BLUEPRINT, CALL TOLL-FREE 1-800-547-5570

 (prices and details on pp. 12-15.)

Built for All Seasons

- Spectacular rear viewing is yours in this exciting, yet homey design that provides comfort in all seasons.
- The heat-absorbing wall in the lower level and the fireplace-to-furnace "tie-in" circulation system help balance mild and cold days during the heating season.
- Two secondary bedrooms and extra storage space are also offered on the lower level.
- The main level features a bright and cheery L-shaped living and dining area with a brick column wall that absorbs heat from the sun.
- The upper side patio deck off the kitchen can be roofed and converted to a screened porch.
- The main level also houses the delightful master suite with dressing alcove and bath with step-up tub and corner mirrored wall.

Plan CPS-1045-SE

Bedrooms: 3	**Baths:** 2½
Space:	
Lower floor:	1,095 sq. ft.
Main floor:	1,040 sq. ft.
Total living area:	2,135 sq. ft.
Garage:	624 sq. ft.
Exterior Wall Framing:	2x6
Foundation options:	
Daylight basement.	
(Foundation & framing conversion diagram available — see order form.)	
Blueprint Price Code:	C

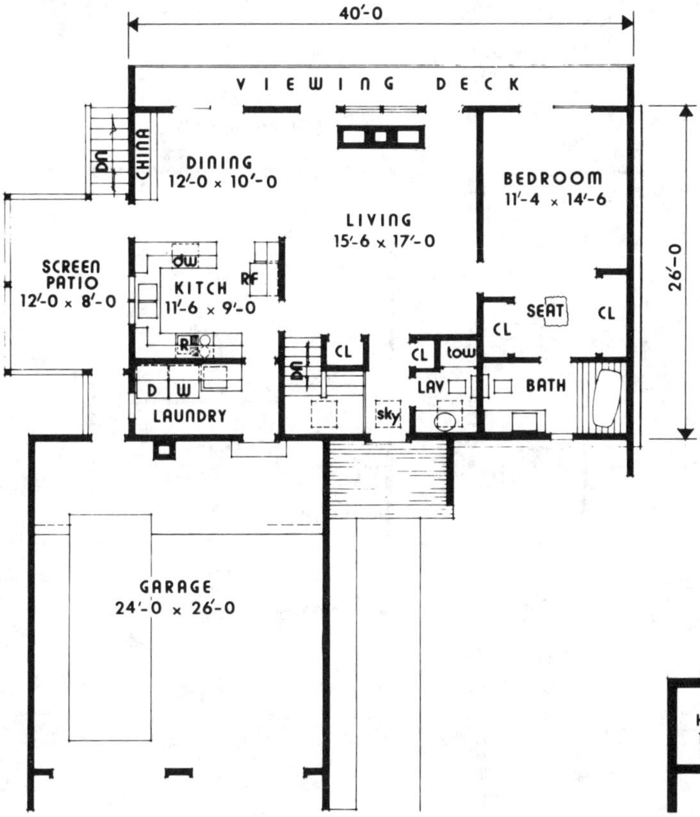

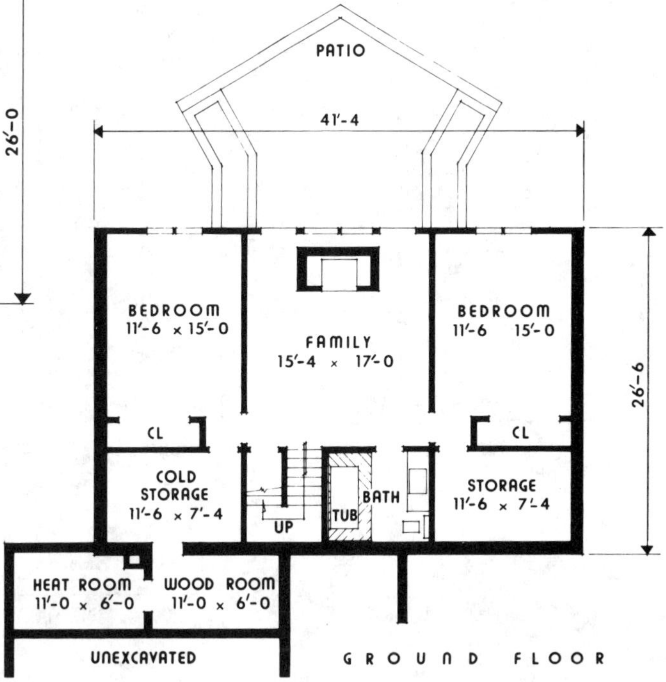

40'-0
VIEWING DECK
CHINA
DN
DINING 12'-0 x 10'-0
LIVING 15'-6 x 17'-0
BEDROOM 11'-4 x 14'-6
26'-0
SCREEN PATIO 12'-0 x 8'-0
DW
RF
KITCH 11'-6 x 9'-0
R
SEAT
CL
CL
DN
CL
CL
tow
D W
LAUNDRY
LAV
BATH
sky
GARAGE 24'-0 x 26'-0

PATIO
41'-4
BEDROOM 11'-6 x 15'-0
FAMILY 15'-4 x 17'-0
BEDROOM 11'-6 15'-0
26'-6
CL
CL
COLD STORAGE 11'-6 x 7'-4
UP
TUB
BATH
STORAGE 11'-6 x 7'-4
HEAT ROOM 11'-0 x 6'-0
WOOD ROOM 11'-0 x 6'-0
UNEXCAVATED
GROUND FLOOR

Plan CPS-1045-SE

Chalet Style for Town or Country

- The exterior features exposed beams, board siding and viewing decks with cut-out railings to give this home the look of a mountain chalet.
- Inside, the design lends itself equally well to year-round family living or part-time recreational enjoyment.
- An expansive Great Room features an impressive fireplace and includes a dining area next to the well-planned kitchen.
- The upstairs offers the possibility of an "adult retreat," with a fine master bedroom with private bath and large closets, plus a loft area available for many uses.
- Two secondary bedrooms are on the main floor, and share another bath.
- The daylight basement level provides space for a garage and large recreation room with fireplace.

Plan P-531-2D

Bedrooms: 3	**Baths:** 2
Space:	
Upper floor:	573 sq. ft.
Main floor:	1,120 sq. ft.
Lower level:	532 sq. ft.
Total living area:	2,225 sq. ft.
Garage:	approx. 588 sq. ft.

Exterior Wall Framing:	2x4
Foundation options: Daylight basement only. (Foundation & framing conversion diagram available — see order form.)	
Blueprint Price Code:	C

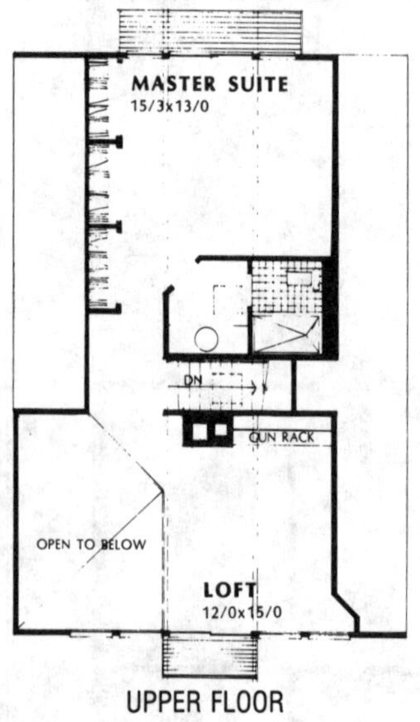

UPPER FLOOR

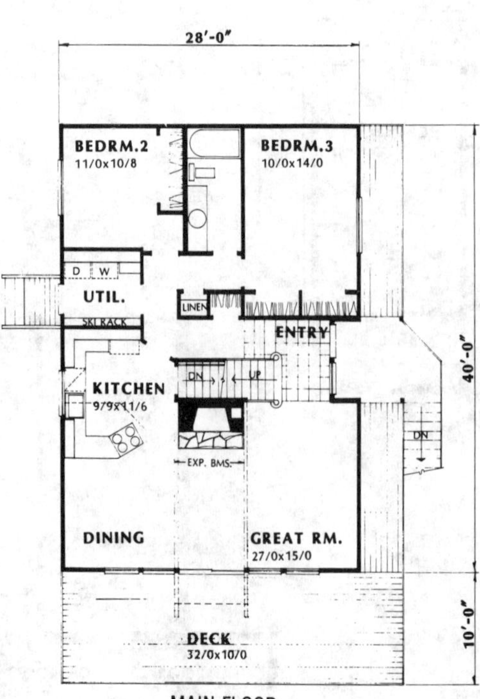

MAIN FLOOR

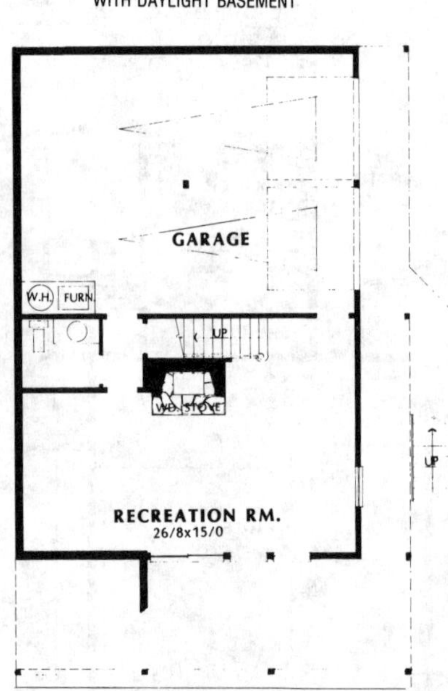

LOWER FLOOR

TO ORDER THIS BLUEPRINT, CALL TOLL-FREE 1-800-547-5570
(prices and details on pp. 12-15.)

Plan P-531-2D

Rear Of Home As Attractive As Front

[T]he rear of this rustic/contemporary home [f]eatures a massive stone fireplace and a [f]ull-length deck which make it ideal for [m]ountain, golf course, lake or other [l]ocations where both the front and rear [o]ffer scenic views.

Sliding glass doors in the family room [a]nd breakfast nook open onto the deck. [T]he modified A-Frame design combines a [2]0′6″ cathedral ceiling over the sunken [f]amily room with a large studio over the [t]wo front bedrooms. An isolated master [s]uite features a walk-in closet and [c]ompartmentalized bath with double [v]anity and linen closet. The front bedrooms [i]nclude ample closet space and share a [u]nique bath-and-a-half arrangement.

On one side of the U-shaped kitchen and breakfast nook is the formal dining room which opens onto the foyer. On the other side is a utility room which can be entered from either the kitchen or garage.

The exterior features a massive stone fireplace, large glass areas and a combination of vertical wood siding and stone.

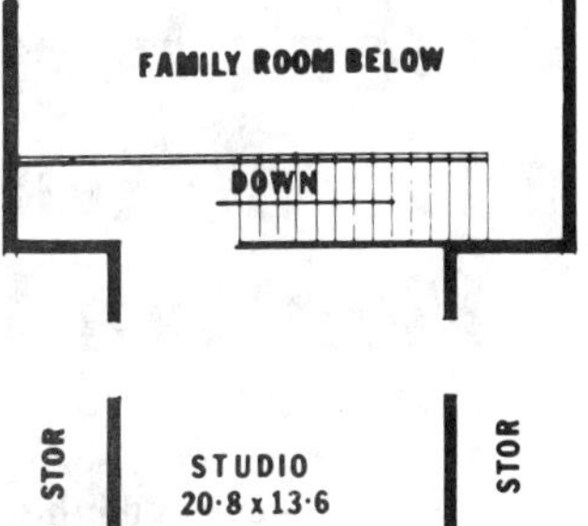

SECOND FLOOR

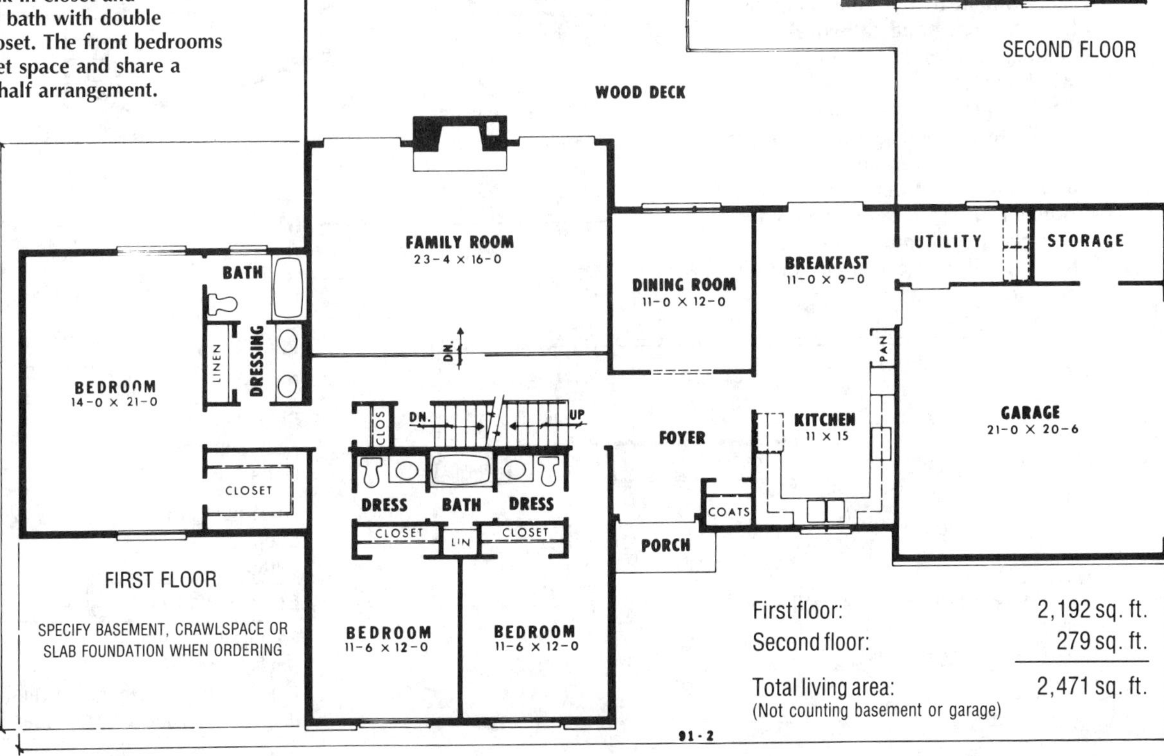

First floor:	2,192 sq. ft.
Second floor:	279 sq. ft.
Total living area: (Not counting basement or garage)	2,471 sq. ft.

Blueprint Price Code C

Plan C-7710

TO ORDER THIS BLUEPRINT, CALL TOLL-FREE 1-800-547-5570

(prices and details on pp. 12-15.)

Deck Wraps Home with Plenty of Views

- A full deck and an abundance of windows surround this exciting two-level contemporary.
- Skywalls are found in the kitchen and dining room; the kitchen also features an island kitchen.
- The brilliant living room boasts a huge fireplace and cathedral ceiling, besides the stunning window wall.
- The master bedroom offers private access to the deck and an attached bath with dual vanities, large tub and a walk-in closet.
- A generous-sized family room and two extra bedrooms share the lower level with a two-car garage and storage area.

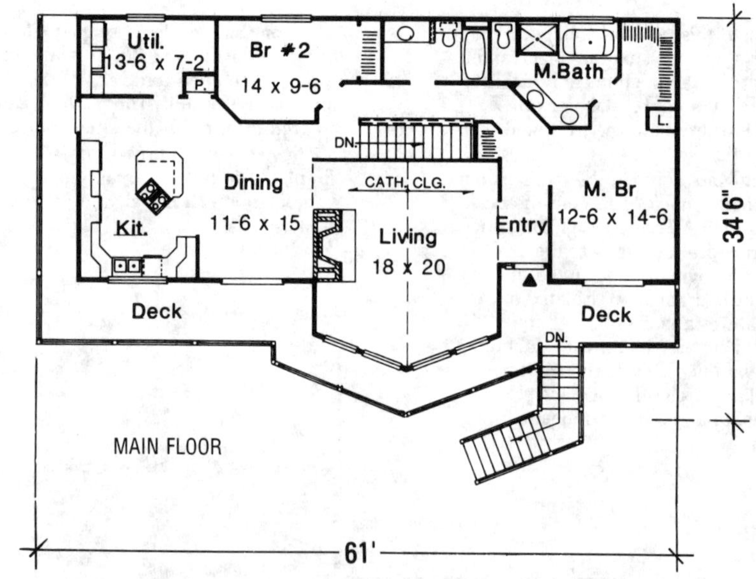

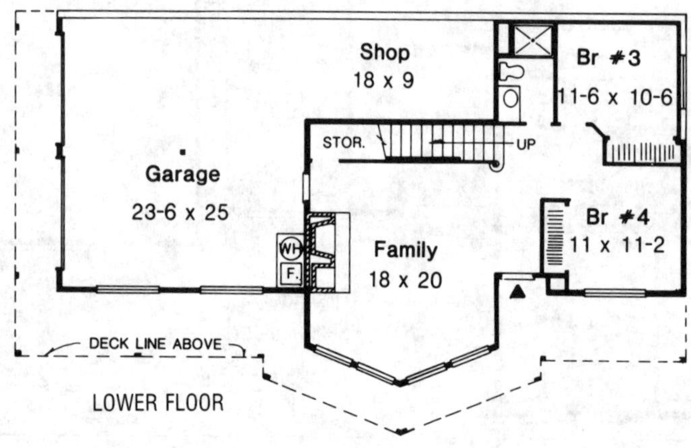

Plan NW-579

Bedrooms: 2-4	**Baths:** 2-3
Space:	
Main/upper floor:	1,707 sq. ft.
Lower floor:	901 sq. ft.
Total living area:	2,608 sq. ft.
Shop:	162 sq. ft.
Garage:	588 sq. ft.
Exterior Wall Framing:	2x6

Foundation options:
Daylight basement.
(Foundation & framing conversion diagram available — see order form.)

Blueprint Price Code: D 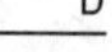

TO ORDER THIS BLUEPRINT, CALL TOLL-FREE 1-800-547-5570

 (prices and details on pp. 12-15.)

Plan NW-579

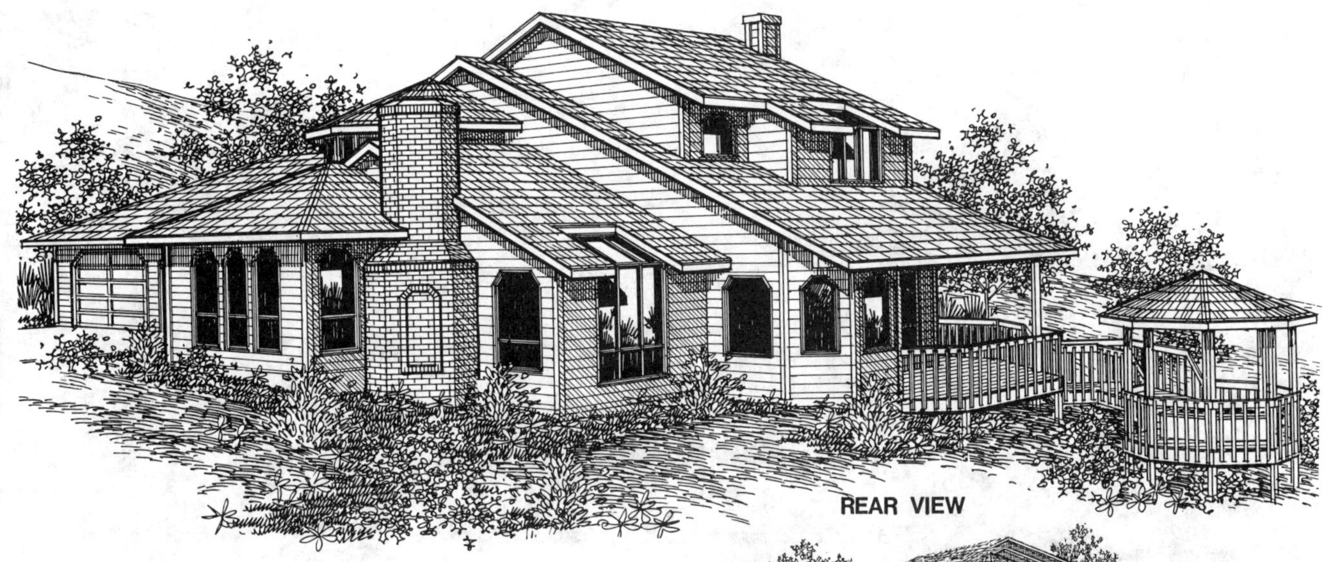

REAR VIEW

FRONT VIEW

Luxurious Living Areas

- This striking exterior design also provides plenty of excitement inside as well, with its angles, curves and bay windows.
- Especially note the eye-popping entry, with its curving stairway soaring through the two-story high foyer.
- The large family room is surrounded by a spacious deck, and a sunny nook adjoins the efficient kitchen.
- The upper floor is devoted mostly to a luxurious master suite with a spa bath and large closet. An adjoining space can serve as a nursery, library or den.

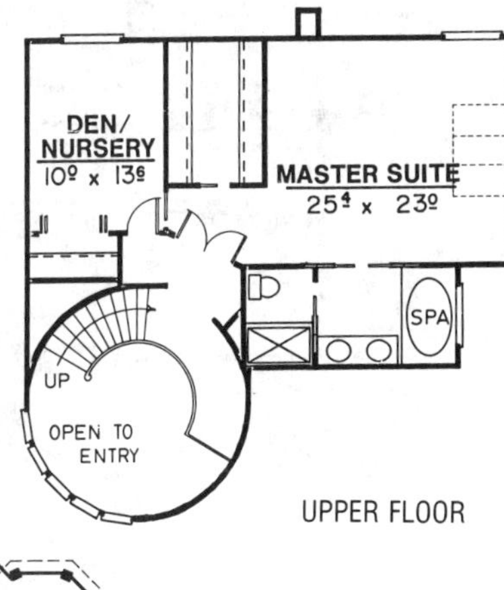

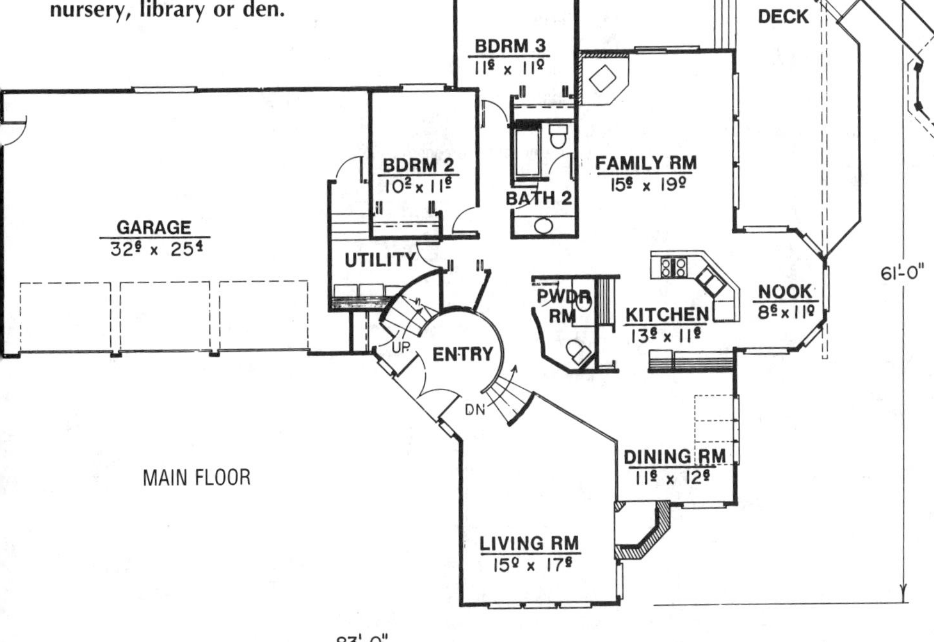

Plan I-2686

Bedrooms: 3	**Baths:** 2½
Space:	
Upper floor:	785 sq. ft.
Main floor:	1,901 sq. ft.
Total living area:	2,686 sq. ft.
Basement: approx.	1,900 sq. ft.
Garage:	823 sq. ft.
Exterior Wall Framing:	2x4

Foundation options:
Standard basement.
Crawlspace.
Slab.
(Foundation & framing conversion diagram available — see order form.)

Blueprint Price Code: D

TO ORDER THIS BLUEPRINT, CALL TOLL-FREE 1-800-547-5570
(prices and details on pp. 12-15.)

Plan I-2686

An Ever-Popular Floor Plan

The basic concept of this plan is to provide a simple straight-forward design for an uphill site. The plan is available with either a family room or dining room adjacent to the kitchen. Other features include a convenient laundry room, three bedrooms and two full baths. The living room features a fireplace and the wrap-around deck has access through the kitchen and laundry room. Total main floor area is 1,664 sq. ft.

Main floor:	1,664 sq. ft.
Lower level:	1,090 sq. ft.
Total living area:	2,754 sq. ft.
Garage:	573 sq. ft.

(Exterior walls are 2x6 construction)

PLAN H-2029-4
MAIN FLOOR
(DINING ROOM VERSION)
1664 SQUARE FEET

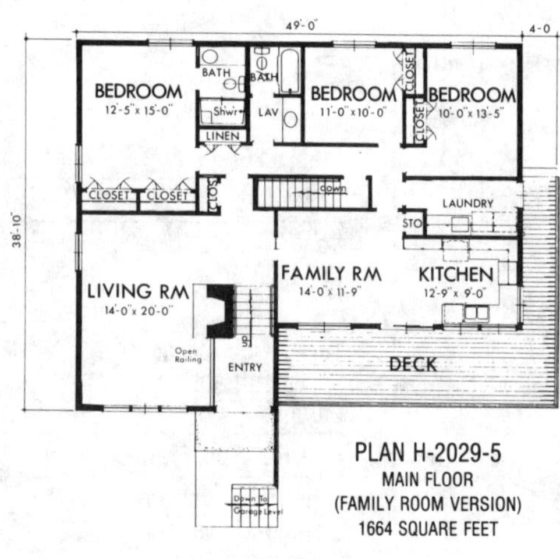

PLAN H-2029-5
MAIN FLOOR
(FAMILY ROOM VERSION)
1664 SQUARE FEET

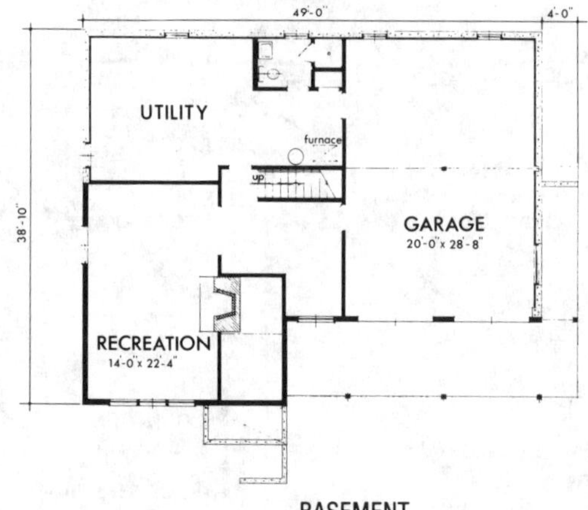

BASEMENT
1090 SQUARE FEET

Blueprint Price Code D

Plans H-2029-4 & H-2029-5

Dramatic Western Contemporary

- Dramatic and functional building features contribute to the comfort and desire of this family home.
- Master suite offers a spacious private bath and luxurious hydro spa.
- Open, efficient kitchen accommodates modern appliances, a large pantry, and a snack bar.
- Skylights shed light on the entryway, open staircase, and balcony.
- Upper level balcony area has private covered deck, and may be used as a guest room or den.

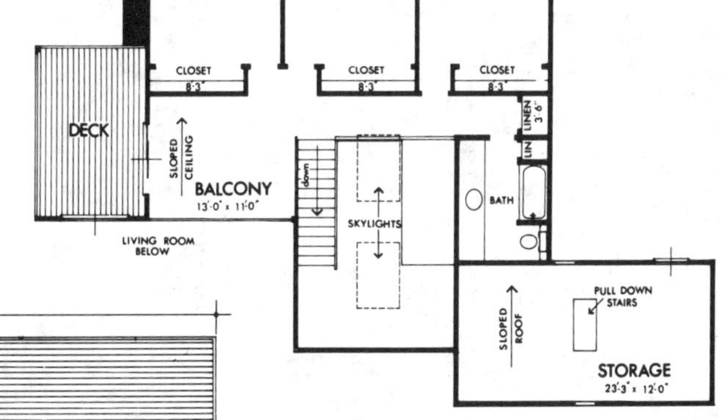

UPPER FLOOR

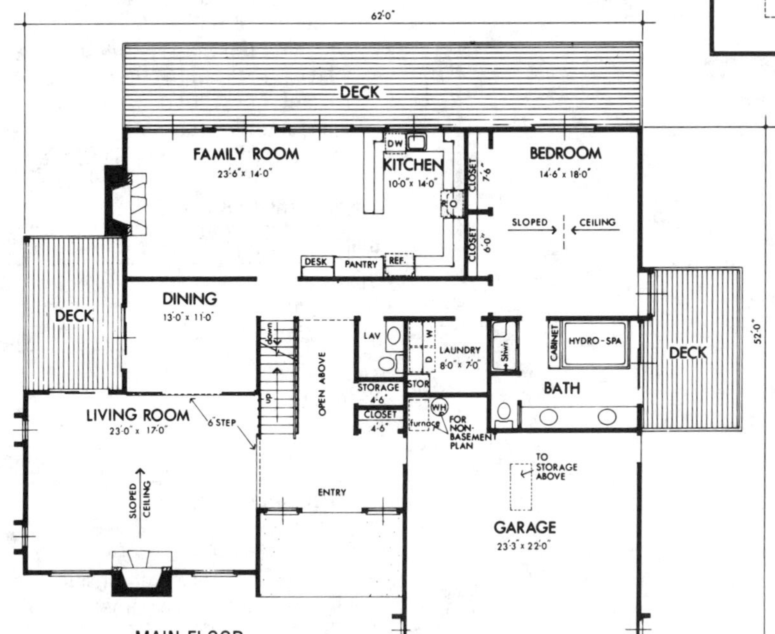

MAIN FLOOR

Plans H-3708-1 & -1A	
Bedrooms: 4	**Baths:** 2½
Space:	
Upper floor:	893 sq. ft.
Main floor:	2,006 sq. ft.
Total living area:	2,899 sq. ft.
Basement:	approx. 2,006 sq. ft.
Garage:	512 sq. ft.
Exterior Wall Framing:	2x6
Foundation options: Daylight basement (Plan H-3708-1). Crawlspace (Plan H-3708-1A). (Foundation & framing conversion diagram available — see order form.)	
Blueprint Price Code:	D

Plans H-3708-1 & -1A

TO ORDER THIS BLUEPRINT, CALL TOLL-FREE 1-800-547-5570

(prices and details on pp. 12-15.)

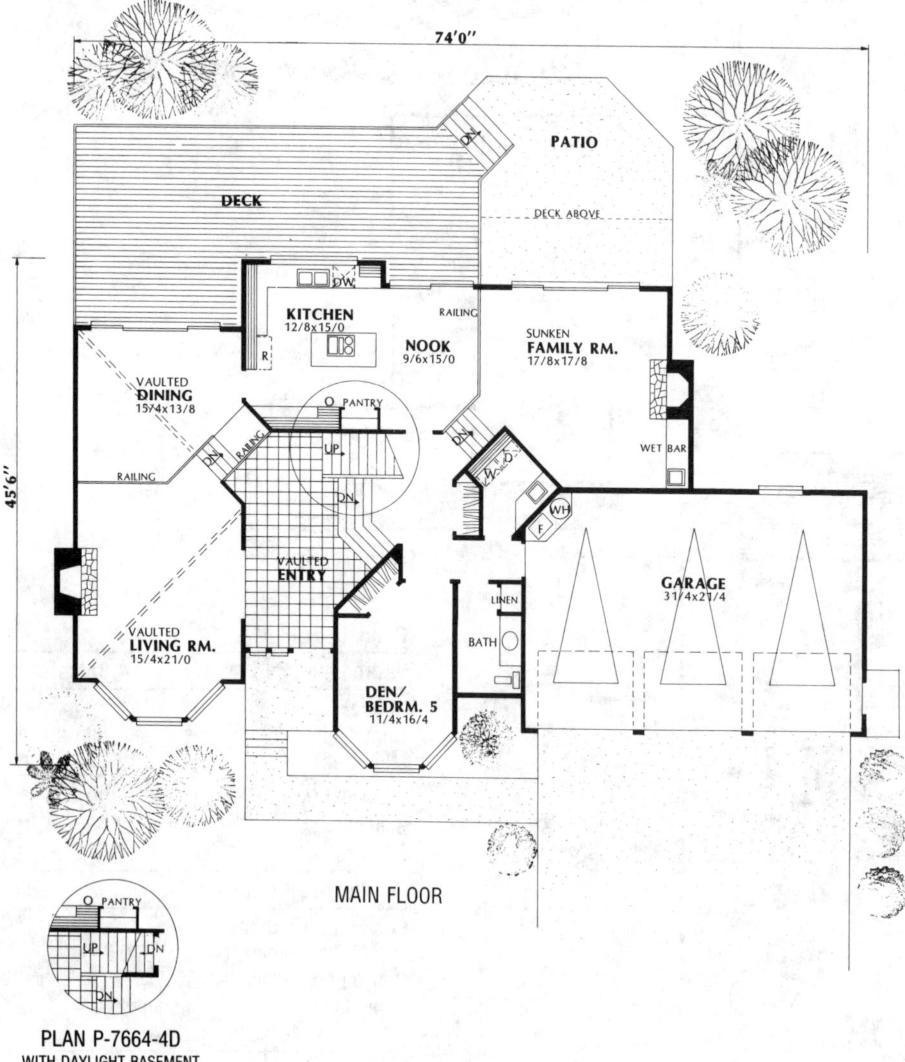

Creative Spaces

- Here's a home that is not only large, but extremely creative in its use of indoor space.
- A huge area is created by the combination of the vaulted living and dining rooms, which flow together visually but are separated by a railing.
- Another expansive space results from the kitchen/nook/family room arrangement, and their easy access to deck and patio.
- Upstairs, the master suite includes a lavish bath and generous closets.
- Three large secondary bedrooms share another full bath, and each has its own unique design feature.

Plans P-7664-4A & -4D

Bedrooms: 4-5	**Baths:** 2½
Space:	
Upper floor:	1,254 sq. ft.
Main floor:	1,824 sq. ft.
Total living area:	3,078 sq. ft.
Basement:	1,486 sq. ft.
Garage:	668 sq. ft.
Exterior Wall Framing:	2x4

Foundation options:
Daylight basement (Plan P-7664-4D).
Crawlspace (Plan P-7664-4A).
(Foundation & framing conversion diagram available — see order form.)

Blueprint Price Code: E

TO ORDER THIS BLUEPRINT, CALL TOLL-FREE 1-800-547-5570

Photo by Kevin Robinson

Popular Plan for Any Setting

- City, country, or casual living is possible in this versatile two-story design.
- A spa room and sunning area lie between the master suite and Great Room, all encased in an extended eating and viewing deck.
- U-shaped kitchen, nook, and dining area fulfill your entertaining and dining needs.
- Two additional bedrooms and a balcony hall are located on the second level.
- Daylight basement option provides a fourth bedroom, shop, and recreation area.

**NOTE: The above photographed home may have been modified by the homeowner. Please refer to floor plan and/or drawn elevation shown for actual blueprint details.

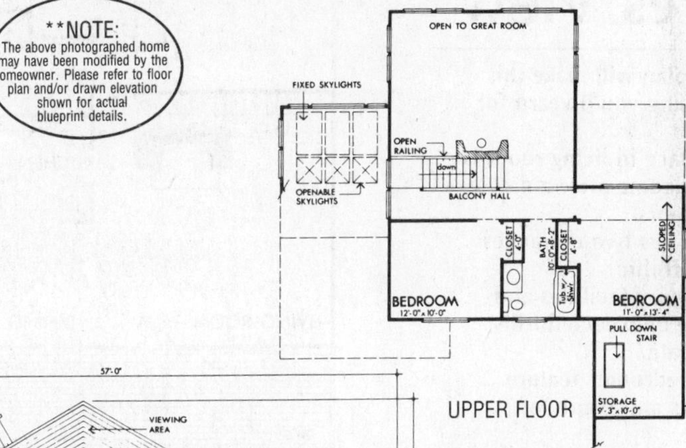

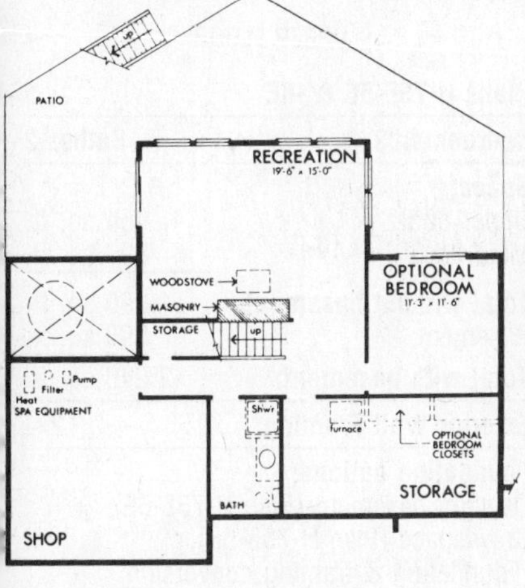

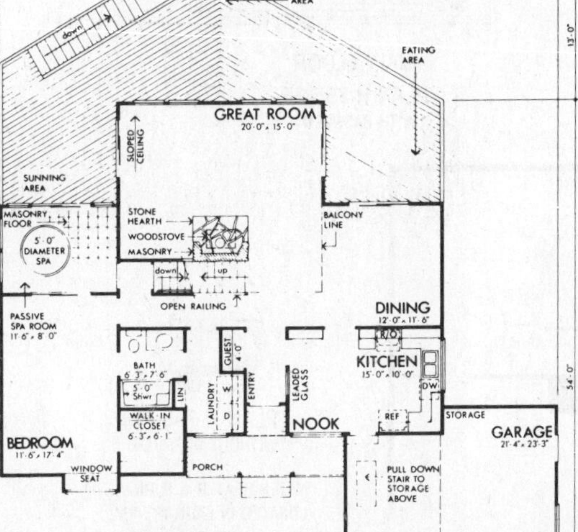

Plans H-952-1A & -1B

Bedrooms: 3-4	**Baths:** 2-3
Space:	
Upper floor:	470 sq. ft.
Main floor:	1,207 sq. ft.
Passive spa room:	102 sq. ft.
Total living area:	1,779 sq. ft.
Basement:	1,105 sq. ft.
Garage:	496 sq. ft.
Exterior Wall Framing:	2x6

Foundation options:
Daylight basement (Plan H-952-1B).
Crawlspace (Plan H-952-1A).
(Foundation & framing conversion diagram available — see order form.)

Blueprint Price Code:

Without finished basement:	B
With finished basement:	D

Plans H-952-1A & -1B

TO ORDER THIS BLUEPRINT, CALL TOLL-FREE 1-800-547-5570
(prices and details on pp. 12-15.)

Handsome Chalet Design Features View

- Roomy floor plan will make this chalet something you'll yearn for all year long.
- Massive fireplace in living room is a pleasant welcome after a day in the cold outdoors.
- Open kitchen has two entrances for smoother traffic.
- Generous laundry facilities and large bath are unexpected frills you'll appreciate.
- Upper floor bedrooms feature sloped ceilings and plenty of storage space.
- Optional basement plan affords more storage and general use space.

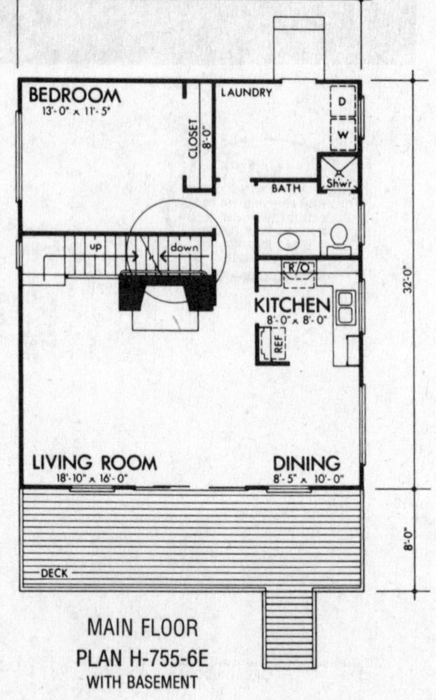

MAIN FLOOR
PLAN H-755-6E
WITH BASEMENT

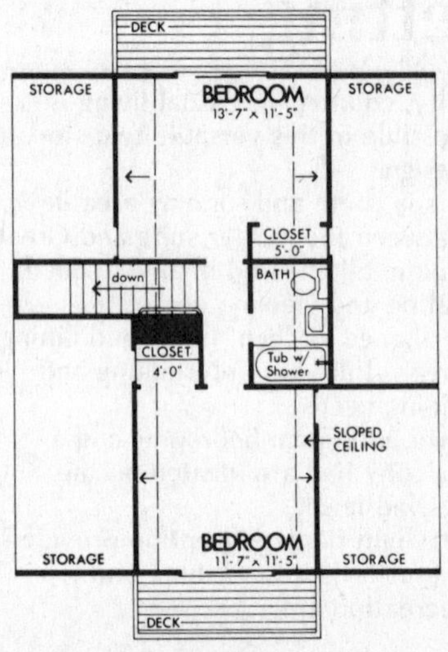

UPPER FLOOR

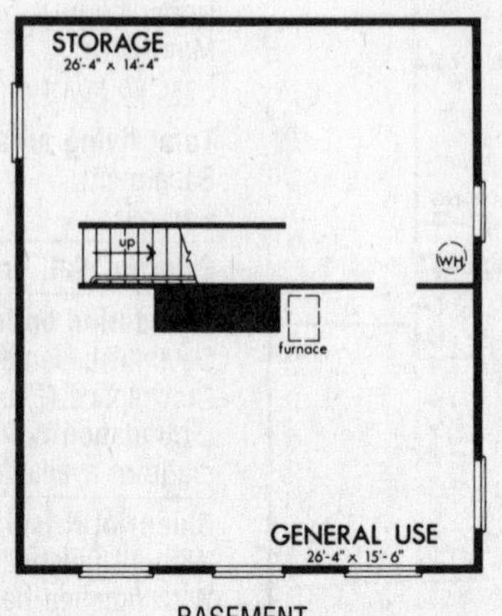

BASEMENT

PLAN H-755-5E
WITHOUT BASEMENT

WATER HEATER & FURNACE LOCATED IN LAUNDRY RM.

Plans H-755-5E & -6E

Bedrooms: 3	**Baths:** 2
Space:	
Upper floor:	454 sq. ft.
Main floor:	896 sq. ft.
Total without basement:	1,350 sq. ft.
Basement:	896 sq. ft.
Total with basement:	2,246 sq. ft.
Exterior Wall Framing:	2x4

Foundation options:
Daylight basement (Plan H-755-6E).
Crawlspace (Plan H-755-5E).
(Foundation & framing conversion diagram available — see order form.)

Blueprint Price Code:

Without basement:	A
With basement:	C

Plans H-755-5E & -6E

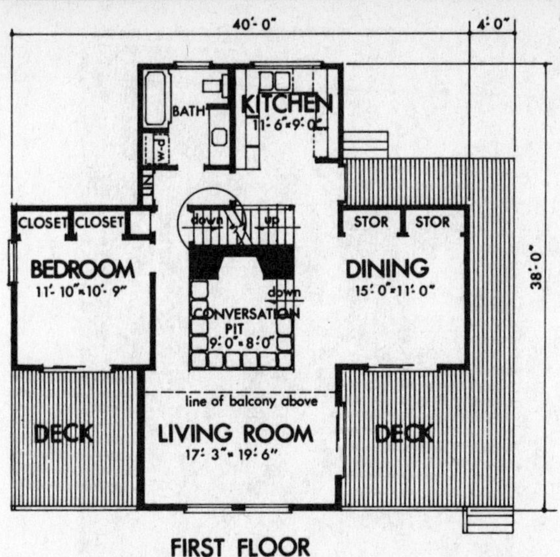

FIRST FLOOR
992 SQUARE FEET

BATH
Shwr
LIN
BEDROOM
11'- 5" × 9'- 0"
CLOS
CLOS
BALCONY BEDROOM
17'- 3" × 10'- 0"
balcony railing
upper part of living room

SECOND FLOOR
486 SQUARE FEET

PLAN H-805-1
WITH BASEMENT

PLAN H-805-1A
WITHOUT BASEMENT
(CRAWLSPACE FOUNDATION)

First floor:	992 sq. ft.
Second floor:	486 sq. ft.
Total living area: (Not counting basement)	1,478 sq. ft.

Coziness and Charm in Unique Plan

This rustic design is keynoted by a cathedral window wall. Handsome from inside or outside, the windows assure that both levels are well lighted.

The focal point of the lower living level is a 9' x 8' sunken conversation area in front of the fireplace. Both living and dining rooms are warmed by this fireplace.

During the summer the home is cooled by breezes coming through the sliding glass doors that serve the decks. The fireplace divides the living area from the master bedroom and bath.

Upstairs a sleeping loft and additional bedroom are served by a second full bath. Other features include the washer-dryer in the bath and the abundant storage throughout.

Blueprint Price Code A

Plans H-805-1 & -1A

TO ORDER THIS BLUEPRINT, CALL TOLL-FREE 1-800-547-5570

(prices and details on pp. 12-15.)

For Full-Time Living or Part-Time Fun

This is one of several plans in this book that can serve as either a recreation home or a permanent year-round dwelling. A large, formal entry hall introduces you to several options. You can turn right into the kitchen, left into your bedroom or the main floor bath, up the stairway to a second floor suite or, crossing the balcony type family room, go down a few steps to the living room. Huge deck areas surround the house. A private outdoor dining deck is immediately off the kitchen-family room complex. On this level you will also find a handy laundry room and access to the garage.

Besides the two good-sized main floor bedrooms, there is a suite upstairs consisting of a 13′ by almost 17′ master bedroom, closet space and a totally private bath. This suite is designed to take full advantage of whatever view you have.

To preserve the possibility of usage as a permanent home, we kept the street side of this plan as conventional as possible, but we designed the rear as a vacation home. The two level house-spanning deck, the cantilevered overhang of the upstairs bedroom and the numerous sliding glass doors all combine to make this a desirable vacation home.

One final note. Space does not permit us to include a picture to show the dramatic openness of the living room-family room-kitchen complex. In reality, this group of rooms forms one large area almost 20′ x 40′ in size, broken only by the floor level difference between living room and family room.

First floor:	1,342 sq. ft.
Second floor:	429 sq. ft.
Total living area: (Not counting garage)	1,771 sq. ft.

FRONT VIEW

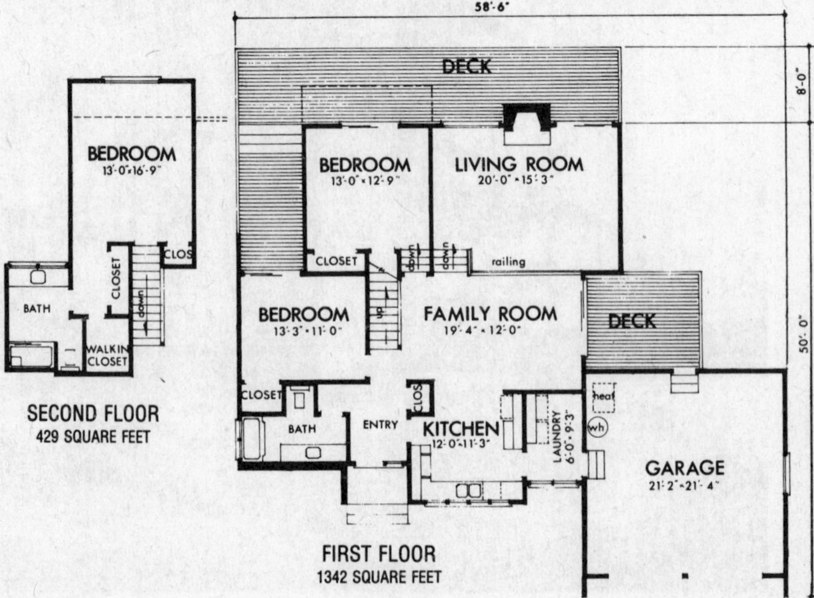

TO ORDER THIS BLUEPRINT, CALL TOLL-FREE 1-800-547-5570 (prices and details on pp. 12-15.)

Blueprint Price Code B

Plan H-911-1A

REAR VIEW

A Striking Contemporary

A multiplicity of decks and outcroppings along with unusual window arrangements combine to establish this striking contemporary as a classic type of architecture. To adapt to the sloping terrain, the structure has three levels of living space on the downhill side. As one moves around the house from the entry to the various rooms and living areas, both the appearance and function of the different spaces change, as do the angular forms and cutouts that define the floor plan arrangement. Almost all the rooms are flooded with an abundance of daylight, yet are shielded by projections of wing walls and roof surfaces to assure privacy as well as to block undesirable direct rays of sunshine.

The design projects open planning of a spacious living room that connects with the dining and kitchen area. The home features four large bedrooms, two of which have walk-in closets and private baths. The remaining two bedrooms also have an abundance of wardrobe space, and the rooms are of generous proportions.

For energy efficiency, exterior walls are framed with 2x6 studs.

First floor:	1,216 sq. ft.
Second floor:	958 sq. ft.
Total living area: (Not counting basement or garage)	2,174 sq. ft.
Basement:	1,019 sq. ft.

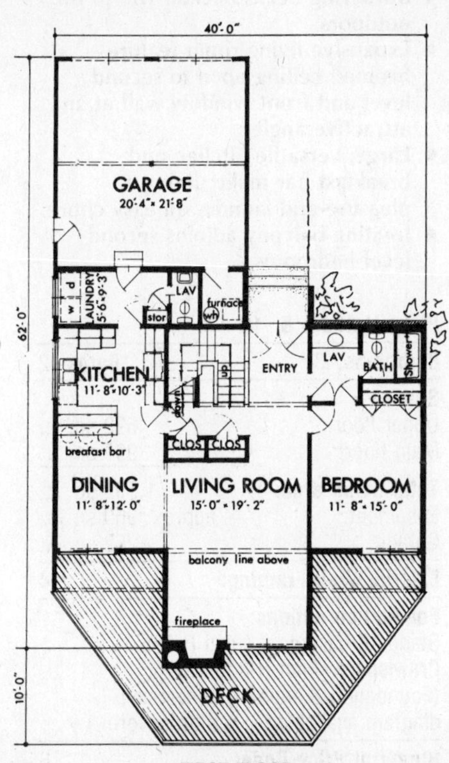

FIRST FLOOR
1216 SQUARE FEET

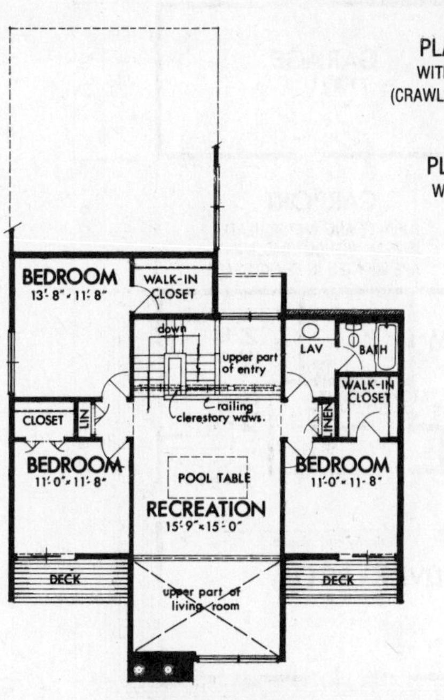

SECOND FLOOR
958 SQUARE FEET

PLAN H-914-1A
WITHOUT BASEMENT
(CRAWLSPACE FOUNDATION)

PLAN H-914-1
WITH BASEMENT

Blueprint Price Code C

Plans H-914-1 & H-914-1A

(prices and details on pp. 12-15.)

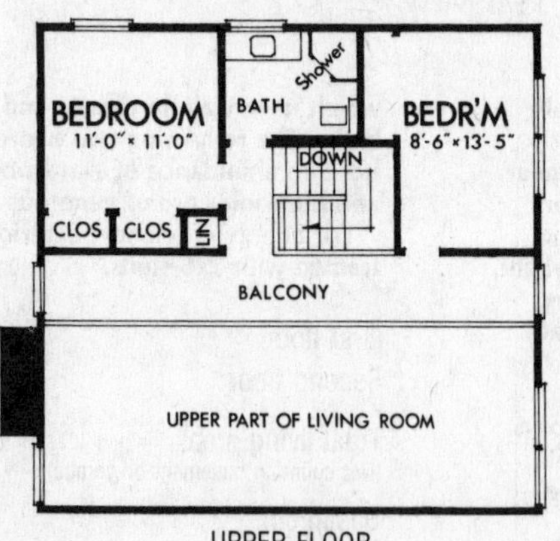

Surprising Spaces via Beamed Ceilings

- Open and spacious floor plan allows for uninhibited movement.
- Bordering decks beckon you to the outdoors.
- Expansive living room features beamed ceiling open to second level and front window wall at an attractive angle.
- Large, versatile kitchen and breakfast bar make dining a pleasure and laundry an easy chore.
- Inviting balcony adjoins second level bedrooms.

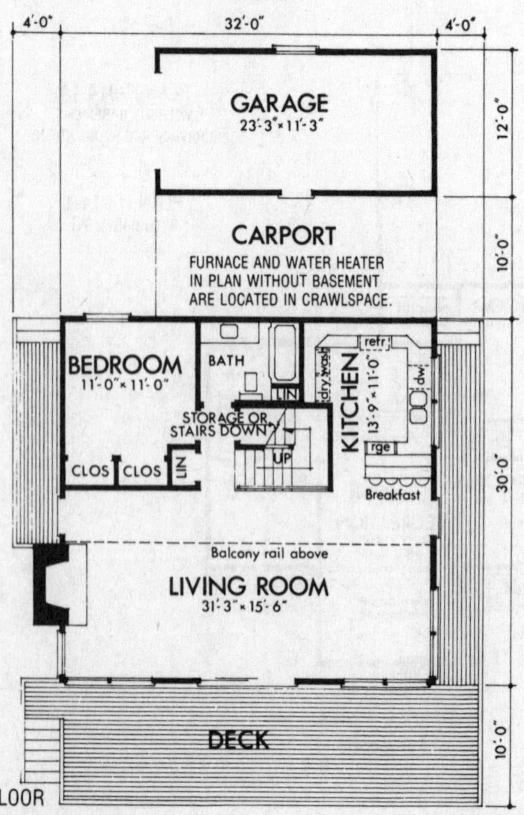

Plans H-876-1 & -1A

Bedrooms: 3	**Baths:** 2
Space:	
Upper floor:	592 sq. ft.
Main floor:	960 sq. ft.
Total living area:	1,552 sq. ft.
Basement:	approx. 960 sq. ft.
Garage:	262 sq. ft.
Exterior Wall Framing:	2x4

Foundation options:
Standard basement (Plan H-876-1).
Crawlspace (Plan H-876-1A).
(Foundation & framing conversion diagram available — see order form.)

Blueprint Price Code: B

Plans H-876-1 & -1A

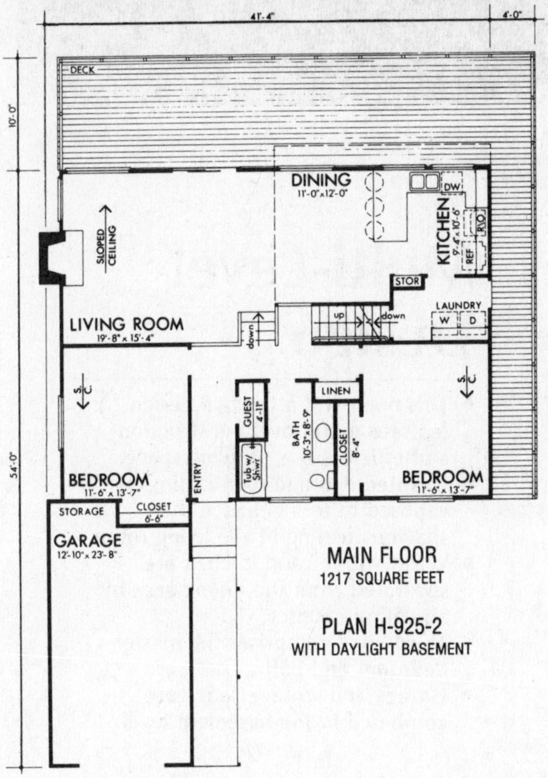

DECK

DINING
11'-0" x 12'-0"

KITCHEN
9'-4" x 10'-6"

LIVING ROOM
19'-8" x 15'-4"

SLOPED CEILING

LAUNDRY

BEDROOM
11'-6" x 13'-7"

BEDROOM
11'-6" x 13'-7"

GARAGE
12'-10" x 23'-8"

MAIN FLOOR
1217 SQUARE FEET

PLAN H-925-2
WITH DAYLIGHT BASEMENT

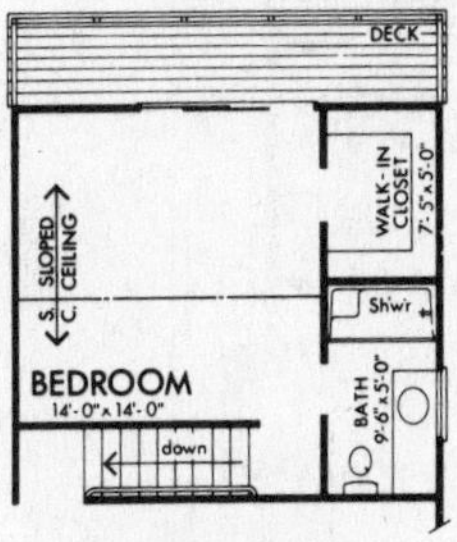

BEDROOM
14'-0" x 14'-0"

SECOND FLOOR
360 SQUARE FEET

First floor:	1,217 sq. ft.
Second floor:	360 sq. ft.
Total living area: (Not counting basement or garage)	1,577 sq. ft.

PLAN H-925-2A
WITHOUT BASEMENT
(CRAWLSPACE FOUNDATION)

Economical and Convenient

In an effort to merge the financial possibilities and the space requirements of the greatest number of families, the designers of this home restricted themselves to just over 1,200 sq. ft. of ground cover (exclusive of garage), and still managed to develop a superior three-bedroom design.

From a covered walkway, one approaches a centralized entry hall which effectively distributes traffic throughout the home without causing interruptions. Two main floor bedrooms and bath as well as the stairway to the second floor master suite are immediately accessible to the entry. Directly forward and four steps down finds one in the main living area, consisting of a large living room with vaulted ceiling and a dining-kitchen combination with conventional ceiling height. All these rooms have direct access to an outdoor living deck of over 400 sq. ft. Thus, though modest and unassuming from the street side, this home evolves into eye-popping expansion and luxury toward the rear.

To ease homemaking chores, whether this is to be a permanent or vacation home, the working equipment, including laundry space, is all on the main floor. Yet the homemaker remains part of the family scene because there is only a breakfast counter separating the work space from the living area.

Tucked away upstairs, in complete privacy, one finds a master bedroom suite equipped with separate bath, walk-in wardrobe and a romantic private deck.

The plan is available with or without a basement and is best suited to a lot that slopes gently down from the road.

Blueprint Price Code B

Plans H-925-2 & H-925-2A

TO ORDER THIS BLUEPRINT, CALL TOLL-FREE 1-800-547-5570

(prices and details on pp. 12-15.)

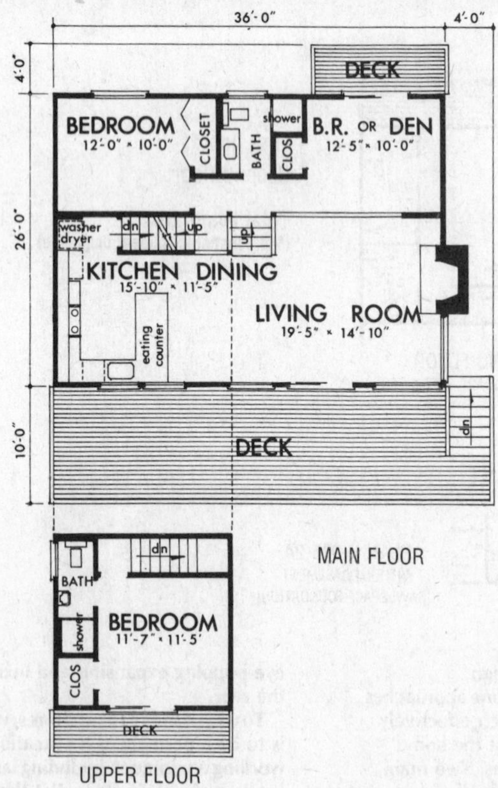

Multi-Level Design

- This open and attractive design features multi-level construction and efficient use of living space.
- Elevated den and high ceilings with exposed rafters enhance the spacious feeling of the living room.
- Washer/dryer and kitchen are separated from the dining area by an eating counter.
- Third level comprises the master bedroom and bath.
- Garage and storage space are combined in the basement level.

Plan H-863-2

Bedrooms: 2-3	**Baths:** 2
Space:	
Upper floor:	252 sq. ft.
Main floor:	936 sq. ft.
Total living area:	1,188 sq. ft.
Basement: (includes garage)	approx. 936 sq. ft.

Exterior Wall Framing:	2x4

Foundation options:
Daylight basement only.
(Foundation & framing conversion diagram available — see order form.)

Blueprint Price Code:	A

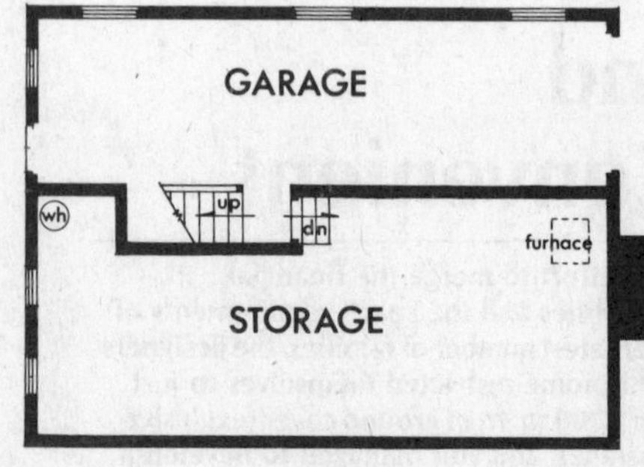

BASEMENT

TO ORDER THIS BLUEPRINT,
CALL TOLL-FREE 1-800-547-5570

Plan H-863-2

Easy Living

- Large, beautiful living area with sloped ceiling and fireplace lies five steps below entry and sleeping areas.
- Attached dining room and kitchen separated by eating bar.
- Convenient main floor laundry near kitchen and side entrance.
- Secluded master suite includes personal bath and private access to sun deck.

Plans H-925-1 & -1A

Bedrooms: 3 **Baths:** 2

Space:
Upper floor: 288 sq. ft.
Main floor: 951 sq. ft.

Total living area: 1,239 sq. ft.
Basement: approx. 951 sq. ft.
Garage: 266 sq. ft.

Exterior Wall Framing: 2x4

Foundation options:
Daylight basement (Plan H-925-1).
Crawlspace (Plan H-925-1A).
(Foundation & framing conversion diagram available — see order form.)

Blueprint Price Code: A

MAIN FLOOR
PLAN H-925-1
WITH DAYLIGHT BASEMENT

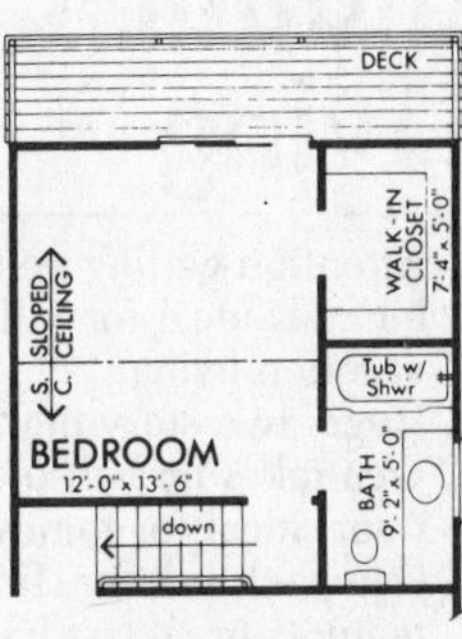

UPPER FLOOR

PLAN H-925-1A
WITHOUT BASEMENT

Plans H-925-1 & -1A

TO ORDER THIS BLUEPRINT, CALL TOLL-FREE 1-800-547-5570
(prices and details on pp. 12-15.)

Indoor-Outdoor Living

- Attention-getting pentagonal-shaped home is ideal for full-time or vacation living.
- Huge, two-story high living/dining area takes up half of the main floor, ideal for family gatherings.
- Compact, but functional kitchen features breakfast bar and adjacent laundry room that can also serve as a pantry and/or mudroom.
- Open stairway leads to second-floor balcony hallway overlooking the main level living area.
- Upper level has room for two additional bedrooms and a second bath.

Plans H-855-2 & -2A

Bedrooms: 3	**Baths:** 2
Space:	
Upper floor:	660 sq. ft.
Main floor:	1,174 sq. ft.
Total living area:	1,834 sq. ft.
Basement:	approx. 1,174 sq. ft.
Garage:	277 sq. ft.
Exterior Wall Framing:	2x4

Foundation options:
Daylight basement (Plan H-855-2).
Crawlspace (Plan H-855-2A).
(Foundation & framing conversion diagram available — see order form.)

Blueprint Price Code:

Without basement	B
With basement	E

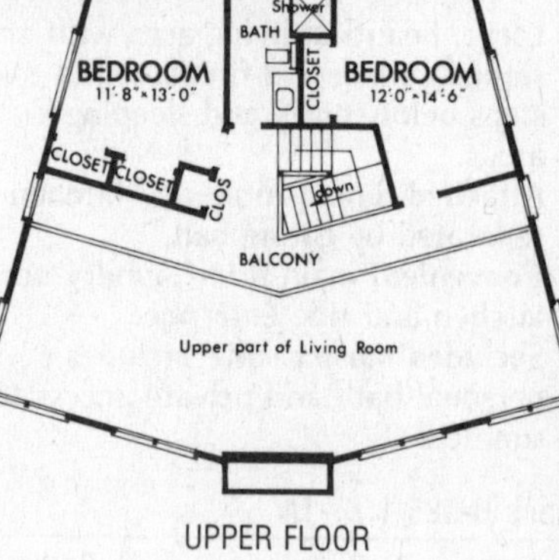

UPPER FLOOR

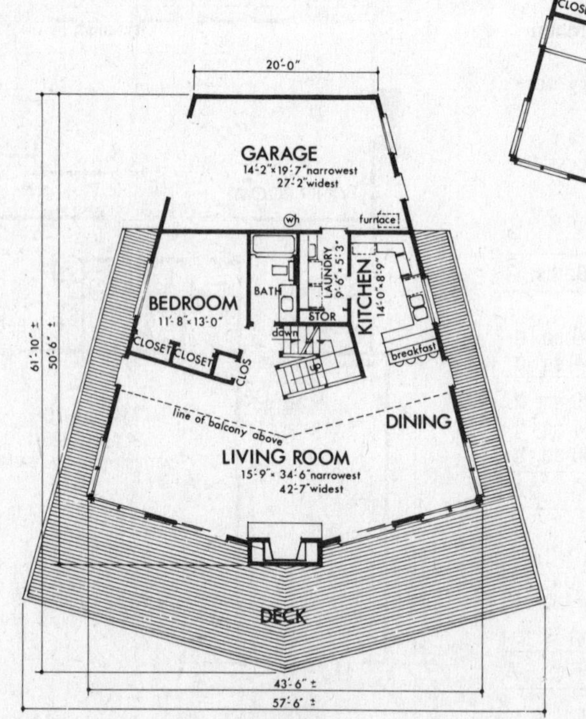

MAIN FLOOR
PLAN H-855-2
WITH BASEMENT

PLAN H-855-2A
WITHOUT BASEMENT

SCALE

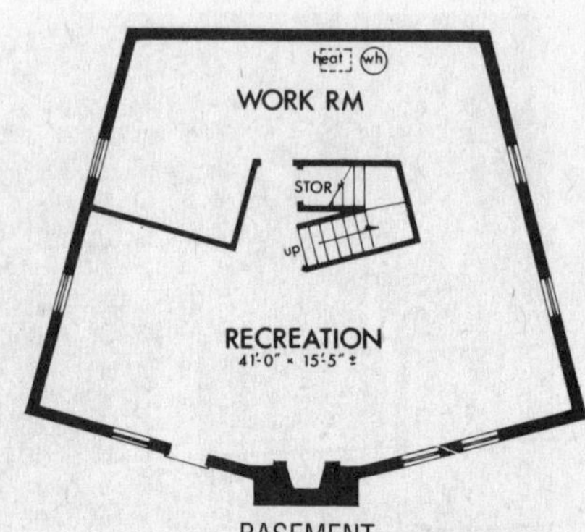

BASEMENT

TO ORDER THIS BLUEPRINT, CALL TOLL-FREE 1-800-547-5570
(prices and details on pp. 12-15.)

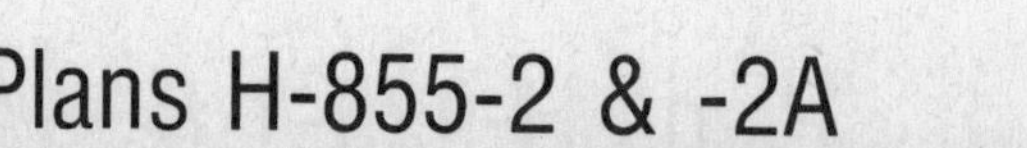

Covered Wrap-Around Deck Featured

- Covered deck spans home from main entrance to kitchen/side door.
- An over-sized fireplace is the focal point of the living room, which merges into an expandable dining area.
- Kitchen is tucked into one corner, but open counter space allows visual contact with living areas beyond.
- Good-sized main floor bedrooms furnished with sufficient closet space.
- Basement level adds a third bedroom and an additional 673 sq. ft. of living space.

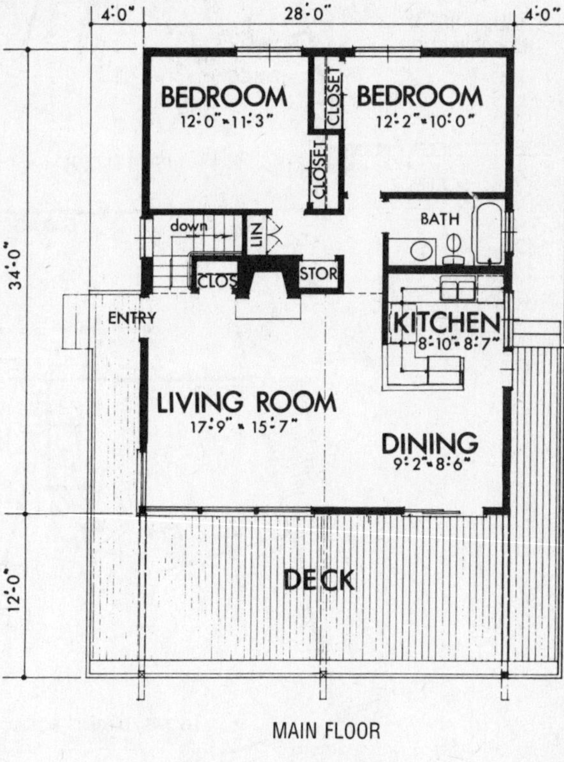

MAIN FLOOR

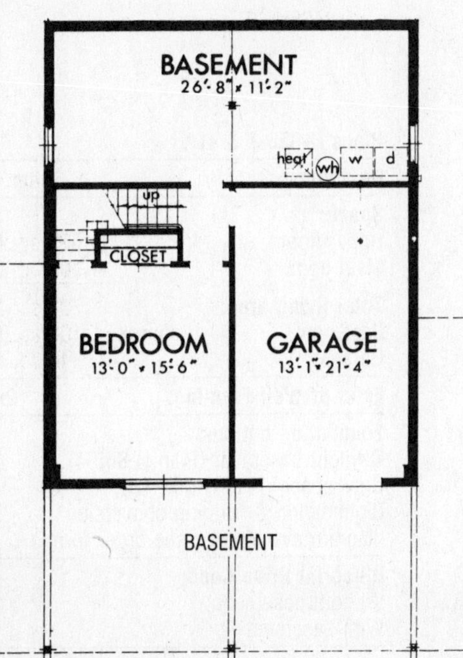

BASEMENT

Plan H-806-2

Bedrooms: 3	**Baths:** 1	**Exterior Wall Framing:**	2x6
Space:		**Foundation options:**	
Main floor:	952 sq. ft.	Daylight basement only.	
Basement:	673 sq. ft.	(Foundation & framing conversion diagram available — see order form.)	
Total living area:	1,625 sq. ft.		
Garage:	279 sq. ft.	**Blueprint Price Code:**	B

Plan H-806-2

(prices and details on pp. 12-15.)

Panoramic View Embraces Outdoors

- This geometric design takes full advantage of scenic sites.
- Living area faces a glass-filled wall and wrap-around deck.
- Open dining/living room arrangement is complemented by vaulted ceilings, an overhead balcony, and a 5-ft-wide fireplace.
- 12′ deep main deck offers generous space for outdoor dining and entertaining.

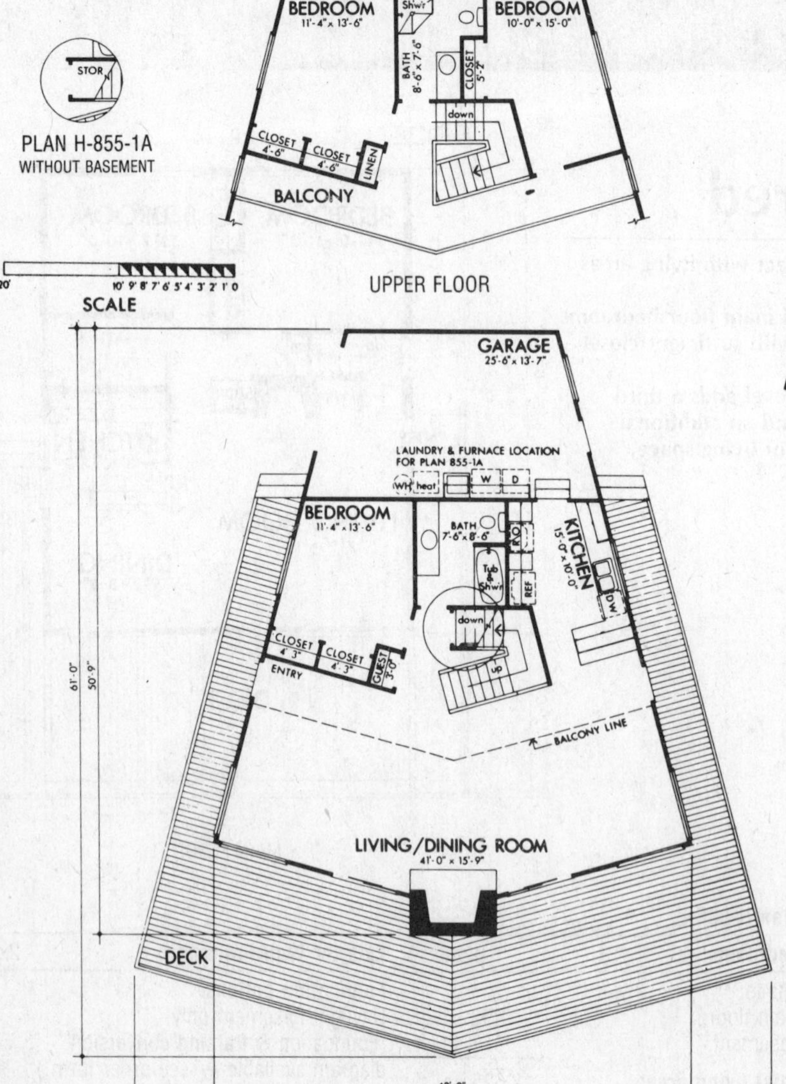

MAIN FLOOR

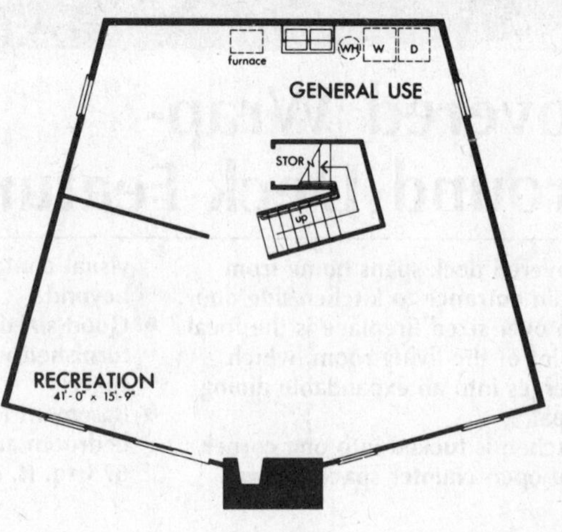

BASEMENT

Plans H-855-1 & -1A

Bedrooms: 3 — **Baths:** 2

Space:

Upper floor:	625 sq. ft.
Main floor:	1,108 sq. ft.
Total living area:	1,733 sq. ft.
Basement:	approx. 1,108 sq. ft.
Garage:	346 sq. ft.
Exterior Wall Framing:	2x6

Foundation options:
Daylight basement (Plan H-855-1).
Crawlspace (Plan H-855-1A).
(Foundation & framing conversion diagram available — see order form.)

Blueprint Price Code:

Without basement	B
With basement	D

TO ORDER THIS BLUEPRINT, CALL TOLL-FREE 1-800-547-5570
(prices and details on pp. 12-15.)

Plans H-855-1 & -1A

Rustic Comfort for Rec Home

- This delightful plan offers striking design inside and out.
- A huge "Grand Room" is flanked by two equally impressive Master Suites, both with walk-in closets and private baths.
- The central kitchen offers easy access from any part of the home.
- Upstairs, a guest suite provides two bedrooms.

Plan EOF-13

Bedrooms: 4	**Baths:** 3
Space:	
Upper floor:	443 sq. ft.
Main floor:	1,411 sq. ft.
Total living area:	1,854 sq. ft.
Garage:	264 sq. ft.
Storage area:	50 sq. ft.
Exterior Wall Framing:	2x4

Foundation options:
Crawlspace.
(Foundation & framing conversion diagram available — see order form.)

Blueprint Price Code:	B

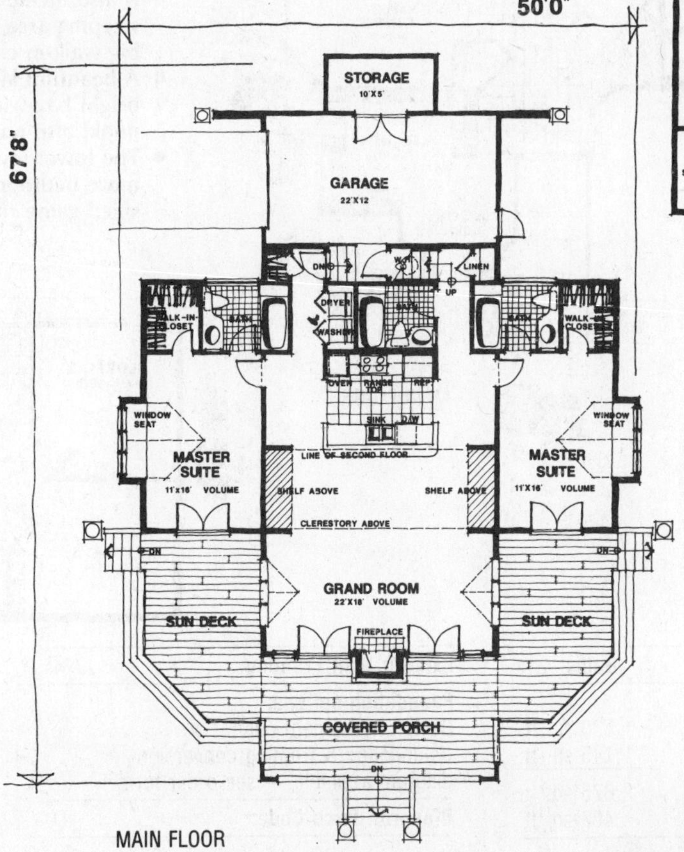

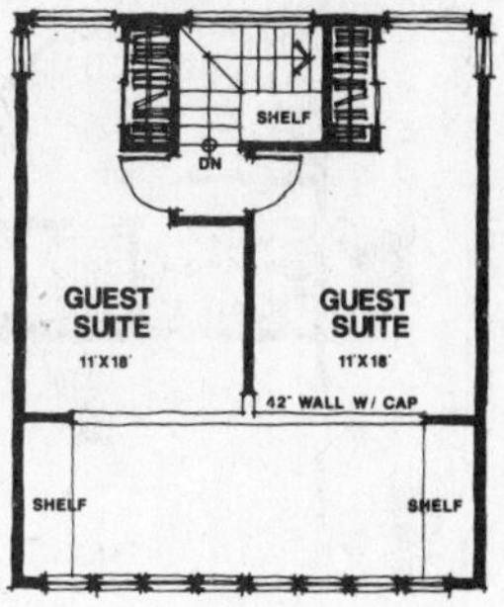

UPPER FLOOR

MAIN FLOOR

**NOTE: The above photographed home may have been modified by the homeowner. Please refer to floor plan and/or drawn elevation shown for actual blueprint details.

Plan EOF-13

TO ORDER THIS BLUEPRINT, CALL TOLL-FREE 1-800-547-5570
(prices and details on pp. 12-15.)

49'3"
RAILING
DN
DECK
HOT TUB
STEP
MASTER
19/0x14/0
VAULTED
GREAT RM.
21/6x17/6
PLNTR.
SUNKEN TUB
STEP
DRESSING
LIN
RAIL
UP
DN
BATH
WALK IN WARDROBE
VAULTED
DINING
14/4x10/6
PANTRY
SKYLIGHT
VAULTED
ENTRY
REF
KITCHEN
13/6x10/6
DW
50'8"
GARAGE
21/4x21/8
NOOK
10/0x10/0

MAIN FLOOR

Simple Exterior, Luxurious Interior

- Modest and unassuming on the exterior, this design provides an elegant and spacious interior.
- Highlight of the home is undoubtedly the vast Great Room/ Dining area, with its vaulted ceiling, massive hearth and big bay windows.
- An exceptionally fine master suite is also included, with a large sleeping area, luxurious bath and big walk-in closet.
- A beautiful kitchen is joined by a bright bay-windowed breakfast nook; also note the large pantry.
- The lower level encompasses two more bedrooms and a generously sized game room and bar.

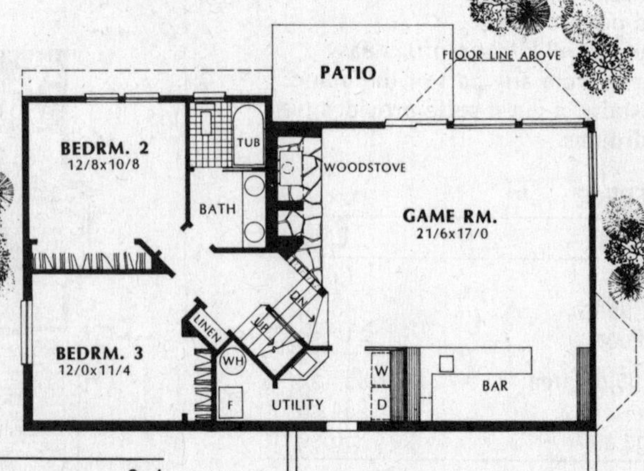

BASEMENT

Plan P-6595-3D

Bedrooms: 3	**Baths:** 2½
Space:	
Main floor:	1,530 sq. ft.
Lower level:	1,145 sq. ft.
Total living area:	2,675 sq. ft.
Garage:	462 sq. ft.

Exterior Wall Framing:	2x4
Foundation options: Daylight basement only. (Foundation & framing conversion diagram available — see order form.)	
Blueprint Price Code:	D

TO ORDER THIS BLUEPRINT, CALL TOLL-FREE 1-800-547-5570
(prices and details on pp. 12-15.)

Plan P-6595-3D

Ideal Home for a Narrow Lot

- This design features a room arrangement that is wide-open, yet confined to an economical width of only 28′.
- The entryway greets you with a balconied staircase and lovely bay window.
- The Great Room, dining area, and kitchen are arranged so no one is excluded from conversation or on-going activities.
- Other highlights include a woodstove/stone hearth in the Great Room, a large outdoor deck off the dining area, and a spacious U-shaped kitchen with breakfast bar.
- Second level features a master suite with walk-through closet and private bath.

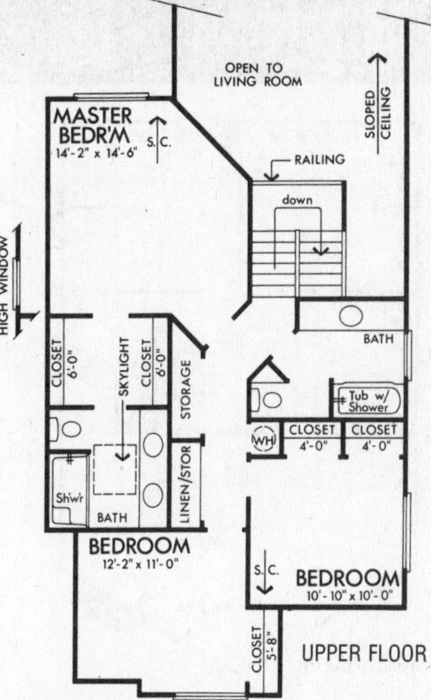

down

CLERESTORY WINDOWS OVER STAIRWAY

down

PLAN H-1427-3B
WITH DAYLIGHT BASEMENT

GENERAL USE

up

WH heat

BASEMENT

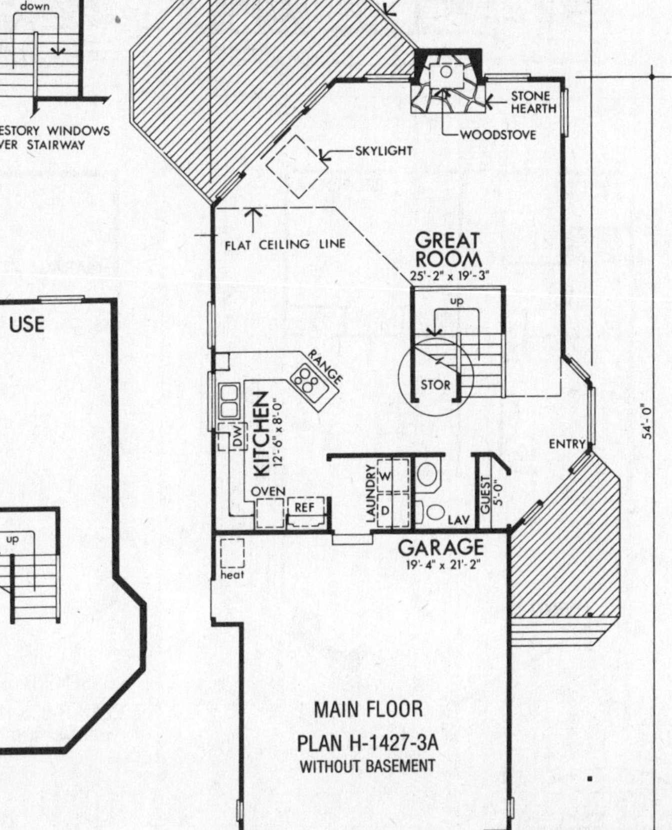

Plans H-1427-3A & -3B

Bedrooms: 3	**Baths:** 2½
Space:	
Upper floor:	880 sq. ft.
Main floor:	810 sq. ft.
Total without basement:	1,690 sq. ft.
Basement:	810 sq. ft.
Total with basement:	2,500 sq. ft.
Garage:	443 sq. ft.
Exterior Wall Framing:	2x4

Foundation options:
Daylight basement.
Crawlspace.
Foundation & framing conversion diagram available — see order form.)

Blueprint Price Code:

Without basement:	B
With basement:	D

Plans H-1427-3A & -3B

TO ORDER THIS BLUEPRINT, CALL TOLL-FREE 1-800-547-5570
(prices and details on pp. 12-15.)

Photo by Bob Hallinen

Soaring Design Lifts the Human Spirit

- Suitable for level or sloping lots, this versatile design can be expanded or finished as time and budget allow.
- Surrounding deck accessible from all main living areas.
- Great living room enhanced by vaulted ceilings, second-floor balcony, skylights and dramatic window wall.
- Rear entrance has convenient access to full bath and laundry room.
- Two additional bedrooms on upper level share second bath and balcony room.

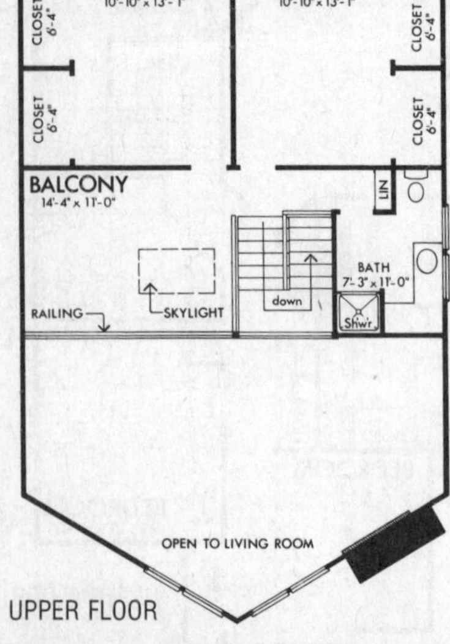

UPPER FLOOR

Plans H-930-1 & -1A

Bedrooms: 3 **Baths:** 2

Space:
Upper floor: 710 sq. ft.
Main floor: 1,210 sq. ft.

Total living area: 1,920 sq. ft.
Basement: 1,210 sq. ft.
Garage: (Included in basement).

Exterior Wall Framing: 2x6

Foundation options:
Daylight basement (Plan H-930-1).
Crawlspace (Plan H-930-1A).
(Foundation & framing conversion diagram available — see order form.)

Blueprint Price Code:
Without finished basement: B
With finished basement: D

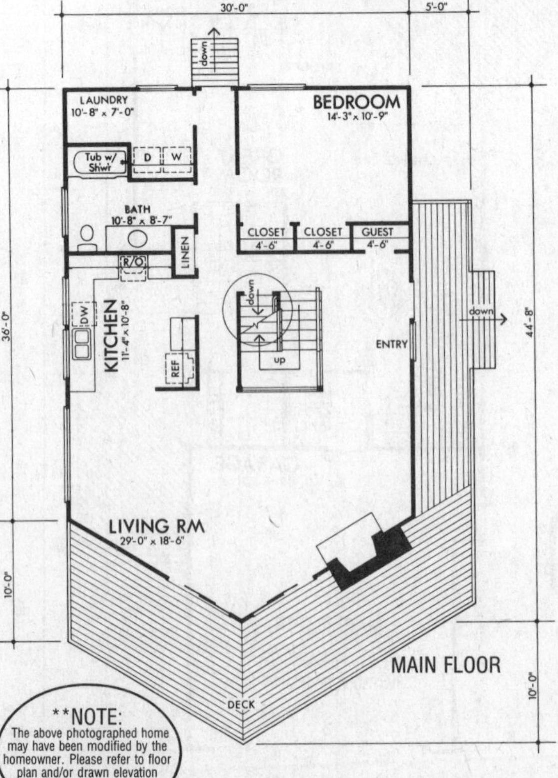

MAIN FLOOR

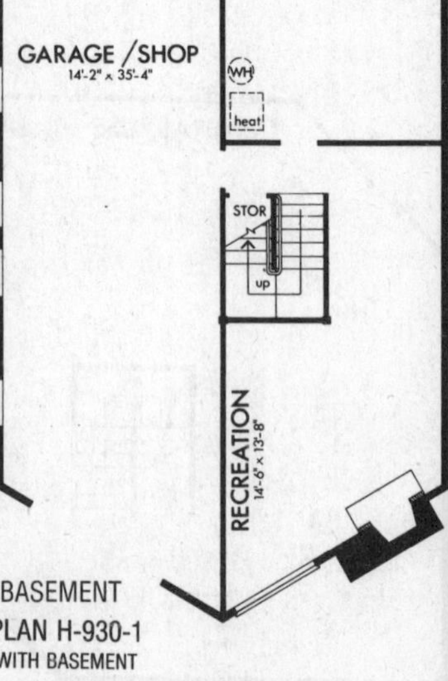

BASEMENT
PLAN H-930-1
WITH BASEMENT

STOR

PLAN H-930-1A
WITHOUT BASEMENT
(CRAWLSPACE FOUNDATION)

**NOTE:
The above photographed home may have been modified by the homeowner. Please refer to floor plan and/or drawn elevation shown for actual blueprint details.

TO ORDER THIS BLUEPRINT, CALL TOLL-FREE 1-800-547-5570

(prices and details on pp. 12-15.)

Plans H-930-1 & -1A